Onondaga Community College

Syracuse, New York

THE CHILDREN
WE SEE

THE CHILDREN
WE SEE

An Observational Approach
to Child Study

BETTY ROWEN

University of Miami, Coral Gables

With a foreword by E. PAUL TORRANCE

HOLT, RINEHART AND WINSTON, INC.
New York   Chicago   San Francisco   Atlanta
Dallas   Montreal   Toronto   London   Sydney

To Janine
Who Is a Joy To Observe

Cover photo courtesy of Suzanne Szasz
Photos for chapter 7 courtesy of Bill Winter
Photos for chapters 8 and 9
courtesy of Thelma Aranha and Leo Karasik
Photos for chapter 10 courtesy of Mark Nankin

FOREWORD

For as long as I can remember, teacher education programs and the textbooks that support them have been criticized for inattention to the development of important teaching skills. Many of the critics have maintained that the most frequently used and critical teaching skills are observing children and making inferences about their behavior. Of course, most teacher education programs have always sent students out to observe teaching. Too frequently, such students have seen very little. Rarely have there been systematic and disciplined attempts to teach students how to observe, what to observe, and how to process the information obtained through observation in such ways as to improve teaching.

An obvious difficulty is that there has been almost no textual material to support this training. In recent years, Amidon, Flanders, Ober, and others have provided support materials for what has been called "classroom interaction analysis," but these systems, while useful in research, have not been used systematically in teacher education, and might have proved to be somewhat "mechanical and superficial" if they had been. In this book, Betty Rowen makes a bold attempt to go beyond previous efforts and provides a variety of aids for building a genuine awareness of children and their development through an observational approach to child study.

As pre-primary and elementary education moves in the direction of individualized instruction, open classrooms, multilevel classrooms, and the like, the kinds of awareness that this book deals with become more important than ever. We have known for a long time that teaching becomes ineffective and teacher-pupil relationships "go wrong" when teacher or pupil behaves as though the other has abilities, motivations, interests, information, and concepts that he does not possess. When this happens, children become "turned off" to learning and, if it happens very frequently, they stop learning and become alienated from school.

The kinds of awareness that this book seeks to build are absolutely essential in creative learning and teaching, which regards the child as a self-acting, creative being and the learning environment as a responsive one— not just a stimulating one. To respond to a child effectively and to create this responsive environment requires the most sensitive and alert type of awareness, guidance, and direction. The teacher must respond to the child accurately in terms of his abilities, interests, motivations, skills, concepts, and so forth. Skilled and disciplined use of this book should certainly increase the reader's chances of attaining such awareness.

E. Paul Torrance

January 1973   *Athens, Georgia*

PREFACE

The idea for this book had its beginnings with case studies that were submitted to me as term papers by my students in undergraduate child development classes at the University of Miami. Some of these studies were so clearly revealing of developmental problems, and presented such insightful views of the children described, that they were used in subsequent classes as a basis for discussion.

Students in my classes are instructed in methods for the study of children through direct observation. I began also to collect their time samples and anecdotal records and to arrange them into developmental stages. These, too, proved to be effective as focal points for discussion about child development.

The need for a text that deals with an observational approach to child study became evident. Before students can effectively report upon their observations of children, they have to develop techniques of observation. They must sense the part that they play as teachers and observers, and must be aware of their own perspectives. They need to know the sources of information available to them and how to tap these sources. They should have information about diagnostic tools and how to interpret them.

This book is intended to prepare students to learn about child development through their own observations. It directs readers to use their own senses to gain knowledge about the children they see. The recognition of individuality is a basic need of our times and, since no two children are really alike, the ability to view children as unique individuals is more essential in teacher education than the study of norms of behavior. This skill in observing, interpreting, and responding to individual behavior can be applied to their future role as teachers in the classroom.

However, the reader of this book will also come away with a knowledge of levels of child development and an insight into various types of behavioral patterns. Understandings will grow as students look at children and compare their findings with those of their classmates. The literature in the field of child study will become more meaningful to them when they view it in the light of their own investigations.

Although the major concepts and principles in the field of child development are discussed in this book, they are dealt with in an informal way. The writing style is direct and simple, and, in many instances, is based upon the students' own expression of what they have observed. Theoretical material is introduced when relevant, as comparisons of observations are made to behavior reported by researchers in the field.

The Children We See is an introduction to child study for use in college and junior college settings. The skills developed through observation of children and the knowledge gained of their behavior can serve as a foundation for further study and research in child psychology as well as preparation for teacher education.

Part I of this book focuses mainly upon rationale and methodology. The rationale behind the observational approach to child study is dealt with in Chapter 1. Chapter 2 emphasizes a humanistic view of the teacher's role in the educative process through the use of self-evaluation techniques, measurements of classroom interaction, and exercises for sensitivity training. A more detailed description of a program to develop awareness in teachers is given in Chapter 3. In Chapter 4, we are concerned with various approaches to observation, methods for recording the behavior of children, ways to use interviews, and techniques for developing a full case study. Chapter 5 discusses and gives samples of the use of the creative arts as a means by which the teacher can gain knowledge about individual children. Chapter 6 presents examples of the observational approach applied to the interpretation of tests and diagnostic tools.

In Part II, Chapters 7 through 10 deal with the levels of development through which the individual evolves, from infancy through the elementary school years, as revealed through observational records of actual children done by students in undergraduate child development courses. Suggested activities are included that will help the reader to observe more astutely and organize observations in various ways. Discussion relates these observations to research findings.

Part III consists of case studies pertaining to specific conditions governing behavior—Environmental Deprivation (Chapter 11), Learning Disability (Chapter 12), Emotional Disturbance (Chapter 13), and Giftedness and Creativity (Chapter 14). Histories of individual children ranging in age from eighteen months to twelve years illustrate some unique characteristics that are related to these conditions. Discussions focus upon the application of insights gained through examination of these cases to the interpretation of behavior of children with similar patterns.

Throughout the text, exercises are given that help the reader to heighten perception and to interpret observations effectively. Thus, the book should not simply be read chapter by chapter, but should be interspersed with activities and field work. Actual involvement by the reader will result in better understanding than simply a passive reading of the text.

I was encouraged to write on this subject by colleagues whom I met at planning sessions for Forum No. 2 of the 1970 White House Conference on Children. Dr. E. Paul Torrance was the chairman of this planning committee, which dealt with "The Emergence of Identity in the First Six Years of Life." The need for an observational approach to child study was emphasized in our discussions, and I was instrumental in designing a video-tape display and matrix form for observations, which were part of our forum's presentation. I am grateful to Dr. Torrance, Dr. Boyd McCandless, Dr. Eugene Howard, and Norman Cohn for the helpful suggestions and support that they gave me at that time.

Since so much of this book is based upon the work of students, it is to them that I am primarily indebted. It would not be possible to mention all of them by name, but I would like to acknowledge those who made vital contributions to this manuscript. Some of these individuals were students in undergraduate classes; some were students working on projects that were part of their graduate programs; some were children I taught years ago in elementary school. To preserve the anonymity of the children discussed in the time samples, anecdotal records, and case studies, I will not make distinctions among these three categories of students. The individuals listed in alphabetical order below represent those whose writings were most helpful to me, and whom I gratefully acknowledge:

Diane E. Baker	Jan B. Hurwitz	John Moore
Suellen Bergstrom	Barbara M. Irwin	Elizabeth T. Morris
Morri Berman	Patricia Jacobs	Ann Rechter
Jeanne Clark	Deborah D. Johnson	Norma Santos
Helen Carol Gates Dunstall	Corinne Judd	Inge Smith
Mary Lou Ennis	Donna Kaplan	Roy Spruyt
Roberta Epstein	Carol Durbin Keiser	Sharon Stickney
Maureen E. Garrigan	Linda Kushner Keyes	Gay Sullivan
Arlene Greenberg	Lucy McCoy	Sarah Sures
Rickey Grotenstein	Martha J. McKinney	Vonnell Tillman
Malcolm G. Hileman	Margaret Michaelson	Paula F. Wollman

My editor at Holt, Rinehart and Winston, Richard Owen, has been most helpful to me throughout the preparation of the manuscript. Dr. Dale Harris of Pennsylvania State University reviewed the manuscript with keen understanding of its intended message, and offered constructive suggestions.

Professional associates and friends have also been helpful. Sources for information on learning disabilities were suggested by Norma Banas and I. H. Wills of Educational Guidance Services, Inc. of Miami, by Dr. Philip H. Mann, and by members of the staff of the University of Miami's Mailman Center for Child Development.

My friend, Edith Weber, inspired some of the ideas that led to this approach to teacher education. She has been my staunch supporter and sincere critic throughout the preparation of the manuscript. My husband Jules Rowen, has shown infinite patience as a frequent proofreader, and has maintained the admirable tolerance that is required to live with an author's absorption with a writing project. My own children, Richard Rowen and Mrs. Lois Winter, taught me more about child development as I watched them grow to maturity than I was able to learn from any book. All of these experiences, as a wife, mother, and teacher, are reflected in my writing, and I am grateful to the people who made them possible.

Betty Rowen
Coral Gables, Florida

January 1973

CONTENTS

THE WHY AND HOW OF AN OBSERVATIONAL APPROACH

A need to look at children as individuals

To know each child as an individual has always been an educational goal, but today it has become an urgent need. Automation has created a situation in society in which youth has to search desperately for identity, often with very threatening consequences. Many forces are at play that are destructive to individuality. There are few jobs that offer the satisfaction of personal accomplishment. Governments and institutions are frequently unresponsive to the members functioning under their control. The individual in today's world has a difficult time finding ways in which he can affect his environment.

Yet this need is with us at birth. The infant is born with a desire to explore the world and to become a person who can affect it. By interacting with his environment, the infant begins to identify himself. As he perceives the response of other human beings to his action, he begins to distinguish himself from the outside world. As he relates to his surroundings with whatever resources and possibilities that exist at the moment, new patterns of expression emerge. Where there is no reaction to his expression, development of ego is atrophied. A baby confined to his crib all day, with little opportunity for stimulation and human contact, becomes apathetic. From the very beginning, the adult's reaction to the infant's explorations is essential for the development of his sense of identity.

The need for recognition of one's individuality is with us throughout life. Healthy personalities develop in a society where the individual feels that he can be himself and where he will be accepted as such. His actions need to be recognized, and he needs to feel that he can interact with his environment and have an effect upon it. It is not by accident that youth today speaks rebelliously of "doing your own thing." Creative young people find adult society frustrating and restricting, and they cry out for opportunities to be recognized as unique individuals.

Children in school need to feel that their uniqueness is accepted and appreciated by their teachers. The atmosphere of the classroom must be one in which a child feels free to be himself. His sense of identity will be strengthened if there are teachers who listen and respond to him as a person.

Educators have given lip service to a respect for individual differences, but there has been increasing recognition of the discrepancies between the facts concerning individuality and the common practices in our schools. Testing programs have pegged children and have placed them into ability groups. But the unique qualities of each individual cannot be classified and categorized. The reader in the slow group may have potentials that cannot be discovered through standard achievement testing. What is he like? What are his special interests? How does he relate to his family, or to the children he plays with outside of school?

Each child must feel that he has a special contribution to make and that what he has to offer is valued. Learning cannot take place where the individual does not feel respected. His own sense of self comes before his motivation to achieve.

There are many facets of human behavior that go unrecognized in the schools. The emphasis upon academic skills has obliterated other potentials which may exist within the individual. Is he sensitive to the feelings of others around him? Does he respond to qualities in music, in art, or in the world of nature? Is he a leader on the playground? Can he make things with his hands? Often teachers never find out about these qualities. There are many areas in which a child's unique abilities can be developed, but his contributions must be valued. They must have an equal chance for recognition along with academic skills. Other kinds of learning will follow in time when a child knows his worth and feels accepted for what he is.

There are no ready-made descriptions, no established norms, that can determine the level at which the child is operating, his learning style, or his view of himself and his world. Keen insight is required by the teacher in order to sense a child's needs—intellectually, socially, and emotionally—and she must attempt to meet these needs in order to help him grow.*

Can prospective teachers develop insight, and can teachers in the field learn to sharpen their powers of observation to assess more accurately their pupils' needs? The traditional program in teacher education is not focused toward this goal. The study of learning theory is of value, but what theory is best to apply to a specific situation cannot be determined in the college classroom. Studies of research on child development familiarize the teacher with behavior of groups in experimental settings, but do not tell her why "Johnny

---

* Throughout this book feminine pronouns are used to refer to the teacher. In most instances, the prospective teachers who did the observations quoted extensively in the text are female.

Another consideration that prompted the above decision was the desire on the part of the author to avoid confusion in sentences where both teacher and child are used. The teacher is referred to as "she" or "her," while the child is called "he" or "him."

can't read." The teacher or prospective teacher should be knowledgeable about curriculum materials and methods in various subject areas; but only through actual classroom experience will she learn how to use them.

Preparing teachers to work effectively with children must involve experiences which develop abilities to look at students as individual human beings. The prospective teacher must be helped to develop insight and empathy. Only then will she be able to relate to each child in terms of his individual frame of reference and only then can she select the methods and materials best suited to his learning style and level of operation.

Not only must teachers see children as individuals, but they must learn to respond to them as they find them. In a sense, the capable teacher functions as an artist. She is aware of the feelings and thoughts of her students. She is able to pick up clues from their movements and gestures as well as their verbal responses. She can select aspects of experience that are meaningful to each child. She can respond to his feelings with empathy and can "tune in" to his wavelength. She can heighten her perception and can synthesize fragments of knowledge into significant wholes. Like an artist, the teacher is a living seismograph that enables those in contact with her to experience, more deeply and more meaningfully, some aspect of life.

Many readers will say that such teachers are born, not made. Sylvia Ashton-Warner was sensitive to the emotional life of her Maori children, and, because of this, was able to involve them fully in their learning activities.[1] One of the early outstanding teachers, Socrates, was able to sense the level at which his students were operating and was able to provide the provocative question that led them naturally to the next step.

It is the opinion of this author that such abilities can be developed. Teachers can become more sensitive individuals. They can learn to sense the level at which a child is operating, and they can provide the stimulation that is geared to that level. They can learn to empathize with children's feelings and can thus respond to them with warmth and understanding. Until recently, little effort has been made to provide this kind of training in teacher education. Artists may be prepared for their work with exercises that include the development of senses and feelings, but educators, with few exceptions, have been concerned mainly with the dissemination of information. The attempt to develop insight and responsiveness in teachers and prospective teachers is, therefore, a main focus of an observational approach to child study.

Changing concepts in theories of child development

Profound changes have occurred in the last decade concerning the way we view child growth and development. These changes are forcing educators to shift their sights, to modify their concepts, and to develop new approaches.

Basically what has occurred is a shift from a static to a dynamic view of the child. Whereas we once felt that intelligence was fixed, we now believe it

[1] Sylvia Ashton-Warner, *Teacher*.

to be modifiable. Where we once conceived of growth as an orderly unfoldment of natural stages, we now see it as an interaction between the organism and its environment. The brain is no longer thought of as a switchboard consisting only of stimulus-response connections but is viewed as a complex computer in which present elements interact with new input in a variety of ways. The organism itself is continually active and selects, to some extent, the aspects of environment it is ready to receive.

To understand more fully this shift in point of view, it is necessary to look briefly at the history of child study and to see it as a reflection of the spirit of the times in which it evolved. A relatively new branch of the behavioral sciences, child study had its beginnings in this country less than a century ago. G. Stanley Hall became president of Clark University in 1889 and quickly made it a headquarters for the intensive study of the child.

Hall was strongly influenced by Darwinism, and he applied evolutionary theory to psychology. His belief that "ontogeny recapitulates phylogeny" assumed that the growth of each individual reflects the evolution of the race. This development, it was believed, takes place through natural unfoldment of predetermined patterns. Hall's genetic approach was followed by his pupils, two of whom were largely responsible for laying the groundwork for further thinking along these lines. Edward L. Thorndike's laws of learning based upon the establishment of bonds of connection between stimulus and response were known to a generation of teachers. Arnold Gesell studied children at various age levels to determine norms of behavior.

Gesell's studies of children at the Yale Clinic placed age as the most important developmental condition affecting behavior. The very organization of his work into ages and stages implies that maturation occurred in an orderly, fixed pattern. Although Gesell himself often stressed the importance of individual differences, he was interpreted by parents and teachers in such a way that his norms became measurements against which to judge the growth of a child. No one seemed concerned about the population Gesell used in his studies. Since he used children from a predominantly academic community, it was not likely that environmental deprivation would be considered as a factor in determining rate of development.

The 1920s and 1930s were times when scientific method was in its ascendancy. Psychologists and educators were determined to make the study of the child as "scientific" as physics or chemistry. The testing movement crystallized the concept of fixed intelligence. Emphasis upon quantitative and objective aspects of behavior supported the static interpretation of Gesell's norms and Binet's IQ.

Thorndike was a firm believer in scientific method and its application to educational problems. Founded upon animal studies, his laws of learning became the basis for a behaviorist approach to education that flourished in the early part of the century. There are some persistent overtones of this approach in current practices. Learning, according to this point of view, consists of impressions of new stimuli upon a passive organism. Repetition, reward, and reinforcement determine the success of the learning, and in this manner habits and skills are developed. In this approach little attention is given to the student's interests, level of understanding, or motivation. The relevancy of the material is not a factor in the conditioning process.

With this static view of child development and learning theory, it is not necessary for the teacher to know the child as an individual. His level and rate of progress can be determined by tests. The selection of materials for the classroom is determined by the goals established for learning at various age levels. The teacher and the child need not be in constant transactional relationship to each other in order for learning to take place.

Fortunately there has been a dramatic shift in thinking in the last decade. Many factors have contributed to this change, among them the focus upon the problems of disadvantaged children, new phenomenological methods in psychology, and the research findings of J. McV. Hunt and Benjamin Bloom.

Bloom called attention to the early years as the most rapid period of development for both intellectual and affective functioning. His book, *Stability and Change in Human Characteristics*, synthesizes research concerned with growth patterns.[2]

Hunt's book, *Intelligence and Experience*, presents a strong argument for the influence of environment upon development. Behavior is not the result of an automatic process of maturation, but "experience, defined as the organism's encounters with his environment, is continually building into the developing human organism a hierarchy of operations for processing information and for coping with circumstances."[3] Thus, experience is a crucial factor in the development of intelligence.

Hunt's work supports the cognitive theories of Piaget, for whom intellectual growth is a developmental process involving interaction between the individual and his environment. Logical thinking evolves from a process of modification of existing internal schema. The reflexive responses of the newborn infant become progressively transformed through contacts with the environment. Continuous transformations take the child through a sensorimotor period, where he begins to organize aspects of sense experience into interiorized schema, to an extensive period of concrete operations, where logical processes develop through direct manipulation. Only after interaction has taken place at sequential levels of experience do these processes become extended toward abstract reasoning.

Although Piaget was developing his theories in Switzerland at the same time that Gesell was working at the Yale Clinic, psychologists in this country paid little attention to his work. Since a more dynamic view of learning has now come into ascendancy, Piaget has been recognized. His thinking is the basis for much of current learning theory and for new directions in curriculum development.

Hunt builds upon Piaget's theory and postulates that there must be a

---

[2] Benjamin S. Bloom, *Stability and Change in Human Characteristics*.

[3] J. McV. Hunt, *Intelligence and Experience*, pp. 246–247.

"match" between the inner integrative patterns a child has achieved and the external circumstances with which he is confronted. Providing him with materials and ideas beyond his level of operation causes frustration and withdrawal. When outer and inner levels are identical, there is no challenge. Promoting the optimum rate of intellectual development requires careful selection of environmental factors and takes into account self-directed interest and curiosity. "Inasmuch as experience and maturation are continually changing the schemata of the child, maximizing the richness of an environment calls for continual concern with the appropriateness of the match."[4]

If teachers are to be in constant transactional relationship with learners, if they are to be able to deal effectively with "the problem of the match," then they need a conscious awareness of learning patterns and some operational tools for diagnosing where children are with respect to their development and intelligence. "A teacher, in selecting his strategy, needs to take into account not only the general principles of learning but also the specific information about the specific pupils in his classroom."[5]

Current learning theory demands knowledge of the child as an individual to be effective in practice. Since it is concerned with process, rather than simply assessing levels, it requires greater insight on the part of the teacher. Teacher education must be concerned with providing experiences which give the teacher and prospective teacher opportunity to develop this insight. Looking at child development as an evolving process which is unique to each individual is an attempt to focus in this direction.

The limitations of measurements

Child development, as an evolving process, is difficult to assess through use of standardized measuring instruments. The same question on an intelligence test can mean different things to different children, depending upon their own frames of reference. A "wrong" answer may be perfectly "right" if the child's logic is determined.

Testing can be an effective diagnostic tool if reasoning and judgment are applied to the analysis of the results. A standardized reading test may determine that Child A cannot discriminate differences in sounds of words, while Child B cannot effectively use context clues. This can help the teacher in planning sequences of language activities for the children involved. The overall score on a test which has many component parts tells the teacher very little. She must take into consideration the background of the child being tested and must analyze responses to various parts of the test in terms of her knowledge about previous performance and the level at which each child is operating. Past experiences must be related to present reactions, for they are often causal determinants of the observed behavior pattern.

From a common sense point of view, we all make judgments that involve

[4] Hunt, *Intelligence and Experience*, p. 272.
[5] Ira J. Gordon, *Studying the Child in School*, p. 5.

an appraisal of behavior based upon our interpretation of the intent of the behavior we are observing. Watching a boy play checkers, we assess the logic of his moves in terms of our own knowledge of the game. We try to determine, from our own experience, what is the sequence of thought behind his action. There would be little sense to much of what we observe about overt behavior if we did not bring our own subjective interpretation to bear upon what we see.

Teachers must apply this subjective judgment to their interpretation of children. The so-called objective test can be meaningful in assessing development only if the tester considers the causal relationships that are determinants of behavior. Gilbert Ryle points out that, in judging whether a performance is intelligent, we must look beyond the performance itself.[6] As in the game of checkers, we consider the abilities and propensities of which this performance is an actualization. To characterize people we go beyond what we see them do or hear them say; we integrate their observed behavior with our total view as we see it and evaluate that behavior accordingly. Since a person is directly aware of correlation between his own private experiences and his overt acts, he therefore has some possibility of understanding the performance of others.

Doctors and psychologists take this total view of the individual into account when diagnosing observable symptoms. Laboratory tests and measurements of body function do not determine a patient's illness. It is the doctor's use of these data, in combination with his own previous experience with similar patterns, that enables him to make a diagnosis. A child analyst observes natural behavior, interviews parents, administers projective tests, and considers previous cases in his experience before making judgments about the child under his care. No one questions the authenticity of this judgment, although ultimately there is a subjective element involved in its formulation.

The same respect must be given to the judgment of the teacher. Educators generally have been so concerned with measurement of results of educational methodology that they have taken the objective data as the end in itself. Scientific method used in the physical sciences has been applied to the assessment of educational programs. By definition, the traditional scientific method of research implies the isolation of a single variable from experience and the control of other factors in the environment. In assessing human behavior this condition cannot be met. No variable can be observed in isolation from other elements. In assessing children's growth a multitude of variables must be considered, and their interrelationships to each other are as important as the awareness of the factors themselves. Until we have measuring instruments which can appraise these complex interrelationships (and I am not sure that day will ever come) we must rely upon human judgment to do the job. Teachers can be trained to make these kinds of appraisals. They must acquire the skills necessary for diagnosis, much as the physician does. They must be prepared to interpret the raw data of test scores and overt actions in the light of their knowledge of the child, his previous experience, his learning style, and his frame of reference. They can learn to use their own experiences to gain

[6] Gilbert Ryle, *Concept of Mind.*

insight into observable behavior. We must accord to teachers the same professional respect we give to doctors. We must consider their judgment as a
valid means of assessing child growth and development, and we must help
them develop skill in judgment by including experience of this nature in
teacher education.

The English philosopher, David Pole, says that a trained mind is chiefly
distinguished by its different and more significant grasp of data.[7] This mind
develops "an organized, acquired bent for interpretation." As men engage
in inquiry, their attitudes and views progressively tend to grow into some
common structure. Thus, investigators with extensive experience in their field
often have similar judgments when they view new phenomena. The more
intense and wide the experience of the individual, the greater his ability to
interpret the performance of others. When teachers have wide experience
with the behavior patterns of children, they will be able to integrate and
interpret what they observe and will bring to their teaching the trained mind
of which Pole speaks. Such a trained mind will be able to interpret tests
effectively, diagnose teaching problems, and prescribe solutions which meet
students' individual needs.

The emergence of individualized programs in today's schools

The emphasis upon individualization of instruction is one of the new directions
in education today. Several types of programs gaining recognition point in
this direction.

The philosophy of Head Start was influential in leading this movement.
Children from poverty areas are considered in terms of their total development. Nutrition and health are significant factors in assessing their potential to
learn. The child's view of himself, his self-concept, is important in determining
his motivation. A main focus of Head Start is parent involvement. The total
life experience of the child is considered as it relates to his ability to learn.

The organization of a Head Start classroom places strong emphasis upon
individuality. For the most part, children are free to choose areas of interest.
Teachers and aides work in small groups or with individual children, using
materials that develop language or number concepts. The selection of these
materials is determined by examination of the child—his interests, his strengths,
and his deficiencies.

When Head Start children moved into the more formal first-grade classrooms, it was discovered that much of the progress they had made was lost. It
was felt that a continued program which met individual needs was necessary
to insure that the benefits of Head Start were not diminished. Thus, Follow
Through Programs came into existence, which carry over the atmosphere and
philosophy of Head Start to the primary-grade classroom.

One of the features of these programs is the employment of several

[7] David Pole, *Conditions of Rational Inquiry*.

adults for a class of twenty to thirty children. Aides and parent volunteers work along with the teacher so that small-group instruction becomes feasible. A one-to-one relationship of student to teacher in beginning learning experiences is often considered desirable.

The use of paraprofessionals in the classroom has spread to other types of schools and other grade levels. Not only does this relieve the teacher of some of the pressures of routine jobs, but, if used to best advantage, the paraprofessional in the classroom can help to individualize instruction. Under the teacher's guidance, she can provide experiences for individual pupils that meet their own special needs. To make the most effective use of the paraprofessional, the teacher needs to assess each pupil's level of ability and suggest activities to the assistant which will enhance the growth of the child she is to work with. Children who need special attention because of emotional problems can also find help through the use of paraprofessionals. But the teacher must be able to assess the needs of each individual in her class to prescribe the type of help that will serve each the best.

Some of the English Infant Schools have operated for some time now with an emphasis upon individualized instruction. Children from ages of five to seven are grouped together in one class. Of course, they do not all function at the same level, and many small-group projects go on simultaneously. Older children are often involved in helping younger ones with a project. There is a free flow of movement in the classroom, the corridors, and throughout the school. Many activities are initiated by the students and are determined by their own interests. The teacher facilitates matters—supplying materials, helping to arrange space and time, and offering moral support and suggestions when needed. Here individualization is an essential element of the program, and the teacher's knowledge of each child is necessary for her to perform her role.

Efforts to initiate programs of this nature in this country are mushrooming. The pod-type building where several rooms can become one by simply sliding open partitions facilitates the extension of the "open classroom" concept. Teachers in these pod-type arrangements may see as many as 75 to 100 children a day instead of the usual 20 to 30. They can arrange for small or large groups to work together, and several activities can be going on at one time. Special skills of the teachers involved can be effectively used, if planning and teamwork are carefully developed. But again, the success of such a program is largely dependent upon the ability of the teachers to assess the levels and learning styles of the children in their groups and to prescribe the best learning environment for each one.

The use of programmed instruction, teaching machines, tape recorders, and listening stations focus attention upon individualizing instruction. Many new schools now have media centers where groups of children can go for a period of time each day and work at their own special programs. Machines can be helpful in providing opportunities for skill development and for enriching curriculum if they are properly prescribed to meet special needs.

All of these developments point up the necessity of having teachers who are aware of the individuality of the children they teach. Without heightened sensitivity on the part of teachers these individualized programs can be disastrous. With teaching machines, television, and mechanical gadgets of all kinds being placed on the market by educational companies, school can become a mechanized kind of factory. But these same materials, if used effectively, can help children to find their own interests and to develop at their own rate. The success of many new programs in the elementary school, such as team teaching, programmed instruction and the open classroom, is dependent upon the sensitivity of the teachers to the children's level of development and to their individual needs.

Knowledge and understanding of human behavior must begin with self-awareness and self-acceptance. In the next chapter we will try to focus attention upon the personality of the teacher. Each teacher, as well as each child, is a unique individual, and she must know herself before she can begin to know others.

REFERENCES

ASHTON-WARNER, SYLVIA.   *Teacher*. New York: Simon and Schuster, Inc., 1963.

BLOOM, BENJAMIN S.   *Stability and Change in Human Characteristics*. New York: John Wiley & Sons, Inc., 1964.

GESELL, ARNOLD.   *The First Five Years of Life*. New York: Harper & Row, Publishers, 1940.

GORDON, IRA J.   *Studying the Child in School*. New York: John Wiley & Sons, Inc., 1966.

HUNT, J. McV.   *Intelligence and Experience*. New York: The Ronald Press Company, 1961.

INHELDER, BARBEL, AND JEAN PIAGET.   *The Growth of Logical Thinking from Childhood to Adolescence*. New York: Basic Books, Inc., 1958.

MASLOW, ABRAHAM H.   *Toward a Psychology of Being*. Princeton, N.J.: D. Van Nostrand Company, Inc., 1962.

MOUSTAKAS, CLARK.   *The Authentic Teacher*. Cambridge, Mass.: Howard A. Doyle Publishing Company, 1966.

POLE, DAVID.   *Conditions of Rational Inquiry*. New York: Oxford University Press, 1961.

PURKEY, WILLIAM W.   *Self Concept and School Achievement*. Englewood Cliffs, N.J.: Prentice-Hall, Inc., 1970.

ROGERS, CARL R.   *Freedom to Learn*. Columbus, Ohio: Charles E. Merrill Books, Inc., 1969.

ROGERS, CARL R.   *On Becoming a Person*. Boston, Mass.: Houghton Mifflin Company, 1961.

RYLE, GILBERT.   *Concept of Mind*. New York: Barnes & Noble, Inc., 1950.

WEBER, EVELYN.   *Early Childhood Education: Perspectives on Change*. Worthington, Ohio: Charles A. Jones, 1970.

2

Looking at the teacher

We view others through our own eyes, and our opinion of others is influenced by the values, the attitudes, and the perspective that are intrinsic parts of ourselves. Any approach to child study, then, which is dependent upon a teacher's view of a child, must take into account the nature of the individual observer.

We have made a fetish of objectivity in our times. As we have seen in Chapter 1, we cannot divorce ourselves from our judgments. We read our own experience into what we observe of others' behavior. To deny this is to depreciate humanness. Arthur Combs says:

What makes people human are matters of feeling, belief, values, attitudes, understandings. Without these things a man is nothing. These are the qualities which make people human. They are also the qualities which, in our zeal to be objective, we have carefully eliminated from much of what goes on in our public schools. The problem of dehumanization is no accident. We brought it on ourselves. We have created a Frankenstein's monster which has broken loose to run amok among us.[1]

If the attempt to become totally objective tends to dehumanize then we must consider the human qualities of the individual who is or will become the teacher. These qualities must be put to work for the benefit of children. Teachers and future teachers must become more perceptive about themselves and others so that they may become aware of the consequences of their own behavior.

The importance of self-knowledge

Self-knowledge helps in the understanding of others. When we know our own motives for behavior, we can more easily infer the motives of those we observe. A teacher who is aware of her own discomfort when she is questioned about her program by the principal, and one who studies the causes of this discom-

[1] Arthur Combs, "An Educational Imperative: The Human Dimension," p. 174.

fort, can empathize with a child who has to justify his action to the teacher. A teacher who is conscious of the involvement that comes with the pursuit of a creative enterprise is less likely to interrupt a child who is absorbed in such a project as building with blocks.

Self-knowledge can also help us to sense when our own biases have influenced our judgment. If the teacher has an attractive sister who has always been favored in the family, she might find that she is easily antagonized by the pretty little girls in her classroom. For another teacher, a child who constantly seeks approval might satisfy nurturant instincts which might prevent the teacher from encouraging independence in the child.

These personal feelings cannot be eliminated, but teachers and prospective teachers can be made aware of them. No one who is human is going to react to all other individuals in the same way. A teacher may say, "I love all of the children in my class," but she is deceiving herself if she believes she really can have the same feelings for each of them. Hopefully, she can respect each one's individuality and can try to understand them all. But, if she is a human being with feelings, she is going to be drawn to some individuals and be annoyed or indifferent to others. Teachers cannot help responding to students in terms of their own personal needs and their own emotional framework.

How can teachers and prospective teachers learn to know themselves better so that they can take into account their own attitudes when they interpret the observed behavior of children? Arthur Jersild has pioneered efforts to develop self-understanding in teachers. As a result of his survey of teacher attitudes in 1952 he concluded that a person who wants to help others to understand themselves must first strive for self-understanding. This has far-reaching implications both for preservice and inservice teacher-training programs. Opportunities must be offered to teachers and prospective teachers which will help them to grow in self-knowledge.[2] Self-understanding, according to Jersild, requires something different from the methods, study plans, and skills that are usually emphasized in education. For a teacher to accept herself, she must identify her own concerns. Only then can she share the concerns of her students and help them to gain healthy attitudes of self-acceptance.

In a later study Jersild used written statements, opinion polls, conferences, and the shared clinical experiences of several thousands of people who were mainly teachers engaged in part-time or full-time graduate work at Teachers College.[3] On the basis of these interviews and related techniques, an instrument was devised called the Personal Issues Inventory. Items appeared on the left side quoting, "What others have said." Teachers were to respond on the right side with a choice of several possibilities offering degrees of agreement or disagreement. This instrument was then administered to other groups of graduate students.

The inventory revealed that teachers were concerned about anxiety, feel-

[2] Arthur Jersild, *In Search of Self*, p. 118.
[3] Jersild, *When Teachers Face Themselves*.

ings of loneliness, the search for meaning, sex, hostility, and compassion. Jersild devotes a chapter of his book to each of these concerns. It is not difficult to see how teachers' attitudes and emotions affect their behavior in the classroom. Anxiety, for example, might cause behavior in which the person who feels threatened seeks to control and vies to rise above others. Scholarship is often motivated by such neurotic drives. Successful academic students who become teachers often strive to maintain their self-esteem by using these strategies with their class. A person who avoids emotional involvement might also be reacting to feelings of anxiety. A detached teacher may be effective in communicating ideas, but feelings remain blocked.

The reader might examine Jersild's Personal Issues Inventory and might make an attempt to understand something of her own attitudes and feelings.[4] If each teacher or prospective teacher can learn to face herself, then she can begin to move toward intimacy and communication with others in her teaching.

Psychological methods applied to teacher education

It has been suggested by some that the best methods for preparing teachers for effective interaction in the classroom would be through group therapy or psychoanalysis. Many teachers have sought such experiences on their own and have found that they were helpful both in personal and in professional ways. Clinical psychologists and psychiatrists are required to undergo some form of analysis before they are qualified to work with patients. Teachers are not psychologists, but their actions have psychological impact. Whether they know it or not, they are practicing psychology in their daily encounters with children. Their attitudes and actions can cause the student to feel humiliation and shame or pride and self-worth. The teacher does not treat mental illnesses, but she must occasionally deal with disturbed children in her classroom. Since she is performing in a psychological role to a greater or lesser extent, she should try to function as effectively as possible at what she is already doing.

Psychoanalysis or group therapy cannot become part of teacher education for very practical reasons. Such treatment is expensive and takes an enormous amount of time. Jersild says, "The genius who can show how the full range of the benefits of psychoanalysis and psychotherapy might be incorporated into the regular educational process has not come along."[5] However, there are some common areas of investigation that would serve well for both the prospective therapist and prospective teacher.

There is good evidence to suggest that effective teachers are personally adequate people. The teacher's personality and mental attitude might, from our point of view, be considered as important as the knowledge of methods and theory that she has acquired. To produce an effective teacher, then, is not

---

[4] Jersild, *When Teachers Face Themselves*, Appendix B, pp. 149–161.
[5] Jersild, *When Teachers Face Themselves*, p. 12.

only a matter of teaching her how to teach; it is also a matter of helping her become a more effective and a more secure person.

In his studies of the helping professions at the University of Florida Arthur Combs has come up with a list of qualities that distinguish a good teacher from a poor one:

> Good teachers feel identified with, rather than apart from, others.
> Good teachers feel basically adequate rather than inadequate.
> Good teachers feel trustworthy rather than untrustworthy.
> Good teachers see themselves as wanted rather than unwanted.
> Good teachers perceive their purpose in teaching as one of freeing, rather than controlling, students.
> Good teachers tend to be more concerned with larger, rather than smaller, issues.
> Good teachers are more likely to be self-revealing, rather than self-concealing.
> Good teachers tend to be personally involved, rather than alienated.
> Good teachers are concerned with furthering processes, rather than achieving goals.[6]

If these are the characteristics that distinguish good teachers, then much more attention must be given to the prospective teacher as a person and to the ways in which she interacts with others.

It would be valuable if prospective teachers were to acquire a strong background in psychological foundations. Courses in normal and abnormal psychology should be taken as electives, if they are not required in the teacher-education program. Study concerned with the source of neurosis, the effects of inner conflict upon behavior, and the ways in which individuals adapt and cope with their environment, develop understandings that can be applied in the classroom. Some of the most discerning teachers that this writer has known began their college careers as psychology majors!

The use of attitude tests and scales in teacher education

Jersild's studies were among the first to investigate teacher attitudes as they relate to the learning process. As educators became more aware of their own role in group interaction, tools were devised which attempted to assess attitudes and to analyze group process. For example, in one personality inventory the respondent is asked to indicate her reaction to a series of statements in terms of how she thinks of herself. In one column she responds to the statement "As I Am," while in a second column she reacts to "As I Wish I Were."[7]

It might be helpful to look at some of these investigations. No doubt, many of the scales and inventories on attitudes would serve us well in assessing the role of the teacher in her interaction with children. However, there are

[6] Combs, *An Educational Imperative: The Human Dimension*, pp. 177–178.
[7] Stephen M. Corey, *Action Research to Improve School Practices*, Chapter 6.

limitations to these efforts at measurement. College students and teachers soon become "test wise" and answer with the desired responses on these questionnaires. It is not difficult to see the kind of response that indicates the acceptable teacher attitude. Even unconsciously, teachers choose the preferred responses, often thinking that these answers truly represent their feelings. Observers of their behavior in the classroom see that their actions belie their chosen attitudes.

A doctoral student known to this writer decided to use such an inventory to assess attitudes of teachers before and after a training program in group dynamics. To validate her instrument, she chose a committee of judges to evaluate the changes in behavior of the teachers in their work with children. Everyone on the committee had worked closely with the training program and was aware of the goals to be achieved. They also had close contact with the teachers and the children with whom they were working.

The attitude test was administered to the group of teachers before and after the training session. Positive changes in attitude were measured. The judges also evaluated the performance of the teachers before and after the training session. Those who showed greatest growth in group-leadership abilities did not show much change on the attitude tests. Those whose pretest and posttest showed the greatest improvement in attitude were among the poorest in performance in group situations with children. It appears that the teachers who related poorly to children had, throughout the training program, learned the right words with which to respond on the attitude test. This knowledge, however, had little effect upon their performance.

It is questionable, therefore, whether measurement of attitude really reveals true attitudes. This is particularly so if the inventory is used to judge competency. If, however, such inventories are used simply to give students greater insight into themselves, they may serve as an effective tool.

The inventory devised by George Stern and Joseph M. Masling is useful for this purpose.[8] Students are asked to put in order of preference statements about teacher roles and feelings selected from interviews with teachers. Each of these ten statements is representative of a particular teacher attitude as defined by Stern. These attitudes are:

1. Practical, detached, no personal involvement
2. Status seeking
3. Nurturant
4. Nondirective
5. Rebellious
6. Preadult fixated
7. Orderly
8. Dependent
9. Exhibitionist
10. Authoritarian, dominant

After the students have placed the statements of feelings in their order of

[8] George Stern and Joseph M. Masling, *Teachers Preference Scale*.

preference, the class discusses the categories devised by Stern and infers the manner in which these attitudes affect the teacher's role in the classroom. No one except the student herself knows the choices that she has made. The discussion of teacher attitudes and how they affect classroom climate have special meaning after the students have identified their own choices. (See Appendix A for selected sections of the Stern-Masling Preference Scale.)

Such a use of inventories can be helpful in developing self-knowledge in prospective teachers. An awareness that attitudes affect behavior, and a knowledge of the manner in which they determine teacher–child relationships, is, in itself, a significant discovery.

The role of the teacher in classroom interaction

Another means by which teachers and prospective teachers can learn more about their role in interacting with students might be through an examination of research studies that have attempted to analyze teachers' classroom behavior. This research ranges from empirical studies that count how many times the teacher performs a specific act such as organizing, disciplining, smiling, and so forth, to views of the totality of teacher performance with inferences concerning her perceptions. Some examples of these types of studies will be discussed here, with a view to assessing the value of such research for developing self-knowledge in teachers.

The first systematic account of teachers' classroom behavior was reported by Anderson and his associates in the middle 1940s and dealt with observations of kindergarten and primary-grade teachers.[9] An interesting generalization was made concerning the effect of teacher behavior on classroom climate. Where the teacher was directive, the class manifested dominative, conflictive behavior. These same children, observed a year later in another teacher's class, did not behave in the same way.

This finding is consistent with the classic study by Lewin, Lippitt, and White of boys' preadolescent group life. Leaders were trained to behave in a democratic, autocratic, or laissez-faire manner, and it was determined that leadership technique, rather than any other variable, influenced the boys' behavior. When the situation was restrictive in nature, the boys became aggressive and less sociable. When the situation was encouraging, free, accepting, and clearly defined, the boys moved toward group cohesion and their behavior became more spontaneous, productive, and integrated. The absence of any guidance in the laissez-faire situation led to much frustration and low morale.[10] (Many years later the writer simulated this experiment, to a limited extent, in her third-grade classroom. The results are reported in the section on role playing in Chapter 5.)

[9] H. H. Anderson *et al.*, *Studies of Teachers' Classroom Personalities.*
[10] Kurt Lewin, R. Lippitt, and R. K. White, "Patterns of Aggressive Behavior in Experimentally Created Social Climates," pp. 271–299.

More specific measuring tools of teachers' classroom behavior have since been devised by many investigators. Perhaps the best-known such instrument was developed by Flanders.[11] In this study Flanders developed a scheme for scoring and analyzing the verbal classroom behavior of teachers. He separated behavior into two major categories, indirect influence and direct influence. The types of behavior to be scored in each area by the observer were defined by subcategories. (See Appendix B for Categories for Interaction Analysis.) Flanders used this scale in field experiments to investigate the relationship between behavior of teachers and academic achievement.

Our concern, in this book, is not the reporting of the results of this type of research, but rather, the application of tools, devised for research purposes, for use in teacher education. The Flanders categories for interaction analysis have been revised for use in such settings. Elizabeth Hunter describes this system and its use in helping teachers and prospective teachers to become conscious of classroom talk in her book, *Encounter in the Classroom*.[12]

Sensitivity training in teacher education

Sensitivity training has become a popular idea in recent years and has taken many forms. During sensitivity training a participant learns about human relations, communication, and leadership skills. Many variations are being offered under such names as T-Groups, encounter groups, personal-growth groups, and marathons. These training programs have been offered at conference centers and in schools, universities, churches, and business organizations. Enthusiastic supporters of the movement claim that the effect of such programs has been to improve relationships between business executives and their staffs as well as to establish more humanistic climates within school systems.

The concept of sensitivity training developed from several sources and is a response to the needs of our times. The impersonal relationships that exist within large organizations have caused a reaction against "establishment" practices. Critics of education, such as John Holt, Paul Goodman, and Herbert Kohl, have emphasized the need for greater human interaction and personal concern in working with children. Ways to effect change are being investigated, and sensitivity training is one such attempt.

Tracing back into its history, sensitivity training has been in practice for quite a while. A group of Gestalt-oriented social psychologists formed the National Training Laboratory for Group Development in 1947, and NTL has conducted summer laboratory training programs at Bethel, Maine, each year since that time. These programs have become known as T-Groups—the "T" standing for training—or "Gestalt" groups. Because they are based upon observation and analysis, rather than upon a mechanical model of receiving and repeating information, NTL training programs are called laboratories. Participants work together in a small group over an extended period of time, learning

[11] N. A. Flanders, *Teacher Influence, Pupil Attitudes and Achievement*.
[12] Elizabeth Hunter, *Encounter in the Classroom*, Chapter 4.

through analysis of their own experiences—including feelings, reactions, perceptions, and behavior. T-Groups are one type of experienced-based learning. These groups are distinguished from group therapy in that they are not intended as a means of correcting significant psychological deficiencies, and persons needing or seeking psychotherapy are discouraged from participating.

T-Groups are conducted by "trainers" who have an understanding of group and individual behavior and are capable of dealing with others in non-punitive ways. Members of the T-Group participate, some trying to organize the group, some responding to each other, and some withdrawing. The behavior of the individuals in the group is observed and analyzed, and these perceptions and reactions become the data for learning in the T-Group setting.

Many of the activities used in sensitivity training are effective in teacher-education settings as well. Here are some ideas that might be tried in the classroom:

> *Listening game*: The class is grouped into small circles with eight to ten members in each. A topic is chosen which is of interest to the group. Before a member can offer his own opinion he must repeat what the person ahead of him has said—paraphrasing it to that person's satisfaction.
>
> *Magic circle*: The group sits in two concentric circles. The inside group discusses a topic selected in advance. The outside group makes observations on the behavior of the inside group and takes notes. Their observations are then discussed with the total group, following which they change places.
>
> *Observer*: A scene is set up for role play. An "Observer" stands outside the scene and comments on what is happening. She may guess at the unvoiced feelings of the participants in the scene.
>
> *Planned roles*: A specific situation is set up in advance for role play, and the players are briefed before the session. The audience does not know what briefings have been given to the role players, and they must guess whom the players represent. For example, one player might have been asked to try to dominate the discussion, another might have been told to play the role of arbitrator, and so on.
>
> *Role reversal*: The parties in a two-person situation change places and try to continue the discussion. This is particularly effective in pointing out what it is like to "be in someone else's shoes," as in a parent-teacher conference.[13]

Readers are encouraged to try out some of these activities and then to analyze and evaluate what happens in the process. While playing the role of children, students might begin to sense how difficult it sometimes is to have to "wait your turn." They might discover an effective way to stop a fight on the playground, or to sense why some teacher behavior is not effective in a particular situation. Behavior at teachers' meetings and at parent conferences is better understood when role playing and its analysis is applied to the situation.

[13] For additional games and activities to increase sensitivity, see Matthew B. Miles, *Learning To Work in Groups*, chapter 5; or Hunter, chapters 2 and 3.

Developing self-awareness

There are many ways in which the teacher or prospective teacher can gain insight into her own attitudes and can begin to understand her own behavior. Such self-knowledge is likely to increase her understanding of children and her ability to empathize with them.

The reader is advised to try some of the activities described in this chapter and to make use of the materials in Appendixes A and B. Teacher attitudes can be identified, and their effect upon classroom behavior can be assessed. The role of the teacher in classroom interaction can be analyzed. Techniques related to those employed in sensitivity training can be used to increase knowledge of group dynamics.

In Part II of this book activities are inserted into the text in **bold-face type,** which should help the reader to empathize with the feelings of the children being discussed. Many of these activities are of the type used in sensitivity training. Before the student reader can perform these freely and sincerely, she needs exposure to some exercises in concentration and observation. In the next chapter a program designed to give teachers a direct experience with these elements of the creative process will be described. It is recommended that readers try some of the exercises. The increase in awareness and sensitivity which is likely to develop will help in the understanding of the children they will observe.

REFERENCES

AMIDON, EDMOND, AND ELIZABETH HUNTER. *Improving Teaching: The Analysis of Classroom Verbal Interaction.* New York: Holt, Rinehart and Winston, Inc., 1966.

ANDERSON, H. H., AND J. BREWER. *Studies of Teachers' Classroom Personalities,* II. "Effects of Teachers' Dominative and Integrative Contacts on Children's Classroom Behavior." Applied Psychological Monographs, No. 8. Stanford, Calif.: Stanford University Press, 1946.

BESSELL, HAROLD, AND UVALDO PALOMARES. *Methods in Human Development Theory Manual.* San Diego, Calif.: Human Development Training Institute, 1970.

COMBS, ARTHUR. "An Educational Imperative: The Human Dimension." *To Nurture Humaneness,* ASCD Yearbook (1970), p. 174.

COMBS, ARTHUR. *The Professional Education of Teachers.* Boston, Mass.: Allyn and Bacon, 1965.

COREY, STEPHEN M. *Action Research to Improve School Practices.* New York: Teachers College Press, Columbia University, 1953.

FLANDERS, N. A. *Teacher Influence, Pupil Attitudes and Achievement.* Cooperative Research Monograph, No. 12, USOE. Washington, D.C.: Government Printing Office, 1965.

FOX, ROBERT, MARGARET BARRON LUSZKI, AND RICHARD SCHMUCK. *Diagnosing Classroom Learning Environments.* Chicago: Science Research Associates, Inc., 1966.

GORDON, IRA J.   *Studying the Child in School.* New York: John Wiley & Sons, Inc., 1966.

HARRISON, CHARLES H.   "The Teacher and the T-Group." *Scholastic Teacher* (February 1971).

HUDGINS, BRYCE B.   *The Instructional Process.* Chicago: Rand McNally & Company, 1971.

HUNTER, ELIZABETH.   *Encounter in the Classroom.* New York: Holt, Rinehart and Winston, Inc., 1972.

JERSILD, ARTHUR.   *In Search of Self.* New York: Teachers College Press, Columbia University, 1952.

JERSILD, ARTHUR.   *When Teachers Face Themselves.* New York: Teachers College Press, 1955.

LEWIN, KURT, R. LIPPITT, AND R. K. WHITE.   "Patterns of Aggressive Behavior in Experimentally Created Social Climates." *Journal of Social Psychology,* X (1939), pp. 271–299.

LIFTON, WALTER M.   *Working with Groups.* 2d ed. New York: John Wiley & Sons, Inc., 1961.

MILES, MATTHEW B.   *Learning to Work in Groups.* New York: Teachers College Press, Columbia University, 1959.

NASH, PAUL.   "Integrating Feeling, Thinking and Acting in Teacher Education." *Bulletin of the American Association of Colleges for Teacher Education,* XXIV (April 1971).

RYANS, DAVID.   *Characteristics of Teachers.* Washington, D.C.: American Council on Education, 1960.

SEASHORE, CHARLES.   "What is Sensitivity Training?" *NTL Institute News and Reports,* II (April 1968).

STERN, GEORGE, AND JOSEPH M. MASLING.   *Teachers Preference Scale.* Syracuse, N.Y.: Psychological Research Center, Syracuse University, 1960.

3

Building awareness in teachers
A personal report*

Many years ago a friend came to visit the nursery school I was directing. She had been an actress, but was, at this time, preparing to teach speech and drama in the schools. In a psychology course that was part of her masters program in education she was required to make observations of children, and so she had come to watch some four-year-olds in my class. She did several ten-minute time samples, recording in detail the overt behavior of two of the children. In her written report based upon these observations, she gave evidence of intimate knowledge of these two children. I had not discussed them with her and was surprised to find that she knew so much about them.

When I questioned her, she answered that she had been trained in observational techniques and in making inferences from observation as part of her preparation for acting.

I thought about this for a long time. If actors can be trained to be more aware, why not teachers? Certainly the need for sensitivity and insight in the effective performance of their role is just as great. I began to investigate methods employed in the training of actors. I read Stanislavski's books and found that much that the famous director of the Moscow Art Theatre had to say about actors' preparation was applicable to teacher education.

I observed my friend as she taught drama classes to children. Much of what she was doing seemed familiar to me. I had studied modern dance and had spent many years working with children in creative movement. Many of the teaching techniques were the same as those used in beginning acting classes. There was an emphasis upon involvement and concentration. Some of the exercises, both in drama and in creative dance, were directed toward the development of greater sense awareness.

* Some parts of this chapter were originally published in an article by this author, "The Creative State of Mind: An Application of the Stanislavski Acting Method to Teacher Education," *The Journal of Teacher Education*, XIX (Spring 1968).

It was, perhaps, seven or eight years later that I had the opportunity to translate some of these thoughts into action. After years of teaching in nursery, kindergarten, and the primary grades, I had begun working in teacher education at George Peabody College for Teachers in Nashville, Tennessee.

In the winter of 1966 I taught a graduate course in Early Childhood Education. In discussing the need for close observation and intimate knowledge of children, I told my students about my friend's visit to my nursery school. The class, consisting mainly of experienced teachers, thought that the idea of applying acting techniques to teacher education was a fascinating one and worth a try! And so, in the spring trimester, a continuation of the graduate course in Early Childhood Education was offered, in which an experimental design for teacher education was to be introduced.

There were to be no specific assignments and no term papers in the course. However, each student was asked to keep a log of her personal reactions to various class activities or to any other relevant experiences outside of class. They were also asked to submit any creative writing that they wanted to, in the form of reactions to readings or original stories and poems. More material was submitted in this class than is normally required for most graduate courses in education!

It is these written logs and reactions that will be used to report the progress of this experiment in this chapter. I will not describe the class discussion that began each session. Much of it concerned reactions to readings, especially books dealing with biographies and personal accounts of children and teachers. I will, however, give some of the exercises used to prepare the students for creative activity in the hope that they can be used in other teacher-education settings.

Acting exercises are often referred to as "theater games." This is an appropriate title, since "the game is a natural group form providing involvement and personal freedom necessary for experiencing."[1]

The theater games described here have been grouped according to the various objectives toward which they are directed. These are: Observation, Concentration, Body Awareness, Sensory Awareness, and Empathy. There is considerable overlap in these categories. Games focused upon observation or sense awareness all require concentration. Body awareness is really one form of sensory experience, and it is an essential element in building concentration. Empathy involves skills developed through all of the other areas, and might, therefore, be the last to be presented to the group. The games, however, need not be offered in the order given below. It might be desirable to alternate areas of focus at each session. The games presented to the class at Peabody College are described below, and reactions of the students follow each category.[2]

---

[1] Viola Spolin, *Improvisation for the Theater*, p. 4.

[2] Additional games and exercises to develop these skills can be found in Spolin's book and in others that deal with the Stanislavski acting method.

Observation

Training in observation is most essential for the teacher, and is, in fact, a major objective of this book. It is equally important for the actor. Stanislavski recognized this when he said:

An actor should be observant not only on the stage, but also in real life. He should concentrate with all his being on whatever attracts his attention. He should look at an object, not as any absent-minded passerby, but with penetration. Otherwise his whole creative method will prove lop-sided and bear no relationship to life.[3]

Stanislavski urged his acting students to observe the petals of a flower or to study a spider's web and then try to express in words what makes these things give pleasure. The attempt to describe causes the observer to notice more closely. When the student has learned to make direct and fresh contact with the environment and the objects and people in it, this broadens his ability to involve himself with his own phenomenal world. Once begun, like ripples on the water, this process continues, and he becomes more aware and more capable of detailed perception.

Teachers must also be taught to look at, listen to, and be aware of all that is going on around them. Young children come to school equipped with this sensory awareness and keen powers of observation. The teacher must heighten her own sensitivities in order to share the child's world with him.

Training in observation begins with simple classroom games that are easy to play and are enjoyable. If they are done in the first few sessions, students often do not see the long-range purpose for these activities, but they enter into them in the spirit of fun, and so this is a good way to start.

Changing appearances: Five or six people are selected to stand in front of the class while the group observes everything they can about them. Then they are asked to step outside the room for a few minutes and to make some minor changes in their appearance. The ladies might exchange jewelry or move a watch from left to right wrist. Men can remove a tie clasp or unbutton a shirt or jacket. When they return, the class is to determine what changes have been made.

Find the objects: Four or five small objects are placed around the room before the class arrives. They might be a paper clip, a bobby pin, a rubber band, and so on. They are put in places where all can see them, not underneath or within furniture. However, they are placed in such a way that they seem like natural parts of the environment, for example, a rubber band looped over a doorknob or on the back of a chair.

Students are informed of the four or five objects and told what they are. Time is given for them to be spotted but not removed from their places.

The first of these games was played at the opening meeting of the Peabody

[3] Constantin Stanislavski, *An Actor Prepares*, p. 86.

class and was its first exposure to theater exercises. A log entry of a third-grade teacher reveals her initial reaction to the class, her response to the game, and its effects upon her after she left the class. This is her first log entry:

I went to class this afternoon with no idea of what to expect. The explanation of the course was interesting and exciting, but I kept feeling inadequate to cope with it. I began to be aware of how little I *was* aware! I recognized none of the changes in the six people who were standing! If this is to develop my awareness in order to help children—then let's go! On the way home I noticed the shapes of tail-lights and colors of cars, also traceries of asphalt in the cracks in the street.

I am excited—keyed up—but also scared of tackling this concept! I think I'll try an experiment tomorrow. Art without motivation—then art with motivation through perceptual awareness.

This third-grade teacher proceeded to try out her ideas for presenting art with her class in the following few days. Her next two log entries reported on lessons on drawing daffodils. The first day the children were simply asked to draw from memory; the second day each child was given a daffodil, and the teacher asked, "How does each petal look, feel? How does it smell? How are the petals different? How can you show this?" There was improvement in the pictures.

Concentration

The ability to concentrate is the beginning step in inducing what Stanislavski called "the creative state of mind." One of the most notable characteristics of persons involved in creative endeavor is the intense degree of concentration that permits them to direct all their spiritual and intellectual forces toward one definite object. All artists must be capable of this concentration if they are to communicate their ideas as well as their feelings to others.

Concentration of attention helps the student to overcome self-consciousness as demonstrated in the first exercise presented below. When one is totally absorbed in perceiving an object, either real or imaginary, he has not time or thought for what he looks like to others. Observation requires a focusing of attention outside the self, but perceiving imaginary objects demands an even more disciplined power of concentration.

Several of the exercises below are focused upon the perceiving of imaginary objects. Stanislavski requested that his students train themselves to recall in detail, what a meal tasted like, what dishes it was served upon, and so on and suggested that they do this kind of thing each night after they have gone to bed. "Inner attention" centers on things we see, hear, touch, and feel in imaginary circumstances. Exercises in concentration, similar to those used by Stanislavski in his training of actors, were used with the graduate students at George Peabody College.

Solving an arithmetic problem: Students work with partners in this exercise. One member of the team is given a fairly difficult problem of addition or subtraction to be done "in her head." While she is performing this task, her partner is to distract her with conversation, questions, and so on.

The students doing the arithmetic problem become irritable or giggly and self-conscious as their concentration is broken.

Roles are reversed, and then the total class is asked to describe their feelings. Those few who were able to solve the problem had maintained a degree of concentration in spite of distractions.

Sensing an object: Each member of the class is asked to take a small object from her pocket or pocketbook. She is to concentrate on it for a few minutes, experiencing it in as many ways as she possibly can. Is it cold, or warm, smooth, or bumpy? Can it make a sound? Does it have an odor? Does it have any moving parts? How heavy is it?

Then she is to put the object away, and try to reproduce, from imagination, the sensations she had when she was holding it.

When a person seems to be able to concentrate enough to do this successfully, she may be asked to do it while others in the group try to guess what object she has in mind.

Pantomime of a daily activity: Several people at a time are asked to do a pantomime of something they do every day, such as making a bed, brushing teeth, setting a table, and so forth. Each student in the audience is to focus upon one of the performers to see if her actions are complete and plausible. Does she walk through the middle of the bed to get to the other side? Did she turn off the water or put the toothpaste down when she completed the pantomime?

Complete concentration is required in order to remember the details involved in such daily activities. This exercise is effective in beginning classes in creative dramatics with children.

The ball of paper: The students sit in a circle, close enough to each other to be able to pass an object from one to the other. The ball of paper is passed, but the students are to imagine it is a ball of fire, a snowball, a bird with a broken wing, and so on.

Silence should be maintained while the paper is being passed, in order for the students to fully concentrate upon the various sensations evoked by the suggestions of the object that the paper has become.

The "Ball of Paper" exercise had particular significance for the class at Peabody. It seemed to mark the turning point at which time the students suddenly perceived what we were trying to do. This came during the third week, and the class was able to focus upon the ball of paper with a good deal of concentration. The sensations of coldness and of burning were real to them. The "bird with the broken wing" evoked feelings of tenderness that were displayed without self-consciousness. I decided to try them out on experiencing a deeper emotion.

I took a ruler from the desk and stated simply that "This is the shotgun that killed John Kennedy." As the ruler was passed around the circle, feelings of revulsion were freely shown. Some refused to touch it. Some were moved to tears.

I felt, at the time, that I was perhaps "going too far," and that the experience was too deeply involving for the class. I dismissed them following this exercise, with no further discussion.

Comments in their logs following this incident revealed that it had special meaning for many of the participants. In the sessions that followed this one, there was never a problem of getting total concentration. Students became absorbed with an idea as soon as it was presented. Here is an excerpt from a student's log.

Working with objects was the first time I experienced beginning concentration. The "ball of paper" pantomime and the group experience of passing objects around a circle let in the light. I will never forget this day. I really saw for the first time what we were trying to do. For the first time, I also began to understand how this applied to "feeling with" young children in order to understand them.

Body awareness

The state of the muscles of the body not only reflect the emotional state of the individual but often determine his reactions. Stanislavski recognized, long before psychological information was common in everyday thought, that physical tenseness paralyzes action. A central idea of his method is that the complex of human psychological life—moods, desires, feelings, intentions, ambitions—is expressed through simple physical actions, and that before such action is possible, the actor must be freed from muscular tautness that interferes with inner emotional experience.

Stanislavski demonstrated the effects of tension by asking his students to do an arithmetical problem while holding up a corner of the piano! In order to answer the question, they had to let down the weight, relax the muscles, and only then were they able to concentrate on the problem at hand.

Lessons in muscle relaxation are part of the training of actors and were given to the teachers in the Peabody class at the beginning of each session.

Tensing the Muscles: Sitting in their seats, students are asked to feel tension in their toes and to tighten, in sequence, the muscles up through the body to the head. Each part of the body is isolated, and students are asked to feel the tension in those muscles separately. No visible motion need be made. Soon the total body is tense and rigid.

Release of tension may also be done by degrees, starting with the head and face and working downwards. Or the students may be asked to release all of the tension at once, "letting it all out" and feeling calm and loose. Images are created by the teacher to induce feelings of relaxation, such as "You are gliding along a stream in a canoe on a lovely day with soft breezes blowing."

Students begin to realize the difference between tension and relaxation, and become aware of the feelings in their own bodies.

Once the students have developed enough concentration to allow them to be free of self-consciousness, they may be asked to explore movement with large muscle activity. They can move freely around the room but must always focus upon the feeling in the muscles (kinesthetic sense).

Back Bouncing and Body Swings: In a standing position, not too close to a neighbor, students are asked to drop backs, heads, and arms forward so that they hang loosely from the waist. In this position, they are to bounce their backs, bending their knees a little to give momentum, but remaining totally relaxed throughout their whole body.

If this is done correctly, arms will swing loosely back and forth as the back bounces. Students are then asked to let the arm swing get bigger, keeping the whole body loose and relaxed. As the swings get bigger, they may come up to an upright position and move around the room.

This is a most freeing and relaxing type of large muscle movement. When students can do this with relaxation they report a great feeling of well-being and freedom.

Ball game: Games of various kinds can be played with imaginary balls. The teacher determines the size and weight of the ball, and the participants must respond with their movement and the amount of energy they use, to the various weights and sizes.

Using a drum to establish a rhythm for the throwing and catching can make this exercise take on the qualities of a dance.

Simulating a team game, such as baseball, requires members of the group to respond quickly to one another in movement. Done in slow motion, and in time to a drum beat, this activity also takes on a dance quality.

Middle-grade school children, especially boys, do well with this exercise. It develops concentration, muscle awareness, and ability to relate to others.

Yoga: Various exercises borrowed from yoga stress the inner experience of the movement and thus emphasize body awareness. Other forms of Oriental exercise also have this quality.

When there is a member of the group familiar with these forms of exercises, she should be invited to teach the class.

The Peabody class was fortunate in having a representation of several cultures among its members. Kyoko, a Japanese girl, had some experience with an Oriental type of exercise, Tai Chi, which she shared with us. We got into the habit of having members of the class take turns in giving a warm-up exercise at the beginning of each session.

A young girl from India had some difficulties with body movement at first, owing to both her sari and to her inhibition! She told of her discomfort in her log entry. Finally she borrowed a pair of slacks from her roommate and became involved in the activity. "Now I feel more active, and whenever I hear music, my feet start dancing and my hands start snapping. . . . I feel that this is good for anybody, either a small child or an adult."

Another student expressed his feelings about the movement experiences with a poem:

IMPRESSIONS

Thrill and excitement of new emotion,
Involving
The boom of a drum that frees from restraint,
Inhibition
Movement away from bald heads and moustaches,
And airless classrooms that reek of the past,
And crusty professors with noses that twitch
With sweet Learning's bitter restraint,
Memorization
Excitement of life with creative
Expression
Bright afternoon sky with a fleecy white cloud,
Expectation!

Sensory awareness

A major part of the Stanislavski Method is concerned with stimulating the senses. In all of the arts, sensory awareness is preliminary to creation. Through heightened perception, the artist is able to capture some aspect of experience and express it through his art form. The teacher's role also involves heightening perception. Like the artist, she must be more fully aware, so that she can help children to synthesize fragments of experience into significant wholes. She must sharpen her own senses in order to penetrate into the nature of things and people.

There are exercises for sharpening all of the five senses. Some of these have already been presented in previously discussed sections. Certainly the sense of sight is involved in all of the observation games. Sight, touch, taste, and smell are all ways of "Sensing an Object," the game described in the section on "Concentration." Here are some other games to develop sensory awareness:

> *Listening exercise*: While remaining in their seats, the students in the class are divided in halves. Those on one side of the room are to listen for sounds within the building. The other half is to concentrate on sounds heard outside the building. They are to do this for several minutes, and then members of each group report on what they have heard.
>
> Students may be asked to do this exercise periodically at home, that is, practice listening to the sounds in the environment.
>
> *Feel box*: Objects of various textures are placed in a box with a hole in one side. Each participant is to put a hand into the box and pick an object. Without looking at it, she is to identify it and describe its qualities.
>
> Another variation is to ask a student to act out how the texture of an object makes her feel, for example, a smooth piece of satin,

sticky fly paper. Other students are to guess what object has provoked this reaction.

Taste exercise: The teacher describes an item of food to be experienced through taste, and the class tries to re-create the taste sensation from memory. The most effective sensations are those evoked by the suggestion of a lemon or peanut butter. It is desirable for the participants to keep their eyes closed while concentrating on the taste sensation.

Smell exercises: The above procedure can be used to evoke experiences of smell, for example, a rose, ammonia, and so on.

Another way to explore the sense of smell is to present the students with several jars of liquid, all having the same appearance, but differing odors, for example, alcohol, water, lemonade, and so on. Students are to guess what is contained in each of the jars.

The students in the Peabody class reported on increased sensory awareness as a result of these exercises. One teacher mentioned that she listens as she walks through the halls of her school, instead of "hurrying deafly through each day." The comment of the third-grade teacher in her first log entry, quoted earlier in this chapter, indicated heightened sensory awareness.

Many teachers found children's poems that deal with the senses, expressing the sound of the wind, animal noises, and so on. They reported that they read these to their classes, asking the children to experience each sensation.

When all of the senses are tuned in to life, we are likely to experience a "high" moment. Some young people today think that this feeling is achieved only through the use of drugs. Heightened sensory awareness produces this feeling of exhilaration, and many of us can recall times when we have experienced it. One student, who had spent her childhood in Germany, recalled such a peak moment.

Thinking back it is hard for me to decide how old I had been then. Perhaps nine or ten? I really can't say. Every winter my parents and I went to a lovely little ski lodge in the Erzgebirge not very far from Dresden, our home town, for a few days of winter sports. The children in that part of the world learn to ski about the same time they learn to walk, and I loved to ski.

This particular morning I had gotten up before anyone, it seemed. It was a brilliantly cold morning. When I emerged from the back door, the glitter of the sunlight on the snow almost blinded me. There had been a light snowfall during the night and all the tracks from the day before had been covered. It was almost like being the first being in a brand new world.

I put on my skis and stood up and looked around me. A strange feeling of exhilaration took hold of me. I began gliding easily and smoothly along the woodland trail. Everything was still—so still. Occasionally some snow would fall off a fir-tree branch with a little clomp, but even the wind seemed to be holding its breath in the stillness. I felt light and free. With every push of the sticks I seemed to be flying smoothly over a brand new world—all mine, all mine.

Empathy

According to Webster, "empathy" is the "capacity for participating in another's feelings or ideas." A teacher must be able to sense the feelings a child has in order to truly relate to him. It is not enough for her to know the reasons for a child's aggressive actions; she must sense what it is like to feel that way herself. "The sudden loss of temper nearly all of us have experienced gives a momentary empathy with the feelings of uncontrollable rage, helplessness, confusion, guilt, and self-hate felt by the child with no impulse control. . . . Each of us contains the whole range of emotional health and disease within himself."[4]

Students in the Peabody class were encouraged to read selections from literature which give insight into the feelings of children. The editors of *Conflict in the Classroom* present such selections to their readers in order to give them the intense experience of how it feels to be disturbed.

Stanislavski attempted to give this experience to his acting students through a method known as "emotional memory" or "emotional recall." When an actor undertakes a new role, he tries to determine the motive or "objective" behind the action of his character. If the actor does not sense the character's emotions readily, he attempts to recall some comparable situation in his own life which will set the climate in which he can experience the emotions of the character he is playing. The actor thus becomes united in feeling with the role he is portraying by finding a comparable experience in his own life and reliving the emotions involved in that personal experience.

Several exercises can help develop the ability to emphathize:

> *Walk as if you were*: After some freeing experiences in movement, the students are asked to walk around the room, feeling as if they were— a proud prince, a man being chased, a child entering a dark cave, a flirtatious woman, and so on.
>
> Each person is to concentrate on his own interpretation, becoming the character in every aspect and feeling the part in every part of his body.
>
> *Recalling an incident*: Students are asked to recall a situation they have observed in which a child was emotionally involved. A kindergarten teacher may remember the fears exhibited by some of the children on the first day of class. A sixth-grade teacher might recall the disappointment of the boy who was not chosen for the ball team. This incident might be written down and brought to class for the next session. Students are then asked to analyze the behavior of the child in the incident they chose, searching out the motive or objective of his act.
>
> The question is then asked, "Have you ever experienced anything like this?" "Have you ever been motivated by these same feelings?"
>
> The personal experience can be recalled from recent events or

---

[4] Nicholas J. Long, William C. Morse, and Ruth G. Newman, eds., *Conflict in the Classroom*, p. 1.

from childhood. Students then role-play some of the situations that they recall. Emphasis is placed upon recalling one's own feelings in the situation.

Students in the Peabody class became quite involved with this last exercise. Starting with an incident of a kindergarten child who wanted a toy possessed by another, one teacher recalled a time when she had found a much-desired old harpsichord in an antique shop. She went home to tell her husband of her discovery, but when she returned to the store a day later, the treasure had been sold! Her anger and frustration were so great that there were tears in her eyes as she acted out the situation!

Several teachers in the class wrote stories which revealed empathy and deep insights into their children. A nursery-school teacher wrote a story about "Herbie."[5]

Herbie noticed the easels and paint the minute he walked into nursery school. Herbie liked to paint. He hurried to hang up his coat. He put on his smock and rushed to the easel. He watched carefully as the teacher wrote "Herbie" in the corner of his paper. Then Herbie took a brush and painted a big red circle around his name. "Herbie," he thought. "I'm Herbie!"

Then Herbie began to paint. He painted large red marks on his paper. He watched as the red paint ran down the paper. Then he put green marks beside the red ones. How nice it was to watch the little red streams of paint hit the green! Soon Herbie had green streams running on his red marks, and red streams running on his green marks. Herbie then took his yellow brush and began to make yellow circles on his paper. "Oh, how much fun!" thought Herbie. "I'm Herbie. Painting is the nicest kind of a game! I like it!"

Herbie looked carefully at his picture. It needed just one more thing. He picked up his orange brush, wiped it free of too much paint. Then he began to throw his brush just a tiny bit. Surprise! Little dots of paint landed on his paper. He made just a few dots and then put his orange brush away.

Herbie wiped his hands on his smock and stood back to look at his picture. "Gee," Herbie thought. "Such nice colors! Yes, I'm Herbie, and I did a good job. I like to paint. Tomorrow I'll use different colors and do something different with paint. I'm Herbie."

Application to teaching

In the second half of the course students were asked to prepare and teach to the rest of the class a lesson from any area of the curriculum or for any age level. The one requirement was that it involve fully and creatively all members of the group, who, at this point, were capable of full participation without self-consciousness.

For one of the lessons a young man brought to class various shaped and sized cartons from the grocery store and asked the group to construct a community on the lawn in front of the college building. Students became excited about different ways of putting on a roof or about the location of the railway station. They mapped out the community, lining up their structures along streets labeled North, South, East, and West. They were so involved in and excited about what they were doing that they did not notice people walking by and were unaware that pictures were being taken of them as they worked.

Several members of the class who had experience with various ethnic groups were able to share these with the class. A young man who had worked on Indian reservations constructed the atmosphere of a Zuni ceremonial rain dance. He had made masks similar to those used by the Zuni and had a recording of their music. He described the feeling of harmony with each other that the Zuni consider essential before the dance can be performed and made the class feel that they were actually participating in the ceremony as they moved to the music.

A young woman from the Fiji islands took us on an imaginary trip to her land. We boarded a plane, experienced the flight, and soon found ourselves walking on the beach, watching the palm trees swaying in the breeze, and feeling the warm white sand between our toes! We then collected objects that can be found along the beach—coconuts, shells, and seaweed—and we made our own souvenirs to take home with us.

Other areas of the school curriculum were also explored. A sixth-grade teacher gave a grammar lesson in which descriptions of the action of horses were derived from looking at pictures and from movement exploration. A third-grade teacher taught a lesson on fractions in which the concept of thirds was discovered by the participants when they cut felt into three parts and bounced balls in time to a three-quarter rhythm.

In all of the lessons the qualities of involvement, discovery, and creative participation were present to a greater or lesser degree.

Some of the students' logs showed that they were already applying their new experiences to their teaching situation. The third-grade teacher who experimented with using movement to discover fractions continued to try out movement ideas with her own class of children. A sixth-grade teacher included in her log pictures of boys and girls in her class participating in dramatization and movement exploration during poetry and social studies lessons. Another student had great success in inspiring her class to write Japanese haiku poems.

Teachers who have experienced elements of the creative process as part of their teacher-education program are likely to be able to evoke greater creativity in the children that they teach. They will also be able to sense and feel along with children and thus will understand them better.

This chapter has described a program that proved to be very effective in increasing teachers' sensitivity and in making them more aware and responsive to children. Some of the same activities and exercises can be used in preservice teacher-education programs. Suggestions for the application of these ideas will be made, when relevant, throughout the remaining chapters.

REFERENCES

ASHTON-WARNER, SYLVIA. *Spinster*. New York: Simon and Schuster, Inc., 1958.

ASHTON-WARNER, SYLVIA. *Teacher*. New York: Simon and Schuster, Inc., 1963.

LINDERMAN, EARL, and DONALD HERBERHOLZ. *Developing Artistic and Perceptual Awareness in the Elementary School*. 2d ed. Dubuque, Iowa: William C. Brown Company, 1969.

LONG, NICHOLAS, WILLIAM C. MORSE, AND RUTH G. NEWMAN. *Conflict in the Classroom*. Belmont, Calif.: Wadsworth Publishing Company, 1965.

MASLOW, ABRAHAM. "The Creative Attitude." In *The Helping Relationship Sourcebook*, Donald L. Avila, Arthur W. Combs, and William W. Purkey, eds. Boston: Allyn and Bacon, Inc., 1971.

MOORE, SONIA. *The Stanislavski System: The Professional Training of an Actor*. New York: The Viking Press, Inc., 1965.

ROWEN, BETTY. "The Creative State of Mind: An Application of the Stanislavski Acting Method to Teacher Education." *The Journal of Teacher Education*, XIX (Spring 1968).

SPOLIN, VIOLA. *Improvisation for the Theater*. Evanston, Ill.: Northwestern University Press, 1963.

STANISLAVSKI, CONSTANTIN. *An Actor Prepares*. New York: Theatre Arts Books, 1948.

4

Looking at the child through direct observation

We have seen how self-knowledge is important to the teacher or prospective teacher, and how sensitivity and awareness can be heightened. It is time now to look at some ways of observing children and some techniques for gathering data about them.

There are many different ways to gather information and no one way is the right way. Some teachers may keep on-the-spot-records, making notes on scratch pads whenever they get the chance. Some, in team-teaching situations, may set aside a special time of the day or week which they save for observing. Sometimes a particular child presents problems, and the teacher wants to know "what makes him tick." At other times, a teacher chooses to observe a child who is unobtrusive, and she feels she knows too little about him.

There are various techniques for acquiring information about an individual child, and, in this chapter, we will examine several of these. The teacher herself must decide which method best suits her purposes. She might try more than one approach to gathering data. Insights gained from one approach might reinforce findings discovered through another means.

It is a good idea to keep an individual folder for each child in the class. Anecdotal records and time samples (discussed in detail later in this chapter) can be dropped into the folder from time to time. Interviews with parents and/or former teachers can be noted, and these can be placed in the folder. Before such an interview takes place, the teacher can review the information in the folder to remind her of incidents she might want to discuss. Examples of children's artwork and/or writings should be included in the collection, as well. Review of the materials in the folder from time to time gives the teacher an awareness of changes in behavior, growth patterns, and persistent problem areas. It is not unusual for an observant teacher to comment to herself, "I had forgotten that he used to be that way!" or to note, with surprise, the immaturity of a child's expression at the beginning of the term as compared to his present state.

Another way of keeping records of behavior is through use of a teacher's log or diary. The teacher might write down the most significant happenings at the end of each day. Where they relate to a particular child, this information can be transferred to his folder at a later time. The log can also help the teacher in planning activities for the next day or week, can provide means for assessing group and individual development, and can help in organizing her class into groups or in selecting leaders.

Tests and rating scales can also be tools for assessing individual development. These should never be considered in isolation but must be integrated into the total picture that the teacher has of the child. Chapter 6 will show how various measurements can be used to provide information about a specific facet of the child's behavior.

For whatever methods are used to gather information, the purpose of the investigation must be clearly kept in mind. Tests, rather than being used as diagnostic tools, can become ends in themselves, whereby the sole concern of the teacher is directed toward increasing scores for her class. Anecdotal records are confidential, yet they are sometimes used as conversation pieces in the teachers' lounge. Parent conferences sometimes provide the teacher with bits of gossip that can color her judgment. But, the discreet and intelligent use of all of these methods can give added insight that assists the teacher in understanding and guiding the individuals in her class. We are concerned with techniques that will give us a realistic picture of a whole human being, as he responds to school and to life in his own unique way.

Time samples

A very effective way of beginning an observational approach to child study is with the use of ten-minute time samples. Here the observer selects a period of time when she can devote her full attention to the task and records every aspect of the child's behavior during that period. Facial expression, use of hands, and whole body movements are to be noted. If the child speaks or makes sounds, the exact expression should be recorded. The time is to be noted in the margin (see example below) at one- or two-minute intervals.

An effort should be made to record only overt behavior in one column. Comments and interpretations should be written in a parallel column or placed at the end of the sample. Ten minutes seems to be an effective amount of time. Less than this does not always allow for enough action, and longer than this is fatiguing to the observer. Watching and notating every aspect of behavior requires intense concentration, and writing everything down as soon as it happens is a strain on the writer.

It is advisable to take two ten-minute samples of the same child within a brief period of time. He might be involved in a different activity during the second observation, but he should be in the same setting on the same day. A lapse of a half hour to an hour between samples usually provides variation in his activity, while preserving some continuity in the observation.

Ten-minute time samples are particularly effective in observing infants. Most students, when asked to record the behavior of a four-month-old, will say, "But he doesn't do anything!" It is only after they have tried to watch every movement and gesture within a brief time period that they begin to realize how much is happening. It is always a source of amazement that they can find out so much about a baby's level of development just by watching closely for so short a time.

The following is a part of a ten-minute time sample done by a student. The baby girl is three months and thirteen days old and was not known to the observer before the time of observation. She had been placed in a crib nursery at a church on a Sunday morning, while her parents attended services.

TIME	OVERT BEHAVIOR	COMMENTS
	Child lying on back in church nursery. Wearing long foot-in pants and long-sleeve top. Folded blanket on left side of head in touching distance of left hand. Pacifier lying in crib by right hand. Row of five bells hanging in eye position above crib.	Physical surroundings are very pleasant. Room is warm and a record is playing softly. There are some disturbing noises occasionally, for example, door slams, crying of other children, movement. Over all, however, the atmosphere is conducive to rest.
9:45	Child lying on back with four appendages spread in relaxed position. Eyes are open and looking up.	Child had been placed in crib at 9:25 following delivery of child to the nursery by mother and father.
9:46	Legs flex and accidently kick bells hanging over crib. Eyes immediately flash to bells as child hears sound. Arms flex and left hand moves across path of eyes. Eyes follow hand for an instant and then return to bells.	Bells hang from one side of crib to the other. Child shows ability to follow objects with eyes. Child also follows her own hand movements. Child is able to react to noises.

In this detailed description of only two minutes of action, we have already begun to see the level at which this baby is operating. She is able to follow a moving object (her hand) and can respond to sounds (the bells). Flexing of arms and legs are part of a total body response to stimulation. Later observations in this same time sample (not given here) reveal that the child relaxes when a pacifier is introduced into her mouth, sucks vigorously, moves to retrieve pacifier when it slips out. The random arm movements are not successful and so she experiences frustration, begins to whimper, and substitutes blanket for pacifier. All of these overt actions are revealing of the stage of development of this infant. A month sooner she might not have been interested in following her hand. Sometime later she will be able to retrieve the pacifier. Movements become more differentiated as the infant matures. Her responsiveness and her unique personal qualities are also revealed in the remainder of this very brief but astute observation. She responds to adult attention (a teacher who strokes her head). She shows a preference for her left hand. Her physical well-being is revealed as she gradually drops off to sleep in her new surroundings.

This and other time samples done by students will be discussed in later chapters when they will be used to illustrate levels of child development as revealed through direct observation of characteristic behavior of specific infants. For the present, this small bit from the observation of a three-month-old demonstrates the effectiveness of the method when used by a keen observer. No action is too insignificant to record. No less than one hundred lines of type were required in this observation to make a record of only ten minutes of action! Not every observer will be as conscientious, and not all are as capable of noting detail. But the more observant the recorder, the greater will be the knowledge gleaned from the experience.

It is advisable to concentrate solely on recording overt behavior in the time spent watching the child. Comments can be added later, and, in fact, much of the meaning of the action is revealed to the observer if she reads over her notes after the observation time. Her total concentration during the time of taking the sample should be focused upon recording all overt responses. Comments have a way of slipping into the observations, particularly with inexperienced observers. Every effort should be made to keep the subjective remarks for later recording in a separate place on the observation report. Qualifying statements such as, "She smiled contentedly" should be changed to "The baby smiled" and "She seemed contented." These comments should be entered in the appropriate columns. Skill in making objective observations of overt behavior develops with practice.

A time sample is a good starting place for the novice observer because it focuses upon no specific incident but requires that she make note of everything that happens within that period. Powers of observation are sharpened. The significance of small bits of action is revealed. Ability to interpret what has been observed develops as the student becomes more aware of the meaning of what she has seen. Sharing these observations with others leads to other hypotheses regarding interpretation of behavior. Follow-up observations on the same child might increase the student's insights, and she will be more aware of details of action in her next observation.

Sometimes a time sample taken at a particularly significant moment in a child's experience reveals not only his level of development and unique way of viewing his world, but also an emotional reaction that is characteristic of him. A student did a time sample of this type, observing a three-year-old neighbor's child who was visiting her. (See time sample at top of page 40.)

This observer, a psychology major, was quite aware of the significance of this incident, which she refers to as a "classic approach-avoidance conflict." No doubt, since it was a recurring event in her house, she chose this moment to do her time sample, anticipating that the conflict would reveal itself in

TIME	OVERT BEHAVIOR	COMMENTS
5:00	Marty, sitting in the living room chair, asks where Guinness (the dog) is. Gets down, goes to window, yells to dog.	Marty exhibits the classic approach-avoidance conflict in respect to the dog. Marty wants dog inside but at the same time is anxious about being overwhelmed by him. Have instructed Marty about remaining quiet around dog which he recalls when reminded.
5:01	Dog comes in. Marty runs for chair, dog at heels. Marty gets into chair. Dog tries to lick his face.	
5:02	Marty hits at dog. Dog snaps at his fingers.	
5:03	At my request, Marty withdraws hands and puts one under each arm. Dog is called away. Marty says, "Bad Guinness" and then "but he-he was just playing with me."	[Marty exhibits] ambivalent feelings about dog. [His reactions include] some stuttering and [he] frequently begins sentences with "but."
5:04	"He only wanted to lick me." Gets down from chair and approaches dog lying on floor. Smacks dog on nose and runs for chair.	Despite anxiety he elicits a new dog confrontation.

Marty's actions. The fact that she kept track of the time, and kept minute records of what happened each moment, added interest and more intimate knowledge of the child's behavior to her observation report. However, this incident is worthy of note, even if the time was not recorded. The student observing such a scene might have written down the incident from memory after it occurred; in this case it might have been an anecdotal record of the kind discussed in the next section.

Time samples need not always be of ten-minute duration, nor need they be organized in columns as illustrated above. Longer periods of time are sometimes required when observing older children, since their overt responses are often smaller and less frequent. That the movements of older children and adults are equally significant cannot be denied. A popular best seller by Julius Fast is concerned with *Body Language*. "Body language can include any non-reflexive or reflexive movement of a part, or all of the body, used by the person to communicate an emotional message to the outside world."[1]

According to Mr. Fast the body can sometimes indicate a person's attitudes—can tell a man whether a girl wants to be approached, can give clues as to how to break through defenses, and so on. Most of the body reactions are not consciously induced, but the sending and receiving of messages occurs daily whether we are aware of it or not. People telegraph their thoughts as they fold their arms, cross their legs, or move their eyes and mouth.

In the following observation of a twelve-year-old girl, done over a period of one hour, this kind of body language is taken into consideration. The ob-

[1] Julius Fast, *Body Language*, p. 2.

server records all overt behavior at five-minute intervals and presents her comments at the end of the observations, using the time designation to point up the evidence for her inferences. The girl was at a rehearsal for a school play when this time sample was taken. A small portion of it is presented here.

2:45 Laura is sitting in the auditorium in an aisle seat down near the front. Her friend, Beth, is sitting to her right. L. sits with her right leg crossed over her left. She is resting her elbows on the arm rests. She is staring in front of her, apparently at nothing. She giggles at something that B. says. L. crosses her arms in front of her at the waist and listen as the teacher gives the cast a pep talk. L. turns her right foot, from the ankle, in a circular motion. She leans to the side and talks to B., tapping her foot in the air. She purses her lips and looks around the auditorium. She pulls the left side of her lip into her mouth. She looks behind her, over her left shoulder, at a girl who is talking quite loudly.

And later:

3:30 The girls are placed in sitting positions on the stage. L. sits with her knees bent in front of her, facing the right side. Her right arm is to the side, and she has her weight leaning on it. Her left arm rests in her lap. L. purses her lips and looks around the room. A girl sitting next to L. says something to her. She nods and smiles but doesn't say anything. L. pushes her tongue against the inside of her bottom lip. She bends her head to the right and gazes at the girl who starts to sing the solo. Her eyes are fixed on the girl, and L. doesn't move except to blink her eyes during the entire song.

3:35 At the end of the song L. drops her eyes. Her mouth is slightly open, and she points her tongue to the right side of her mouth. She looks up at the girl singing the solo, as she starts to sing again. The girls get up. L. crosses her hands in front of her. She sways slightly from side to side. She grabs her nose briefly between [the] thumb and index fingers of her right hand. Then she drops her hands behind her back. She watches the action of the play and laughs at the comedy in the scene.

3:40 L. looks to the right and to the left. She pulls at the flesh of her right arm with her left hand. She is blinking rapidly. She folds her arms in front of her. She is pulling at the inside of the left side of her mouth. L. fingers the buckle of her belt with her right hand. B. comes over to L. and L. begins talking animatedly. She pushes the fingers of her right hand back, one by one, with her left hand and laughs as she listens to B.

All of this may seem like a great deal of irrelevant detail, and the reader may be wondering what can be accomplished by noting such minutiae. However, the inferences made from an hour-long observation of this girl gave a clear picture of her that was readily validated by those who knew her intimately. After twelve five-minute recordings such as the three cited above, the observer wrote:

In this observation Laura appears to be a mild-mannered, soft-spoken, quiet, and reserved girl. She is not the center of attention, does not initiate friendly advances, and remains in the background. She does not seek out people but will wait for them to take the initiative (see 2:50, 3:25, 3:30, 3:40).

She is the leader within a small select circle of friends, and they seek her out (see 3:05, 3:15, 3:30, 3:40).

L. is comfortable and relaxed with people she knows well (see 2:50, 2:55, 3:15, 3:20). But she is ill at ease in a larger social situation that does not include intimate friends (see 3:00, 3:05, 3:20, 3:25, 3:40).

L. has a good sense of humor, grasps the comedy in a situation quickly, and is quick to point it out (see 2:50, 2:55, 3:15, 3:55, 3:40). She has excellent powers of concentration, and her attention is direct and can be held intently (see 3:25, 3:30, 3:35).

L. is conscious of her body, not ashamed or uncomfortable about it, but sensitive to her physical development (see 3:00, 3:20, 3:25). When she gets tired or bored, she uses body movement as a means of relaxation (see 3:00, 3:10, 3:15). L. does not seem at ease in this situation and appears anxious, tense, and nervous (see 3:10, 3:15, 3:20, 3:25, 3:40).

Although the whole observation is not presented here, the reader can readily see that there is specific evidence cited for each of the observer's inferences. Had she not given as much detail, and were she less skilled in observation, it is unlikely that the observer could present such an insightful profile of this twelve-year-old.

Anecdotal records

The time sample is only one way of recording direct observation. As stated above, it can be distinguished by the fact that every detail of action within a given period of time is noted.

An anecdotal record need not note every detail of action but is a report of a specific incident. Teachers may make these notes at the end of a day, recalling, from memory, a happening in the class that may have significance. It may also be an on-the-spot record which the observer jots down as it happens.

Anecdotal records may be organized into overt behavior and comments columns as was done with the time samples discussed in the previous section. Students are sometimes assigned the task of recording a group-play activity in this way. The following observation was done on the playground at a private nursery school.

OVERT BEHAVIOR	COMMENTS
A group of three- and four-year-old boys were trying to get berries to fall from a tree. They threw rocks at them. One four-year-old was in the tree. He yelled, "Gimme a rock!"	The younger children did not talk to the older children. When they attempted to play, they were not received very well.
A three-year-old extended a rock. He was ignored, and he wandered off. The other boys kept throwing rocks at the berries. The boy in the tree got down. No one would give him a rock.	The boys seemed [to act] like it was a contest to be the one who knocked the berries down. They were not going to help the boy in the tree, who already had the advantage.

The student who did this observation did not know the children in this scene. She therefore could not refer to them by name. Her comments were based purely on her observations during the brief time she visited the school. She inferred relationships between age groups and between individuals that might have had more significance if she knew the children in the group.

Anecdotal records may include subjective statements when the background or previous experiences of the child are known to the observer. A good example of this is taken from one of the case studies by a male student, reported in chapter 13.

Wilma Adams did not arrive at school at her usual time on the day of my seventh observation. She came shortly after I did, and I had the opportunity once again to see her with her mother.

A good amount of time had passed since the incident which I described in my second observation where both Wilma and her mother became quite upset at having to leave each other in the morning. Wilma's teacher had pointed out that there had never been a recurrence of this incident. Shortly after this Mrs. Adams had stopped following her into the schoolyard but would leave her at the gate if the teacher was near. As of late, the teacher commented, there were mornings when Wilma seemed to barely acknowledge her mother as she said good-bye.

Mrs. Adams drove into the schoolyard and parked her car. Before she had even gotten out of the car, Wilma was halfway to the gate. Mrs. Adams hurried to catch up with her and when she did, Wilma paused only for a minute to kiss her good-bye. Mrs. Adams' face had traces of the same urgent look I had seen there before. The hug she gave Wilma seemed to convey some of this urgency, but Wilma appeared unaffected. She ran off to the swings and, as her mother drove off, turned and called, "Good-bye, silly Mommy."

In this observation, there is no attempt made to separate overt behavior from subjective judgment. The observer gives some background information based upon previous observations. He infers emotional reactions of the mother from her facial expression and identifies this as "the same urgent look." He injects his own perspective into the record and speaks in the first person.

Some excellent writing has been done by students when they report things as they see it, using a narrative style, as in the above example. Although the more scientific approach, when observations are objectively stated with comments on the side or below, gives the student practice in sharpening her powers of observation, the more subjective narrative account frequently conveys more of the flavor of the incident. Students should be encouraged to try both methods of presenting anecdotal records.

The choice of language in reporting often helps to convey a clearer picture of the child. A child may walk across the room, but HOW he performs that act tells us more about him than the act itself. Observers might be reminded that words like *saunters*, *bounces*, and *shuffles* help create a picture of the action for the reader. Qualifying words in narrative-type observation reports give life to the writing. If the child reaches for a block, does he do it *hesitatingly, angrily, stealthily,* and so on? The description of the quality of his action gives meaning to the report. It is this type of writing that makes literature so effective in creating characters that appear to the reader to be "true to life."

We have come a long way from the objective reporting of overt behavior recommended for the time-sample type of observation. Many kinds of reporting are possible, and, after experience with several forms, students should be permitted to choose the method that best suits their purposes and the situation they are observing.

Coding behavior records

There are occasions when the observer is interested in tracing a particular type of response in a series of behavior samples. The child might be known to be aggressive, for example, and the teacher may want to determine what situations most frequently provoke aggressive acts. Or, an investigator might want to know what kinds of teaching situations produce the greatest number of creative responses in a child or in a group.

After several observation sessions the investigator might decide to isolate certain behaviors to be noted and/or tallied. She then defines these behavior patterns in her own terms, or she might use coding systems developed by researchers such as Prescott or Gordon. (See *References* at end of chapter.)

Subsequent observations are coded according to the established system. Tallies can then be made as to the frequency of a particular behavior pattern. Changes occurring in the child with respect to a specific trait can be noted.

A student had been observing a child who was known to be hyperactive and to have a learning disability. The student, in reading about problems of this nature, found that the recommendation was frequently made that such children do better in structured situations. She decided to observe the child in two types of settings, a structured climate and a freer climate, and to record and code his behavior in each. The code was established based upon known behavior patterns of the child, and the student set up her own categories. They were:

CB: Compulsive behavior (typical of a hyperactive child)
LR: Learning response (involved in activity)
Cr: Creative response (verbal or nonverbal)
LD: Learning disability (perceptual-motor or auditory)
Att.: Seeking attention from teacher or peers
       1. Through constructive behavior
       2. Through misbehavior
PA: Peer association
Em: Emotional response (related to emotional problems known to the observer from previous history)
       1. Seeking male model

2. Rejection of females
3. Protection of self
4. Pleasure response

The child, an eight-year-old boy, was then observed for several sessions in each of two learning situations, a structured physical education class and a creative movement class.

The coded observations helped the student to see the number of constructive behavior responses and the number of disruptive ones in each of these two settings. The total case history would have to be reported here in order to assess adequately the results of this survey. But, for our purposes of examining a technique for observation, it will suffice to give an example of the coding as applied to one part of a creative movement lesson.

The class was in the gymnasium where they were seated against the wall. The teacher led a discussion about the circus and asked the children to think of a circus act they would like to portray.

LR: Tommy quiet—listening to discussion.
PA: Bob and Tommy want to be partners.
Att.: Tommy pokes Bob as discussion goes on.
PA/Em4: Looks pleased at being Bob's partner.
Em2: "Oh, pew"—says as little girl walks by.
PA: Whispering to Bob, hand over Bob's ear.
Cr: Tommy says, "You could swing on the inside bar of jungle gym and use it as a trapeze."

(Class is to practice with partners, one person to act while the other accompanies him on a drum.)
Att2/CB: Tommy runs around the room wildly.
CB: Pushes aside little girl and climbs to top of jungle gym and leaps off.

(Class is called to attention. They are to take turns presenting their acts to each other.)
LR: Sitting at wall with knees up, apparently listening.
Em2: "She'll probably kill herself," he says, as little girl is performing. "She'll slip"—smiling.
PA: "Could us two do it together?" [He] points to Bob.

(Everyone claps after girl's performance.)
Em2: Tommy says, "Boo."

(Lapse of time.)
(Tommy and Bob to perform.)
LR: Walking on balance beam.
Att1: "I'm gonna jump off now."
Em4: Jumps and smiles.
PA: Plays drum for Bob on jungle gym.
PA/Cr: Changes beat to follow swinging movement.
LR: Playing intently.
CB/Em4: Runs to wall beating drum. Gives it to teacher.

(All march to circus music.)

LR: Marching in circle to music.
CB: Goes out of circle and falls on floor.
Att2/CB: Acts like a monster, making faces.
CB: Runs to jungle gym, leaps up on bar.
CB: Climbs rope.
Att1/LR: Runs over to put on shoes. Says, "I'm ready to go."

The coding of this behavior record was very helpful to the student in her effort to determine the effects of this type of program on the child she was observing. Her coding categories are her own, and we may disagree with some of her descriptions and question how she determined what behavior fell into each category. However, this was not intended to be a scientific research study, but simply a device for helping the student to observe and interpret what she saw in some systematic way. As such, the coded behavior report served her well. It is a technique that might be applied to similar situations, where the observer seeks to isolate certain behavior patterns for special consideration.

Establishing criteria for observations

Another method of focusing upon specific behavior characteristics is by means of establishing, in advance of observation, a set of criteria. The investigator might be interested in noting specific types of behavior, as in the example above using coding. In using this technique, however, not all behavior is noted, but only those actions are recorded that seem relevant to the characteristics being studied.

These characteristics are established in advance of the observations, and observers are asked to keep them in mind while watching the class or the individual child. When a behavior related to a specific category is noted, the observer records it in anecdotal style. A collection of such anecdotes is made for each child being studied. These are then used to tally the number and intensity of responses under each category of the established criteria.

An action-research project done by this writer uses this technique for evaluation of observations. Two trained observers were provided with a set of criteria for observation, and were asked to record, in anecdotal style, every incident of significance relevant to these factors. (See Table 1.) A tape recorder placed in the room recorded children's verbal expressions, from which data relevant to the criteria were also selected. The investigator acted in the capacity of a visiting teacher in the classroom, presenting various activities related to aesthetic concepts to a class of seven-year-olds. Responses recorded for each child in the study were then tallied according to the established categories and also according to the intensity of response, ranging from "not at all" to "decidedly," in five degree steps.

The establishment of criteria must be based upon previous experience of the investigator and must involve research into the area under consideration. In the example being cited the investigator devised the list of criteria after surveying writings in aesthetics that describe components of the aesthetic response. She was aided, also, by authorities in the field of art education and by her own extensive experience in working with children in movement expression. Each category is accompanied by a list of questions related to the child's performance which is relevant to that category. Incidents which reveal elements of behavior in that category, that is, behavior patterns which answer one of the posed questions, are noted and then tallied in the appropriate column. A folder containing a tally sheet such as the one shown in Table 1 was kept for each child in the study.

At the conclusion of the action research, an attempt was made to evaluate the program based upon the evidence which appeared on these tally sheets. Although some quantitative measurement was possible, the scores, in terms of number and intensity of responses, were meaningless unless viewed as part of the total picture for each child. Thus, twenty-two case studies were developed, in which evidence from the evaluation sheets was used to describe the child's reactions to the program.

TABLE 1
*Evaluation of observations**

	NOT AT ALL	NO	SOME-WHAT	YES	DECIDEDLY
I. DEGREE OF INVOLVEMENT					
a. Does the child ignore outside noises, conversation of classmates, etc.?					
b. Is he anxious to continue working beyond the allotted time?					
c. Is his attention focused on this activity?					
d. Is he enjoying this activity?					
II. INTENSITY AND SCOPE OF SENSORY PERCEPTION					
a. Does he recognize changes in rhythm, tempo, volume?					
b. Is there a feeling response to kinesthetic sensation?					
c. Is there a feeling response to line, color, or texture?					
d. Is there a feeling response to quality of sound?					
III. POWERS OF OBSERVATION					
a. Does he notice things in his environment without having the teacher point them out?					
b. Does he observe differences and similarities?					
c. Does he perceive detail?					
d. Are associations formed from observations?					

TABLE 1
*Evaluation of observations**

	NOT AT ALL	NO	SOME-WHAT	YES	DECIDEDLY
IV. RECOGNITION OF AESTHETIC COMPONENTS IN VARIOUS MODES OF EXPRESSION					
a. Does the child perceive rhythm visually?					
b. Does he recognize pattern or the ordering of elements?					
c. Does he recognize change in dynamics? Can he use accent effectively?					
d. Does he show evidence of being aware of line and shape when it is not in a painting or drawing?					
V. ORIGINALITY AND IMAGINATION					
a. Are the child's ideas his own?					
b. Are they different from others in the group?					
c. Do they depart from stereotyped responses?					
d. Do they depart from his own previous responses?					
VI. MISCELLANEOUS (Fill in suitable categories for this child not included above)					

* From Betty Rowen, *An Exploration of the Uses of Rhythmic Movement to Develop Aesthetic Concepts in the Primary Grades,* Cooperative Research Report, no. ED 020770, USOE, (Washington, D.C.: Government Printing Office, 1966).

An example from the case history of one child will illustrate the way this technique works, when applied to observations. Rosann was particularly responsive to stimuli related to texture. Many of the anecdotes recording her behavior, therefore, were scored under the category II c on the tally sheet. The following are some samples of her verbal expression.

In looking at a collage design, she-said, "I think it's kind of nice, because here it's bumpy, and in other places it's like—smooth, and in other places it's rough."

When asked to move to colors, Rosann described her feeling about "pale blue" as "smooth" and moved in that manner.

Music was described by her as feeling "like silk against my skin," and she reacted to another selection by saying that it was "rough." Still another piece of music made her feel as if "bees were stinging you."

Because of her intense reactions to sensory experiences, Rosann had one of the highest scores (fifty) in the class for that particular category on the evaluation sheet. Although she was not a particularly outgoing child, she expressed herself frequently in some kinds of situations and revealed herself to be deeply sensitive and responsive to sensory stimuli. In other categories of the selected criteria she tended toward the average. Her scores were:

I.	Degree of Involvement	11
II.	Sensory Perception	50
III.	Observation	13
IV.	Recognition of Aesthetic Components	8
V.	Originality	9

It can be seen that the use of a tally sheet based upon an established set of criteria helped the observers to focus upon particular aspects of behavior and helped the investigator to evaluate responses in some meaningful way. Rosann was not a particularly outstanding child, and were it not for her high score in sensory perception, the evidence of her sensitivity might not have been noted. The number of responses that fell into the category of "Sensory Perception" and the intensity of her responses in this area far outweighed other types of response for her.

Other children in the study had higher scores in other categories. Strongly verbal children were able to express ideas related to "Observation" and the "Recognition of Aesthetic Components." Many observations for quiet, sensitive children were recorded under the category of "Degree of Involvement." The quality of response to the program was different for each child, and the evaluation of observations tallied in this manner was helpful in substantiating this fact.

Using cumulative records

Up to this point we have been concerned with various methods of direct observation of children. The author feels strongly that this is the primary source for building understanding of an individual child. However, other sources of information are available to most teachers, and, used in conjunction with direct observation, these sources can fill in the gaps in a teacher's knowledge about a child.

Most school systems keep permanent files in the office which contain various kinds of information about each student enrolled in the school. These files are available for the teacher's use, and, as a matter of fact, she is often required to make entries from time to time, for each of her students. The files are composed of several types of records; each is kept on a separate card on which relevant entries are made periodically.

Thus, these files are known as cumulative records and usually consist of:

1. *Health record*: including acute-disease history, immunization data, limitations of eye and ear functioning, dental history, and measurements of height and weight. Entries are made on this card by the school nurse after scheduled periodic checkups. Teachers might also

be required to make entries regarding number of absences during the term and/or frequency of absence due to illness.

2. *Family data*: including the names, marital status, educational level, and occupations of the parents; number and order of children in the family; and their current and previous addresses. The degree of mobility of the family, as well as their socioeconomic level, can be gleaned from this record.

3. *Test results*: including various intelligence, aptitude, and achievement scores obtained over the period of time since the child entered school. Some tests, such as IQ batteries, are administered at particular grade levels, such as kindergarten, third, and fifth grades. Standard achievement tests of one kind or another are usually administered at the end of each term. In addition, the results of special tests administered to a child by a consultant, such as a reading specialist or school psychologist, are also entered on this card.

4. *Report card grades*: usually entered at the end of each term by the child's teacher. Grading systems vary from school to school and even are different for various grade levels in the same school. Sometimes these grades reflect the work habits of the child and his personality traits, and sometimes they simply record his achievement in curriculum areas.

5. *Teacher's comments*: usually included, either on the record of report card grades or on a separate card in the cumulative folder. Comments may vary from one or two lines to a detailed description of the child's behavior, as perceived by each of his teachers.

Cumulative records can be useful to the teacher, but some caution must be applied in interpreting the information contained in them. For example, teachers' comments are subjective statements and must be considered in the light of the point of view of the commentator. Previous test scores and report card grades often affect the current teacher's opinion of the child before she has a chance to observe his behavior. There can be no doubt that knowledge of family background is useful, but other methods of obtaining this information can yield more fruitful results (see section on Interviews below). The health record is, of course, important and the teacher should be aware of handicaps and physical limitations of students in her class. But even this information might be more meaningful *after* the teacher has gotten to know her pupils.

It is strongly recommended that teachers consider cumulative records in the light of their own perceptions of the child. For this reason it is advisable to wait until the second or third week of school before examining the previous records of the child that are filed in the office. Even at this time an open-minded view must be taken, so that the child's cumulative record does not determine the teacher's expectations of him for the future.

A perceptive statement by Herbert Kohl points out the dangers in the use of cumulative records.[2]

When the teacher meets his class on the first day of the school year, he is

2 Herbert Kohl, *The Open Classroom*, p. 18.

armed with all of this "professional knowledge" [acquired through use of school records]. Anticipating a dull class, for example, a teacher may have spent several weeks preparing simple exercises to keep his students busy. On the other hand, faced with the prospect of teaching a bright class, he may have found a new and challenging textbook or devised some ingenious scientific experiments.

If the record cards indicate that several pupils are particularly troublesome or, what is more threatening, "disturbed," the teacher will single them out as soon as they enter the room and treat them differently from the other pupils. He may do the same with bright students or ones rumored to be wise, funny, lazy, violent, scheming, deceitful. The students will sense this and act in the manner expected of them. Thus, the teacher traps both himself and his pupils into repeating patterns that have been set for years.

Further evidence of the effect of teachers' preconceptions is given in the report of Robert Rosenthal and Lenore Jacobson.[3] Here teachers were informed that certain children were "underachievers" and that their IQ level was considerably higher than previous performance indicated. Although this information had no validity in the record, these children subsequently received deferential treatment by the teachers thus informed. This, in turn, led to higher achievement for the students under consideration.

Despite all this evidence to the contrary, the use of cumulative records can still be of benefit in helping the teacher understand the child. Caution must be exercised as suggested, but generally, the knowledge contained on school records expedites the work of the teacher. She should use this information, already collected and available to her, with discretion. She should put her own judgment of the child, based upon direct experience with him, ahead of other considerations. The information in his cumulative folder can help to explain and interpret some things that she already knows about him or can give her deeper insight into causes of his behavior.

Interviewing techniques: with children

Interviews are planned or spontaneous conferences during which the teacher tries to acquire additional information about the child under consideration. Whether the teacher is speaking to others about the child or in direct interaction with the child himself, there are some generalizations that can be made about conducting a successful interview.

1. Interviews should be informal, relaxed, and casual. There should be no list of prepared questions to be answered. Ideas should flow as the discussion ensues. The interviewer picks up suggestions for proceeding from statements made by the person being interviewed.
2. Every effort must be made to make the participant comfortable in the situation. It is not advisable for the teacher to be seated behind her desk, because this, in itself, presents a barrier. An informal arrangement where each party meets each other at the same eye

[3] Robert Rosenthal and Lenore Jacobson, *Pygmalion in the Classroom.*

level should be maintained. This may mean that the teacher sits on the floor with a kindergarten child, or that she uses the same size chair at the side of a table (not the head!) when speaking to adults. The physical surroundings have a great deal to do with the establishment of a relaxed atmosphere.

3. Learning to listen attentively is a special skill to be developed by the interviewer. Genuine interest and the suggestion of empathy encourages the person being interviewed to be less reserved and to feel comfortable about expressing his feelings.

4. Respect for the opinions of others is essential. The teacher must make the parent or the child feel that he is a partner in the efforts to solve a particular problem. Everyone has a unique contribution to make regardless of his educational background or social standing. The interviewer must assume that the person interviewed has some bit of knowledge which can be helpful, and it is her role to find out what it is.

Therapists, when working with young patients, use a technique that can readily be adapted by the classroom teacher. The therapist reinforces what the child has expressed by repeating his words after him, giving heightened meaning to them by inflection or by emphasis. The following is an excerpt from a conversation between a principal and a group of students from the fourth-grade class that was having difficulties in school.

BOB: Today I was picked on by the teacher. I didn't have my assignment done and she knew it, but called on me anyway. I don't think that's fair.

MR. BELL: *You think Miss Norris called on you purposely to make you feel bad.*

BOB: Yes (a pause).

BILL: Bob had plenty of time to do his work. He was showing off.

MR. BELL: *You think he just wanted to show off?*

BILL: He's usually wasting time. He could have done it.

MR. BELL: *Uh-huh*[4]

In this brief passage from an interview the principal, Mr. Bell, uses the reinforcing techniques of the therapist to encourage the boys to talk freely. By rephrasing what Bob had said, he shows that he is listening, but he places no value judgments on what he has heard. Another student, Bill, makes the condemning statement, but again, Mr. Bell reinforces him by simply rephrasing his statement as a question. Even the final "Uh-huh" shows the principal's interest and empathy and allows the boys to discuss freely their own feelings, and, ultimately, to solve the problems themselves.

Interviews with a child can take place on the playground, on a special trip, at the time of a home visit, or whenever the occasion arises that seems appropriate. Direct questions, such as "Do you like school?" should be avoided. A better approach might be to discuss something that is happening in class and let the child respond with his own reaction to it. Similarly, questions about parents' attitudes might embarrass the child or simply make him

[4] Clark Moustakas, *The Authentic Teacher*, p. 167. Italics are mine.

withdraw. A question to the child of divorced parents about the fishing trip he took with his dad might reveal more of his feelings about his parents' relationship than a direct question.

Fantasy in a child's response should be accepted without question. Victor, a boy from a disadvantaged background, was staying in a foster home in a middle-class neighborhood. When other children told of trips they had taken over the weekend, Victor volunteered a story involving wild exploits with bandits. In this story his father was the hero, and Victor drove the car in the pursuit. In an interview with the child at a later time on the playground the teacher accepted the story and allowed Victor the ego gratification of bragging about an imaginary father.

Once rapport has been established by accepting the child's statements and encouraging him to further expand on his feelings, it is possible to confront him with more direct questions. In the case study of Peter reported in a later chapter the student teacher took the boy to the zoo. While viewing the animals, the student teacher maintained a supportive role, even when Peter pushed people rudely to get closer to the cages. She observed his behavior and made mental note of his comments for later recording. On the way home she asked him directly how he liked school and was rewarded with a frank answer, "I like it except no one likes me."

Interviewing techniques: with adults

Adults respond much as children do to the type of atmosphere established in the interview. If they are given the feeling that their ideas are accepted and valued, if they are relaxed enough to speak freely about personal concerns, and if the interviewer listens attentively and with empathy, the adult will reveal much about his relationship with the child that will be helpful.

Even colleagues in the same school deserve this kind of treatment when they are interviewed about a child. A former teacher does not want to know how much better the interviewing teacher is handling the situation. She needs to feel that her ideas and her problems with the child in question are worthy of consideration. Sometimes, without stating them directly, the former teacher's attitudes are revealed, explaining quite clearly why Johnny has such a poor self-concept. Even in these instances the interviewer should not make value judgments but should allow the former teacher to talk freely, expressing her own feelings which the interviewer can note for later recording.

The guidance director, reading consultant, or school nurse often is a valuable source of information. For one thing, these specialists can help in interpreting test scores and other data that are related to the child's development. Sometimes it is necessary for special tests to be administered in order to evaluate the child further. The classroom teacher should discuss these test results with the specialist and share with him the results of her own observations and classroom interactions. Advice from consultants can be helpful but need not always be totally accepted and enforced. It is important to respect the opinions of experts and to let them know, as in every interview situation, that their ideas matter. The classroom teacher must maintain her own judgments based upon her own store of information and her direct contact with the child. No one has a better opportunity to see the child in various situations than his classroom teacher, especially if she is a sensitive observer and maintains good rapport with the child himself.

Interviews with parents and other family members may take place in either the home or the school setting. Home visits are especially helpful, since they allow the teacher to observe much about the home background and family relationships. By just looking around and listening to what takes place in the home setting, the teacher can find out more about the child in one visit than she might discover after several school interviews.

After arranging for the visit by phone or with a brief note, the teacher should enter the home setting much as if she were a guest. Casual comments about family portraits, the baby's diet, or any observable interest of the mother, help to "break the ice" and lead to free-flowing conversation. The teacher might ask to see pictures of the child when he was a baby and then encourage the parent to talk about when he began to talk, sit up, walk, and so on. It will not be long before the parent is giving the teacher valuable information about the child's attitudes, his relationship with siblings, his work habits, and so forth.

As a good guest the interviewing teacher does not take down notes while the parent is talking but listens attentively and adds comments of a neutral nature to the discussion. She might even share some of her own experiences with the child's mother, that is, what her own family life is like or how her own children developed in their early years. It is much easier to share personal information with an individual who is also willing to reveal something of herself in the conversation. Statements of a judgmental nature about the child in question should be avoided, however. Even if the mother makes the condemning statement, the teacher should refrain from being critical of the child.

With regard to schoolwork it is better for the teacher to avoid, for the most part, evaluations to the effect that the child is good at this or poor at that. Most parents expect some kind of evaluation of their child from the teacher and usually anticipate the worst when the teacher visits the home. The total tone of the interview should be casual and friendly with evaluations reserved for some later date. The purpose to be served by the visit is mainly to procure information that will be helpful to the teacher in working with the child. The parent must be made to feel that she can contribute to the child's success in school by providing the necessary insights into his needs and feelings that the teacher is seeking.

The school interview with the parent, better known as a parent-teacher conference, should maintain, as much as possible, the free-flowing conversation and relaxed atmosphere of the home visit. This is not always possible. The school is a frightening place to some adults, who perhaps remember, with trepidation, their own unpleasant school experiences.

Many school buildings have foreboding appearances, and parents are hesitant to enter, to apply to the principal's office for a pass, and to make that long journey down the dark, narrow corridors. If they are greeted at the classroom door with a friendly smile and a handshake, they may begin to relax. If, however, the teacher remains behind the desk and asks that the parent please wait outside until she calls him, the image of an outsider invading foreign territory is reinforced.

This feeling is most prevalent among members of subcultures who are awed by the school and the teacher and may possibly feel insecure about their ability to communicate in English. In a role-playing session during the orientation of Head Start teachers in New York, one trainee took the role of a Puerto Rican lady who was invited to visit her child's teacher for the first time. Another trainee, playing the role of the teacher, greeted her with, "Mrs. Lopez, I asked you to be here a week ago. Why didn't you come at that time?" Interestingly, the "teacher" in this role-playing situation was from a subculture herself and was familiar with the problems and feelings of people from poverty backgrounds. Her pedantic manner was a result of her years in a traditional classroom setting and carried more weight than her insights into the feelings of the parent in this situation. She demonstrated, quite unconsciously, that intellectual understanding of a problem does not necessarily create an atmosphere for its solution.

Hopefully, Head Start and other programs of this nature have broken down some of the barriers, and teachers are beginning to welcome parents into the classroom both for conferences and for participation. The freedom of the parent to be within the school setting, and the fact that their contributions are welcomed in the classroom should make it easier for a teacher to discuss a child with his parent in a friendly and relaxed manner.

Do we always accept, as fact, whatever the parent tells us? That depends very largely on the teacher's insight into the parent's motives and emotional needs. It has been suggested that the interviewer listen attentively and with empathy, regardless of whom she is interviewing. Just as she accepts fantasy in children's stories and encourages them to continue, in order to get to the roots of their feelings, the interviewer should also accept subjective judgments on the part of a parent. It is difficult to see one's own child objectively, and many parents project their own frustrations and desires upon their children. The interviewer must listen, reserving judgment for some later time when she can review, in solitude, the information imparted to her.

Nancy was not doing well in her sixth-grade class and seemed to have little motivation to learn. According to the parent this had been a consistent pattern since Nancy entered school. She never reached her potential owing to lack of interest. Of course, her mother knew she was a gifted child. Some emotional block, or possibly a learning disability, was hampering her performance.

It didn't take the teacher long to surmise that the difficulty was with the parent herself. Both mother and father were highly educated and successful people with great pride and interest in academic achievement. Nancy was a late-in-life child, being born fifteen years after her parents' marriage. She received much attention as an infant and was the object of great expectations from her family from the moment of birth. Needless to say, she had difficulty living up to all that was expected of her and so had stopped trying.

It would be foolish for the teacher to communicate her sudden insights to the parent during the interview. She might suggest that the parent see a psychologist and discuss the matter with him. But the information gleaned from the interview, far from being a clear statement of fact, casts new light on the child in her class. Parents' attitudes are revealed through discussions of this nature, and this may be more helpful to the teacher than the actual information imparted.

Some parents show more understanding and acceptance of their child than the school authorities give them credit for. Kathy was an underachiever in her third-grade class. (Her story entitled "In the Field" appears in Chapter 5.) Because Kathy was a daydreamer, who never finished her work, and was always a "loner" in the classroom, the principal had suggested that she be referred to the school psychologist. After an interview with her mother, the teacher decided against this. Kathy's parents accepted her as a sensitive little girl who needed time to be alone with her thoughts. Her mother said she had a "beautiful soul," and was different from her younger sister who was lively and outgoing. Each child in this family of five was considered to be a separate individual with needs and feelings of his own. No expected patterns of performance were established, and each child was free to be himself. The interview with the mother assured the teacher that Kathy had a loving and accepting family. Kathy would be able to work out her school problems if teachers would try to understand her as well as her family did.

Developing the case study

The case study is a way of collecting and organizing all of the information gathered from the various sources discussed in this chapter. The process of summarizing and synthesizing information is the same regardless of the age of the individual or the experience of the investigator. Case studies have been used extensively in clinical settings and in the study of abnormal behavior where they are useful to social workers, psychologists, and special educators. It is the contention of this author that a similar approach to normal behavior will be of equal benefit to those dealing with children in the classroom setting.

Of course, teachers do not have the time, nor are they in a position, to gather information as intimate and personal as that which the psychologist has available to him. Clinical tests and measurements cannot as easily be used. This should not discourage the case-study writer in the classroom. The information that is available can be organized in some meaningful way so that new insights are brought to bear upon the behavior of the child.

The manner or organization is at the discretion of the writer and is influenced by the type of data she is able to procure Different kinds of data lend themselves to different kinds of summarization. The writer's own style also plays a part in the selection of her method of organization. Students are encouraged to use a narrative style, if they feel they can express themselves well in this way. Some have even portrayed the child in the first person, as if the student were living inside the child's skin.

Several examples of different types of case studies are presented in later chapters of this book. As a way of illustrating the various means of presentation, we will cite them here and describe their internal organization.

The case study of Billy (Chapter 11), age eighteen months, is based upon direct observation plus interviews with members of the family. There is even a time when the student writer involved herself in direct interaction with the child as a way of providing stimulation. The case study is written from the point of view of the observer, and she uses the first person to describe her experiences with the family. The first part of the study gives background information about each member of the family since it is felt that this is vital to understanding the situation involving the child being studied.

The case study of Peter (Chapter 12) includes a time sample done in the classroom and an interview with the child while on a trip to the zoo. Following these direct observations, the student observer gives information based upon interviews with the child's teacher, his mother, and the school psychologist. The summary at the end of her case study lists Peter's traits in categories of motor skills, mental ability, and emotional aspects.

The case study of Wilma (Chapter 13), age five years, is made up solely of a series of subjective anecdotal reports. The student observed Wilma at her nursery school eight times. Some of the observational reports include information received through discussion with the teacher. Most of the report is based upon pure observation of what happened during those visits, and the student observer brought his own insights, gained through the early observations, to bear upon his interpretation of later events.

The case study of Brian (Chapter 14), age nine years and eleven months, is organized into aspects of his development, that is, physical, intellectual, social, and emotional. Information gained through observations and interviews with teachers is divided into these categories and reported accordingly. An introduction tells of first impressions and family background, and a summary gives the student observer's interpretation of what she has reported upon.

As can be seen from these examples, there is great variety in the methods of organizing case studies and many writing styles are acceptable. What is important is that the student or teacher try to convey to the reader of the case study as much insight into the child's nature and way of behaving as is possible, based upon the data collected. Not every observational report needs to be included. Much can be synthesized for more effective transmission of ideas. Key bits of dialogue can be included and often add flavor to the reporting. The choice of what to include is purely at the discretion of the observer and reporter. It is for her to decide what information gives the most insight into the child and what can be most helpful to the teacher in her efforts to understand and guide him.

REFERENCES

ALMY, MILLIE. *Ways of Studying Children.* New York: Teachers College Press, Teachers College, Columbia University, 1959.

BRANDT, RICHARD M. *Studying Behavior in Natural Settings.* New York: Holt, Rinehart and Winston, Inc., 1972.

COHEN, DOROTHY H., AND VIRGINIA STERN. *Observing and Recording the Behavior of Young Children.* New York: Teachers College Press, Teachers College, Columbia University, 1958.

FAST, JULIUS. *Body Language.* New York: Simon and Schuster, Inc., Pocket Books, 1971.

GORDON, IRA. *Studying the Child in School.* New York: John Wiley & Sons, Inc., 1966.

KOHL, HERBERT R. *The Open Classroom.* New York: Random House, Inc., 1969.

MILLARD, CECIL V., AND JOHN W. M. ROTHNEY. *The Elementary School Child: A Book of Cases.* New York: Holt, Rinehart and Winston, Inc., 1957.

MOUSTAKAS, CLARK. *The Authentic Teacher.* Cambridge, Mass.: Howard A. Doyle Publishing Company, 1966.

PRESCOTT, DANIEL A. *The Child in the Educative Process.* New York: McGraw-Hill, Inc., 1957.

ROSENTHAL, ROBERT, AND LENORE JACOBSON. *Pygmalion in the Classroom: Teacher Expectation and Pupil's Intellectual Ability.* New York: Holt, Rinehart and Winston, Inc., 1968.

ROWEN, BETTY. *An Exploration of the Uses of Rhythmic Movement to Develop Aesthetic Concepts in the Primary Grades.* Cooperative Research Report, no. EO 020770, USOE. Washington, D.C.: Government Printing Office, 1966.

TORGERSON, THEODORE L. *Studying Children: Diagnostic and Remedial Procedures in Teaching.* New York: Holt, Rinehart and Winston, Inc., 1947.

WHITE, VERNA. *Studying the Individual Pupil.* New York: Harper & Row, Publishers, 1958.

5

Looking at the child through the arts

The arts in the classroom offer the teacher a unique opportunity to gain insight into the child's growth, his experiences, his emotions, and his interests. A child's drawing may reveal how he feels about his world and the people in it. His picture may also show his level of maturity by indicating the detail he was able to observe, his muscular coordination, and his sense of organization. Response to music often reveals to the teacher hidden depths of feeling that she could not perceive in other classroom activities. The child's way of moving tells something about him even when he is just performing routine functions of walking, putting things away, or working at his desk. When he is given the opportunity to express his ideas in movement, as when he acts out a story, interprets an idea from a social studies lesson, or moves to music, then certainly he is saying something about himself which the sensitive teacher can perceive. When children are old enough to put their ideas in writing, their stories and poems provide the teacher with a rich source for developing insight and understanding of the child. Each of these means for self-expression will be discussed in this chapter, and examples will be given of ways in which children reveal themselves through the arts.

The young child expresses himself more freely than the child in the middle years. He freely responds with his whole body to sensory stimuli. He can move like the wind or grow like a flower. He chants as he swings on a swing, jogs along when he is happy, kicks the dirt when he is angry. Elementary forms of music, poetry, and dance can be found in the performance of his daily activity. Teachers only need to observe and to be aware to find expressive acts and self-revelation in the behavior of young children.

But as they get older, expression becomes inhibited. The nine-year-old is not so free in the use of his body. Feelings are not so easily discerned. Drawings become more realistic, revealing less of a personal nature. Writing is more often factual rather than expressive. It is possible that the emphasis in education has been too exclusively upon one type of experiencing. Methods of analysis and generalization have replaced sensory experience and have dulled capacities for alternatives. Education has imposed limits upon response and has thus conditioned ways of thinking.

Expressive qualities develop and thrive upon opportunities for recognition. Were we to encourage various forms of expression in the classroom, it is likely that the expressive acts of early childhood would not become atrophied. If teachers were aware and responded to expressions of feeling, children would continue to express themselves more freely. It is said that communication is a two-way street. If we talk, we want someone to be listening. If we express ideas in nonverbal forms—painting, music, dance— we want an audience to sense our meaning. Teachers who are responsive to these forms of expression have artistic children in their classes, and it always happens this way. Visiting a classroom where interesting artwork is displayed is not an indication that this group of children is more talented. It is more likely to be true that this teacher responds to the meaning and quality of children's drawings and has thus encouraged further expressive efforts.

Children's art

Many teachers have recognized that children's drawings are a way of communicating ideas. The class is often asked to "Draw a picture of what you saw on our trip to the zoo" or "Draw a picture of what you did last summer." The resultant drawings reveal how much the children observed and what was important to them about their experiences.

But children's artwork also shows their emotional reactions to their world. A child's painting is not an objective representation. "On the contrary, it expresses his likes and dislikes, his emotional relationships to his own world and the world which surrounds him. It also expresses not only what he knows, but also what he feels, sees and touches, if he has become sensitively aware of it."[1]

What can a teacher see in children's drawings and paintings? What can she learn about the young artist? First of all, she can see what is important to the child. He is likely to draw those items larger, or in greater detail, if they have greater meaning for him. A picture by a seven-year-old girl entitled, "I Am Throwing Something into the Trash Basket," shows the hands and arms enlarged. They are of significance, therefore exaggerated.[2]

Observations of detail and organization of a picture often reveal the conceptual level at which the child is operating. "In his drawings only the active knowledge, or what actively motivated the child, can be seen. This is of decisive significance, because it permits the educator to record how far the child has proceeded in the grasp of himself and of the surrounding world. A knowledge of what actively motivates the child further reveals to the

[1] Viktor Lowenfeld, *Creative and Mental Growth*, p. 7.
[2] Lowenfeld, p. 142.

educator the emotional significance which the represented objects have for the child."[3]

Lowenfeld has described levels of development in children's drawing. A familiarity with the characteristics of children's drawing at various age levels would be helpful to the teacher in assessing the maturity of the child. For example, the representation of a man which simply shows the circle for the head, and legs and feet extending down from it, is common for a five-year-old. But were this type of representation to be found in the drawings of an older child, the teacher might note some immaturity and would adjust her expectations and her program in areas of reading and writing, possibly, to a less mature level.

The level of maturity in drawing can be used as a diagnostic tool in working with handicapped children or with children who are having learning difficulties in the classroom. An eight-year-old child who can draw a detailed picture of a baseball game, showing all of the players in accurate relationship to each other, is not a "slow" child, even if he has not yet begun to read. The teacher might refer such a child for further testing or might look for other factors to find the reason for his learning deficiency.

Rawley Silver, an art teacher working with aphasic and deaf children in New York, kept sequential drawings that her subjects made over a period of several years.[4] The drawings revealed conceptual development and growth in ability to organize ideas in spite of the fact that these children could not communicate verbally.

It is helpful for the teacher to keep folders of children's artwork throughout the term in order to assess their growth and development. Questions might be asked, such as:

Does the child relate colors to objects?
Does the child use base lines?
Does the child show visual awareness by drawing distant objects smaller?

The answers to these questions can help to indicate the level of maturity the child has achieved.

The collected artwork of the children can also reveal what is of greatest interest to them. A boy who always draws airplanes can be stimulated to further observation by referring him to books concerning types of planes. This can increase his motivation to read as well as broaden his knowledge and visual perception of his favorite subject.

Selected subject matter for drawing will sometimes help the teacher to find out more about the child and his relationship to his environment. At the beginning of the term it is a good idea to ask primary-grade children to "draw a picture of your family." Each drawing can then be saved and referred to when the teacher reviews her records on the child. Pictures like this will

---

[3] Lowenfeld, p. 110.

[4] Rawley Silver, "The Role of Art in the Conceptual Thinking, Adjustment, and "Aptitude of Deaf and Aphasic Children," unpublished doctoral dissertation (New York: Teachers College, Columbia University, 1966).

Figure 1   Drawings of families

Figure 1 (continued)

often reveal how the child feels about his parents, his siblings, and other important people. It is very likely that he will place himself close to the favored member in his drawing. The size of the drawing of himself in relation to his siblings tells something about his self-concept as well as his feelings about his brothers and sisters. Inclusion of an aunt or a grandfather has significance as well. The teacher might discuss the picture with the child, learning the reasons why he included certain things. She might also use the picture as a focal point for discussion in a parent conference. It is amazing how much can be discovered about family relationships using this device! (See Figure 1, pp. 62–63.)

Art is useful in psychotherapy, since drawings and paintings permit direct expression of dreams, fantasies, and other inner experiences that are more likely to occur as pictures than as words. Pictured projections of inner thoughts and feelings are also more likely to escape the self-imposed censorship that often inhibits verbal expression. Interpretations of these drawings are often obvious even to an inexperienced eye. There is a danger that the classroom teacher, once aware of children's art as a projection of inner conflicts, will interpret what she sees too freely. We have all heard the story of the child who was referred to a psychiatrist because all of his pictures were painted in black. It was later discovered that all of the other colors had been used up, and black was the only paint available!

We do not want teachers to become alarmed at every scary monster drawing done by a child or to rush him off for psychological examination the first time his picture reveals an inner fear or repressed emotion. However, there are opportunities to perceive disturbance in children's drawings. Tenseness can be sensed in the rigidity of style or in the limited use of space. Fixations upon certain ways of viewing things are often indicative of disturbance. Of course, it is essential to view a series of drawings by a child before such qualities can be identified. These symptoms must be viewed in the light of further knowledge of the child and cannot be considered in isolation. With the assistance of a psychologist the drawings of a disturbed child can help to indicate areas for investigation as well as show growth and improvement in a patient under treatment.

A good example of a child's problem revealing itself through her artwork can be found in the case study of five-year-old Wilma Adams in Part III of this book. Wilma had suffered a traumatic experience at the death of her father through drowning. She never discussed this loss, but her drawings consistently concerned themselves with water and boats. Experimenting with plastic snowflakes, a creative construction toy, she made a boat for the teacher that "wouldn't ever sink." One day, when the class was told they could color as they wished, Wilma

began coloring and did not join in any of the conversation. Her silence seemed heavier than usual, and her face appeared troubled. When Wilma's teacher approached her and commented on her picture, Wilma did not give her customary response. Instead of smiling and hugging her teacher she just looked up into her face, her expression unchanged. The teacher asked if "there was something wrong today." When there was no immediate reply, the matter was not pursued. The teacher told me later that she felt that Wilma would come to her if and when she chose to.

Wilma's sullen attitude continued as she finished her paper. She seemed to be coloring only in blue and green and to be working much less rapidly than she usually did. She appeared instead to be taking great pains with her picture as if she were seriously pondering its contents. Her head was close to the paper and she showed none of her usual good posture and movements. The intensity she displayed was not of the eager nature with which she usually worked.

After the papers were collected and the children were sent out to the playground, I asked to see Wilma's picture. Set in among many large blue and green waves was a drawing of a sailboat with no one aboard.

The student making this observation had no training as a psychologist. He was not experienced in classroom teaching, being an undergraduate who just returned to college after military service. But his astute observations of this child revealed a great deal about her. He was concerned not only with the content of the drawing, but with her attitude and body movements while engaged in the act. We get a view of the significance of the drawing through the many clues provided by the observer.

Art expression is an important source of information about a child, but it must be taken within a frame of reference to be interpreted meaningfully.

Music and dance

Young children express their feelings readily in the ways that they move. Long before they are able to communicate in verbal ways, infants use gesture and body movement to tell adults of their needs. No one can mistake the message which signals "Pick me up" or "Bye-bye," even if no sounds are uttered. When a toddler is fearful or unhappy, his emotion is revealed through a total body response. Joy is equally manifested throughout his body as he bounces gleefully, waving his arms vigorously.

And young children respond to music and rhythm. The baby rocks back and forth in his crib and accompanies his movements with vocalized rhythmic sounds. Children on the playground chant as they play circle games. When they hear music or even the rhythmic sounds of a washing machine, young children respond with body movement.

Teachers of young children can encourage these responses by allowing children to move freely to music in the classroom. Watching them as they move, teachers can sense the emotional reactions of the children to the various qualities of the music. Lyrical, quiet music will elicit soft and flowing movements. Sharp, percussive sounds will cause the children to react with strong, vigorous thrusts of arms and legs. Some children respond more than others, and some have stronger responses to particular qualities in the music they hear. All of these kinds of reactions give the teacher an opportunity to sense a little more about the children with whom she is working.

Feelings are more easily expressed through movement and through a response to music than they are through verbal expression. Although this is universally true for the preschool child who has limited verbal ability, it is often true for young school-age children as well.

This writer did an action study involving second-grade children in a suburban community.[5] The study was concerned with aesthetic responses, and so it was necessary for the children to describe their feelings to the investigator. In an initial interview they were asked about how a particular movement made them feel. It became evident that the children needed some clarification as to what was meant by "feeling." These seven-year-olds did not expect this to be an area for discussion in the school setting. In answer to the question, "How does it make you feel?" many of the children replied, "I am fine."

At later sessions of the action study the children were still unable to define in words the emotions they felt when listening to music. Even after inhibitions were released and the children were able to express feelings about the quality of their movement response, they had difficulty in describing verbally what they were experiencing.

One boy, Steven, in responding to the feeling of the color red, wrapped himself up in a large red scarf, and did sharp arm and leg movements as if trying to get out. When asked what kind of music he would like to accompany him, he chose sad music, only to find it did not fit the quality of his movement improvisation at all. Later it was determined that he envisioned himself caught in a fire and was trying to get out of it. Angry music fitted his mood much better, as the connotation of "sad" was not a true description of his feeling.

The beauty inherent in the free movement of children has been most eloquently expressed by Sylvia Ashton-Warner as she describes a scene in her New Zealand "Infant Room" on one spring morning.

Having settled them all down busily and noisily writing stories, feeling keenly myself the spring in the air, with the sun pouring across the prefab through the generous windows, I ran over to the piano and began playing, "Hark, Hark the Lark." Then something happened which is the highest peak of achievement in what I, for want of the real word, call my teaching.

Whether it was the genius of Schubert speaking over the century through his inspired music, whether it was the spring in the air after the unprecedentedly cold winter or whether it was ripe to come anyway, it came.

There was a flash of yellow at my right; I looked round. It was Twinnie dancing. I thrilled violently. It was not hula or any native dance. It was a fine, exquisite expressive dance, such as is cultivated these days as something new but which belongs to the days before time. It was perfectly in rhythm with the music and followed the feeling of it. Up floated the other Twinnie. They danced to each other, from each other, their arms expressing, their hands and their small bodies. Two small brown spirits with bright yellow jerseys like jonquils. . . .

[5] Betty Rowen, *An Exploration of the Uses of Rhythmic Movement to Develop Aesthetic Concepts in the Primary Grades.*

They had never heard this music before. They had never danced in that wonderful way. It was purely spontaneous. Purely *organic*.[6]

Where there is an accepting atmosphere, where teacher and children share ideas and feelings, where children are encouraged to express themselves, in such classrooms, dancing is likely to happen. Natalie Cole says, "The beautiful dancing is in the child already. What the teacher does is to remove fear and embarrassment and help it come out."[7]

Mrs. Cole, although no dancer herself, certainly knew how to free her children to express themselves through movement. And through their expressive dancing, she was able to discover more about each one. She was able to catch a child in a sincere moment and praise him for "how beautifully José was feeling the music. . . ."[8]

She understood the silliness that might necessarily follow as José tried to cover his feelings of embarrassment. As children become more comfortable, the silliness passes. Acceptance by the teacher and the other children frees a child to express response to beauty, joy, sadness, or comedy through his dance.

Once such faith is established, and children feel free to express ideas in movement, many deep-seated thoughts and emotions may be revealed. Often the quality in a selection of music suggests ideas to the children. After they have moved to the music, they may want to talk about the feelings they had, or the things that the music suggested to them.

This was one of the activities presented to the second-grade class in the action study previously mentioned.[9] Three selections of music were played, each having a distinctive quality and contrasting sharply with the others selected. The children were not told the titles of the music, nor was there any discussion prior to hearing it. They were invited to move to the music as they liked and then to talk about their feelings or the images they saw.

Manuel, a usually lively, mischievous boy, seemed very pensive while listening to the *Bydlo* theme from Moussorgsky's *Pictures at an Exhibition*. This is heavy, slow music descriptive of an old ox cart being pulled by an ox. Manuel's response to the music was that it made him think of "a giant crying." Later he was asked to act out his impressions. An observer recorder noted "Manuel does a slow, heavy walk, hands over eyes. Duane plays a bass drum in slow marching time with the music. They repeat [this] with no variation of movement throughout [the] music—but with decided quality. Manuel called this a 'sad parade' in which a giant was crying."

The intensity of this portrayal was evidence of the emotional meaning it had for the child. Manuel was a bright, active seven-year-old, of Portuguese descent, who participated readily in creative activities and was both verbal and rhythmic. But never before had he displayed this somber, serious quality. The classroom teacher commented:

[6] Sylvia Ashton-Warner, *Teacher*, pp. 190–191.
[7] Natalie Cole, *The Arts in the Classroom*, p. 69.
[8] Cole, p. 85.
[9] Rowen, pp. 105–108.

Manuel's "sad parade" may stem from his recent experience—the death of a grandfather whom he dearly loved. The whole class was affected, also, by the televised scenes of Churchill's funeral, which brought back recollections of Kennedy's funeral. There is an unusual preoccupation with this in some of these children.

Children's response to music is natural and real and often involves them deeply. Movement interpretations only externalize what many children instinctively feel in the quality of the music that they hear. A perceptive teacher can find these moments of great interest and can gain new insights into her children's feelings by observing them as they listen and respond to music.

Creative drama

The use of creative drama gives the teacher a laboratory for observation of human behavior. Children reveal themselves as they play out roles, and as they discuss the interpretation others have given to a role. Note paper should be handy, so that the teacher can jot down her observations, for this activity is a rich source for anecdotal records that can be filed in a child's folder for reevaluation at some later date.

Many fine books have been written that will help the teacher begin creative dramatics in the classroom. Our purpose here is not to present methods for developing a creative drama program but rather to demonstrate ways of perceiving the expressive acting of children as a means of knowing them as individuals. Of course, experience on the part of the teacher helps her to develop insight. If she has acted in a school play, taken classes in drama, or worked with a community theater group, she will be more capable of directing children and leading them to a point of emotional involvement. Such experiences are strongly recommended for all who plan to work with children.

Children sometimes need the opportunity of identifying with characters in a known story in order to sense their own feelings and understand them. By putting themselves into the roles of the characters, they begin to sense that their feelings are not unique to them. Others have experienced the same anger, frustration, or joy that they have known. Emotions, both of a negative and positive nature, can be accepted more readily.

In the aforementioned action study the investigator devised a lesson which would help the children to identify and accept their own emotions and to clarify the meanings of words that describe feelings.[10]

She chose the story of *Hansel and Gretel* to tell to the class, since it contains so many of the emotions familiar to children. As she told the story, the children acted it out in pantomime, the boys playing the parts of Hansel and the father, the girls playing Gretel, the mother, and the witch. The investigator described some scenes in greater detail, pausing to allow time for

[10] Rowen, pp. 146–149.

the children to develop the dramatic quality suggested. Many of the children became quite involved. The observer recorder reported:

Lynn seems to become more alive as she plays the part of Gretel. While weaving the brooms, she frowns at the trouble she seems to be having putting them together. Later loses concentration, giggles as "Mother" scolds.

Duane, as Hansel, walks to other side of room to get milk, responds to drum beat indicating milk was dropped, goes back to "kitchen" to get rag to wipe floor, looking reluctant.

Susan is sneaking up with finger to mouth to silence Hansel. When witch comes, she hugs Annette, sits down with hands in prayer attitude, chin trembling. She is serious throughout the action.

All of the children acted at the same time, taking cues from the story being told by the investigator. A discussion then followed, in which scenes in the story were used to identify emotions aroused by those situations. The children recalled what it felt like to be lost. Although they had never been lost in the woods like Hansel and Gretel, they did remember—"not being able to find my mother in the movies." Finding the candy house was associated with opening surprise packages at Christmas time.

At the next session children did individual pantomimes recalling something that had happened to them which made them angry, surprised, or fearful. The observer recorder reported:

Lorraine told about how she had once been playing at the beach, and a big wave had come and "drowned" her. Although her action was small, her facial expression made us really believe her.

Eddie told about how his brother was teasing him one day, and he did a very convincing pantomime of anger.

Rosann ran to do her pantomime and fell. The observer recorder thought she had really hurt herself, but it was part of her story. Her face was contorted, she rubbed her hip, her eyes looked anxious.

Not all of the children were able to maintain this degree of concentration in doing their pantomimes by themselves. Surprisingly, Lorraine and Eddie, who were usually shy and self-conscious, became completely absorbed in the scene they played. Many of the more outgoing children overplayed their parts and were not sincere.

In these instances situations in a well-known story triggered off emotional reactions in the children, and they were able to associate their feelings with personal experiences of their own. Professional actors sometimes use this method of association to give life to the roles they play. Recalling one's own experiences creates empathy with the character and allows the actor to identify more closely with his role.

Creative dramatics in the classroom can allow the teacher to develop greater empathy with her children. The knowledge that Eddie, for example, was capable of such intense anger in reacting to the imagined scene when he was teased by his brother, gave his teacher a new view of this child. Perhaps this quiet, rather dull-appearing boy has greater potential, which has been over-shadowed by the image of an older brother. The teacher, in this case, resolved to pay more attention to this child who previously had demanded so little of her.

Other quiet and unobtrusive children have revealed themselves to their teachers through dramatization. Such an instance occurred when Robbin became *The Little Match Girl.*

Robbin is a first grader who barely speaks above a whisper. She never volunteers for any activity. She seems happiest during rhythms sessions, when the children are allowed to skip, run, and gallop around the room. Even then, however, her movements are restrained and self-conscious. Sometimes when the children are all swinging freely, or skipping in a circle, she seems more relaxed.

The class had talked about "acting out" some of their favorite fairy tales after one of these freeing sessions. Everyone had suggestions to make. They might be Cinderellas or Princes. Some wanted to be Papa, Mama or Baby Bear.

Robbin came quietly to the teacher's desk. "Would it be too sad to do "The Little Match Girl?" she asked. Her mother had read the Anderson fairly tale to her the night before. "Sad things are sometimes beautiful, too," the teacher told her.

It was hard for Robbin to get started. The teacher helped. She described the way the Match Girl looked, the way she was dressed. Soon Robbin was moving as the Match Girl might move. Her small, timid steps, so much a part of her, might have been made by this other child. The class listened and watched, for this was a story that was new to most of them. Then the Match Girl lit the match in which she was to see such lovely images. Robbin's face lit up, and her body unfolded. The movement was not big, but there was a change from the huddled position to the open one that started within the child. The teacher's voice went on, setting the mood, creating a rhythm with her pauses. Robbin's movement developed; she reached out; she turned. Finally she sank down quietly, and the dream was gone.

Robbin had forgotten about herself, and she blushed when the class applauded. This was a day she would remember.[11]

The classroom teacher need not be a psychologist to be able to sense the contributions to personality growth evidenced in this dramatization. Self-consciousness was momentarily overcome as Robbin became absorbed with the story. Her own beautiful dreams came to life as she reenacted the visions of *The Little Match Girl.* The sincerity of her performance was communicated to the children watching, and they were carried along with her. Recognition by classmates for a performance such as this often changes a child's peer relationship in the weeks that follow. Robbin became much more involved with her classmates and developed closer friendships possibly owing to her own rise in self-esteem.

[11] Betty Rowen, *Learning through Movement*, pp. 57–58.

Puppets

It takes a while to free children enough for them to become deeply involved in dramatic portrayal. Some less outgoing children might respond more when puppets are used to tell the story than when they act it out themselves.

A language-arts consultant used this approach to encourage language-deficient first graders to express feelings and to develop greater language fluency.[12] She presented original marionette shows, each of which was focused upon an emotion familiar to the children. Following the presentation small-group discussions were led with ten children participating at a time. The children were from an academically low group of first graders in a predominantly black community, who had been selected for language enrichment experiences. In these discussion groups an attempt was made to explore the feelings of the children as they related to what happened in the marionette show. The following questioning technique was used to accomplish this exploration.

1. Enumerate ideas from the story.
2. Make inferences about the feelings of the characters in the story.
3. Explain why the characters in the story might feel as they do.
4. Compare the feelings of the characters in the story to similar emotional experiences the children have had.
5. Have the children describe how they felt.
6. Explore the reasons why they felt as they did.
7. Come to conclusions about the point of the story and see if the point seems valid to the children.

In the group discussion following the show the marionette characters became real people to the children. The characters had feelings similar to those that the children had experienced. In one of the stories several animal characters argued over what was inside an Easter egg. Using the children's language patterns the investigator asked, "Have any of you ever had a fuss with anybody?" This led to a very revealing discussion about arguments the children had overheard at home and the way that this "fussing" made them feel.

The investigator encouraged the children by accepting their language patterns, reacting to their feelings, and by leading them to further expression with her questions. The amount and quality of the resultant conversation indicated the high level of interest that the marionette show elicited. While many of the children told of incidents that were meaningful to them, others tended to repeat what had already been said in an attempt to maintain their place in the group. Were this investigator to work with this group of disadvantaged youngsters on a regular basis, the insights gained from these discussions could help her to motivate them in other areas of learning.

Drawings of the marionette characters, done by some of the children, are shown in Figure 2. The level of performance in artwork seems to be

[12] Helen Carol Dunstall (Dade County School System, Miami, Florida).

Figure 2   Drawings of puppet characters

Figure 2 (continued)

Figure 2 (continued)

miss cat thee bee fussing about the egg with the mother dragon.

Figure 2 (continued)

higher for these children than their verbal ability. This is an interesting fact and indicates that various modes of expression should be available for children with language deficiencies. Puppets are one way to free them for greater expression in both verbal and nonverbal forms.

When children operate the puppets themselves, there is sometimes even greater opportunity for the teacher to gain insight into their feelings. A family of hand puppets in the classroom gives the children the chance to enact some of their own life experiences. Many times a child, playing with a mother or father puppet, will reveal submerged feelings about his own parents or will portray the way he perceives the adults in his life. Puppets have been used in play therapy for this purpose and have helped the therapist to understand something of the emotional problems of the young puppeteer. The classroom teacher can use this technique just as effectively. All children, the well-adjusted as well as the disturbed, have some emotional conflicts. It helps to act out the feelings that are bothering them, and the understanding adult can lend support. The teacher, like the therapist, can acknowledge the feelings expressed and can help the child accept them.

When children create their own puppets, the choice of the character they decide to make is, in itself, revealing. The small child who consistently makes lions, monsters, or gorillas is very likely trying to identify with strength through his puppets. The little girl who is preoccupied with making fairies has a lively fantasy life which serves some emotional purpose for her. A psychotherapist, who frequently uses puppets in his work, says:

It is assumed that each child identifies himself, in a manner specific to him, with the puppet characters and with the actions portrayed by them. It is further assumed that this identification leads to projections in the sense that each child projects his own feelings, desires, wishes and anticipations into the puppet show.[13]

The teacher can also interpret something of the feelings of children through their reactions to various puppet characters and through observation of their selections of puppets to make or to play with.

Role playing

Role playing differs from creative dramatics or puppet shows in that it is aimed at solving particular problems. We have discussed the use of role play in teacher-education programs. By acting out the parent-teacher conference, teachers gain new insights into the feelings of parents. Reversing roles gives them a chance to see things from another person's perspective. This technique can be used with children as well.

Many classroom problems lend themselves to role playing, and solutions are often found as a result of this. Children begin to see the need for rules when they act out situations in which no rules are enforced. Playground con-

[13] Adolf G. Woltmann, "The Use of Puppetry in Therapy," p. 203.

flicts can be acted out, discussed, and often resolved when children begin to see what the other person is experiencing. Solutions to problems become clearer when the class is asked to finish a story by acting it out, thus coming up with various possible outcomes.

In a third-grade class taught by this writer, a problem became evident when some children became "too bossy" while working with their committees on research projects. Role play was used as a way of demonstrating the effects of this behavior upon the group.

The teacher picked two capable chairmen one day and called them aside for some preliminary discussion. "I know that you both know how to be good chairmen," she said. "You know how to take suggestions from the members of your group and to put them together so that the best ideas are used. You know that the more you let each member contribute, the better the group will work together. I'd like to try a little experiment this morning, to show the class that this is true.

"Ned, I'd like you to be the best chairman you know how to be. Let everyone have a part in making your play. Let the group decide who should play each part. Vote on things if there is disagreement. Try to give everyone something important to do.

"Charles, I'd like to see if you could act differently, just for today. You select the story, and tell each member of the group what he is to do. Be as bossy as you can be. Do not let anyone else have a chance to give an opinion. Let's see what happens."

Ned and Charles enjoyed the secret that the teacher had entrusted to them, and they carried off their roles well. Ned's group went off to one side of the room and proceeded to plan. There was lively discussion, some noisy, enthusiastic voices raised, and then a quieting down as each member began to work on his own part.

Charles selected a story he knew but which was unfamiliar to the others in his group. He was trying to tell it to them, but already there were voices raised in protest. The children ran to the teacher's desk, complaining that "Charles is unfair,"—"He won't listen to anybody." "He won't let us talk." The teacher shrugged her shoulders and told them that they must do as their chairman tells them.

There was some grumbling, but the children sullenly complied. When it was time to show each other what they had done, Ned's group performed with enthusiasm and both performers and audience enjoyed it. Charles had actually devised a better play, but his group was listless in its performance. The audience was quick to sense this, and to comment about it during the discussion that followed.

"Can I tell them now?" Charles asked. "I don't want everyone to think I'm really that bossy!" The secret was told and everyone thought it was a great joke.[14]

For the teacher this experiment served many purposes. It demonstrated the value of democratic methods to the children. It showed the bossy ones (who were *not* the chosen chairmen in this role-playing scene) what it felt like

[14] Rowen, *Learning through Movement*, pp. 31–32.

to have someone giving orders all of the time. And, it gave the teacher the opportunity to observe a group-dynamics situation which revealed a good deal about each child's personal reaction to types of classroom atmosphere.

Creative writing

If art, music, and drama are natural means by which young children reveal themselves, then creative writing is the most accessible means of self-expression for the older child. "Writing is a way of discussing things with themselves, seeking meanings, clarifying values, considering their own relationships with the world, and pondering the meaning of life and its implications for their own future."[15]

Autobiographies may offer the teacher a means of collecting data. But asking children to write about themselves does not always open secret doors. Students can often be self-conscious and constrained when they are writing if the stage has not been set for openness and confidence.

A creative writing lesson should never be focused upon grammar or punctuation. These things may come later, but the first concern of the teacher must be an interest in the child's ideas. This is a time for quiet in the class-room, and no set limits can be placed upon time. One way of dealing with this is to allow the children to take as long as they like, using yellow "first draft" paper to encourage them to "get their own ideas down" in whatever way they come. When they are finished with the first draft, the children may come to the teacher's desk and take a number, as they might do at a crowded bakery or supermarket counter. When their number is written on the blackboard, they may have a private conference with the teacher, sharing ideas with her and listening to suggestions for improvement. Content is never criticized, but the order of ideas or the need for a stronger statement at the end might be suggested. When the writer is satisfied with his composition, he is given white paper and a dictionary. His final copy will be neater with words more carefully spelled.

Opportunity for sharing compositions with others encourages creative writing. A weekly class newspaper or a magazine with "our best stories" stimulates children to write more frequently. A box should be placed some-where in the classroom to receive contributions whenever authors feel the urge to write.

Mrs. Cole made a wall newspaper, mounting selections of the children's writing on special topics; she always tried to "find something good from each child."[16]

To learn about some of the deeper feelings of her children, she asked them to write about things that troubled them. By discussing her own child-hood experiences, she gave them confidence to communicate personal stories of their own. Children were told to write at the top of their stories, "O.K. to

[15] Daniel Prescott, *The Child in the Educative Process*, p. 188.
[16] Cole, pp. 98–101.

read out loud" or "Just for Mrs. Cole." Children's confidences must be respected at all times. The teacher's use of methods like these will encourage the children to do much personal writing, and the teacher can increase his depth of understanding of her children as a result of it.

This writer has had some surprising experiences when children expressed themselves in writing. Tom was a freckle-faced, wiry eight-year-old who had little interest in school. He was absent often, but when his mother was contacted she never knew where he was. When he was in class, he didn't talk much, did his work in an off-hand manner, and managed to do passable work with little interest or enthusiasm. One day he wrote:

> Listen to the birds sing over the trees
> Listen to the water flowing through the
>   mountain tops and through the
>   forest meadow
> Into the ground
> Into rivers
> And into the oceans and seas
> Following the land and the breeze.

The guidance worker later discovered that, when Tom played hooky, he went fishing down by a brook that leads into the bay near his home. Tom's experiences while absent from school provided inspiration for his poetic expression.

With Skippy, there was another story. Skippy liked school, was a good student, and was somewhat of a show-off. Teachers in the faculty room often talked about him. Many were impressed by the bright, sophisticated humor of this pint-sized eight-year-old. Others thought he was too fresh and difficult to control in class. His wit, self-concept, and opinions about school and teachers were revealed in this story about:

The Owl That Went to Medical School

I am Joe Owl and this is how I went to medical school. First period was how to give a shot. My teacher was not very smart. When the teacher was just about to give the shot, I said, "Excuse me, teacher, but the needle is upside down!" Then the bell rang for lunch.

In the cafeteria I had a bowl of bird seed and chicken soup.

Next period was how to pull tonsils. I said, "Excuse me, teacher, but why are you going to pull tonsils with a stethoscope?" Then the bell rang.

Now I am a doctor. How I am, I'll never know. Now you know what happened in a medical school for the birds!

The most observant teacher may not know the potentials of all the children in her class. Kathy's creative writing was a surprise to many who had been watching her. Kathy was the eldest of a family of five girls. She was a delicate-looking, fair-skinned, dark-haired Irish beauty, but she was an outsider in her third-grade class. On the playground she could be found off by herself, quietly swinging on the swings. In class, she rarely finished her work, and would be found absent-mindedly looking out of the window when others were involved in lively discussion. The principal noticed that she always walked alone, following the class as we left the building, often gazing at the ceiling as she strolled along. He suggested that she be referred to the school psychologist for examination.

One day, during creative writing, Kathy seemed very absorbed in what she was doing for the first time. When she brought her story to the teacher's desk, it was poorly written, with words strung together and many misspelled. (See Figure 3 for a sample of the child's writing.) It was hard to decipher her meaning, although many of the so-called "errors" added rhythm and quality to her writing. It is presented here in its corrected form.

In the Field

Once upon a time there was a lovely field that had a beautiful name.

It was a very wonderful place to be.

It was not a place to live. It was only a place for flowers and other things that belong in a field.

In the field were flowers that were the most beautiful flowers to see. The most beautiful butterflies flew all over the field. There were white and blue, green and pink butterflies.

Every day there was a party. But it was not a party that you have when you are going to have a party. It was just a party of being happy. Every day there was happiness going on.

Until one day the sun went, and the birds flew away. The people that were not too far away, and the people that were far away closed their doors as tight as they could.

And it was a little bit dark.

Then the most rain and wind came. It was a half of a hurricane. Oh, how much it rained and oh, how much it blew.

Then finally, the half of a hurricane was over.

But the field was not happy because all of the flowers were very much dead. The whole field was all rotten.

Then came the winter. Oh, how it snowed.

Then came the spring, and then came the summer.

The dead, rotten field was all right. All the field was well taken care of.

All winter the flowers grew more and more better.

So then, at summer, the field was very, very happy. And every day there was a party. And it was not a party that you would have. It was a party where you threw confetti up, up into the air.

Kathy was a dreamer, and the world needs more of them. Her teacher came to respect this quality in her. She was spared the discomfort of lengthy psychological tests and involved questioning, which would certainly have made her more self-conscious.

Creative writing can give the teacher knowledge that can change her total picture of a child. But again, as in all interpretation of expressive forms, no one factor can be the determining one. Art media sometimes reveal hidden qualities in children and make us view them in a new light. But the child's

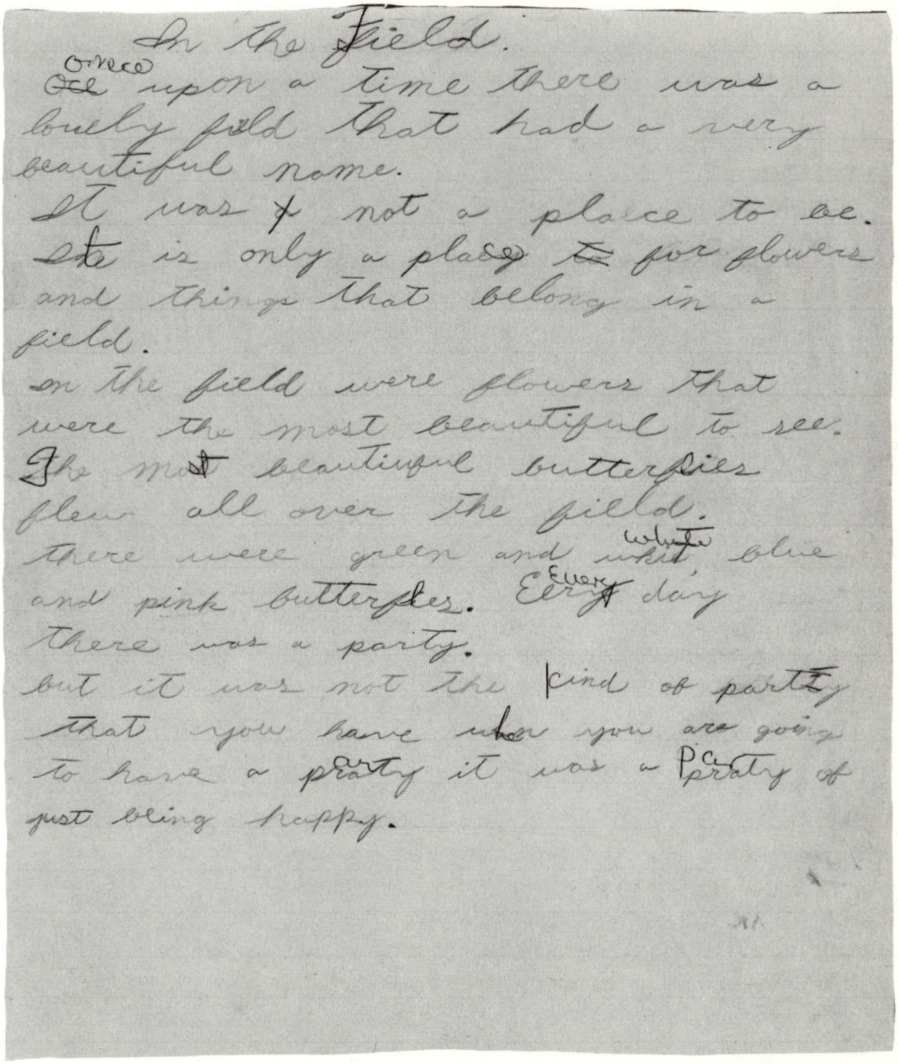

In the Field.

Once upon a time there was a lovely field that had a very beautiful name.

It was not a place to be. It is only a place for flowers and things that belong in a field.

In the field were flowers that were the most beautiful to see. The most beautiful butterflies flew all over the field. There were green and white, blue and pink butterflies. Every day there was a party.

But it was not the kind of party that you have when you are going to have a party it was a party of just being happy.

Figure 3   Creative writing: "In the Field"

Every day there was happening [~~happening~~] going on. Once [~~Until~~] one day the sun went down. and the birds flew away. The people that were not park away and the people the were park away closd their doors as tight as they could [~~cold~~]. And it was alittlebit dark. Then the most rain and wind came [~~blew~~] It was a half of a hurricane. Oh how much it rained and Oh how much it blew. Then finally the half of hurricane was over but the field was not happy because all the flowers were very very much dead. The old field was all rotten. Then came the winter Oh how it snowed! Then came the spring and then came the summer.

Figure 3 (continued)

the dead rotten field was all
~~right~~. right
All the field was well taken
care of.
all winter the flowers grew
more and more oedter.
So then at summer the field
was very very happy.
Also evry day there was a
party.
and it was not the kind of
party that you have.
It was a party at which you
threw confette up, up, up
into the air.
For ever the great field and the
great butterflies and flowers were
happy.

The End

Figure 3 (continued)

picture or story must always be considered as part of an observational approach to his total behavior.

REFERENCES

ASHTON-WARNER, SYLVIA.   *Teacher*. New York: Simon and Schuster, Inc., 1963.

AXLINE, VIRGINIA.   *Play Therapy*. Boston: Houghton Mifflin Company, 1947.

COLE, NATALIE.   *The Arts in the Classroom*. New York: The John Day Company, Inc., 1940.

LOWENFELD, VIKTOR.   *Creative and Mental Growth*. 3d ed. New York: Crowell-Collier and Macmillan, Inc., 1957.

MEARNS, HUGHES.   *Creative Power: The Education of Youth in the Creative Arts*. 2d rev. ed. New York: Dover Publications, Inc., 1958.

MEARNS, HUGHES.   *Creative Youth*. New York: Doubleday & Company, Inc., 1931.

MIEL, ALICE, ed.   *Creativity in Teaching*. Belmont, Calif.: Wadsworth Publishing Company, 1961.

PRESCOTT, DANIEL.   *The Child in the Educative Process*. New York: McGraw-Hill, Inc., 1957.

ROWEN, BETTY.   *An Exploration of the Uses of Rhythmic Movement to Develop Aesthetic Concepts in the Primary Grades*. Cooperative Research Report, No. ED 020770, USOE. Washington, D.C.: Government Printing Office, 1966.

ROWEN, BETTY.   *Learning through Movement*. New York: Teachers College Press, Columbia University, 1963.

WOLTMANN, ADOLF G.   "The Use of Puppetry in Therapy." *Conflict in the Classroom*. Edited by Nicholas J. Long, William C. Morse and Ruth G. Newman. Belmont, Calif.: Wadsworth Publishing Company, 1965.

Looking at the child
through the use
of diagnostic tools

Much can be learned about individual children through direct observation of them. Their expressive acts in writing, art, or movement also reveal unique qualities that may not be perceivable in more academic classroom situations. We cannot overlook, however, the knowledge about children to be gained through the administration of tests and through the use of diagnostic procedures.

Tests and measurements of various kinds have become a standard practice in the school setting. In many instances, the outcomes of such an application of diagnostic tools are considered to be ends in themselves. Educators and psychologists have operated as though the ability to perform tasks on tests were an independent faculty apart from the rest of the child's existence and experience. When the teacher categorizes pupil behavior simply on the basis of tests, placing children in ability groups according to final scores and ignoring their motivation and style of thinking, she is performing a meaningless operation. Testing can be functional only when the results are considered in the light of the total behavior of the child. The teacher's personal evaluation and her interpretation of the factors operating in the way a child performs in a test situation must be taken into account.

In this chapter we will examine some of the areas in which children have been judged on the basis of tests, and we will try to establish ways in which teachers' insight in the interpretation of test results can add to the diagnostic value of the test itself.

Children's logic

The noted Swiss psychologist, Jean Piaget, has strongly influenced our thinking about the development of logic in children. Piaget believes that there is a sequence of developmental steps in cognitive growth. The chronological age at which these stages occur may vary, but the order of progression is fixed.

In the first stage, called the sensorimotor period, the child's thinking is based purely upon perception. He must organize various sensations into internal "schema" or structures and must coordinate one sensory image with another to determine the nature of reality. He gradually develops from a state where the world is undefined to one in which there is a knowledge of self and of outside objects.

With the first representational activity of the toddler, a preoperational stage begins. Objects gradually begin to take on symbolic meaning, and gestures, words, and pictures begin to stand for something. Concepts begin to form, but thinking is largely intuitive, that is, based upon the child's perception of things rather than on logic. Through interactions with the environment a series of cognitive structures begin to develop, and the child enters the stage of "concrete operations." Thoughts revolve around the experiences the child has had, and, in cases where he has had no direct experience, he can deal with concepts only through analogy to something with which he is familiar. He develops logical processes only when dealing with concrete objects.

The child can deal with abstraction, according to Piaget, only after he has passed through the various preceding stages and has entered the stage of "formal operations." Logical deductions can now be made without reference to empirical evidence. This usually does not occur before the age of eleven or twelve.

Piaget's conception of logic is very much dependent upon his own scientific orientation. In determining whether a child is functioning at the intuitive or the concrete stage of operation, in deciding whether he is logical or sublogical, Piaget applies his own, adult conceptions to his view of the child's thinking. In his early writing Piaget observed his own children, and others, in small groups and tried to determine what made them answer questions about space and matter in the way that they did. Later studies involved large groups of children who were interviewed after seeing demonstrations of specific scientific principles. The stages in the development of logic that Piaget evolved from the earlier studies were applied to the children in the later studies, and the children were thus classified according to the level of logic at which they were operating.

Piaget's conclusions have been criticized because it is felt that what is lacking in children is not logical processes but rather direct experience with the principles involved. The children's lack of understanding of Piaget's reference points when he questioned them also accounts for some of their misconceptions.

These criticisms of Piaget's conclusions have validity when they are applied to many other adult attempts to assess children's logic. Does the child always perceive the question in the way the adult intended it? It is possible that the constructs we are looking for in children's thinking are merely products of our own adult experience, and thus exist only in the investigator's mind, not in the child's.

A graduate student, who is a school guidance counselor experienced with testing procedures, devised a project which replicated some of the tests described by Piaget.[1] She then attempted to find out, by direct elicitation from the child, just what assumptions the child was making about the problem presented and the child's reasoning behind his answers.

One exercise, common to many forms of intelligence testing, concerned transitive relationships. The child is shown a picture of a little girl standing between a black dog and a brown dog and is told that she is pointing to the black dog because that is the one she wants to play with. In the second picture the girl is standing between the brown dog and a white dog and she is pointing to the brown dog because that is the one she wants to play with. Finally the child being tested is shown a picture of the little girl standing between the black dog and the white dog and is asked which one he thinks she will choose and why. (See Figure 4 for test illustrations.)

Seven-year-olds in the University of Miami campus elementary school were questioned about their reasons for their answers to this question. They were, of course, to select the black dog as being preferred to either the white or the brown dog. This choice was the correct one on the basis of the adult conception of logical transitive relationships inherent in the test. But Andy, a bright, black child from a professional family, said that the little girl would choose the white dog, because "she likes dogs and doesn't want to make one of them unhappy." Therefore, she will give all of the dogs a chance to play and the white dog is the only one which had not had a turn yet. David, a handsome blond boy, described by his teacher as a very good student, decided that the little girl pictured would choose the white dog, since she had chosen the dog on the right of the picture on two previous occasions and could, therefore, be expected to do so again. This was a relationship which had not been noticed by the investigator and certainly constitutes a decision based upon a logical procedure.

Another question dealing with transitive relationships had to do with various colored cars. Instead of following the adult logic several children gave reasonable answers of their own. One child decided that the brown car appeared to be on rougher terrain and therefore could not go fast. Another child, who was accustomed to visiting the auto races with his father, decided that "little cars go faster than big cars," and therefore, the smallest car was the fastest. These answers cannot be considered nonlogical since the children obviously did not accept the experimental premises.

[1] Barbara Irwin (Dade County School System, Miami, Florida).

Figure 4   Test of Transitive Relationship

Experiential background seems to play a part in a child's perception of a test situation, as the last example above indicates. Limitations in experience also are significant factors.

Hattie, a black child with considerable poise and charm, did well on all parts of the testing program except one. She was shown ten strips of paper, varying in length progressively, which were scattered at random on the table top. She was given paper and pencil and asked to draw a picture of the way the strips would look if they were arranged in order of size. Hattie was completely unable to do this, even though she was able to place the strips in the correct order when allowed to manipulate them. This leads to the speculation that experience may have a great deal to do with this problem. Since middle-class children have a great many opportunities to work on jigsaw puzzles or construct objects from tinker toys, they find it relatively easy to visualize the results of manipulating the objects in various ways. It is at least possible that Hattie, being the fifth child in a low-income family, may be lacking in this type of experience.

Angela, another child of similar background, also was unable to draw the strips as they would look if arranged in order. Unlike Hattie, she was also unable to construct the arrangement. Others in this testing program were all able to perform both of these tasks. Angela, however, was one of only two children who recognized, in another part of the test, that the question "Are all the circles blue?" is not the same question as "Are all the blue ones circles?" When asked to explain the difference, she said, "They're not the same question because two blue ones aren't circles." This explanation makes it obvious that she really understood a logical relationship that was comprehended by only one other child, a girl who had no difficulties with any part of the test.

Many children who took the test did not appear to hear the question correctly at first and changed their answers after they realized how they had misinterpreted the investigator's meaning. Even the teacher of this class, when questioned by the investigator, made one error which she immediately caught and corrected. Children, and adults, tend to hear what they anticipate the question might be, but this does not mean that they are incapable of making the kinds of discriminations necessary in order to perform the selected tasks.

This study has been reported here, not to refute any of Piaget's work, or to deny his contributions in describing the development of logical thinking in children. Rather, it is our intent to show that all testing programs can be misjudged by investigators if they do not take into account the perspective of the child who answers the questions. This perspective can be determined only through direct knowledge of the child and his previous experiences. Piaget used these kinds of tests to determine the stage of cognitive development of the child but did not take into account other determining factors, such as the child's previous exposure to manipulative toys, and so on.

Writers of intelligence tests very often assume that the child is familiar with the objects pictured and can thus classify or group them according to specifications. As indicated in the case of Hattie, unfamiliarity with objects of a similar nature makes it difficult for a child to visualize the construct required to complete the item on the test. Then, too, questions asked about the cars or the little girl's choice of a dog to play with, assumed that the child being questioned perceived the problem as being the same problem perceived by the investigator. This is very often not so, and administrators of intelligence tests would do well to take this factor into consideration.

Teachers might make a practice of trying to determine the reasons for children's choices in answering test questions. They might find that some incorrect answers are given for some very logical reasons. Taking into consideration the perspective of the child might change the teacher's opinion about that child's abilities. It might also give her insight into the type of thinking of which the child is capable. Investigators of creativity (see Appendix E for samples of questions from creativity tests) have informed us that many creative individuals do not perceive problems in the way that the majority of people do. Divergent thinking should be respected in children who do not conform to the standards in test situations.

Logical thinking in young children can also be effectively determined through direct observation of their activities and attention to their verbalization while they explore their environment. Even Piaget, in his later writing, implies that the child's own demonstration or experimentation provides a better index to the nature of his thinking than do verbal responses to questions.

Navarra approached the study of the development of scientific concepts in young children by using a case-study approach involving his own child. He and his wife observed their infant son from approximately one to four years of age. During this time anecdotal records were kept of the child's activity and verbal expression when he was involved with exploration of his physical environment. These observations were then classified according to the subject matter which the child was concerned with. When these observations were placed in chronological order within the subject areas, it was possible to see the growth of logical thinking related to the subject over a period of time.

An example[2] of the development of a scientific concept is illustrated by the boy's interest in the origin of water from the faucet. Taking a bath one night, he asked his mother, "Where does the water come from—the wall?" Since he did not see the pipes behind the wall, his information had been logically deduced from what was before him. Nevertheless, he voiced his answer in a tentative way, as if presenting a hypothesis.

This concern for the source of water in the house lay dormant for a while. In the summer he visited his grandmother where he saw water pumped from a well. He was allowed to work the pump handle in order to get a drink. Some months later, the boy again raised the question, "Where does the

---

[2] John G. Navarra, *The Development of Scientific Concepts in a Young Child*, pp. 19–74.

water come from?" His mother replied, "From a large lake." The boy now asked, "How does it get into the house? Is there a pump in there?"

The development of a scientific concept is characterized by long periods of integration during which the child pulls together diverse and interlocking experiences. Four months elapsed between the time of the child's first query and his later discovery. That children as young as three and a half are capable of logical deduction is clearly evident here. The relationship of experience to the development of a concept is also clearly demonstrated.

Wann and his associates recorded the behavior and language of children in several nursery-school settings,[3] and then classified these observations into the types of thinking that they illustrated. It was determined that nursery-age children were capable of associating ideas, classifying information, generalizing, and attempting to reach logical conclusions. Anecdotes recorded reveal the children trying to see likenesses and differences and working on cause-and-effect relationships. Many of the incidents which adults perceive as amusing are really efforts on the part of young children to associate present with past experience, a basic process in the development of logical thinking. For example, "In preparation for George Washington's birthday, pictures of Washington had been displayed in the nursery schoolroom. When the children were told that it was George Washington, Henry said, 'I have been over his bridge.' "[4]

Henry had thus put together two bits of information in his growing concept of George Washington. The fact that his association of ideas is not totally correct does not matter at this point. His teacher will help to clarify that for him. But, the relating of ideas is an important part of the process by which most concepts are built and must be respected by teachers as an indication of logical thinking.

Whether in assessing test results or in interpreting children's verbal expression, it is important for teachers to try to see things from the child's perspective. When a teacher laughs at the naïve associations of young children, she discourages them from further attempts at logical thinking. Rejecting an incorrect answer without probing for its meaning to the child discourages the pupil from developing further hypotheses. If a teacher wants to encourage the growth of logic in her students, then she must try to perceive their answers from the individual child's point of view and respect the reasons behind those answers.

Reading readiness

Readiness for reading can be defined as that state which enables a child to learn to read without unwarranted strain or difficulty. For many years this readiness was considered to be closely tied to age. Until a child reached the

[3] Kenneth Wann, et al. *Fostering Intellectual Development in Young Children.*
[4] Kenneth Wann *et al.,* p. 29.

mental age of six years and six months, it was not deemed advisable to introduce reading skills to him. The thinking today is that reading readiness is dependent upon many factors, and it occurs at different times for different children. (See Appendix C for a "Checklist to Identify Interferences in the Learning Pathways.") A child is developing readiness for reading from the time of his birth, and preparedness for learning to read is the result of a combination of maturation and the learning experiences provided within his environment.

It is important, therefore, for a teacher to know which readiness skills the child possesses, and which areas need further development before printed symbols can be meaningful for him. Although the teacher might be able to determine these factors by direct observation of the child, tests are helpful and time saving. At the beginning of a term, before detailed observation of individual children is possible, readiness testing can give the teacher an idea of the range of maturity of her class. She will obtain an indication, also, of the learning problems the children will have, if she analyzes the sections of the test diagnostically. Then, through observation of pupils in their classroom occupations, she should carry on a perpetual inventory or check up on the preliminary test findings.

There are many tests available which attempt to determine readiness skills. Perhaps the most widely used in school programs are the Metropolitan Readiness Tests which attempt to measure a variety of traits and achievements of school beginners. The subtests are directed toward measurement of:

> Linguistic maturity
> Visual and auditory perception
> Number knowledge and readiness
> Information about common subjects
> Ability to pay attention and follow directions
> Ability to handle paper and pencil
> Ability to sustain interest in looking at pictures and responding to them

The Metropolitan Readiness Tests, administered at the beginning of the first grade, correlate very highly with achievement tests given at the end of the year. Thus, readiness testing is considered by most educators to be of great predictive value. But there are many factors which enter into the possible success or failure of school beginners that cannot be ascertained by testing. Emotional factors may make a child "unready" in spite of good test results. Poor health may cause prolonged absences or fatigue, which limit learning ability. The type of curriculum, the relationship of the child to the teacher and to his peers, the situation in the family during the school period—all have influence upon the child's success in learning to read. A combination of test results and teacher ratings, observations, and informal evaluations furnishes a more reliable basis for determining readiness than the tests alone.

A student in a graduate class in child study, who had been a kindergarten teacher for several years, decided to compare the results of her personal evaluation with test scores.[5] Toward the end of the kindergarten term, she selected three children whom she classified as: (1) likely to be successful in a formalized reading program, (2) might possibly be successful, and (3) will probably not be successful. She then developed three case studies for each of these children, collecting data based upon her knowledge of the children and their environment, some informal evaluations made from class exercises, and information on the children's cumulative records. Each of these children was then given a standardized readiness test, and the teacher's evaluations and the test results were compared.

The Clymer-Barrett Pre-Reading Battery was used. This test includes parts on:

Visual discrimination, including letter recognition and word matching
Auditory discrimination, including beginning and ending sounds
Visual-motor coordination, including shape completion and a copy-a-sentence test

The Clymer-Barrett materials also include a Pre-Reading Rating Scale to be filled out by the teacher. She is asked to rate the children as below average, average, or above average on such items as familiarity with words, listening abilities, work habits, social skills, and attitudes. This form, with the additional information developed in the case studies, was then compared with the results of the readiness test for the three children selected for study.

The first child considered was a boy of six years and three months who had two younger sisters. Both of his parents had completed senior high school, were in excellent health, and showed an active interest in their children. Although he was a shy child, his teacher rated him as above average on most of the items on the Clymer-Barrett Pre-Reading Rating Scale. He did well on all parts of the Pre-Reading Battery and was in the 88th percentile rank according to national norms. The teacher's estimate of this child's ability was confirmed by the test scores. She commented that his only area of weakness was his small muscle control, and the visual-motor score was his lowest on the subtests. At the teacher's suggestion the mother had worked with the boy at home in helping him to handle scissors and crayons. The interest of the parents was considered to be a major factor in his superior performance.

The second child, whom the teacher felt "might possibly be successful in a formalized reading program," was a six-year-old girl from a middle-class family background. She was considered to be very mature emotionally and was a leader of the other children in the class. Her rating by the teacher on the Pre-Reading Scale was highly scattered. She was considered above average in oral language and social skills, below average in work habits, and average in listening skills and attitudes. She scored in the average range on all of the subtests of the Pre-Reading Battery, and her final score placed her in the 42nd percentile rank. Her teacher's comments, based upon observation of classroom behavior, throw much more light upon her possible success in reading than do her test scores. She says about this child:

[5] Rickey Grotenstein (Dade County School System, Miami, Florida).

When she wants to use her abilities, she accomplishes her goals. She is perceptive and can see relationships and causes and effects that most of the other children do not see. Unless she is forced to complete her work in an acceptable manner, she will turn in sloppy, half-finished papers. The one incentive that will make her begin learning to read will be the fact that other children are ahead of her. Since she seems to need to be a leader, she will have to learn in order to retain her respect in the group.

The third child, considered by the teacher to be "unlikely to succeed in a formalized reading program," was a girl of five years and five months, who has a sister one year older than she. The mother expressed concern over the fact that this girl, unlike her sister, would not sit with the mother to be taught. The child was rated as poor in oral language, average in concept and vocabulary development, and above average in listening skills. Social and emotional development fell in the average range, but attitudes toward reading were considered below average. Her work habits were rated above average, and, in general, she received more high ratings than average or low ones. The results of the Clymer-Barrett Pre-Reading Battery showed her to be below average in all of the subtests and in the 23d percentile rank in her total score.

The teacher diagnosed her problem as relating to her older sister, whom, the teacher feels, is a threat to her. The child being considered here is bright, does well in creative art and in block design, and appears to be quiet but strong willed. The teacher feels that she will not do well in a formalized reading program because of lack of motivation and fear of not being able to measure up to her sister.

It can be seen, from this brief summary of this kindergarten teacher's study, that the case histories were more meaningful in explaining the children's reading readiness than the tests. The tests seemed to verify the teacher's predictions, but her insights and knowledge of each child were necessary for an understanding of the test results.

Readiness tests, when used diagnostically, can be very helpful to the teacher in her attempt to determine various approaches to be used in reading programs. A child who has difficulty hearing differences in sounds needs more practice with this skill. A child who has difficulty printing his name needs further experience with small muscle activities. Perceptual-motor programs can be introduced to the child who does not perceive spatial relationships with ease.

It has recently been discovered that some children have inherent learning disabilities that make reading difficult. These children may be of average or above average intelligence and may have had all of the necessary experiences provided in prereading programs. Special diagnostic techniques must be applied to determine ways of approaching reading for these children. Philip Mann says that each teacher must be a kind of "detective" and must be able to decode each child's individual learning style.[6]

Some children respond more to one type of sensory stimulus than to

---

[6] Philip Mann, "A Learning Problems Approach to Education."

another. A child who is having difficulty with putting things in sequence might be asked to arrange things in order, using his tactile sense, his olfactory sense, or his kinesthetic sense. Once he has grasped the idea, he might find it easier to do auditory or visual sequencing.

If teachers want to individualize instruction, then every possible method must be used to assess differences in abilities and in learning styles. Many tests are available which help screen out children who have difficulties. Teachers should use these tests analytically and should combine them with their own observations and knowledge of individual children.

Peer relationships

The child's relationship to his peer group is likely to influence his self-concept and therefore have an effect upon his achievement in school. The more knowledge a teacher has of a child's social situation, the more effective she can become in guiding his school activities. Unfortunately, however, teachers are usually inaccurate in assessing the peer culture. This can be attributed to the tendency of teachers to overestimate the social status of the pupils that they themselves prefer and to underestimate the status of those that they least prefer. This being so, scales for assessing peer relationships can be very helpful to the classroom teacher who wants to know her children more fully.

The sociogram is the technique most frequently used for this purpose, and there are a variety of ways it can be administered. The children may be asked, "Whom would you like to have as chairman of your committee?" or "We are going on a field trip. Next to whom would you like to sit on the bus?"

The choices of the various members of the class are then plotted, using circles and arrows to show relationships. (See Figure 5.) Questionnaires in which children are to select the person who most fits a given description are also often used.

There are limitations, however, to conclusions that can be drawn from sociometric tests. The circumstances under which the tests are administered often affect the results. Situations in classrooms change, and choices are sometimes made to satisfy specific needs. Sociograms only indicate persons who are preferred or rejected for a particular kind of relationship or activity. Then, too, a child who is relatively well liked by everyone may not necessarily be chosen as a best friend or as a chairman. The chief function of sociometric devices is to provide leads for further investigation and to raise questions to check against further evidence.

A student teacher, observing a fifth-grade class, made a study of ten of the children using sociometric techniques.[7] In addition to the sociogram she used a "Guess Who" questionnaire with instructions to "write down the names of the persons whom you think each description fits." She then analyzed the

[7] Elizabeth Morris (University of Miami, Coral Gables, Florida).

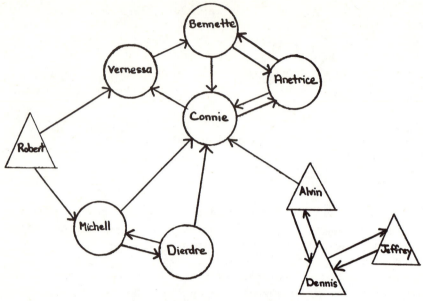

Figure 5   A Sociogram

results, comparing them to her observations of the children involved, and to the description of these ten children given by the regular classroom teacher.

A "star" or several "stars" are usually evident in a sociogram. These children are frequently above average in intelligence, successful in school, and have pleasing personalities. The star in this group, Connie (see Figure 5) fulfills this description.

Underchosen, rejected, or isolated pupils tend, in varying degrees, to be the opposite. In particular, they lack social skills, are overage for their class because of slow progress, and are below average in intelligence and physical skills. Robert, the isolate in this sociogram, generally fits these descriptions.

Robert was chosen most often in the "Guess Who" questionnaire. His name was given thirty-six times by his peers, but only one of the descriptions accorded to him was positive. Robert was judged by his peers to be a "troublemaker" who was known for "picking fights." According to his own reply on the "Guess Who" questionnaire, Robert was aware of his problem. This investigation led to some discussion in class and a private conference with the teacher. Robert began showing improvement, and appropriate grouping served to supplement his own efforts to raise his social status.

Dennis had a poor self-concept, as indicated by his answers on the questionnaire, where he chose himself as the child whom no one cares for. However, he had two mutual choices, in Alvin and Jeffrey, when the sociogram was compiled. This data was used to arrange appropriate grouping for Dennis. He worked more effectively when placed in combination with one of the children who had positive reactions to him.

It can be seen, therefore, that sociometric techniques can help the teacher with grouping and can add to her effectiveness in guiding children's social and academic development. Social growth is a necessary concern of the teacher, and sociometric tests can provide valuable clues for analysis and interpretation of behavior.

We have looked at various techniques for acquiring knowledge about children. Beginning with the teacher and her need for heightened awareness, we have moved into an examination of methods for observing the child. We have made use of various kinds of creative expression and the results of testing programs as well as standard observational procedures. The remainder of this book will deal with information about children obtained from these sources.

REFERENCES

ALMY, MILLIE.   *Young Children's Thinking*. New York: Teachers College Press, Columbia University, 1966.

BALES, ROBERT F.   *Interaction Process Analysis*. Cambridge, Mass.: Addison-Wesley Publishing Company, Inc., 1950.

CLYMER, THEODORE, AND THOMAS C. BARRETT.   *Clymer-Barrett Pre-Reading Battery*. Directions for Administrating. Princeton, N.J.: Personnel Press, 1967.

GORDON, IRA J.   *Studying the Child in School*. New York: John Wiley & Sons, Inc., 1966.

HILDRETH, GERTRUDE.   *Readiness for School Beginners*. New York: Harcourt Brace Jovanovich, 1950.

INHELDER, BARBEL, AND JEAN PIAGET.   *The Early Growth of Logic in the Child*. New York: W. W. Norton & Company, Inc., 1964.

ISAACS, SUSAN.   *Intellectual Growth in Young Children*. New York: Harcourt Brace Jovanovich, 1930.

MANN, PHILLIP.   "A Learning Problems Approach to Education." Speech read at the University of Miami Desegregation Conference, Miami, Florida, August 14, 1971.

Metropolitan Readiness Tests.   Directions for Administering and Key for Scoring. New York: Harcourt Brace Jovanovich, Inc.

NAVARRA, JOHN.   *The Development of Scientific Concepts in a Young Child: A Case Study*. New York: Teachers College Press, Columbia University, 1955.

PIAGET, JEAN.   *Judgment and Reasoning in the Child*. New York: Harcourt Brace Jovanovich, Inc., 1928.

WANN, KENNETH *et al*.   *Fostering Intellectual Development in Young Children*. New York: Teachers College Press, Columbia University, 1962.

PART

STAGES OF DEVELOPMENT AS REVEALED THROUGH OBSERVATIONS OF CHILDREN

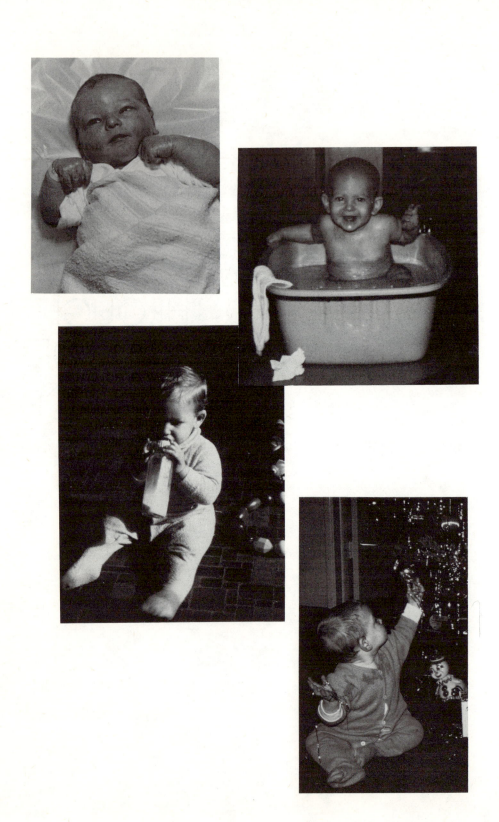

7

Observing infants

It is hoped that, after reading Part I of this book, the reader and student of child development will be prepared and eager to do some observing on her own. The reader might try her own hand at doing observations of children of various ages, prior to reading the chapter relevant to that age level. Observations can then be compared with those included in the following chapters, and, based in part upon personal experience, insights can be developed.

Part II of this book will include some of the findings about the behavior of children which have been obtained by college students using the observational approach discussed in previous chapters. The time samples, anecdotal records, and case studies contained in this and succeeding chapters were done mainly by undergraduates in college classes in child development. None of these observers were professional researchers or clinicians. They had no training other than the preparation given to them in class sessions preceding the observations. Many of the students had little or no experience with children prior to these observations, since this course is offered before their student teaching. Some were baby-sitters and some had brothers, sisters, nieces, and nephews whom they knew intimately. Observations have been selected, from the many student reports available to this writer, which seemed to be particularly significant in revealing patterns of behavior. Only the most detailed and perceptive observations were chosen for inclusion here.

Each of the following chapters begins with time samples or other forms of direct observation of children within a particular age range. Variations are great, even within a relatively short age span, and the focus is upon individual behavior, rather than the establishment of norms for each developmental level. However, some form of comparison or summary of characteristics seems almost inevitable. Several methods for arriving at a synthesis of the findings are discussed below.

When the reader is ready to examine some of the observations presented here, she should ask herself:

Did the child I observed do this?

How is the child I observed different, more or less mature, more or less socially aware, better or not as well coordinated, and so on?

Are some of the behaviors characteristic of this age level present in my observation?

What factors might account for some of the differences?

From time to time throughout the chapters in this part of the book, suggestions will be made for activities in which students might participate. These activities will be related to the discussions of children that precede or follow them and should be done by the class prior to intensive study of that particular stage of development. The activities are numbered and are set in **bold-face type.**

No attempt has been made in this book to cover all of the research findings related to child development or even to summarize the most significant aspects of this research. Occasionally, in the forthcoming chapters, references will be made to studies of children by psychologists, and comparisons will be drawn to children observed and described in these pages. These references are by no means all inclusive. They are made by this author on the basis of her own subjective judgment of their relevance. The reader might very well find sources of her own to confirm or to negate some of the findings of the observations.

There are a number of excellent books (some listed in the reference section at the end of each chapter) which provide résumés of available research in child development, and some that describe fully the characteristics of various age levels. It is strongly recommended that students use these sources as supplementary to their work in learning about child development through direct observation.

After some introduction to observational techniques students of child development might very well begin at the beginning and view human life at the point of its entrance into the world. Can you sense what the world is like for a newborn infant? Keen observation can provide clues to internal sensations if the observer brings with her imagination and insight.

ACTIVITY 1

Close your eyes, and try to become aware of the sensations in your muscles as you move your hands and arms. This is your kinesthetic sense, and it is the most highly developed sense mechanism with which the infant is born.

Are you aware of how much we all rely upon kinesthetic sense? With eyes closed, raise your arms in front of you so that they are parallel to the floor. Open your eyes, and see how close you have come. Did you see where to place your arms? Did you touch anything? How did you know where your arms should go?

The nerve endings in your muscles relayed to the brain the amount of contraction in the muscles, and the degree of rotation in the shoulder sockets. From experience, you knew where your arms were in space.

Because of the highly sensitive kinesthetic equipment an infant is born with, he can learn about his body in space and his relationship to the world around him.

The neonate

"Neonate" is the term applied to the infant immediately after birth. The period usually is considered to extend from birth to the end of the second week. Before studying the behavior of neonates, it would be desirable to see some in the flesh. There is great variation in the skin tone, facial features, amount of hair, and in the observable behavior of infants at this stage. Students might compare these likenesses and differences.

ACTIVITY 2
The child-development class might arrange for a field trip to a local hospital to see neonates in the maternity ward nursery. If the class is large, several groups might arrange to go on succeeding days.

If the time is established in advance of the visit, the nurses will gladly make the infants as observable as possible. Cribs can be wheeled to the viewing window, and coverings can be removed. A good time for viewing might be when the babies have just returned from visits to their mothers' rooms, or when they have just been changed and diapered.

Many students may be surprised at the sight of these young human beings. They are frequently red, squirming creatures, not at all like the babies in magazine advertisements. Some of the little faces are twisted and wizened, resembling small monkeys. The stub of the umbilical cord may not have healed and may be a dark, unsightly tube extending from the baby's abdomen. In order to avoid shock students who plan to observe neonates should be prepared for what they are likely to see. (A student in one child-development class nearly fainted and had to be led away from the viewing window on a nurse's arm.)

Each student should concentrate her attention upon one of the babies in the nursery and should do two ten-minute time samples of the activities she observes. These observations can then be compared and contrasted when the students return to class.

Several classes of students taught by this writer have made field trips to hospitals to observe neonates. The experiences of one such group will be discussed in the following pages. Readers might compare their findings to those described below.

There were eight babies in the nursery on the day that the child-development class observed. Each student selected one infant to watch, so that there were approximately two students focusing on each child. The babies were quite different from each other, yet the students were able to note many patterns that were common to all of them. The students later compared their findings to descriptions of neonate behavior found in child-development literature, and some of these comparisons will be cited here.

Here is a sample from an observation of a three-day-old baby girl, Jane.

TIME	OVERT BEHAVIOR	COMMENTS
11:06	Baby placed on her back, feet and legs kicking hard, toes curling and then un-curling. Head moving from side to side very rapidly with eyes open. Hands go from a grasping position to an extremely open position.	Highly energetic.
11:08	Baby is trembling; hands and arms show the quiver more than legs. Hands now in grasping position and baby is starting to cry.	Possibly due to insecurity.
11:09	Baby is now wailing instead of just a soft cry. Hands are positioned closer to her body and her feet and legs are curled around her buttocks. Face very red from crying and tongue is moving about quite rapidly within mouth.	Possible frustration due to separa-tion from mother. Nurse explained that babies feel less secure when un-covered.
11:11	Eyes blinking open and closed. Right arm moving about more than left; left arm pulled close to body, feet in a hook-line position close to body; crying is ceasing.	Possible favoring of one side but not predictable yet.
11:12	Hands moving randomly about face. Fingers touch her mouth but no re-sponse is seen. Eyes are closing and baby is less active.	Random movement and not yet aware of body. Seems more content.
11:13	Baby is quiet. Head is resting on her right side. Hands near body across her chest. Feet are turned in and legs in a hook-line position near buttocks.	Resting (possible position in the womb).
11:14	Baby in next crib begins to cry. Jane, in turn, starts crying. Flushed face and hands and arms moving about rapidly. Legs extend out straight in front of her body and toes are curled. Head is rock-ing from side to side.	Response to other baby's crying may arouse babies (nurse says this often happens). While crying, Jane is quite active and energetic.
11:16	Still crying as nurse goes to baby. Baby is patted on her back by nurse. She is gradually quieting and her bodily actions are less frequent. Nurse tucks blanket loosely around baby.	Nurse's patting may have a soothing effect. More security may be devel-oped as baby is wrapped in blanket which provides warmth and protec-tion.

In this brief ten-minute observation the student has noted many of the characteristics of neonates. The position of the legs and feet are aptly described. Most of the babies observed assumed the position of feet turned in toward each other and toes curling in and out. In some, however, the position of the feet were parallel, and the legs were less curved. The hands were observed to be grasping and opening frequently. One student observer noted the position of the thumb as being held inside the closed fist.

The quiver or tremor noted at 11:08 is a commonly noted reaction. At one point another baby was observed to "Jump, arms outstretched, fingers of right hand then brought in close to face." The student observer's comment was that "He jumps as though something scared him." This is what the psychologists have termed the "Moro response," or infantile startle pattern. It can be set off by any sudden stimulation such as a loud noise. The neonate reacts by stretching wide his arms and legs, often crying at the same time, and then hugging himself together again. The tension subsides visibly within a few seconds.

The total body response, when the baby is crying, was noted by many of the students. Arms and legs stretch and bend, and, as one student noted, "seem to punch the air." Facial muscles work vigorously, and the tongue is noted "moving quite rapidly within the mouth." An observer commented that the baby she was watching "can't cry or yell without total body muscle contraction."

Many babies were noted as "trying to put hands in mouth." Although this action appeared to be random in the baby observed above (Jane), other babies were seen actively sucking their hands. One student, who was herself the mother of five, noted that it was quite common for babies to "move their head in any direction toward something that touches the side of the mouth or jaw." Psychologists have reported that

Tactile stimulation of the lips or cheek causes the baby to turn his head toward the source of stimulation. . . . If one wants to turn a young infant's face in a given direction, as for nursing, it does no good to push against the baby's cheek, he turns his head in the direction that the push comes from. One should, it follows, touch the cheek on the side toward which one wants him to turn. If restraining a baby's head causes him distress, it may conceivably be because he is being stimulated to turn his head in two directions at once.[1]

Many of the student observers noted that the babies they were watching stopped crying when they were picked up by the nurse or when they were patted on the back. Psychologists agree that babies, at birth, are responsive to human contact. Not only do they stop crying when they are picked up, but they exhibit reciprocal adaptations, interacting with the adult in a kind of snuggling action. For example, when it is carried against the adult's shoulder, the neonate presses his cheek against the adult's. One student observed that as the nurse picked up the baby she was watching, the baby stopped crying

[1] Joseph Stone and Joseph Church, *Childhood and Adolescence*, p. 16.

and grasped the collar of the nurse's uniform, clinging tightly even after the nurse tried to put the baby down. This resembles the "rooting" behavior observed in newborn mammals. The baby searches the adult body, clutches firmly at whatever handholds he finds, and propels himself, if not restrained, with trunk, arms, and legs, exploring with his mouth as though seeking the nipple. The adult's reaction to this infant exploration is the first opportunity for communication with the neonate. Whether the baby is displaying affection, or is capable of emotion at this point, is not known. But the more the adult seeks to respond to the movements and gestures of the neonate, the more opportunities there will be for socialization and for the development of human feelings.

In general, it can be said that the students' observations of the newborn babies at the hospital nursery were keen and detailed, and that they were able to pick up in a very short period of time much of the behavior attributed to neonates by researchers in the field. In their comments or inferences the students tended to credit the babies they were observing with qualities of mind and of purpose that the scientific observer is unable to verify. Such comments as, "The baby seems frustrated at being separated from his mother," or "He wants to put his fingers back in his mouth," reveal attempts on the part of the students to give adult interpretations to the actions they observe.

There is no evidence that a baby of this age has any memory of previous events. Since he does not know the satisfaction of sucking on his hand a second after it occurs, he could not "want to put his fingers back." The security of mother's arms is not directly associated with the person of the mother, since the neonate cannot distinguish one person from another and is not even aware of a world with people in it existing outside himself.

It is difficult for the student, or for the research psychologist, for that matter, to reconstruct the experiences of the newborn child. None of us can recall our own existence at that time of life. No neonate has been able to tell us what he is experiencing. We have had to rely on evidence gathered by researchers working in laboratories. Measurement of heartbeat, brain waves, and respiratory rate have given some indication of how babies are reacting to stimuli presented to them. Studies of animal species shed light on human development, since many early characteristics are similar. But the best we can do is to guess at some of the answers by placing together information from various sources.

A question that was of concern to the students, as to all observers of young infants, is whether the babies they are watching can see. The nurse informed us that, in her training, she was told that neonates perceive only shadows and do not see color at all. Infants, however, do react to color. A recent scientific investigation has established the fact that, at birth, normal babies possess organically complete visual equipment. Although their sense organs are in good working order, they provide only limited information owing to the fact that the baby does not have the experience necessary to make sense out of what he sees. A few babies, right after birth, have been known to turn their heads to follow a moving object.

ACTIVITY 3

Working in pairs, students in child-development classes may simulate the experience of the infant in following a moving object. One student holds a pencil and moves it in a small arc before the eyes of her partner. Each time, she makes the arc larger, so that the viewer must turn her head, or increase the rotation of her eyes. The two students then change places. (This activity is used in training children with some types of learning disabilities and is known as "tracking.")

Fantz developed an apparatus that made it possible to measure how long an infant looks at either of two stimuli.[2] Using this technique, it was determined that the newborn baby spends more time looking at black and white figures than at unfigured colored areas, and a crude approximation of the human face is looked at significantly more than is a nonsensical arrangement of the same features. There is evidence, however, that the neonates' eyes have a fixed focus for objects at a distance of about seven and one-half inches, which may mean that more distant objects are seen as blurred. It has also been observed that neonates often do not focus both eyes in the same direction. However, studies have shown that an infant can fixate at least one eye on a source of light within hours after birth.

Researchers also disagree about the neonate's ability to hear. It was originally believed that fear of loud noises was a basic, inborn emotional response. Experimental results and direct observation of babies reveal that no two children react in exactly the same way to any stimulus including sudden sounds. Where one child may show what we judge to be real terror, another may sleep unperturbed through almost any degree of intense noise. Our student observer reported that the baby, Jane, began to cry when other babies near her began crying. The nurse verified the fact that this is often the case in the hospital nursery. If crying sets off a chain reaction among the babies, then surely they are capable of hearing each other. It has been noted, however, that babies are often impervious to stimuli which adults and older children are very aware of. The young baby may not react at all to thunder, fire sirens, or the clatter of trash cans. On the other hand, the baby may react very negatively to stimulation that seems innocuous to adults such as the crackling of stiff paper.

ACTIVITY 4

If neonates respond differently to various types of noises, it is likely that adults have various innate responses but have learned to react in culturally well-established patterns. Try to hear the sounds in the room as if you have never heard them before. How do they make you feel?

Introduce new sounds, such as crackling paper, using rhythm instruments of various types, dropping objects made of different substances. While one member of the class makes the noise, the rest of the group is to keep their eyes closed and to report upon the sensations and thoughts aroused by each particular sound.

[2] R. L. Fantz, "Pattern Vision in Newborn Infants," pp. 296–297.

It can be seen that, even at this early stage, neonates demonstrate individuality. The babies observed at the hospital nursery had unique individual characteristics that distinguished one from another. Some babies had loud cries, while others had softer tones, moaning and whimpering, in contrast to their more vigorous neighbors. Some babies' cries were sharp and staccato, while others were smoother. The actions of the arms and legs showed differences not only quantitatively but also qualitatively. Newborn babies are decidedly different from each other in terms of energy output, speed at which they move their limbs, and sensitivity to various stimuli. Gesell found that persisting traits of behavior individuality are observable within the first sixteen weeks of life.[3] These traits related to energy output, motor demeanor, self-dependence, and emotional expressiveness. Part of these differences may be attributed to physiological makeup, but other factors relating to interaction with the environment soon come into play.

Although emotional expressiveness is listed by Gesell as one of the traits which reveal the infant's individuality in the first few weeks of life, it is extremely difficult to clearly define the emotional responses exhibited. General excitement is displayed by crying and bodily activity, but emotional reactions are less specific and defined than will be true at a later time. Infants often seem undisturbed by somewhat drastic treatment, as when an experimenter, dropping babies for a distance of two feet, elicited little overt response from them. Thus, only very general categories of emotional response can be defined for the neonate. He exhibits withdrawing and rejecting reactions by squirming, twisting, tensing, and crying. On the other hand there are reactions of acceptance and contentment, when the child seems to be at peace with the world.

Such questions as "Is the neonate conscious of what is going on around him?" "Does he experience emotion?" "Does he possess personality?" are not easily answered. Strict behaviorist psychologists consider these questions to be beyond the realm of scientific investigation, since they cannot be determined from behavior but must be inferred. The words themselves imply an acceptance of the fact that mental events take place in the body and cause behavior. Introspection can reveal internal characteristics, but this is not applicable to the neonate. Freud and others have attributed strong emotions to the infant, but these feelings are deduced from observations of adult behavior and introspection of adult patients. Although babies exhibit responses similar to those related to emotions in older children and adults, these responses seem to occur randomly in neonates, rather than as reactions to external stimuli. The neonate may smile, for example, but this early facial expression must be distinguished from the social smile, which appears during the second month as response to a human face or voice. Most current researchers agree that, in spite of the intensity of crying, kicking, and thrashing about, the neonate is blankly unemotional. Feelings comprise an essential element of awareness of self, which the baby at this stage still does not possess.

[3] Arnold Gesell, *Studies in Child Development*, pp. 128–130.

Since so many of these questions concerning the internal world of the neonate cannot be answered through any kind of scientific investigation, we are fully justified in suggesting that students observe closely and make their own inferences. The most knowledgeable investigators in the field admit that the world of the newborn infant can only be imagined. Fraiberg claims that we can only find analogies in the world of the dream. "Dim objects swim into view, then recede and melt into nothingness. A human face hovers over him like a ghostly mask, then dissolves. Events in his life have no connections. Even the satisfaction of his hunger has not yet been connected with the face of his mother, not to mention the person of his mother."[4]

In the next few months the infant will begin to make sense out of the jumble of impressions he perceives as a neonate. The important initial stage of learning has begun.

The first five months

If we try to reconstruct the perceptual experience of the very young baby from his behavior, we must imagine the world to be a diffuse field where objects, shapes, and colors are not clearly distinguished and exist in no stable framework. The baby is aware of sensations. He sees and he hears, but sounds and sight images are unrelated to each other. He experiences wetness or hunger, but he has no knowledge of himself as a person and no ability to separate himself from the outside world. His experience, thus, is focused in his own body. All he knows is what he feels—that is, his own sensations. Piaget calls this "egocentrism."[5] He states that this sensation, that the world is centered in one's own experience, stays with the young child and is the basis for much of his sense of reality during the first two years of life.

The baby now embarks upon a major task of research. He must put together elements of sensory experience to create an image of himself and the outside world. He must find out, for example, which oral sensations accompany which visual stimuli. He learns, within the first month, to recognize the bottle visually and can direct his mouth toward it without the random searching of the neonate. The following observation of a one-month-old reveals many changes from the behavior of the newborn babies the class recorded at the hospital.

ACTIVITY 5
Read the time sample below and make notations of behavior which was not evident in the previous study of neonates.

TIME	OVERT BEHAVIOR	COMMENTS
6:30	Baby wakes from nap, stretches, throws hands around, makes sounds with mouth,	

[4] Selma H. Fraiberg, *The Magic Years*, p. 36.
[5] Jean Piaget, *The Construction of Reality in the Child*, p. 352.

TIME	OVERT BEHAVIOR	COMMENTS
	eyes wide open, lips moving in all directions.	
6:32	Mother picks baby up. Looks at mother, then looks around the room. Sticks fingers in mouth.	Seems to like being held on shoulder. Seems to be hungry. Hands find mouth immediately.
6:35	Mother places her in infant seat. Feet curl up.	Feet curl toward each other as observed in newborn.
6:37	Mother feeding her cereal and bottle. Baby takes spoonful of cereal and sucks it into mouth.	
6:40	Looks for bottle. Grabs it in her mouth. Hand waves, touches bottle, and grasps it in holding position.	It is very clear that she wants the bottle and seems to know how to get it.

Although the student observer in this case may be attributing purposeful action to this one-month-old prematurely, still the behavior of the baby gave every indication that she could seek the bottle, find it with her eyes, bring her mouth to it directly, and even try to hold it with her hand. The coordination of visual, oral, and kinesthetic sensations was necessary to perform in this way. Since the bottle represents the main source of gratification, it is the natural stimulus around which these learnings begin to take place.

The sucking action is used for the cereal, as well as for the bottle. Babies at this age have also been observed pursing lips at the touch of an object. The muscles of the mouth region are the most active and adept.

The muscles which control eye movements are brought under increasing control. The one-month-old described was able to fix her gaze upon the face of the mother when picked up and then seemed to look around the room. Gesell states that the visual field of a four-week-old child can encompass a small arc of ninety degrees.[6] This is determined by the tonic-neck-reflex—the combination of averted head, extended arm on the side the head is turned to, and the flexed opposite arm, which is the main position of the infant during his waking hours in the first twelve weeks of life. Later the infant will be able to follow an object with his eyes through a wider range.

The baby observed also made sounds with her mouth that were not crying sounds. These small throaty noises, and the accompanying lip movements "in all directions" are the precursors of babbling. At about two months the baby begins to respond to an adult who leans over and talks to him by working his mouth in what appears to be an attempt to answer back.

It is at this time (two months) that the infant gives his first response smile to the sight of an adult. This is particularly significant since it indicates that the foundations of memory have been established. The satisfactions of

[6] Arnold Gesell, et al. *The First Five Years of Life*, p. 10.

nursing have become associated with the sight of the human face, and the visual image is enough to evoke a mental memory of pleasure. Thus, the smile that originally was an instinctive reaction to satisfaction in nursing now precedes the satisfaction and appears at the sight of the human face. A student recorded this behavior in the three-month-old child she observed.

TIME	OVERT BEHAVIOR	COMMENTS
6:30	The baby is staring intently at the new face belonging to the observer. Very little movement is taking place, except for blinking and drooling.	The baby seems to be sizing up the observer before communication will be initiated.
6:33	The baby begins to smile, still looking at the observer.	
6:34	Her mouth starts expanding and contracting, while a steady stream of sounds is also coming from the nostrils. She continues her stare for the duration of her sounds. Her eyebrows and forehead are in motion.	All of the facial expressions and vocalizations seem to be an attempt to communicate with the observer.
6:36	She starts flinging her appendages widely and making new sounds that accompany her rapid breathing.	She seems to have become very excited by her own activity and the current situation.
6:38	The baby is now placed on the floor on her back. She starts flailing her tightly clenched fists as she makes a coughing sound. Her rigid legs are in the air at right angles to the floor. Her face begins to redden as she continues making coughing sounds between tearless crying.	
6:40	Her rage is interrupted when her grandmother picks her up. Her crying immediately ceases.	Her rage is composed of cries and coughs all apparently turned on as a means of communicating her anger and frustration at being placed on the floor.

The three-month-old had obviously developed considerably in the social domain. Not only did she smile at the observer and seem to enjoy communicating with an adult, but she had also developed what appeared to be the voluntary use of crying and coughing as a means of communicating her anger when social interaction ceased. It is at about this age that babies have been known to indulge in bedtime screaming, as a protest to the end of companionship and activity. The baby who acts this way does not just go on crying. He stops, as though listening for a reaction, and then continues if he does not hear footsteps heading in his direction. This is not a cry of pain or discomfort so much as it is an attempt at social interaction.

This action is not common in all babies at this age. Some are quite placid during their first few months, are content to sleep most of the time and lie quietly in their waking moments. Some are highly active, waking frequently and clenching fists and waving arms and legs at frequent intervals between sleeping periods. Individual differences are noticeable even at this early stage. These differences in general temperament tend to persist through early childhood. A consistency of behavior patterns was reported by Lois Murphy when she kept longitudinal records of children from infancy through preschool years.[7] Highly active babies tended to be outgoing and aggressive when they entered nursery school. Babies who reacted with whimpering rather than sharp cries were withdrawn and timid when entering the new preschool situation.

Babies at two or three months are known to stare at moving objects or to look intently at new and interesting objects. One three-month-old observed by a student spent three minutes gazing at a curtain that was blowing in the wind. If she looked around for a moment, she turned right back to the moving material that was hanging next to her crib as if fascinated by it. Another baby was observed staring at a rattle that was placed in his grasp.

At this time the baby becomes intrigued with the sight of his own hand and can be observed watching it frequently.

ACTIVITY 6

Look at your own hand as if it is the first time you have ever seen it. What can it do? Move your hand in front of your eyes, observing the shape it takes as you close and open your fingers. Close your eyes and try to concentrate on the sensation in your muscles as you perform these acts.

The infant, at about three or four months, discovers that the hand which occasionally passes in front of his eyes is the same object that he introduces into his mouth. He finds that there are special feelings that accompany contacts between his own hands that are different from those he experiences when he takes his mother's finger.

With eyes closed, grab the finger of one hand with the other hand. Concentrate upon the sensation. Now grab the finger of a partner. How is the sensation different?

Although eye movement appears to be quite well-coordinated by the age of three months, hand movements are somewhat less well-developed. The baby of this age can spread his fingers to grasp, and might reach out for something within his range of vision, but his thumb is usually not yet opposed to his fingers, and the attempt at grasping is not always successful. The baby may seem capable of purposeful action, however. A three-month-old observed by a student had difficulty retrieving a pacifier when it fell out of her mouth, although she seemed to know what she wanted. Another three-month-old was seen to rub her eye with a fisted hand as she appeared to become sleepy.

Hands become very important objects for investigation and for experimentation as the baby approaches five months of age. He studies and plays with his fingers, inspecting them visually and carrying them to his mouth for further investigation. Soon he not only can grasp objects but can hold on

[7] Lois Barclay Murphy, *The Widening World of Childhood.*

and manipulate them. Here a four-and-a-half-month-old son of a student demonstrates this.

Baby is on his back in playpen beneath a cradle gym.

TIME	OVERT BEHAVIOR	COMMENTS
5:00	Baby has both hands on rings of gym, stares fixedly at right hand, as it manipulates various rings and dangling toys.	Seems to enjoy touching, grasping, and turning the rings.
5:01	Both hands in fists touching each other, long sigh, fast up and down movements.	Acts excited and happy about his manipulating skills.
5:02	Back to manipulating rings and toys. Watching right hand, more leg movements, then feet together, toes touching.	Seems to prefer watching right hand although both are clasping rings and doing approximately the same things.

The student mother commented that her son seemed to be attempting to establish the fact that his hands are a part of his body and that he can control them. In her second observation, the baby was placed on his stomach and exhibited a characteristic attitude with legs and head held up in the air and body rocking on his belly. In this position he seemed to be trying to move forward but was "grounded by his stomach." Later he looked in the direction of sounds, even though they came from another room, and responded to his mother's voice by making sounds of his own. His attempts to affect his environment at four-and-a-half months included both manipulation and vocalization. Obviously his responses are much more specifically coordinated to distinct environmental events than they were a few months earlier.

Sixth through ninth month

As the baby gains control of his arms and legs, his motions become more purposeful. At six months he can reach out and grasp an object that is within his range of vision. What was first random activity becomes something he can do at will. He can examine objects, bring them to his mouth, feel their qualities, bang them, transfer them from hand to hand. When given a rattle by his mother, one six-month-old observed by a student "smiled and began to bang the rattle against the side of the stroller." A minute later, he "stopped hitting the rattle and began to look at it, touching it with his left hand while holding it tightly in his right hand." Another student noticed that, in reaching for the bottle, her baby was able to "move fingers individually" and made use of "opposing position of thumb" in grasping. This perceptual-manipulatory exploration is a strong characteristic of children at this age and is indicative of intellectual process. The infant is now controlling his own actions and making discoveries about his environment as a result of them. He is well on his way to becoming a person.

It is at about this time that the baby is also likely to discover his feet.

At first he stares at them, as if they are not really a part of his own body. He clutches them with his hands and may bring them to his mouth for sucking and chewing. He is surprised if this causes pain, and this is one indication we have that knowledge of his own body is not present at birth but must be learned through experience. He may use his feet as prehensile tools, reaching out and grasping things with them. Here is a six-month-old involved in such activity.

TIME	OVERT BEHAVIOR	COMMENTS
1:00	Mother and baby are in a park. Baby is lying face up in a stroller.	
1:01	Baby moves leg out of leg hole in stroller with a jerk of the leg at the knee. She puts her feet on the handlebar. Toes are bent inward as if to grasp the handlebar.	Baby seems to have control over toes and is able to place feet where she wants them.
1:08	Baby has lifted right leg up with right hand and placed foot in mouth.	Feels moisture on toes. Enjoys sucking.
1:09	Mother takes foot and taps it gently against baby's nose and mouth. Baby enjoys the game and smiles and makes gurgling noises. Mother lets go and baby remains smiling, then stops.	Feels the touch and withdrawal of her foot. Tries to continue sucking after foot is withdrawn. Smiles at this as a kind of game with mother.

And the same baby observed a few minutes later:

TIME	OVERT BEHAVIOR	COMMENTS
1:20	Baby has been placed face down on a blanket in the shade. Head is lifted up in what appears to be a very uncomfortable position. Arms are bent at elbows and hands are pushing against the ground.	Appears to be straining muscles to remain in this position.
1.23	Turns head to right, and arm appears to be under head. In one push baby is lying face up.	Baby has accomplished act of turning over.
1:25	Legs are bent at knees and lifted off ground. Baby appears pleased. Grabs right foot with left hand and puts it in mouth.	Now foot is grabbed by hand on opposite side of body. Appears to be easier.
1:28	Baby turning toward right and bending inward. Head appears to be placed on belly and body all bent inward on right side. Rolls in that direction and baby is now sitting up.	Goes through contortions to get to sitting position!

TIME	OVERT BEHAVIOR	COMMENTS
1:29	Not sitting for very long because she turns to her left and falls over. Tries to repeat previous action.	Sitting appears to be a new experience. Coordination not very good.
1:30	Mother reaches for baby and sits her on blanket in more stable position. Baby now bangs hands against the ground on either side of her. Rattle in front of her. Bends forward to reach it, with one throw of arm and open hand. Gets it and falls to side again.	Mother helps and gives support. Baby accepts, is pleased, but falls again as she throws herself off balance while reaching for the rattle.

This time sample reveals a great deal of new activity for the six-month-old. She discovers her feet, plays with them, sucks them, and uses them for grasping the handlebar of her stroller. She experiments with the use of her body and maneuvers it into various positions. She can roll over from belly to back, although for many babies turning from back to belly comes first. She can manage to sit up by herself, even if her efforts are still somewhat awkward and uncoordinated.

Once the baby has learned to sit by himself, new vistas open up for him. His hands are freed for manipulation, and, with improved sedentary balance, his prehensile approach upon objects becomes less bilateral. He reaches for objects, and can grasp them more effectively by using his thumb in opposition to his other fingers. He practices picking up small objects with precise pincer action. He uses his index finger to pry and poke into things. He transfers objects from one hand to another. He begins to discover, in playing with a string, that moving the string causes the attached plaything to move. Here is an observation of a seven-month-old involved in this discovery.

George is sitting on the living room floor. A turtle pull toy is nearby. His grandmother and the student observer are present.

TIME	OVERT BEHAVIOR	COMMENTS
12:30	Rolls on his side, sits up, smiles at his grandmother. Gets onto knees and crawls.	He sees the pull toy and goes to it.
12:32	Sits up, grabs turtle's head, releases it, and holds cord with one hand, pulls the turtle.	He pulls the turtle while sitting by moving his whole arm backwards.
12:33	Shakes arms while holding cord, smiles, drools, gets on knees, crawls.	He appears pleased and satisfied; crawls toward me with his toy.
12:34	Reaches, grabs my dress, makes noise, sits up, puts his hand on his leg, and smiles.	He moves quickly, says, "Ah," happily; seems pleased with everything.

TIME	OVERT BEHAVIOR	COMMENTS
12:35	Squints, smiles, picks up cord to toy turtle.	
12:36	Drools, makes a noise, shakes arms up and down, puts cord in mouth.	It sounds as if he said, "Ah," with satisfaction.
12:38	Looks around, holds cord with both hands, makes it taut and then loose several times, makes noises, shakes arms up and down.	Experimenting with cord; seems like he is exerting himself when he makes noises.

In these eight minutes George made many discoveries about the cord attached to the toy turtle. He found that he could make the turtle move by pulling the cord. In order to do this he had to use a whole arm movement, pulling it backward behind his seated body. He found out that he could make the string taut or loose and tried this several times. The drooling and accompanying noises seemed to express satisfaction with his own accomplishments.

Social interaction took place at several moments when he smiled at his grandmother, crawled to observer and grabbed her dress, and looked around for approval when he moved the cord. Oral activity was still very predominant in his behavior as he put the cord in his mouth to explore it another way and drooled with accompanying sounds as a sign of satisfaction.

Much of the action described in the time sample above involves manipulation of objects which would not have been possible a few months sooner before the baby learned to sit. Grasping becomes a source of great satisfaction, and he will try to grab anything within his range of vision. What was first random activity becomes something he can do at will. As a matter of fact, "will" becomes quite strong when baby is denied the opportunity to grasp things. Anything and everything is a temptation. Here an eight-month-old demonstrates this.

Teresa, eight months old, is sitting on her mother's lap.

TIME	OVERT BEHAVIOR	COMMENTS
1:10	Mother holding baby, supporting her under arms as she tries to stand on mother's lap. Grabs mother's hair, bouncing on her knees as she stands.	Stretching her limbs; bouncing causes mother's hair to be pulled. She opens child's fist and releases hair.
1:11	Mother runs finger from top of baby's head to chin, tickling her. Baby laughs.	Distracted from grasping activity. Responds to mother's playing.
1:13	Baby sits down, grabbing mother's necklace, making sounds, pulls at necklace.	Mother takes necklace out of baby's hand and tries to give her stuffed bear.

TIME	OVERT BEHAVIOR	COMMENTS
1:14	Grabs necklace again.	Cannot be distracted by offer of toy.
1:15	Mother again takes necklace out of her hand and puts it inside her blouse. Baby cries.	Frustrated at not having necklace to grab.
1:16	Mother picks her up, walks around the room, shaking her up and down playfully. She stops crying.	Enjoys playing with mother. Forgets about necklace as she is carried around room.

In the second half of the first year infants are developing rapidly in social, interpersonal ways. The baby above was excited about grasping things, but playing with her mother distracted her from her original impulses, strong as they were. Mother becomes very significant at this time. It is only at about the beginning of the second half of the first year that the infant comes to recognize mother as a special person. Pleasure of eating is not just a biological need but is bound to the person of the mother, herself. As long as she is there, the baby is willing to greet others with pleasure. He is adventurous only when mother's presence gives him security. Here is a time sample of a nine-month-old child which illustrates this point.

Corey is sitting on his mother's lap, drinking milk from a bottle.

TIME	OVERT BEHAVIOR	COMMENTS
7:50	Pulls mother's hair as he drinks.	
7:51	Begins to kick foot while drinking milk. Looks at me and smiles.	Contented and secure. Not drinking vigorously. Seems more interested in sucking and fondling mother.
7:54	He pulls mother's blouse. Smiles, looks at me, begins to move toes.	Seems to enjoy watching me.
7:56	Bottle is taken away. Mother gives him diaper. He plays peek-a-boo with her.	Seems to know what to do with diaper, as if he has done it before.
7:57	Smiles as he plays peek-a-boo with sister.	
7:58	He pulls the diaper apart.	
7:59	Mother calls his name, "Corey," and his nickname, "Boo." He looks at her.	Seems to recognize both names. He is quite alert.
8:00	He utters sounds and offers diapers to me.	

This little boy is really a very social creature as many of his responses above indicate. He enjoys physical contact with his mother. He initiates social games (peek-a-boo) and he is friendly to the observer. It is doubtful if, in a less secure situation, he would be as relaxed and sociable. A baby observed in the waiting room of a doctor's office was sitting on the floor, tearing and twisting pages of a magazine. She looked around at other people in the room but kept glancing back at her mother each time. Before she moved off to explore another area of the room, she sought the reassurance of her mother's presence.

The link to the mother, the recognition that this face, this person is unique, and responsible for much gratification, is an essential element in the socialization process. Only when a baby begins to love a person outside himself, the mother or permanent caretaker, is he ready to venture forth and explore the outside world more fully.

The baby at this age is just beginning to find out that objects have permanence, and that they exist even when they are out of sight. At six or seven months he will snatch at an object in sight but will not try to find it when it is hidden. This was true in the time sample above, when the baby stopped looking for the necklace when her mother placed it inside her blouse. Teresa simply did not conceive of the necklace existing when she did not see it. At about nine months old the baby will try to find an object that has been hidden, if he sees where it has been placed.

ACTIVITY 7

Try to arrange for a baby, between the ages of six to nine months, to be brought to class. Play the game of the vanishing object with the baby. Show the baby the object (ball, beads, rattle, and so on) and let him play with it. Then hide it under a blanket or behind a screen. See if the baby can find it.

Now place the object in a second hiding place still within reach of the seated baby. He will probably go to the first place where he found it previously.

It takes some time before the baby can find objects that have been placed in several hiding places. Gordon has designed games for mothers to play with babies and has established the fact that object permanence can be learned at earlier stages than usually anticipated, with practice.[8]

This concept of object permanence is essential to the baby, not only for the understanding of physical realities, but for the development of socialization as well. Because he feels that his mother will not exist if she is out of his sight, the nine-month-old feels anxiety when she leaves him. Up to that time he may not have distinguished strange faces from familiar faces and was content to be left with anyone. But at about the time that the baby has learned to love his mother as a person, he is beginning to be concerned with objects disappearing.

---

[8] Ira J. Gordon and J. R. Lally, *Intellectual Stimulation for Infants and Toddlers.*

One of the Gesell films made at the Yale Clinic shows the difference when six-month-olds and nine-month-olds are left with the experimenter.[9] This capacity to perceive strangeness (at approximately nine months) is itself a symptom of social maturity. Mothers create a "sense of trust" in their children, and this "forms the basis in the child for a sense of identity which will later combine [with] a sense of 'being all right,' of being oneself, and of becoming what other people trust one will become."[10]

Tenth through fourteenth month

At about this time the baby becomes fully mobile. Not only can he sit up and turn over, but he can get around, usually quite rapidly, in his own special style of locomotion. At seven or eight months he may begin crawling, dragging himself along with his forearms and pushing with his feet. Or he may use a caterpillar motion, reaching out with arms and pulling his body up to them. Or he may start from a sitting position and propel himself, feet first. A few babies neither creep nor crawl but stay put until they are able to walk.

Whatever the pattern of locomotion, the ten-month-old usually can get from one place to another at will. By this time he is probably creeping, moving in various ways on all fours, with stomach off the ground. He is capable of deliberate action, deciding where he wants to go and heading for it, sometimes with surprising speed and determination. Here an eleven-month-old uses creeping to attain specific goals.

Baby is on the floor, several toys around her.

TIME	OVERT BEHAVIOR	COMMENTS
12:33	Creeps after ball that is under the bench; reaches for it, pushes it; it starts rolling.	Moves quickly as if she knows where she is going.
12:35	Creeps around leg of bench and goes under it, gets ball, looks toward mother and smiles, leaves ball, and creeps to mother.	Is able to avoid bumping into leg of bench. After reaching ball, seems to lose interest in it.
12:36	Reaches for edge of bench, uses it to help herself up, falls down, gets back up again.	Can stand when holding on to something.
12:37	Mother tells her to dance. Big smile, bounces knees up and down, standing and holding onto bench. Very happy and laughing.	Understands mother's request and follows directions. Enjoys rhythmic activity and game with mother.

[9] Arnold Gesell, "Early Social Behavior of Infants" (Film by Yale Clinic of Child Development, New York: Encyclopedia Britannica).

[10] Erik Erikson, *Childhood and Society*, p. 249.

TIME	OVERT BEHAVIOR	COMMENTS
12:38	Grabs for ball again, this time firmly with two hands, makes "O" motion with mouth, throws ball.	
12:40	Creeps to doll, picks it up and hugs it, looks toward mother, babbling.	Imitating adult action with baby, tries to talk (language her own).
12:42	Drops doll, creeps toward glass door, hits head on it several times, cries. Mother picks her up.	Does not perceive glass as a solid that cannot be penetrated.

It can be seen that creeping leads to all kinds of new discoveries. Even the accidental fall becomes a learning experience. One twelve-month-old crept toward a step and fell down it. When adults laughed, he repeated the motion several times until the laughter stopped.

Babies at this stage are capable of communicating with adults in many ways. The little girl described above responded to her mother's request to dance and performed admirably. By reaching up with their arms, children indicate to adults when they want to be picked up. Waving "bye-bye," playing peek-a-boo, and throwing kisses are all favorite games at this age. Some one-year-olds say a few words, and many understand meanings. They can point to their noses, fetch their toys, go to daddy, and so on. The extent of the understanding is dependent upon many factors. Maturation plays a significant part, but the experiences the baby has had accounts, to a large extent, for the degree and nature of his understanding. The interests and life-style of the parents play a part. A one-year-old whose father played on the college football team could follow the directions, "Get the football." He "grabs it with a tight grip, fingers of both hands spread wide, and grins." No doubt the parental reinforcement for such actions encouraged this youngster to be alert to these kinds of social and physical stimuli.

The pots and pans in the kitchen closet seem to intrigue babies at about this age. No expensive toy or plaything seems to have the fascination that kitchen utensils hold. This, again, may be in imitation of adults he has observed. But the baby learns to manipulate pots in ways all his own. He can crudely recognize difference in size. He can put a smaller pot inside a larger one, but he is sometimes baffled when a slightly larger pot will not fit inside a smaller one. He even begins to build towers, placing one pot on top of the other, and precariously balancing it there. Here again, he responds to attention, and will imitate building operations performed by an adult. Or, if mother is writing a letter, he can scribble a few lines on paper with a crayon. When she feeds him, he wants to use the spoon himself, even though he is not always successful in getting the food to his mouth.

Generally speaking, the one-year-old is perfecting patterns that came into being all during the last half of his first year.

ACTIVITY 8

Make a table showing the behavior patterns seen in one-year-olds. List the observed activities on the right side of the page. These might be classified under headings of sensorimotor activity, adaptive behavior, socioemotional behavior, and language development. Then draw a time line to show when this behavior first occurred.

AGE IN MONTHS	4	5	6	7	8	9	10	11	ONE YEAR
Sensorimotor									List
Adaptive									Observed
Socioemotional									Activities
Language									Here

Compare your findings with Gesell's in his book, *The First Five Years of Life*.

We can see that the one-year-old has gained considerably in manipulative skills, but the things he is able to do are simply developments of earlier accomplishments. He became mobile at about ten months, and his mode of locomotion varies. Most one-year-olds still rely heavily upon creeping to get from one place to another. But usually, they can pull themselves to a standing position and can move along sideways, holding on to a playpen railing or a bench for support. They seem to have an irresistible urge to rise to two feet. Babies will practice getting up for hours on end, even if their precarious balance lands them back upon their well-padded seats within a few seconds. Many mothers have reported that their babies, at this stage, refuse to go to sleep. They insist upon practicing standing up in their cribs, sometimes for hours into the night, long past the point of exhaustion.

This is an interesting phenomenon to observe, since educators have said for decades that the young child has a short interest span. This seems to be true when the adult introduces the activity, but when it is of the child's own choosing, he can remain interested for long periods of time. Jersild refers to this as "indigenous motivation" and says that the young child has an innate impulse to practice any newly acquired skill.[11] This repetitive behavior is quite evident in a one-year-old. Standing up is one evidence of it, but the one-year-old will also repeatedly drop an object from his high chair, cry until an adult gives it to him, and then drop it again. Or he will give an object to an adult, wait for it to be returned, and then gave it back. Social games such as peek-a-boo and pat-a-cake need to be played over and over again. New words and new sounds are also repeated constantly.

The one-year-old understands more than he can say. He is, however, beginning to make language a part of his life, and thus, it becomes a means of incorporating himself into human society. Language helps him to clarify his sense of self. As other objects become identified through attaching words

[11] Arthur Jersild, *Child Psychology*.

to them, the child himself becomes more clearly an object that can be symbolized to himself. He responds to his own name, and even learns to call himself by name, or simply "baby." He explores the adult's features with his hands and then feels his own face to see if there are corresponding features. If placed before a mirror, he seems to recognize himself. His behavior will progress from simple interest, to playfulness, to clear recognition, which may be manifested by his touching a part of the image in the mirror and then touching the same part on his own person. It can be seen, therefore, that in this first year of life the infant has evolved from a living organism capable only of perceiving sensation to a human being who perceives the world and can try to affect it, and who even recognizes his own self as existing within it.

REFERENCES

BIJOU, SIDNEY, AND DONALD M. BAER. *Child Development*. Universal Stage of Infancy, vol. II. New York: Appleton-Century-Crofts, 1965.

CHURCH, J. *Three Babies: Biographies of Cognitive Development*. New York: Random House, Inc., 1966.

ERIKSON, ERIK. *Childhood and Society*. New York: W. W. Norton & Company, Inc., 1951.

FANTZ, R. L. "Pattern Vision in Newborn Infants." *Science*, CXL (1963), pp. 296–297.

FRAIBERG, SELMA H. *The Magic Years*. New York: Charles Scribner's Sons, 1959.

GESELL, ARNOLD *et al. The First Five Years of Life*. New York: Harper & Row, Publishers, 1940.

GESELL, ARNOLD *et al. Studies in Child Development*. New York: Harper & Row, Publishers, 1948.

GESELL, ARNOLD, CATHERINE AMATRUDA, BURTON CASTNER, AND HELEN THOMPSON. *Biographies of Child Development*. New York: Paul B. Hoeber, Inc., 1939.

GORDON, IRA J. *Human Development: From Birth through Adolescence*. 2d ed. New York: Harper & Row, Publishers, 1969.

GORDON, IRA J., AND J. R. LALLY. *Intellectual Stimulation for Infants and Toddlers*. The Institute for the Development of Human Resources, University of Florida. Gainesville, Florida, 1967.

JERSILD, ARTHUR. *Child Psychology*. 5th ed. Englewood Cliffs, N.J.: Prentice-Hall, Inc., 1960.

MURPHY, LOIS BARCLAY. *The Widening World of Childhood*. New York: Basic Books, Inc., 1962.

MUSSEN, PAUL HENRY, JOHN J. CONGER, AND JEROME KAGAN. *Child Development and Personality*. 2d ed. New York: Harper & Row, Publishers, 1963.

PIAGET, JEAN. *The Construction of Reality in the Child*. New York: Basic Books, Inc., 1954.

SPITZ, RENE A. *The First Year of Life*. New York: International Universities Press, Inc., 1965.

STONE, JOSEPH, AND JOSEPH CHURCH. *Childhood and Adolescence: A Psychology of the Growing Person*. 2d ed. New York: Random House, Inc., 1968.

STOTT, LELAND H. *Child Development: An Individual Longitudinal Approach*. New York: Holt, Rinehart and Winston, Inc., 1967.

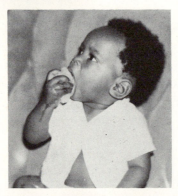

8

Observing toddlers

Once the child is up and about, once he prefers the upright position and uses it for most locomotion, we no longer think of him as an infant. Other characteristics also indicate a new stage of growth. Language has begun to develop, and the baby can make his needs and wishes understood. He is becoming a person in his own right, with a decided will of his own, as we shall soon see. "Toddlerhood" may not be a term acceptable to all developmental authorities, but it does describe a period in the life of the child that is distinct from infancy. The baby has become a walking and talking individual but has not quite reached the preschool period known as early childhood.

We shall consider babies in this chapter who range in age from fifteen months through two-and-a-half years. Since development varies so much from one individual to another, we will not specify behavior by months as we did in the chapter on infants. Many children are walking before they reach fifteen months, while some continue creeping long past that time. Some year-old babies are talking in sentences, although most communicate through gesture, jargon, or one-word expressions, well into the second year of life. Because of these differences, we will not describe a typical eighteen-month-old, or twenty-four-month old but will give time samples and anecdotes of various children, discussing the categories of observed behavior within the toddler age span.

There is, however, a sequence or progression in development. Babies babble before they talk. They crawl and creep before they walk. They communicate with adults before they seek the companionship of their peers. These progressions will be followed in discussing the babies observed, even though the chronological ages may not be in sequential order.

Observing toddlers can be a very delightful experience, as most students have reported. Toddlers have a babyish appeal. They still have the same round softness of infants, but they are not as delicate looking, and inexperienced adults feel more comfortable handling them. They are not as unfathomable, also, and it is relatively easy to perceive what they are trying to do and what they are thinking. College students enjoy their observations of this age level and come to class bubbling with stories about the toddlers they have observed.

ACTIVITY 1
In addition to taking time samples of the behavior of toddlers it would be a good idea for students to become directly involved with the children they may be observing. Play with the child, using a toy (rattle, toy truck, doll, and so on) and let the child react to you as you do it. Peek-a-boo is an ever-popular game at this stage. Hide behind a piece of furniture and see if the baby can find you. Use your hands to cover your eyes and call to the baby as you remove your hands. Record the toddler's reaction at a later time, in anecdotal form.

Here is a sample of a nineteen-month-old in a day nursery, who provided an amusing half hour for the student observer.

TIME	OVERT BEHAVIOR	COMMENTS
10:03	Kimberley is staring at the observer from a spot on the floor behind a crib. She is holding onto some plastic blocks.	Kimberley is not sure what to make of the stranger (me).
10:05	Kim puts a dump truck in the observer's hands, and offers a plastic block also. (Observer puts block in truck.) Kim takes the block out of the truck and offers it to observer again. She repeats this three times.	Kim takes the initiative and uses the truck-block action as a means of learning about the observer.
10:12	Kim takes the block from the truck and throws it. She picks it up, puts it in the truck, and then throws it again.	Kim is less inhibited now and takes delight in her block throwing. She seeks approval or disapproval from the observer.
10:15	Kim fetches the block again, toddling to retrieve it, and then throws it again. This time she hits another child. She retrieves it again, and throws it, aiming at the child. The block hits him, and the nurse reprimands Kim.	She is unaware that hitting the other child might hurt him. Excited about her own activity.
10:25	Kim is playing hide-and-seek with the observer. She gets behind the chair and then moves slowly around to the observer's side of view. She does this several times and laughs very hard each time she is seen.	Kim initiated this activity and seems to know how to play it. She thoroughly enjoys the game.
10:29	Kim stops the game to investigate a large toy she discovered under the chair.	

TIME	OVERT BEHAVIOR	COMMENTS
10:31	Kim resumes the hide-and-seek game.	The toy is not as interesting as her involvement with another person.
10:32	Kim hides in a new spot, this time farther back behind the crib. She cannot see the observer for her view is blocked by a part of the crib, yet her body is in clear view.	
10:33	Kim is peeking around the crib and she laughs quite loudly when she sees the observer looking at her. She repeats this again.	Because she cannot see the observer, Kim assumes that she is well-hidden.
10:34	The observer announces that she is leaving and Kim waves good-bye to her.	Seems to have understood what the observer said.
10:35	The nurse unlocks the side door, and Kim begins to cry as the observer walks out. She starts to cry louder after the door is closed.	It seems the observer has gained a friend! Kim is quite upset that her new playmate is abandoning her.

The student observer did not know this child before she began her observation. Characteristically, the baby began the episode by observing the newcomer with concentrated interest. She then "tested her out" in a play situation with the truck and blocks. Finding a responsive companion, she continued to play with the observer by initiating the game of hide-and-seek. She played it rather crudely, however, since she considered herself hidden from view as long as she could not see the observer, even though most of her body remained exposed. When the observer left, the baby cheerfully waved bye-bye, as if this were another game, signaled by the announcement of departure. But when the observer went out of the door, the cheerfulness turned to tears.

Much of this behavior is characteristic of one-and-a-half-year-olds. Toddlers love adult companionship, and this is one reason why adults enjoy them so. Their use of language, however, is limited, so that even if they use some words and gestures appropriately, they do not always thoroughly understand their meanings. Waving bye-bye did not make this little girl actually anticipate the fact that the observer would disappear! Words apparently meant little when Kim was reprimanded by the nurse for throwing the block. Her own enjoyment of her activity was her sole consideration. Still not able to experience very much beyond his own sensation, the early toddler is as egocentric as he was during infancy.

Motor activity

Motor activity is a source of great joy to the toddler. As can be seen in the time sample above, Kim enjoys throwing the block regardless of its effects on others. Throwing is a new discovery at about this age. Until approximately eighteen months babies can be observed carefully picking things up, but putting them down is a different matter. The prehensile release is exaggerated. It is difficult, therefore, to place things carefully, and so objects are simply dropped. Now the baby is learning to release a hold at will and throwing is part of the practice. Students have observed babies this age throwing toys, spoons, and sand in the sandbox, all with great joy and abandon.

ACTIVITY 2

Take an object from your pocket or pocketbook and experiment with the various ways you can pick it up and drop it. If your thumb did not work in opposition to the other fingers, could you still pick up the object?

Try releasing the object slowly, putting it down with care and precision. Now pick it up again, and drop it with a sudden release. Which way is easier for you?

Locomotor movement has many forms and styles during this second year of life. Once the baby has achieved enough balance to get around on two feet, he is likely to be found running or trotting, eagerly and excitedly pursuing his goals. Even when he is sitting on the floor, he will get up to go after something he has spied and then sit down to play with it. The preference for the upright form of locomotion is clearly shown in this time sample of a fifteen-and-a-half-month-old child.

TIME	OVERT BEHAVIOR	COMMENTS
7:08 PM	Matthew is sitting in the middle of the floor with feet tucked under him. He catches sight of a brightly colored handle of one of his push toys. He places both hands on the floor in front of him and leans forward toward them. His feet quickly come out from under him and he leans on his knees. With one quick boost from his hands and his right foot, he is standing up and rapidly walking toward his push toy.	This baby is more advanced in motor-sensory control than in language. He is still babbling with the exception of one word, "Dada." He has excellent control over his body, in balancing his weight and placing it in the proper position for standing.
7:10	After pushing the toy back and forth in front of him, without moving his body a step, he drops the toy to his right side and abandons it.	Good balance to be able to stand for so long, moving the toy without falling.
7:13	Matthew glances around the room while still in a standing position. His eyes focus upon various things mostly bright colored. A peacock blue vase on a shelf above his head holds his attention.	He seems to be intrigued with shapes and objects seen from various positions.

7:15	Matthew then heads in my direction. I am sitting in the rocking chair, and Matthew tries to climb on my lap. Standing on the toes of his right foot, he places his left knee on my knee. His right hand grabs the side of the rocker, while his left hand is in his mouth. With a push from his right foot and a pull from his right hand, he falls face down into my lap. I turn him around and support his head and body against myself.	The rocker is one of Matthew's favorite places, and he had been held and fed in it throughout infancy. He has been trying to climb into it by himself since he was a year old but has only recently succeeded. He tries to move the rocker himself, but realizing it doesn't work, he communicates his desire very strongly and clearly to the observer. Once rocking he relaxes.
7:16	He attempts to push the rocker into motion. At first I do not help at all, as his body rocks forward and backward. He turns to me and lets out an extremely loud babble. I begin to rock. He discontinues his rocking motion and leans against me with his left hand in his mouth.	He seeks security in this position with hand in mouth.

Rocking is, of course, a favorite activity at this age. Possibly because it is reminiscent of earlier infant comfort or simply because the physical movement is enjoyable, toddlers love to be rocked by adults or to use rocking toys themselves. They love to ride a rocking horse, and once they get used to it, they propel themselves quite vigorously sometimes. It is possible that some of the appeal of rocking is its rhythmic quality. Toddlers can be seen responding to music and bouncing rhythmically in time to it.

A twenty-three-month-old, while playing with blocks in the living room, was observed to "move her blocks up and down following the rhythm of a song on TV." A twenty-four-month-old, visiting the zoo with his parents, clapped his hands in time as he imitated the sounds of the caged birds. Any excitement is likely to cause a bouncing and jogging kind of behavior. Two-year-olds have been observed "jumping up and down," bouncing along or "galloping."

ACTIVITY 3

Play some highly rhythmic music (percussion or rock music is fine) on a phonograph. Experiment with bouncing in time to the music. In a seated position, bounce your shoulders, your head, your elbows, and so on. Then bounce on your seat, letting your body move freely in time to the music. Now stand up and continue bouncing as you move about. Your locomotor activity will greatly resemble the action of toddlers as they jog along gleefully. Do you feel the enjoyment of rhythmic activity that toddlers do?

(If you can have a child join you in this activity, so much the better!)

Sometimes the toddler may attempt to jump down a single step. At the beginning of toddlerhood steps are still climbed from a forward creeping position, going forward on hands and knees. Coming down presents more of a problem, and the baby is often afraid to attempt descent from a height by himself. Later he may learn to reverse his position and come down backward, on hands and knees, as he did in climbing up the stairs. Or he may sit on each step and bump his way down. At about two and a half he can walk up and down the steps, one step at a time, holding on to a rail.

Fear of height is sometimes exhibited when the child first gets to the top of a ladder, or when he is swinging too high on a swing. On the ground, however, the toddler appears to have little awareness of impending danger. A year-and-a-half-old girl, observed at a park, had to be rescued by her mother as she "ran after the ball, apparently not seeing the swing coming right toward her." A seventeen-month-old, who had a pool in her backyard, "walked to the pool's edge, got down on her stomach, leaned over the edge, splashed water with hands, and smiled."

It has been observed that spatial awareness is still somewhat primitive at this stage. Babies do not always distinguish two-dimensional from three-dimensional objects. They may still be seen trying to "pick spots off a rug," as infants under a year are prone to do. They are intrigued with pictures in a book, since they seem to be just beginning to make distinctions between them. Peek-a-boo and various forms of hide-and-seek remain popular activities throughout toddlerhood, partly for their social appeal, but also because the baby is still finding out about the appearance and disappearance of objects.

In both of our previous time samples the toddlers were involved in their own kind of "space exploration." Matthew looked at objects around the room, particularly brightly colored things that were above his eye level. Kim played a hiding game, even though she, herself, was not really hidden. Many of the student observers commented that the baby they observed began a kind of peek-a-boo game as soon as they noticed that they were being watched.

By bending over from a standing position and looking through his legs, the toddler gets an upside-down view of the world that seems to intrigue him. If the baby loses balance in this position, he may end up in a somersault, which may be additional cause for glee. Being vigorously tossed in the air, or rough-housed by daddy, appeals to many babies this age, as it provides new motor sensations as well as different views of the world.

Toward the end of the toddler period, babies often have enough coordination to scoot along on a kiddie car or to pedal a tricycle. Student observers have noted pedaling in a two-year-and-four-month-old child. Maneuvering in various directions is sometimes a problem, and the toddler frequently bumps into walls. He may get off the tricycle and turn it around if he cannot turn corners or move backward. But, regardless of his level of coordination, the two-year-old enjoys large muscle activity and is constantly on the go. A student observer, watching three children playing in a sandbox, noted that the two-year-old climbed in and out and was rarely still a minute, while his slightly older companions remained where they were for most of the observed time.

Skill development

While large muscle activity is predominant in the life of the toddler, skills involving small muscles are also developing. Toys become not only things to be looked at and held but manipulated as well.

ACTIVITY 4

Try to assess the level of skill development of a toddler you are observing by making a graph of his accomplishments on such a screening device as the Denver Developmental Scale. (See Appendix D.) You might test your baby, in an informal way, by seeing if he can perform the tasks corresponding to his age level on a scale of this type.

At the age of two years the toddler has greater small muscle coordination and can deal with smaller objects. While watching television, a two-year-and-three-month-old girl was observed playing with large beads.

TIME	OVERT BEHAVIOR	COMMENTS
7:47 PM	Runs to bedroom to toy chest, bends from waist, rummages through toys, pulls out Tinker Beads in large can, goes over to observer. "Open, open." After it was opened, says, "Thank you."	Chooses beads herself. Good language and social development.
7:48	Takes beads and half hops and half jumps back to TV. Holds box with two hands. Drops to floor, still on feet, knees bent. Then drops to sitting position, handling beads while watching TV.	She seems able to amuse herself while her mother is busy with baby sister.
7:49	Right hand takes a bead, left hand picks up a string; looking at beads, mouth open. Starts to pull bead through string, hands fumbling together while now watching TV; mouth closed. Smiling at something on TV; hands, beads, and string are on lap.	

Again we can see how easily a toddler can be distracted. The beads were selected by the little girl, but they held her interest for a very short time. She asked for help in opening the box, but the observer noticed later that she was able to put the top back on by herself. She also demonstrated that she was able to use a wrist-turning motion as she turned the dials from right to left on the TV set.

The two-year-old, however, can make no great claims to manual dexterity. When he uses his fingers and hands to manipulate objects, it is done rather crudely. A boy in the park was observed as he killed an ant. "With palm open, he bangs it three or four times. Then he looks at his hand." The keys of a toy piano are also hit "several times with the whole hand." Another two-year-old, playing in a sandbox, was shoveling sand into a pail. The observer commented that this was a hit-or-miss operation. When the pail was partially filled, the boy showed it to his mother with great pride.

One of the most challenging manipulative tasks for the toddler is the attempt to feed himself. Mother often has to make concessions during feeding time by giving the baby a spoon of his own, while she tries patiently to get some food into his mouth with another spoon. Hands are also used freely for feeding, as can be seen in this time sample of a two-year-old having lunch in his high chair.

TIME	OVERT BEHAVIOR	COMMENTS
11:30	Mark begins eating by taking fistfuls of hamburger, shoving it into mouth. His mother offers him applesauce from a spoon. He grabs for the spoon.	Seems very hungry, and is quite serious and intent about getting first bites into his mouth. Wants to feed himself.
11:31	Mother gives him another spoon while feeding him applesauce. Puts spoon into applesauce and then into mouth.	Mark uses his spoon, but mother gets food into his mouth using another spoon.
11:32	Continues picking up and eating chunks of hamburger. Picks up cup with both hands and drinks milk.	Drinks very well from a cup. Holds it about the middle, not by handle.
11:34	Bangs spoon on tray. Kicks feet against chair. Throws hamburger. Beats spoon on cup.	As he becomes less hungry food becomes something to play with.

The baby knows, even before he is two years old, what a spoon is for, and he may practice using it even when it is not mealtime. While playing with a plastic spoon on the living room floor, one seventeen-month-old "picked up the spoon carefully with his thumb and forefinger. He placed the spoon in his mouth, opening very wide to meet its entrance. Then he took the spoon out and made circular movements in the air in front of him with this object. He uttered the sound, 'Ummmm.' The spoon was returned to the mouth, as before. Sounds of 'Ummmm' made as the spoon approached. Hand grasped the spoon tightly."

Another seventeen-month-old was observed in a cafeteria playing with a straw. She "peels the paper off the straw. Holding it in her right hand, she places it in the glass and begins to drink. After she finishes drinking, she pushes the coke away. She lifts a spoon out of a dish filled with jello and whipped cream and begins to stir the jello around." The observer commented that she seemed to be using the straw and the spoon both functionally and as toys.

The last little girl described seems to have rather well-developed manual dexterity. She was able to peel the paper off the straw and could stir the jello with the spoon. Rates of development in this area differ widely. In general little girls seem to develop dexterity at an earlier age than little boys. This may be due to the fact that girls, even as babies, are given more toys which are meant for sedentary activities; or, it may have genetic roots.

This difference between the sexes shows up when children begin to write. All babies like to scribble with crayons and pencils when they see adults doing these kinds of things. Although girls seem to be more adept, boys show an interest in writing too. A curious fifteen-month-old boy was fascinated while watching the observer writing on her pad.

He came over and put his hand on my pen. I let him have it. I was writing in a notebook that had holes on the side, and he tried to stick the pen through the holes. After a few seconds, he did it. I ripped out a sheet of paper for him and gave it to his mother. I asked her to show him how to move the pen and to draw a few lines so that he could imitate her if he wanted to. Naturally, he did. Mark held the pen with his whole hand as if it were going to be taken away from him. His lines were long, vertical strokes. This was a totally new and exciting experience for him.

ACTIVITY 5

Hold a pencil in the hand that you use least frequently. Experiment with making lines on a piece of paper. Which kinds of lines are the simplest to make? Can you make a smooth circle? Try making big ones and then little ones. Which is easier? Can you make a triangle? A square? A diamond shape?

Look at Viktor Lowenfeld's stages of development in scribbling in his book, *Creative and Mental Growth*. Compare your scribbling to that of toddlers.

Children will imitate the behavior they see around them, and in this way many adaptive responses are learned. In homes where reading is done a good deal, babies will hold books, turn pages, and babble. We mentioned earlier that a one-year-old son of a football player was already learning to handle a ball, as he attended football practice with his father. It is in this way that the baby begins to reflect the cultural patterns of his environment. "Children growing up in societies in which dancing is an intrinsic part of life become proficient dancers at an early age."[1] But we have noted that the potential for rhythmic response is there, whether the culture encourages it or not. Similarly, stringing beads and drawing with crayons are enjoyable activities for both boys and girls at the toddler stage. If encouraged and praised, children will continue to develop those skills that bring them adult recognition and reinforcement.

[1] Joseph Stone and Joseph Church, *Childhood and Adolescence*, p. 226.

Imitative behavior

We have already implied that much of the learning that takes place during toddlerhood is learning by imitation. Two-year-old children, and babies even younger, are little mimics. They copy every kind of adult action, in real "monkey see, monkey do" fashion. Boys, as well as girls, will be seen following mother around the house, imitating her as she goes about her domestic chores. Girls, as well as boys, will mimic daddy in the act of shaving, reading the newspaper, or mowing the lawn. In one observation, lasting a total of twenty minutes, Jimmy, age two years and four months, is found to imitate the following activities.

1. Imitates father mowing the lawn, by pushing his stroller along the grass next to daddy.
2. Watches sister using a pencil and paper. Tries to take them from her. Mother intervenes and hands Jimmy another pencil and paper. He scribbles on the paper and then turns to his sister and babbles at her in a harsh tone.
3. Follows the mailman, picks up the mail that is left, and hands it to the observer.
4. Goes to kitchen and brings out a broom. He tells his mother he is going to sweep outside. He gets busy sweeping up the make-believe grass from the sidewalk.
5. He hears his sister playing piano inside. He runs in the house and tries to sit on the piano stool with his sister. She won't let him up on the stool, and Jimmy breaks out in a temper tantrum.
6. Finally his mother puts him on the piano stool and his tantrum ceases. He and his sister pound the piano together as if nothing had gone wrong.

All of that imitative activity took place within twenty minutes, so we can see that Jimmy certainly was a busy boy. His anxiety to be able to do whatever his sister was doing led to some frustration and display of temper. He won out, however, and this might encourage the use of a tantrum to get what he is after next time. But we can see that the eagerness to perform all the tasks of his elders is an intense drive, and it is in this way that the toddler learns to do many things and begins to find out about the various roles played by members of his society.

Toddlers' imitative behavior is sometimes amusing to adults, since it appears to be somewhat incongruous with their small size. While observing a two-year-old with his father in the park, one student noted, "Wherever his father goes, Jerry goes. Father puts hands in pockets. Jerry puts hands in pockets almost simultaneously." A little girl was observed answering the telephone. "She stood with one hand on her hip, one foot crossed over the other at the ankle, just as she has seen her mother stand. She picked up the phone and said, 'Hi!' " It is at this stage that dramatic play begins to take shape.

Toddlers, boys as well as girls, enjoy playing with dolls. Scenes from everyday life are enacted as the dolls are fed, bathed, and put to bed. A twenty-three-month-old girl was observed "wiping the doll's face with a cloth. Paula then fixed the doll's dress, fussing with it, straightening it out. She hugged her, then she sat the doll down, saying, 'Good girl.'"

Imaginative play, which reaches its peak during the preschool years, begins to develop during toddlerhood. Police or fire sirens are imitated and identified, and often the tricycle or kiddie car becomes the fire engine. This dramatic play is likely to be sporadic, however, and to consist of only one brief episode. The fireman does not continue to the fire to follow a sequence of activities there. For this kind of activity, we must wait for another year or so of development.

Language

The development of language during toddlerhood represents a major change in life-style. The true beginnings of language took place before this time during the baby's first year. It was then that the infant first began to know the meaning of symbols, as he learned to wave bye-bye, or to lift his arms to tell his mother that he wanted to be picked up. Sounds, too, had been explored previously, but now some of them are beginning to take on meaning. With language the child can move from a primitive system of thought to an identification of objects and categories and thus to higher thought processes.

The toddler is fascinated with picture storybooks and can sit on an adult's lap for long periods of time pointing to the pictures.

ACTIVITY 6
During one of your observations of toddlers try reading a picture story-book to the child. Note his reactions. Compare them to those of the eighteen-month-old girl described below.

Usually the same book is preferred to a new one, and the same words must be repeated by the adult over and over again. A student observer reported her experience while she was reading a story to an eighteen-month-old girl.

After completing the story and closing the book, the child immediately reopened it and tapped the pictures. She kept pointing to the objects until the student observer identified them for her, then she moved to another page and pointed again. She was able to make the sounds of the animals she saw in the pictures, and she tried to say their names. When the student observer suggested that she read another story, the little girl said, "No!" and again turned the page of the book that had been read. She seemed to prefer familiar pictures and could go through the process of identifying them over and over again, until the student observer, not the baby, got tired of the activity.

Even before the toddler learns to say words, he understands words that are spoken to him. Sometimes a single word is associated with a series of ideas within the child's experience. Fifteen-month-old Mark was eating his lunch when a student recorded the following episode.

Mark was having hot dogs for lunch which were cut up in small pieces for him. Mark picked up one piece at a time and ate it. He took out the first piece as his mother came over to him. She said, "Hot, it is hot, Mark. Blow on it." Mark picked it up, blew on it, and then put it right back into his mouth. He babbled a good deal while eating and seemed to know exactly what he was talking about.

He noticed that I was drinking some water with ice in it. Mark pointed to the glass and said, "Ice." I asked his mother if he could have it, and she said he could, so I gave it to him. Mark's mother then related this story to me.

Whenever Mark would fall down or bang into something, he would cry. His mother would put a piece of ice on the sore spot and would often give Mark another piece to eat. Now he frequently goes over to the refrigerator, saying, "Ice, ice." He will bang on the bottom half of the refrigerator where the ice is kept.

It is logical that the first words that babies learn to say are words that have emotional meaning for them. The *ice* Mark learned to ask for was a source of comfort to him. *Mamma, Daddy, up, out, bye-bye, hi,* are among the first words spoken. Often they stand for whole ideas or sentences. "I want to go out," is expressed as "Out;" "Pick me up" is expressed as "up." Toddlers learn the meaning of words when they are recognized by adults who respond to them. Sometimes the baby accidentally makes a sound which is associated with a particular meaning. If the adults in his environment understand this meaning, the baby will use the sound again even if it is not a real word. In such a way "baby talk" comes into being and may persist as long as adults accept it and respond to it.

Even before words are spoken, some babies communicate in a kind of jargon that so strongly resembles language that strangers often take it for actual speech. Student observers have commented that the baby spoke to his mother, and the mother seemed to understand, but the observer could make no sense of it. Such private language systems often come into being and prove to be quite effective. Janine, age fourteen months, carried on this conversation with her mother.

Janine picks up a stick and holds it out to mother, saying, "Eh deh deh?" Mother answers her, "That is a stick." A few minutes later, Janine climbs up the steps, bangs on the door, and says, "Abba jaba jin," in a rather strong tone. Mother comes to the door and asks, "Do you want to come in, honey?" and opens the door.

There can be no doubt that there is conversation taking place here. Janine's mother responds to the baby exactly as if she had talked to her in an intelligent language. Janine's intonation patterns so strongly resemble speech that it is not difficult to guess at her meanings. The mother has encouraged the communication by answering the baby in a logical way. Soon Janine will be substituting real words for the ones she has invented.

Sprinkled in with the babbling, we often hear a few words, as we did when fifteen-month-old Mark said the word *Ice*. A student observer reported the behavior of Jenny, age nineteen months, who "dropped a cereal box she was playing with. She said, 'Oh, oh.' A dog then barked outside. She listened and said, 'Goggi.' She then went to the TV, played with the knobs, all of the time, babbling to herself." This interspersing of words with babbling is characteristic of a period right before speech develops. The babbling is often so expressive that the listener cannot help but believe that the baby has meanings for everything she is saying. Gesell calls this phenomenon "expressive jargon."

At some time, usually after two, babies begin to form sentences. At first these are crude, and words are often misplaced. Two-year-old Jerry, who was observed with his father in the park, "sees a fish in the lake, and runs back to daddy to report excitedly, 'A fish there! A fish there!' "

By two and a half, most children are using sentences, but they may still revert to babbling as they play by themselves. Michael, observed by a student in the park, "picked up a flower and told his father, 'Here's my flower. Here's my flower.' He repeated the words over and over again. He then proceeded to put the flower through a hole in the bench, concentrating as he squeezed it into the narrow space. As he did this, he babbled to himself freely." It seems as if language is something for the toddler to play with, making sense of it at some times, and enjoying it just for its sounds at others.

Some children, by two and a half, have a rather extensive vocabulary and have mastered the structure of our language quite well. When we think about how they started talking so short a time before, it is amazing how much has been learned. The following observation illustrates this point about language development.

Billy, age two and a half, was observed at a restaurant where he sat at a table behind the observer with his mother, father, and grandmother.

When his ice cream cone comes, he says, "Look at that!" His father helps him at first and then Billy holds it himself. He turns around to us and starts licking it and smiling at us. He turns back to his father, who starts to help him with the cone. Billy says, "Please, don't," and continues to lick his cone. Again his father tries to fix the cone where it is dripping, and Billy says, "What are you doing? No!" My friend asks him, "What is that?" and he replies, "Cone." "What kind of cone?" "Strawberry." He drips ice cream on his hand and says, "Cone dripped on my hand," and laughs. He stands up and looks out of the window again and says, "I want to see a train. The train is sleeping. Moon is up." He refuses the rest of his ice cream when it is offered but asks for "*My* water." He tries to crawl over the seat but his father says no.

He wipes his mouth with his hand, turns to father and says, "I have to wee-wee." He puts his arm around father and says, "You'd better take me, there'll be an accident."

As soon as he comes from the bathroom, he turns around and looks straight at us. He sits down and then pops up right away. He starts jumping up and down, and dancing on his seat, smiling and looking out of the window. He is singing, "da-dee-dee."

The family is ready to leave, and Billy says "bye-bye." While standing up and waiting for his parents, he looks around and smiles and dances. He reminds his father to "get ice cream for brother." His thumb then goes in his mouth. He keeps looking around and says "bye-bye" to all of the people. He grabs onto his mother's pants as they begin to walk out. He is given candy and says to father, while holding it up, "Daddy, look what I got."

This child exhibits a very mature speech pattern for his age. He uses words like "strawberry," "dripped," and "accident" all in the correct context. His grammatical structure is advanced too. Such expressions as "Look at that!" "Please, don't," and the compound thought "You'd better take me, there'll be an accident," show that he has absorbed the phrasing and placement of words that are rather complex in the English language. Yet, he still plays with language, as when he sings "da-dee-dee" as he looks out the window. He also expresses imaginary ideas, when he talks about a nonexistent train that is "sleeping."

His vigorous motor activity is evident throughout the anecdotal record. He bounces up and down in his seat. When he finally sits, he pops right up again. He dances on his seat and dances in the aisle, as he stands up and waits for his parents. At the last moment he grabs onto his mother's pants and leans against her, as younger toddlers are prone to do.

Several emotional and social responses are revealed in this anecdote, and these will be referred to in the next section.

Socialization

Toddlerhood appears to be a period of happiness and excitement. New horizons open up every day, and each new discovery and new skill acquired is greatly enjoyed by the baby and by his family. The toddler has become a responsive and communicative individual, and attention and affection are showered upon him.

But not every aspect of toddlerhood is joyous. This is the time when the socialization process begins. Adults try to impose their ideas upon the baby, to make him conform to standards set by the culture. As Fraiberg put it, "The missionaries have arrived."[2] Some conflict is inevitable. The baby has strong impulses and drives, and these must be restricted to comply with parents' wishes. The baby wants to win the approval of his loved ones. At the same time the urge to explore, touch things, and investigate the world around him is so strong that he cannot always do what his parents want him to. Even though he understands their requests, he does not always comply.

A two-year-old, observed while playing in a sandbox, began picking up the sand and throwing it. He seemed to enjoy this, because the action was accompanied the entire time with "laughing in a high-pitched, excited voice." His mother told him not to throw the sand, but he "continued, as if not hearing his mother. This behavior was brought to a quick stop, however, as his mother

[2] Selma H. Fraiberg, *The Magic Years*, p. 62.

reached over from where she was sitting and gave him a tap on his rear. He yelled out, 'No,' but surprisingly did not cry or seem disturbed." There is no doubt that this toddler was capable of understanding, and this was demonstrated at a later point in the student's observation. As adults sometimes do, the toddler seems to "block out" what he does not want to hear.

When the impulse is too strong, the two-year-old may ignore parental request, or he may respond with a decisive "NO." So many necessary restrictions are placed upon him at this time! His new mobility takes him to all kinds of places, and his curiosity involves him in some dangerous undertakings. Of course, he may not touch the electric outlet or daddy's phonograph records! He may not run into the street or too near the lake in the park. He must learn to use the toilet instead of urinating when he feels like doing it. He must wait for his dessert and must go to bed when he is still busy with a game or activity. If two-year-olds are known to be willful, stubborn, and negative, there is good reason for it. Negativism is a natural reaction to all of the restrictions placed upon the toddler. He is simply saying "No" to all of the No's imposed upon his will.

There are many instances of this negative type of behavior in the students' observations. Some of them are:

1. Jerry, the two-year-old at the park with his parents, "wandered down toward the edge of the lake. His mother called a warning. Jerry laughed, approached closer to the water, then turned around and ran back to his parents."
2. The same boy played a game of peek-a-boo with the observer, displaying a friendly and sociable nature. When it was time to leave, however, he would not say good-bye, and "just stared without blinking an eye, no matter how many times his mother requested him to respond to the observer."
3. A boy, two and a half, playing ball with his sisters, "hid his arms and hands behind his body" when his sisters wanted him to try to catch the ball. He had been able to catch a ball since he was one and a half, so this behavior was a kind of teasing. When one of the sisters tried to pull his arms out from behind him, he yelled, "Carolyn, stop it!"
4. A temper tantrum resulted when Jimmy, who was imitating his sister playing the piano, was taken away to the bathroom.
5. When Billy's father tried to help him with his ice cream cone Billy told him, "Please, don't" and later, "What are you doing? No!"

ACTIVITY 7

Have you ever experienced strongly negative feelings? Think of an instance which happened recently that made you feel somewhat like the children did in the examples given above. A few volunteers might be asked to pantomime or to act out these experiences for the class. Can you guess what caused these negativistic feelings?

Negativism is often the result of a strong urge for independence and autonomy, as in the last example given. Billy wanted to take care of feeding himself and would accept help from no one. He was strongly independent until a few moments later, when he asked to be taken to the bathroom and clung to daddy as he took him. As he left the restaurant, he grabbed onto his mother's pants. Characteristically, he vacillated from vigorously asserting his autonomy to a sudden dependence and need for parental support.

Erikson has called this the struggle between autonomy and guilt.[3] We have seen how the infant needs to establish a feeling of trust in the adult who cares for him. Once this feeling is established, he is ready to venture forth to explore his world. The conflict of the toddler is between his desire to please the loved ones that he has come to trust, and his strong urge to become a separate person with wants and desires of his own. The conflict may lead to feelings of guilt. Thus, the toddler seeks reassurance from his loved ones, and his behavior alternates between self-assertion and dependence.

This assertion of will, therefore, is really the two-year-old's healthy attempt to establish his own identity. He is struggling to be himself and to comply with adult wishes as well. Sometimes the conflict manifests itself in a kind of teasing behavior, as when Jerry went closer to the water before meeting his mother's request to come away from it. The teasing of the little brother while playing ball probably stems from a similar source. The two-year-old, not unlike his adolescent counterpart, is saying to the world, "I want to do my own thing!"

Another evidence of this self-awareness is found in the frequent use of the words *my* and *mine*. Billy, the boy at the restaurant, asked for "*My* water" with a strong emphasis upon the possessive pronoun. Another two-year-old, observed by a student, insisted that "I will not spill *my* milk," implying that some other child might do this, but not she!

Two-year-olds frequently refer to themselves by their own name or confuse the use of pronouns such as, "*Jimmy* do it," or "*Me* want the ball." The language may be incorrect, but there is no denying the assertion of self in these statements.

In spite of his willfulness and self-assertion the toddler wants and needs adult support. His newly acquired ego is easily disturbed, and he often seeks reassurance that he is a "big boy" or that she is a "good girl." While bold and self-confident one minute, the toddler may be clinging and dependent the next minute. Left to play by himself, he will do very well as long as mother is within easy reach. The boy in the sandbox refused to comply with mother's request to stop throwing sand, but he ran to her for approval a moment later. "He ran to her and showed her the shovel, handed it to her, but then abruptly grabbed it back. He returned to play with the other children." The student observer commented that, "Throughout the entire time of observation, the child always made sure his mother saw and knew all that he was doing."

Learning to use the toilet is, perhaps, one of the most difficult restrictions that the toddler must deal with. When he first becomes aware that adults

[3] Eric Erikson, *Childhood and Society.*

should be told of his need, the toddler may impart the information *after* the fact. Even this delayed communication is a source of satisfaction, and he may enjoy "wiping up the puddle" he has made. Soon the toddler learns to announce his desire to urinate and asks to be taken to the bathroom. Once control has been acquired, however, then he will probably assert his independence and will want to take care of the operation himself. A student observer was told to "Go away" by her niece, who wanted the privacy of a closed bathroom door when she urinated. Toilet training can thus be a matter of pride for the toddler and can serve as a badge of his independence.

The toddler is interested in other children and seems to enjoy being with them. Usually, however, he will play by himself. He rarely enters into exchange with his neighbors but enjoys doing things alongside them in a manner that educators have referred to as "parallel play." But two-year-olds are not quite independent, as can be seen from the action of this little girl, age two years, and one month.

TIME	OVERT BEHAVIOR	COMMENTS
5:17	Tara is coloring (scribbling) in a book with several other little girls sitting near her.	Tara enjoys what she is doing. Seems unaware of others.
5:21	After a while she throws her crayons down, leans over to get up, and stands.	Unhappy as she looks around.
5:23	Looking at other girls, calls, "Mommy?" in a questioning voice and looks around.	
5:24	Calls and looks for mother. When she spots her mother, her pace quickens to a stumbling run. Smiles and reaches for mommy to pick her up.	Though the other girls tell her to stay, she calls and looks for mother, paying no attention to them.

Although socialization is well under way by the end of toddlerhood, the behavior of two-year-olds can still be very babyish. The little girl above was content to play alongside other children, but when she tired of her activity she wanted her mother. In her first moments of anxiety she looked at the other children, possibly to see if mother was there, but then turned away. She did not respond to the calls of the other children to stay.

It is not until approximately the three-year-old level that children truly engage in peer-group activity. We will be examining how this comes about in the next chapter.

REFERENCES

ALMY, MILLIE. *Child Development.* New York: Holt, Rinehart and Winston, Inc., 1955.

BRUNER, J., R. OLIVER, AND P. GREENFIELD.   *Studies in Cognitive Growth.* New York: John Wiley & Sons, Inc., 1966.

CHURCH, J.   *Three Babies: Biographies of Cognitive Development.* New York: Random House, Inc., 1966.

ERIKSON, ERIK.   *Childhood and Society.* New York: W. W. Norton & Company, Inc., 1951.

FRAIBERG, SELMA H.   *The Magic Years.* New York: Charles Scribner's Sons, 1959.

GESELL, ARNOLD et al.   *The First Five Years of Life.* New York: Harper & Row, Publishers, 1940.

GORDON, IRA J.   *Human Development: From Birth Through Adolescence.* 2d ed. New York: Harper & Row, Publishers, 1969.

JERSILD, ARTHUR.   *Child Psychology.* 5th ed. Englewood Cliffs, N.J.: Prentice-Hall, Inc., 1960.

LOWENFELD, VIKTOR.   *Creative and Mental Growth.* New York: Crowell-Collier and Macmillan, Inc., 1957.

MCCANDLESS, BOYD.   *Children: Behavior and Development.* 2d ed. New York: Holt, Rinehart and Winston, Inc., 1967.

PIAGET, JEAN.   *The Language and Thought of the Child.* New York: Harcourt Brace Jovanovich, Inc., Meridian Books, 1955.

STONE, JOSEPH, AND JOSEPH CHURCH.   *Childhood and Adolescence.* 2d ed. New York: Random House, Inc., 1968.

VYGOTSKY, L.   *Thought and Language.* Cambridge, Mass.: MIT Press, 1962.

YAMAMOTO, K.   *The Child and His Image.* Boston: Houghton Mifflin Company, 1972.

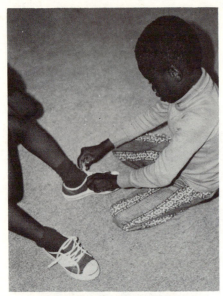

Preschoolers and school beginners

In this chapter we will be concerned with young children at the point where they emerge from total dependence upon home and family and become members of the larger world. We cannot actually distinguish preschoolers from school beginners, since many children begin school at two or three years of age, while others do not enter an organized group situation until four or five. But at some time about three years of age, the child becomes interested in adults outside his family sphere, and he also begins to relate to his peers in various ways. These socialization patterns change in the period from three through five, but, as at the toddler stage, there seems to be a sequence of development that can be followed in spite of the many variations due to individual differences.

Three-year-olds

The three-year-old generally is much easier to live with than he was at two or two and a half. He has learned certain rules of behavior and is ready to comply with them. As Gesell puts it, "You can bargain with Three."[1] The forces of socialization have won out. The three-year-old is amenable to most demands and will even sacrifice immediate satisfaction for some future gratification. Of course, this change in behavior is, in part, the effect of training. Manners must be taught, and the delay of gratifications must be practiced. Children from disadvantaged environments often do not display these same characteristics. Gratifications must be immediate, so that teachers resort to candy and trinkets as rewards for learning to get responses. The amount of interaction with adults at this stage determines, to a large extent, the degree to which socialization patterns will be internalized.

[1] Arnold Gesell *et al., The First Five Years of Life,* p. 44.

The three-year-old still needs to be assured of his own identity, and he struggles for autonomy; but his desire to please the important adults in his world seems to be his primary consideration. Three-year-olds often display amazingly good manners or, at least, will accept gracefully any adult suggestions about their social behavior. In the following time sample this is demonstrated.

Karen, age three, has just arrived at the playground with her mother and two other mothers with their children, who are older. Karen walks along with her mother, holding onto her hand.

TIME	OVERT BEHAVIOR	COMMENTS
1:15	The mothers stop in a shaded area of the park, and they take out a blanket to put on the ground. Karen, looking up toward her mother, asks, "May I?" She seems to want to put the blanket down by herself. Her mother tells her, "You may help."	Apparently, Karen had come to the park before, so she knew what the blanket was to be used for. I noticed that throughout the observation Karen was a very patient child and very eager to help. She did not put up a fuss when told that she could not put the blanket down by herself. She complied with her mother's suggestion to help.
1:20	After getting settled, Karen sits down quietly on the blanket. She notices that the older children have gone off toward the swings, and she gets up to follow them.	
1:22	Karen watches the older children for a while, then decides that she, too, would enjoy swinging.	
1:24	Karen is swinging, while the older child is pushing her. She glances over to the child swinging next to her.	She patiently lets the other child push her, but it appears that she would like to try it herself.
1:25	She tells her friend, "No more." She continues to sit on the swing, rocking back and forth and kicking the dirt with her legs.	
1:30	Karen has gone back over to her mother sitting on the blanket. She goes over to the picnic basket, opens it, and begins to take things out of it. She places paper plates on the blanket, then pauses, turns toward her mother, and asks, "Mommy, okay?"	It seems to me that three-year-olds aim to please. Karen is a very good child.

This time sample points up, not only how good this three-year-old is, but also her desire to do things alone and her beginning interest in her peers. "Mommy" is still the central figure in her life, but Karen is interested in what the older children are doing and attempts to join them for a while. At the swings she seems to want to push herself, just as she had wanted to put down the blanket without help when she first arrived at the park. The three-year-old has a strong desire to do things by herself and particularly to imitate adult behavior. At the end of the observation, we find Karen laying out the plates on the blanket, just as "Mommy" might do.

Three-year-olds love to do grown-up things, and can often be observed setting the table, washing the dishes, imitating daddy mowing the lawn, and so on. They take their own tasks very seriously and make sincere efforts to dress themselves with care. They even try to undertake tasks for which they are not quite ready. But, at three, we are less likely to observe the stubborn persistence and negativism that we noticed at the toddler stage. Three-year-olds accept help politely as can be seen in this observation.

Janis is sitting on her chair, bending over to put on her shoes and having a little bit of difficulty. She asks me to tie them for her. Her mother asks, "What do you say?" Janis then says, "Please." I tie her shoes and she says, "Thank you."

Observers are sometimes amazed at the precision of three-year-olds. They are likely to clean up their room in a very orderly fashion, carefully putting each thing in its place. In this observation, Larry, a three-and-a-half-year-old, is getting ready for bed.

Larry is cleaning up his toys. He pulls his plastic train track apart and places each piece in the box. He makes sure it is neat. He works for about four or five minutes, constantly looking up to receive his mother's approval. Larry has finished and is told to go brush his teeth. He stands up and walks to the bathroom. His actions are completely organized. He brings his stool over to the sink. He stands on it, on his toes. He takes down his toothbrush and toothpaste. He puts them down and then fills his paper cup with water. He puts the cup down and then wets the toothbrush. He takes the paste and opens it; then he puts the paste on the wet brush. He puts the brush down, closes the paste tube, and returns it to where it had been. He picks up the brush and brushes one side of his mouth. He takes the cup and gargles with the water and then spits it out. He does this twice. Then he brushes the other side of his mouth and repeats the gargling. He then washes the toothbrush and returns it to its holder. He throws the cup away and climbs off the stool. He wipes his mouth on a towel.

He smiles at me and seems to have enjoyed the whole operation. I tell him how perfectly he had done everything, and he is elated. Only big boys can brush their teeth by themselves!

Three-year-olds take great pride in their accomplishments, as this student observer was careful to point out. It is very possible, that, by four, this same little boy will have to be reminded several times to do the things that he performed so precisely at three!

ACTIVITY 1
Do a pantomime of a daily activity, such as brushing your teeth, making a bed, and so on. Concentrate upon remembering each detail of the

action. Using no words, and no props, see if you can make your audience know exactly what you are doing.

As one student performs a pantomime, the class can guess what she is doing. They should look to see that precision is used. Did the student turn off the faucet? Did she put the toothpaste down? This kind of precision is required by three-year-olds performing these tasks for the first time.

Motor development

One of the reasons that three-year-olds perform routine tasks with such great care is that the tasks are new to them. They have just achieved the state where small muscles can be coordinated well enough to execute such tasks, and they thoroughly enjoy practicing these accomplishments.

While the toddler is busy banging kitchenware and grasping at any object within range, the preschooler is more absorbed with the manipulation of mechanical toys or playthings designed for building. He lines blocks up in a row. He puts circles, squares, and triangles in the right places on a form board. He can match simple forms, and can work puzzles that have large, easily assembled parts. He can fit together pieces of a plastic train track, as Larry was doing before he so carefully put them away.

Sometimes three-year-olds are observed manipulating materials they find on the ground, but, even then, the ways in which they handle these objects are much more defined than they might be at the toddler stage. Stones are likely to be arranged in neat lines, or in circles, with a bigger stone in the middle. Sometimes imaginative play accompanies this activity, and the child can be observed, "moving the stones around, laughing and talking to himself as he does it."

A three-and-a-half-year-old boy was observed playing with plastic tubes of assorted sizes and colors. He "frowns as he struggles to make two difficult pieces fit together. He tries various sizes until he is pleased with the selection. He smiles when he succeeds in putting them together, looks around and holds up the finished product. 'There it is; it's to run water through. You put water in here and it comes out here.' "

Although three-year-olds can remain for longer periods of time at sedentary activities, they still have a preference for large muscle movement, as they did during toddlerhood. A three-year-old was observed playing a card game with her older sister. Although she could recognize the numerals on the cards and was quite able to play the game, she frequently dropped the cards to run over to rough-house with Daddy. When asked by the observer if she was still playing cards, she answered, "Yes, but Daddy sent me up here on his chest!"

Another three-year-old was riding her tricycle, going both backward and forward. When she backed her bike into the wall, she "looked at the observer with sudden surprise and said, 'Oh-oh!' "

Bike riding becomes more than just a motor activity. Bicycles often become fire engines, as three-year-olds imitate the sound of the siren as they pedal around. Sometimes an imaginary friend joins in the activity as well.

A three-and-a-half-year-old boy, riding his tricycle in his backyard, called to his imaginary friend, "Tom, come play with me." The boy, himself, was then observed riding around and motioning for his friend to follow, although no one else was there!

Another student observer recorded, "When I drove up to his house, Ron (age three years and nine months) was playing by himself, but was talking to an imaginary friend. He was saying, 'Come on. You can't outrun *me*. You can't outrun *me*. I'm the fastest guy around!' "

Practice with an imaginary friend may prepare the three-year-old for later social activities with his peers. It seems so much safer to play with a make-believe person, who will take orders, and who will act as a sounding board for the three-year-old's ideas.

Fantasy and fears

It is at the three-year-old level that fantasy life is at a peak. Perhaps, as Fraiberg explains, the socialization process has the necessary component of producing anxiety.[2] This anxiety may be dealt with effectively through the invention of imaginary playmates. If the three-year-old always wants to please the adults in his life, he may blame his transgressions on an imaginary friend. If the conflict between impulse and conscience has produced anxiety, which might lead to fears, an imaginary monster is easier to deal with than the conflict itself. This is a creative way of coping with a problem. Fantasy and imagination often are means of serving other needs, such as curiosity, an explanation for the unknown, and so on.

Fear of animals is common at this age, even though the neighbor's dog is a constant source of fascination. The observation cited in Chapter 4, in which three-year-old Marty teased the observer's dog and then withdrew in fright, is a typical example of approach-avoidance behavior. Other instances have been cited by student observers. "A three-year-old girl calls to the dog, 'Come here, Coco!' When the dog finally comes, and stands up to lick her face, she begins to laugh, then screams and runs to her mother."

The developing awareness of his own body is sometimes a source of fear to the three-year-old. He is aware of his own vulnerability, and he worries about his intactness. A visit to the dentist, or the anticipation of a tonsillectomy, can be traumatic to a preschooler. It is as if any loss of a part of his body diminishes the self that he has just come to know as an entity.

A three-year-old girl was observed while getting a haircut. "She sits very quietly as if she is afraid to move. Her hands clench the sides of her seat. Her eyes are held closed very tightly. She asks anxiously if the cutter is finished. She does not make one move. She obviously is very frightened."

[2] Selma H. Fraiberg, *The Magic Years.*

This concern about loss of any part of one's body may be related to a developing sense of personal identity. The child has come to differentiate himself from others. He begins to distinguish external events from internal ones. "The three-year-old knows, with clarity, that he is a person, and that you are a person."[3]

Identity and imitation

The preschooler, however, is still setting up experiments which help to define himself. He muses about how he appears to others. He examines his peers, touching faces and bodies to see if they resemble his own. He loves to have adults make faces at him and imitates their expressions in a reciprocal face-making game that he wants to repeat again and again.

ACTIVITY 2
Working in pairs and with eyes closed, run your fingertips lightly over the face of your partner. Now examine your own face in the same way. How were they different?
Tactile sense is strong in young children. They discover more sometimes by feeling and touching than they do by looking.

Tommy, age three years, was observed playing in a puddle. As he played, his hands splashing in water, he seemed to notice his reflection. He "stared at it for a minute, then he began to make faces." He continued this activity for a while, splashing and making faces, and then called a friend over to join him in the game. When he came into the house, he told the observer that he had "found himself" and that he wanted to show her. The observer commented that the reflection was like a mirror and got one out of her pocketbook to show to Tommy. His first reaction was to slap at it, as if he was splashing in the puddle. Then the observer showed him a reflection in a window, and Tommy "made faces into it." Later he was observed watching his reflections on pots and pans, silver, and polished wooden tables.

The fact that the three-year-old still has some confusion about identity can be seen also in his language patterns. Many preschoolers still confuse the use of "I" and "me" and can be heard to say "Me do it" or "Bobby wants to slide," referring to themselves by name, much in the manner of two-year-olds.

Most three-year-olds are beginning to establish sexual identity and are starting to know the difference between mommy's role and daddy's role. Boys, as well as girls, will use dramatic play with dolls to clarify their understanding of mother's role in caring for the baby. They like to dramatize all jobs that involve clearly visible and functional activities and will readily play at being filling-station attendants, bus drivers, doctors, and nurses. This dramatic play offers the preschooler the opportunity to simulate the activities of the adults he sees around him. Thus, he begins to understand aspects of our complex society and how grownups function in it.

[3] Gesell *et al.*, p. 44.

The preschoolers' understanding of social role is sometimes complicated by the effects of divorce. Three-year-old Ann was spending the day with her daddy at his apartment, when this conversation took place.

She walks onto the playground, holding daddy's hand and says, "Me glad to see Daddy." Smiles, gives daddy a hug and says, "Swing me, Daddy."

An eight-year-old begins to swing on the swing next to her. Ann says to the other girl, "My daddy's pushing me." Ann smiles at the girl and says, "Who you?" The girl answers that her name is Jane. Ann says, "You live here?" Not waiting for an answer, she continues, "I live with Mommy; Mommy working, huh, Daddy?" Daddy nods. Ann says, "Daddy live here, huh, Daddy?"

Later on, as she climbs up the steps of the slide, Ann says to Daddy, "Mommy say you not work, Daddy. Mommy work hard." There is no comment from Daddy.

What has happened to the image of daddies who go to work and of mommies who take care of the house? The world has always been a confusing place to three-year-olds, and it takes a great deal of dramatic play and first-hand experiences for them to begin to define social roles. In our era of changing values it becomes even more difficult for preschoolers to understand adult relationships. In spite of the sophistication of some of their comments their confusion is evident and in some cases is somewhat touching.

Peer relationships

In several of the observations above we have seen three-year-olds beginning to communicate with other children. Ann conversed with the older child who was swinging on the swing next to her, but she did not wait for a reply before going on with her own train of thought. Karen, the little girl in our first time sample, joined her older companions for a brief time and then went back to her mommy, who was sitting on the blanket, and began to arrange paper plates for the picnic.

Three-year-olds seem to enjoy acting out adult roles, but they are more likely to engage in this activity in a solitary way than to become involved with others. Even where two or three preschoolers inhabit the "housekeeping corner" at a nursery school at the same time, they are likely to work next to each other, each pursuing his own task, and paying little attention to what the others are doing. Conversation may take place, but what one child says seems to bear no relationship to what the other child says. These conversations have been called "collective monologues," since the aim is less the exchange of information than the pleasure of affective communication.

But there is no doubt that three-year-olds are beginning to enjoy being with each other. They will congregate in the same place, all running to the sandbox at the same time. They love to swarm over climbing apparatus together, babbling and shrieking in an expression of shared feelings. They often communicate a kind of silliness to each other, clowning as they fall to the floor, and laughing heartily as their companions do the same. Communication seems to be nonverbal. Even where language is used, it is the quality of the three-year-old's sounds, rather than the meaning of the words, that seem to affect their peers.

We have spoken about imaginary companions, and these seem to be evident even when three-year-olds play together in groups. They can be heard conversing with an imaginary playmate, while actual playmates are sitting right next to them, engaged in their own solitary play. Soliloquies serve the purpose of helping to clarify ideas and of perfecting speech patterns.

Three-year-olds become interested in the activities of older children as well as those of their peers. They often are seen, standing on the outskirts of a group of children who are playing, trying shyly and without skill to become part of the group. They are often proud of having older companions and remember their social experiences with them long after they occurred.

A student observer, who was the mother of six-year-old Carl, recorded this conversation with three-and-a-half-year-old Ron. (Carl and his mother had visited Ron's house six weeks before.)

"You know me. My name is Ron, remember? Where's Carl?"
I answered, "At home."
"Why didn't you bring him to play with me, like you did last time? I like him. He's nice and friendly."
Ron continued to talk about how he had been sick and had to stay in the house and take medicine. "Do Carl stay in?" he asked. I said, "Yes." Then Ron said, "Do Carl take medicine when he don't feel good?" I said, "Yes." Ron said, "I am going home now. When you come back, bring Carl 'cause I like him. My Mommy said I could keep him as my friend. Good-bye."

We can see here the respect that three-and-a-half-year-old Ron had for six-year-old Carl. He was proud to have an older companion and had even asked his mother if he could "keep him as my friend" like some prize possession!

It is usual to see three-year-olds following older children around, sometimes taking directions from them and often imitating what they are doing. In the following observation, Debbie, age three, was at the park with other children. She was observed relating to them in the following ways:

1. Debbie crawled into the blimp, a large piece of fiberglass equipment in the playground. When she saw some teen-age girls rough-housing in it, she quickly climbed out.
2. She ran to the slide, where the observer's daughter, age five, was playing. When the observer's daughter hitched up her shorts, Debbie also pulled up her shorts.
3. She then ran to the merry-go-round. When her older sister came over and tried to push, Debbie said, "Don't do it, I do it."
4. Debbie then ran over to the maze where she found a boy her own age playing. She announced (to no one in particular) that she was going to play with her friend. She followed him into the maze, pushing him through the holes to reach a higher level. The two children poked

their heads through adjacent holes and began to play peek-a-boo. Debbie then took the boy's hand and said, "See my friend."

5. Debbie found a little girl about two years old. She took the little girl's hand, and, in a motherly tone, said, "Let's go, honey." She followed the younger girl and climbed back into the blimp. The two played alongside each other, not talking but enjoying each other's company.

Much of the social behavior of three-year-olds is revealed here. Debbie shies away from play with much older girls, but she imitates another older child as she pulls up her shorts in a similar manner. She asserts her independence when she refuses her sister's help on the merry-go-round. She is pleased when she finds a friend her own age and shows him off like a proud possession. She treats a younger child much as an adult would, being protective and somewhat patronizing toward her. She then engages in parallel play with the younger child.

A great deal is being learned about social encounters at this age. Children are practicing what they observe their elders doing. They imitate the adults they see performing social roles. They play next to each other and enjoy the companionship of their peers. Often they become involved with the play of older children and take direction from them willingly in order to be part of the group. They are proud to have a friend, especially if that child is somewhat older than they are.

But individual differences become more evident as children begin to play together in groups. The roles of leader and follower are more likely to be dependent upon the nature of the child than upon his age. Three-year-old Marty, who was the teaser of the student observer's dog in Chapter 4, was playing with four-year-old Angela. From the beginning, Marty seemed to dominate the situation, as the following conversation reveals.

Both children are seated at the piano, pounding on the keys.

MARTY: Angela, 'member what I told you. You can't play when I am playing.
ANGELA: I know. (Removes hand from the keyboard. Watches for a few seconds, then joins in again.)
MARTY: It ain't your turn.
ANGELA: I know. I just want to play.
MARTY: But you got a little one. (Meaning a toy piano that Angela has at home.)
ANGELA: Uh-huh, but they put it up because I broke it. (Parents are referred to as an omnipotent "they.")
MARTY: (Hits Angela's arm.) Stop it. (Hits keys with palm of hand. Puts elbows on keys. Angela copies actions.)
ANGELA: Let's sing a momma song.
MARTY: Be quiet. Be quiet.

Although a year younger, Marty seems to dominate in the play situation. Even when Angela tries to take the initiative, Marty does not follow her lead. Angela generally complies with Marty's instructions.

As children begin to interact with each other, the nature of their unique personalities becomes more evident. The question of leadership in group play comes into greater focus as we examine the behavior of four-year-olds.

Four-year-olds

There is quite a contrast in the group-play patterns of four-year-olds as compared to three- or two-year-olds.

ACTIVITY 3
Visit a playground and observe the differences in the types of play of children of different ages. Record some of the conversations you overhear.
When you return to class, sort out the incidents and conversations recorded by age level. What differences do you note among the play activity of two-, three-, four-, and five-year-olds?

At a nearby day-care center students in a child-development class were able to observe mixed age groups of children of black, low-income families playing together in the play yard. It was not difficult for the student observers to distinguish the two- and three-year-olds from the four-year-olds. Here are some of their observations.

1. The two-year-olds were sitting on the ground, near each other, playing silently with blocks and toys.
2. Three- and four-year-olds were climbing jungle gyms and coming down the slide. They made some noises but apparently were not talking to each other. Remarks were occasionally addressed to a teacher standing nearby.
3. Two four-year-old girls were playing pat-a-cake.
4. A group of four-year-olds, about fifteen children, were on the merry-go-round. They were talking to each other. No one wanted to get off to push. Finally two boys got off, pushed a few times, and jumped back on. The children then pretended that they were going to the beach.
5. Three four-year-olds and one five-year-old were crawling through the sewer pipe. One four-year-old began calling the five-year-old a "dumb bunny," and the five-year-old responded with more name calling.
6. A four-year-old was building a wall of sand with a five-year-old. Another four-year-old knocked it down. This action was repeated several times. Soon the five-year-old left; the four-year-old who was knocking down the sand wall now began to help the other four-year-old to build it. The five-year-old then returned to build and took the shovel from the boy with whom he had previously been building. The four-year-old said, "Give me that, boy" but continued to work without it. The five-year-old joined in building, using the shovel formerly possessed by the four-year-old.
7. A group of three-, four-, and five-year-olds was trying to get berries

to fall from a tree. A four-year-old yelled, "Gimme a rock!" A three-year-old extended a rock to him but was ignored.

The play patterns of four-year-olds are quite clearly defined in these observations. Unlike the two-year-olds, who played contentedly by themselves, or the three- and some four-year-olds, who sought the attention of an adult while climbing and sliding, most four-year-olds seemed to initiate their own activity and were busy interacting with each other. It appeared that they had developed friendships, perhaps based upon age grouping, and these small groups related to each other and ignored the intrusion of others. The four-year-old in the tree did not accept the rock offered to him by a three-year-old, even though he had just asked for a rock. The four-year-old who had destroyed the sand wall became more cooperative when the five-year-old left. The five-year-old was in control again, when he returned and took the shovel from the four-year-old he had been playing with.

Four-year-olds seem to be very concerned with positions of leadership in a group. They tend to challenge each other with name calling; they seek to get recognition from peers by giving orders; and they brag freely about their accomplishments. They have entered a competitive world of play, and their social behavior seems to be dominated by their need for self-assertion.

Self-assertion

Patterns of self-assertion are evident in the home environment as well as in group play. The three-year-old who seemed so anxious to please adults may become a four-year-old who is much more concerned with making his own demands and asserting his own will.

Four-year-old Tommy was observed in a restaurant, where he had come with his mother, older brother, and another family.

TIME	OVERT BEHAVIOR	COMMENTS
4:24	When asked by his mother what he wants, he snaps, "I want ice cream" and points to the woman at the counter.	His choice did not take much thought!
4:26	Waitress brings a menu and he yells, "Me, Me" and grabs it from his brother.	Seems to be ignored by all in his party.
4:31	He grabs the spoon, curling his fingers around it and shoves it into his mouth. As he raises the spoon to his mouth, his hand falters and the ice cream spills onto the table.	Still seems unruffled and unaware of those around him.
4:32	He puts his spoon down and stares at the mess. Lifts his napkin and very carefully wipes the table clean.	He can perform careful operations.

TIME	OVERT BEHAVIOR	COMMENTS
4:33	Then he stops and looks around the room again, lifts napkin to his face, and licks the ice cream from it, smiling all of the while.	He seems to carry this out almost devilishly, glaring around the room and smirking.

We might consider this the behavior of a naughty child, but this same child, a few months earlier, might have been very polite and amenable. At four, the child seems less concerned with pleasing adults and more interested in pleasing himself! He even enjoys a little mischief, since he knows very well that licking the napkin is not approved behavior. That he is capable of performing tasks with care is demonstrated by the manner in which he wipes up the table.

Four-year-olds are less likely than three-year-olds to perform routine tasks with precision. The behavior of four-year-old Roderick, while washing up, is quite different from the careful seriousness of three-year-old Larry, whom we previously observed while he was brushing his teeth. "Roderick went inside to eat dinner. He rushed to the bathroom, wet his hands, but didn't dry them. His mother asked him to go and do it the right way, and he did."

Roderick does not always take suggestion readily. When his older brother tried to show him the correct way to catch a football, Roderick insisted that his way was right. Four-year-olds need to be reminded often to complete tasks they have started and can be quite exasperating for parents to deal with.

A student observer recorded the behavior of David, age four, playing with play-dough with his younger friend, Joseph, age three. As the play-dough was divided, David complained that "You gave Joseph more!" David left the activity to watch television, and when he returned, he accused Joseph, saying, "Joseph stole my play-dough. Where's my play-dough?" He kicked Joseph as he climbed into a chair, but said he "didn't mean to do that." When it was time to leave, David was reminded to clean up the mess. He did so but threw his ball of play-dough down on the paper. When told that he hadn't finished cleaning up, he said that he did. He left, saying "Good-bye," not closing the door.

Aggressiveness and activity seem to be a part of being four. Doors are either left open or are slammed shut. Running and bouncing on furniture seem to be natural to them. Reminders to clean up or to sit still may be heeded, but an aggressive act often follows compliance with an adult suggestion. Aggression toward younger children, especially siblings, is common at this age.

Sibling rivalry

If self-assertion is evident in the group play of four-year-olds, it is equally obvious in family settings. The four-year-old wants to make sure that he is getting his share and is quick to challenge the judgment of adults who may seem to him to be favoring the younger child. Four-year-olds are often heard to exclaim, "Mine's better!" or "I have more," whether these remarks are addressed to a friend or a younger sibling.

When company comes, the four-year-old is likely to put on a show, making sure that he gets at least as much attention as his sister or brother. But four-year-olds know the rules of good behavior, and sometimes they use this information to show off how nicely they can act toward the baby. Shelley was observed as she greeted visitors who had brought presents for her and her younger sister Lynn.

TIME	OVERT BEHAVIOR	COMMENTS
7:30	Opens door and says, "Hello."	Shelley looked puzzled when she saw us but soon became more lively as we gave her the gifts.
7:33	Screams and smiles, "Look, Lynn, we got presents!" as she runs to the living room to her sister.	
7:35	Gives one package to sister, placing it on high chair table. Asks, "May I open mine?"	
7:37	Grabs package and begins to tear it apart, at first carefully, then rapidly, throwing wrappings to floor.	Eagerness wins out over composure.
7:39	After the excitement of discovering a toy she wanted, she suddenly lifts her head, widens her eyes, and says, "Let's help Lynn. Can I open her present?" She runs over to Lynn and carefully opens the package, taking care not to rip the paper.	Shelley seems really sincere in wanting to help her sister. She is aware, however, of everyone watching her.
7:40	She shows Lynn the puzzle and demonstrates how to place the pieces. Then she drops it over the tray and shows her again.	Shelley displays an extraordinary amount of patience while playing with her sister.

Shelley gave a very convincing performance of being the loving older sister. The exaggerated kindness, and the care with which she opened the package and demonstrated how to work the puzzle gives us the impression of premeditation, however. Shelley was also keenly aware that she was being watched, and she knew that everyone was thinking what a good girl she was!

Four-year-olds are very often protective of their younger siblings. In some large families four-year-olds are responsible for care of younger children. They often do a fine job, treating the younger child much as they might treat their dolls in dramatic play. But such care and concern may not be consistent. Playing with dolls is only one interest of four-year-olds, and other activities might distract them. The baby being cared for might then be resented.

A four-year-old was observed returning from a day-care center with her younger sister. She carefully helped the younger child down from the bus. But when her mother picked up the baby, the four-year-old "extended her hands upward for her mother to pick her up also."

Younger siblings are often used as scapegoats for the four-year-old's own transgressions. When Susan spilled some glue, she ran to her mother, claiming that "Brother did it." But later, when her brother let out a scream from his room, Susan ran immediately to "Go and help him." As she was performing for company, dancing to some music, her brother made an unexpected entrance. Perhaps because she anticipated an interruption of the attention focused upon her, Susan announced, "Ladies and gentlemen, brother will do a dance on the green rug."

ᐧWe can see evidence of mixed emotions toward younger siblings. The four-year-old may show resentment and jealousy one minute and be loving and protective the next. It is quite possible that all of these emotions are sincere at the time that they occur. Fours are very volatile, and their moods shift easily from one state to another.

ACTIVITY 4
Can you think of an incident within your recent experience, when you had ambivalent feelings toward another person? Perhaps your sister won an award, and you felt both proud of her and envious also. Perhaps you resented your parents' intrusion into your affairs and yet were pleased about their concern for you. Describe some of these incidents to other members of your class. Role-play some of the situations.

Skill development

Four-year-olds enjoy accomplishments of all kinds. On the playground they can be seen climbing to the top of the jungle gym, and shouting, "Look where I am!" Their ecstatic expressions seem to indicate that they feel they have conquered the world!

The four-year-old runs with great agility and spends much of his time moving in highly active ways. Often he has learned to skip, although, in many cases, this does not happen before he is five. He can hop on one foot. He can walk on a walking board. He can push himself on the swing, or he can play on the seesaw.

He finds pleasure in feats of fine coordination as well. He can button his clothing, and he can pull up zippers. He can do simple puzzles, and he can put pegs into a pegboard. In his drawing he can make representative pictures of people and of things.

His skills are demonstrated, perhaps most clearly, by the way in which he handles blocks. Twos handle blocks with random activity; threes will build towers, knock them down, and then rebuild them; fours will build tunnels and bridges with the blocks and then use these in dramatic and social play. Here is a conversation between two four-year-old boys in the block-corner of a nursery school.

JOHN: Take this.

PETER: No, that truck is mine. Let's make a bridge.

JOHN: Let's make a highway with a bridge.

PETER: What do you think you are doing?

JOHN: I'm tearing down your highway. . . . Let's build a bridge. . . . Look at this bridge you can go under.

We can see in this dialogue the way in which fours play together, using the same materials but not always operating on the same wave length! The boys were working together quite well, handing blocks to each other to complete the construction. Their conversation, however, indicated some competition for leadership and possessiveness about the ownership of the truck.

Some of the structures that fours build, cooperatively or individually, are quite complex and ingenious. They can figure out exactly which size block will balance the structure or will accommodate the weight of the next block. Some four-year-olds exhibit such skill that they appear to be budding engineers.

Four-year-olds use every kind of available material in competitive games. Some were observed on the playground throwing sticks. Jimmy said he could "beat them all!" He experimented, using sticks of different sizes and weights to see which would go the farthest. The sticks were then hit against the monkey bars to see which ones would break. Jimmy decided that the thicker, dryer sticks were easier to break than the thin, greener ones. When one of the boys climbing on the monkey bars asked him to stop shaking the bars, Jimmy said he would "shake them softly."

Blocks and sticks and rocks and shells all make excellent materials for experimentation. Fours are young scientists, using every available resource for finding out more about their world.

Imagination is helpful in this exploration as well as in manipulation of materials. The block corner is often the scene for some lively dramatization, as blocks are built into rocket ships, racing cars, or gasoline stations. Boys role-play the exciting events that they see or hear about in the real world, and thus they come to understand them a little better.

Another area for dramatic play is, of course, the housekeeping area in the nursery school. Three-year-olds enjoy imitating mother washing the dishes or setting the table. By four this kind of activity has taken on social dimensions, as children interact with each other. Here is a typical conversation.

RUTH: Let's be dressed up!

ELIZABETH: No, it's not time yet. I am just about to make the breakfast. I'll put this on the table (sets out the coffee pot).

RUTH: See? The mothers put things on like this, don't they, Gail? (Addressed to a little girl standing nearby. Gail makes no response, but stands and stares. Eugene is busy opening and closing the oven.)

RUTH: There are four people in this house (counting out plates and spoons).

EUGENE: One, two, three, four.

Again, as in the block-play conversation, we can see that the communication is fragmentary. But the children are aware of each other, and roles of leaders and followers are beginning to emerge. Ruth takes over from Elizabeth and tries to involve the onlooker, Gail. Eugene becomes attracted to the group at the mention of numbers.

Social skills are involved in this activity, but also language and number concepts are being developed. Play situations provide many opportunities for learning for four-year-olds.

Imagination runs strong in the dramatic play of fours. Roles are easily reversed, and "the baby" may jump out of the cradle and decide that he is the "daddy" and is "going off to work." Dolls and stuffed animals are invited to the "tea party." One four-year-old invited the student observer's dog to have lunch with her!

Dressing up in adult clothing is a favorite activity. Susan got dressed up in a pair of fishnet stockings and high-heel shoes. She tied a diaper to her head and called it her "pretend hair." She paraded around the room, singing nonchalantly, with a crayon in her fingers as if it were a cigarette!

We cannot neglect the area of children's paintings, because it is here that some four-year-olds show remarkable talents.

ACTIVITY 5
The class might collect a series of paintings done by nursery-school children. Examine the paintings to note the use of color and space. When representational pictures are included, what ideas are expressed? What is the most important part of the picture to the child who made it? What concepts is the child dealing with?

When the painting was done by a child whom a student has observed, the student should tell the child-development class about that child. How does the painting reflect his level of development or his emotional concerns?

The use of color and space on some free-form paintings may resemble the efforts of modern artists. We may wonder if these artistic endeavors are purely a matter of chance, but some children consistently produce beautiful paintings. There seems to be an instinctive sense of design in young children, and, if given the opportunity, it will show itself in their artwork. Rhythm is also an inherent quality of young children. This, too, may account for some of their success in this area. Here, Peter and Jill are talking as they paint.

PETER: We're just making colors and colors and colors.
JILL: Look what I'm making . . . pit, pat, pit.
PETER: I'm going back and forth and up and down.
JILL: See what I do . . . I jump and paint. . . .

Peter and Jill are enjoying the painting as a motor experience. The rhythm of their motion with the brush is reflected in the rhythm of their talk: "pit, pat, pit," "back and forth and up and down," "I jump and paint." The color enhances the experience. They are very proud of what they have made. It is as if a part of themselves is reflected in the painting. (See the nursery-school teacher's story of "Herbie" in Chapter 3.)

Language and concept formation

Language development is closely related to the development of logical thought. As children learn the names for things, they begin to be able to classify them. As language develops, children begin to make associations between past and present experiences. The four-year-old might proclaim that a stranger "must be a nurse, because she is wearing white shoes." This linking together of experience often leads to amusing errors of judgment, but the child is testing out his ideas. His assumptions are logical based upon his limited experience, and they should be taken seriously by adults.

Kenneth Wann and his associates recorded the conversations of preschool children in three different settings. They visited an upper-class, middle-class, and lower-class nursery or day-care center and then analyzed their findings to see what children were thinking about and what thought processes were in operation. "We have evidence that children were associating ideas; they were trying to see likenesses and differences in things and events; they were working on cause and effect relationships; and they were drawing conclusions and generalizing about their activities."[4]

ACTIVITY 6

Make a collection of the amusing sayings of four-year-olds. Report on these in class. What concepts is the child grappling with? Is he associating past experiences with a new experience? Is he making a generalization, or placing things in categories? Is he sensing likenesses and differences?

Many verbal expressions of four-year-olds reflect the development of logical processes. Students should be able to identify these and should learn to listen seriously to these profound but sometimes amusing statements.

The following time sample of Lori, observed in the veranda-type hallway of a middle-class Miami apartment house by a student, reveals many of the characteristics of language development and concept formation that are typical of four-year-olds.

TIME	OVERT BEHAVIOR	COMMENTS
1:21	When Lori sees me coming up the stairs, she calls out my name. I ask her how she is feeling because her mother told me that she was sick yesterday. She answers that she "has a headache." I ask her where it hurts. Putting her hand on her stomach, she says, "Here!"	COMMENTS She probably has heard her mother say that she had a headache but does not know what it is or where it should hurt.
1:23	She runs back to where I am standing and tells a little boy who is looking for his mother, "Your mother is in here, dum-dum."	Confident and superior manner with other child.

[4] Kenneth Wann *et al., Fostering Intellectual Development in Young Children,* p. 28.

TIME	OVERT BEHAVIOR	COMMENTS
1:24	She asks me, "Who drived you here?" I tell her my friend brought me. She asks if my friend "drived me here yesterday." I say, "No," and she asks me, "Where is your car?" I tell her it is at school. She asks, "Are you going to leave it there?" I tell her I am going to get it when we leave.	Lori is definitely at the question-asking stage. She wants to know the why, how, and what of everything! When she says "yesterday," she refers to the time I was here two weeks ago.
1:25	She mentions that my girl friend and I "are both wearing the same pants."	She is very observant. We both are wearing dungarees.
1:26	Her girl friend walks by and Lori grabs her and hugs her.	Lori is affectionate and demonstrative.
1:27	She sees her friends going into an apartment down the hall, and she says, "All my friends are going down there." I ask her to stay with me for a while, and she says, "O.K."	She wants to follow her friends but is willing to do what I ask and stay a while longer.
1:28	She hears an airplane and looks up and sees two planes. She says, "They are following each other!" I ask her where she thinks they are going. She answers, "They are going to New York." She continues "When I was on a plane, the stewardess told me that we were going to New York." She says that planes go to Georgia, Forest Hills, "where I used to live," and, searching for the right word, "other states in Florida."	She speaks of airplanes from her own experience. She has flown to New York from Miami with her parents. Obviously these are places that are familiar to her. She has heard of states but does not distinguish them from cities.
1:29	She asks us, "Why did you bring an umbrella?" I tell her we don't want to get wet. I ask if she likes to be wet. She makes a face and says, "No! My feet get shriveled up in the rain!" She picks up her feet and shows me her toes, "When I get out of the bath, my feet and my fingers get shriveled up."	She is very curious and is discovering many things. She is aware that water will make her skin wrinkled.
1:30	I ask how old she is, and she answers, "My birthday just passed and in ten weeks I'll be four and a half."	Knows terminology for time, but concepts not clear. Actually, Lori is four years and one month at this time.
1:31	She walks up to a little boy, puts her hands on her hips, sticks out her stomach, and asks what his name is. She then tells us she knows all of her friends' names and "Rusty" is her "boy friend."	She is being coy. She does know this boy's name. She is aware of male-female relationships.
1:32	A woman standing in her doorway asks	She enjoys conversation with adults

TIME	OVERT BEHAVIOR	COMMENTS
	her how she is feeling. She answers, "I took my medicine. I laid down on the couch and now I'm all better."	and is quite polite. But she is anxious to be with her friends. She asks permission before she leaves.
1:33	She asks if she may join her friends at one of their apartments. I tell her, yes, and she leaves, skipping down the hall. She turns, looks back, waves, and says, "Bye!"	

This time sample really gives us the opportunity to get to know Lori quite well and to see many of the characteristics of four-year-olds that we have been discussing in this section. We are amazed by her physical energy and by the agility of her mind. It is hard for her to sit still. She runs and skips back and forth, swinging her arms in well-coordinated movements. Her coy posturing with the little boy is an imitation of adult behavior. Her facial expressions and gestures are lively as she talks.

But it is her conversation that is most intriguing. She asks many questions and is curious about the student observer. She wants to know how she got there, why she brought an umbrella, who her friend is, where she left her car, and so on. She is most observant and notices that the observer is wearing pants like her friend. She notices airplanes flying by. Very little escapes the attention of an alert four-year-old!

Her concepts of time and place are not yet clear, but her conversation reveals that she is thinking about these things and is beginning to figure them out. She refers to the observer's last visit as "yesterday," which is the way many four-year-olds refer to any event that is in the past. She uses time concepts in telling her age, although she is not accurate about this either. She knows the names of places that are familiar to her, and she even knows that a state is a term for a place. It would be too much to expect her to know that Forest Hills is not a state!

She has other misconceptions, such as where a headache is located. Her language is highly developed, but she uses some incorrect forms of the past tense, such as "bringed" and "drived." These errors actually reflect the logic that is inherent in the speech of four-year-olds. They have learned the rule of grammar, that adding an "ed" sound to the end of a verb makes it refer to action that has passed. If our language does not always comply with this logic, it is not the fault of four-year-old thinking!

Logic is also exhibited in the association of the student's visit with the last time she was there, when she came to observe Lori's younger sister. She noticed, also, that the airplanes were "following each other." Perhaps her sharpest observation, and her most descriptive use of language, was when she associated the effect of rain with the way her feet and fingers "get shriveled up" after she takes a bath. This observation was based upon a series of experiences which Lori was able to put together in her own mind.

Children, like scientists, collect information based upon their own experiences and then apply this information to develop hypotheses about physical causality. Lori's deduction about the effects of water upon the skin of her hands and feet is an illustration of the logical process of association, and is another example of the remarkable discoveries that four-year-olds are capable of.

Four-year-olds have been called "frustrating" by adults because of their hyperactivity and their assertiveness. But they are equally fascinating. An observation of a child like Lori reveals the intricate thought processes in operation at this stage. If we consider the limitation of experience of the four-year-old, his observations and his logical deductions can be a source of constant amazement to adults. Not all four-year-olds are geniuses, but if we can penetrate their world, if we can gain their perspective, then we can see intellect in action. Children with fewer advantages than Lori also make active use of their experiences to figure things out at this stage. It is for this reason that it is so very important to enrich the experiences of four-year-olds, to give them opportunities for verbal and artistic expression, and to provide a receptive atmosphere for their discoveries and their self-expression.

Five-year-olds

If four seems to be a period of self-assertion and discovery, then, by contrast, five is a more stable, leveling-off time in a child's life. The five-year-old seems to have a better understanding of his world, and has, to some extent, found his own place in it. He is willing to accept rules of behavior and will conform to a group much more readily than he did at four. Five-year-old Bobby told a student observer who was baby-sitting with him that "You can't talk loud when people are reading." And, a little later, he told her that, "I play with John a lot, but when I pinch him, he won't play with me." Bobby has begun to realize the consequences of antisocial behavior and has accepted them as reasonable.

Most five-year-olds are willing to take turns and can wait in line in an orderly fashion. When a child is not ready to accept the rules, the other children may be critical of him. Cherie, a little girl with some emotional problems, rushed over to the door to be first in line when her kindergarten class was dismissed. The teacher explained that it was "not her turn to be first," and Cherie began to cry. The other children called her a baby.

But, generally speaking, the five-year-old is a self-contained and independent individual. He can leave the home setting without difficulty, and he enjoys the companionship of his peers. He has learned to take care of himself in dressing, feeding, and toileting. He is reasonable, and often tactful and polite, in his dealings with others.

Language and reasoning

The language patterns of the five-year-old have matured considerably since he was four. He speaks in sentences and uses adult grammatical structures. He uses all types of sentences including those with conditional clauses. He is familiar with adult idioms and is less likely to take their meaning literally.

Conversation in dramatic play is likely to be more communicative than it was previously, although a certain amount of collective dialogue is still heard. Language is used to express ideas and feelings, and the five-year-old is less reliant upon facial expression and physical gesture to convey meanings.

Once language has developed sufficiently, it may be used to inhibit physical aggression. Kindergarten teachers encourage the child to "stop fighting, and tell Johnny what is making you angry." This often works in limiting the use of punching and slapping, but language, itself, may become a form of aggression. Five-year-olds, especially little girls, are frequently observed using name calling in social interaction. Language and reasoning is sometimes used to exclude a child from a group. In the following dialogue, Ronnie, a newcomer to the playground, is trying very hard to be included.

RONNIE: Can I play?
TOM: No.
RONNIE: Why?
TOM: The toys aren't yours.
RONNIE: They aren't yours either; they are the school's.

Language has become a weapon to exclude Ronnie from the game. In a sense this is a more adult way of handling the situation than the fist-fighting of fours!

ACTIVITY 7
Have you ever experienced what it is like to be excluded from a group? Several members of the class might form a circle holding hands and standing fairly close to each other. A single class member is to stand outside of the circle. She is to try to break into it, while members of the circle try to keep her out. This exercise could be done either in pantomime or with dialogue. Have several students try to break into the circle and then let them discuss their feelings with the class.

The five-year-old asks fewer questions than four-year-olds, and his questions are more succinct. He seems to be more interested in obtaining information, rather than experimenting with language or trying out his own ideas. Questions are concerned with "What is this for?" or "How does this work?" The five-year-old has learned that most events in this world are caused by something. When he asks questions it is to find out about causes and effects.

At this time many children begin to wonder about their own origin. If everything has a cause, and one can find out how things are made, then it is logical to question how "I" came into being and "Where did I come from?" Even parents who give the most reasonable and truthful explanations of the beginnings of life find that the child cannot always accept the answer. Fraiberg gives an example of five-year-old Sally who asked: " 'Where was I before I was born?' 'Don't you remember?' says Mama. 'I told you.' 'Oh, I don't mean that!' says Sally crossly. 'I mean *before* I grew inside of you.' 'Well,' says

Mama lamely, 'you were a tiny, tiny egg.' 'I don't mean *that*. I mean *before* I was a tiny, tiny egg.' 'Well, you were —well, you see, you were nothing.' 'Nothing!' Sally is horrified. 'How could I be *nothing*!' "[5]

The miraculous process of procreation does not seem reasonable to a five-year-old. He has just arrived at a point where he has become aware of his own identity. He knows that he exists, as a being apart from other human beings. How, then, can he accept an explanation that says that he did not always exist?

The five-year-old is a realist. He wants to see proof before he believes. It is little wonder, therefore, that stories describing the sexual act in terms of "the birds and the bees" sound to him like fantasy and fairy tales, which he has, just recently, begun to identify as outside the realm of reality.

The realistic quality of five-year-olds is exhibited in their play activity. They act out roles but are more likely to interpret adults behavior accurately as they play. A five-year-old was overheard saying to his companion, as they were playing in the block corner, "That's not the way to lay those bricks! You have to mix up the cement first!"

Because of their reality-based approach to play, activities in kindergarten can be introduced that expand a child's understanding of the real world. While playing store the five-year-old can learn about job differentiation, about producers and consumers, and about supply and demand. It is not too early to introduce children to economic concepts, if these ideas are introduced by means of play activity. Fives are very interested in how society functions, and there are many opportunities when dramatic play can be used to enhance concept development.[6]

In spite of his sophistication in language and seeming understanding of reality the five-year-old's thinking is often confused. Here is a conversation between a mother and a son that a student observer recorded.

Richard wanted money for a new toy. "We can't buy the toy," said his mother. "We don't have enough money."

"But you can get some," said Richard. "You can go to the store and get some."

"We don't get money at the store, Richard. We have to give the man money."

"But he gives you lots and lots. I seen him," said Richard.

In Richard's eyes, the man in the store gave money to his mother. When she handed him a bill and got back change, the coins seemed more valuable to the five-year-old; therefore, it seemed logical to think that mother could get money from the store!

As can be seen, the relationship of cause and effect is sometimes peculiarly twisted within the minds of five-year-olds! When Michael bragged that he had

---

[5] Fraiberg, *The Magic Years*, p. 196.

[6] For example of how this can be done, see Helen Robison and Bernard Spodek, *New Directions in the Kindergarten*.

lost his tooth and was going to put it under his pillow for money, his friend, Bobby, reasoned that Michael had lost his tooth because he had dark hair. When asked how he knew this, he said he "just figured it out." Bobby's cousin, who was the same age, had dark hair and had lost a tooth. Bobby thought that when his hair, which was blond, turned dark, then he too would lose a tooth!

Skill development

At five, most children are very proud of their developing skills. Many can handle scissors and paste very well and can make scrapbooks, cutting pictures from magazines. They can do puzzles and can discriminate sizes and shapes. Their awareness of number relationships has developed considerably. While four-year-olds may be able to count, fives can usually establish a one-to-one relationship in counting as high as ten. Even counting backward becomes a task accomplished. Five-year-olds may imitate men in space as they count, "10-9-8-7-6-5-4-3-2-1-blast off!"

Many five-year-olds can write their name, and most are interested in the writing process. Student observers were often questioned about their writing when they did their observations.

Although five-year-olds show a lively interest in writing and in developing other academic skills, they are frequently not ready for a formalized program in these areas. Many kindergartens today emphasize reading and writing skills, owing, in part, to the pressure for achievement that pervades the schools in these times. Because five-year-olds are willing to conform and are interested in developing skills, schools often take advantage of these characteristics and subject them to various kinds of intense instruction.

ACTIVITY 8
Visit a kindergarten during an instructional period and observe the behavior of a five-year-old child during a formal lesson. Compare this observation to the description of Jeff, given below.

But although the five-year-old may be quite mature in many ways, he is far from grown-up in others. Lengthy periods of sedentary activity bore him. Here is a description of a typical five-year-old, as he sits in a group circle during a discussion about the calendar.

While sitting cross legged at the calendar, Jeff is pulling on his right sock with his hands, not seeming to pay any attention to the teacher. He does not respond to questions about the calendar. He yawns and blinks several times while he continues playing with his sock. He rubs his eyes with both hands.

Jeff chews on his nails while he puts the other fingers on his nose. He then bites his thumb and moves so that he is sitting on one hand. He stretches out his arms and holds his hands above his head. He sits on the edge of his seat and looks at the faces of other children. He makes a series of facial expressions—frowns, smiles, and contortions—while listening to some of the discussion.

Jeff is doing nothing to call special attention to himself. He is not a trouble maker, but it is obvious that he is not getting very much out of the discussion. The observer comments that some of his facial expressions show that "he latches onto a few words of what is going on." But he does not participate, even though he may understand. He seems much too uncomfortable and restless after prolonged sitting to be very much concerned with learning anything. When the group is finally dismissed, he "gets up, whistles, and swings his arms freely as he moves toward the block corner."

Jeff is not an unusually restless child. His behavior is common to many five-year-olds, and student observers frequently describe similar actions while watching children in kindergarten. There is a need for motor activity, and loss of interest is likely to occur when young children are required to remain still for very long. Notice the difference when these same children are on the playground. When they are moving, their faces are animated; their whole bodies are awake and full of life.

Learning can take place while children are actively involved. Children can act out stories; they can learn about numbers while moving to rhythms; they can dramatize things they have observed in nature.[7] A five-year-old asked a student observer, "Want to see how an inchworm crawls? It goes like this." And he proceeded to demonstrate on his hands and knees. Kindergarten children are observant, and, if given the chance, will use movement to express what they have observed.

The following observations were recorded by a group of student observers at an academically oriented kindergarten class in one morning.

1. The children were given dot-to-dot paper to work with at their seats, while the teacher worked with a small group. Dianne said, "Oh, no, not writing!"
2. Tommy picked the toy duck from the tray of objects, but, incorrectly, pointed to the letter *b* as the beginning sound of the word *duck*. After he took the toy duck to his seat, he played with it instead of paying attention to the beginning sounds of other objects being displayed.
3. Mark began to read very slowly. He looked around to see the other children—where they were sitting, and what they were doing.
4. As she looked at the book, Sally looked around, at first chewing on her nails, then wiggling and pulling at her clothing.
5. Hazel said she "doesn't like to read." It makes her "real tired."

If teachers are sensitive to children, if they are capable of picking up clues and interpreting body expression, then they will know when a program such as this one is not reaching many of the children in their class. Unfortunately, teachers are often so concerned with the body of knowledge they wish to impart that they do not take the time to observe children and to learn from their observations.

[7] Betty Rowen, *Learning through Movement.*

Two school beginners

Experience becomes an increasingly important determinant of behavior as the child progresses from infancy to school age. If children have not played together, they do not begin their play by realistically dramatizing events they have observed. Children who have not been exposed to many language experiences do not have use of complete language forms at five. The experiential background of the child has a great deal to do with how he will function as he enters a kindergarten program.

ACTIVITY 9

Visit two kindergarten classrooms in differing socioeconomic settings. Are the children you observe there operating at the same level of development? What are the differences?

Make a chart comparing the behavior of two children you have observed, one from each of these differing settings. If you prefer, you might chart the differences of the two children, Dinah and Jane, reported below.

Dinah and Jane are two little girls who were observed on their first day of attendance at a summer kindergarten program. All of the other children in the group had been in a school situation throughout the school year. These two girls were to enter school in the fall but were permitted to attend the summer session because they each had brothers who were in the group.

Here is a description of Dinah on her first day at school.

When the children arrived, the teacher asked them to please be seated. Dinah sat at a table all alone until the teacher asked her if she wouldn't like to sit with her brother. She nodded her head, yes, and moved near to him.

After the opening exercises the children were asked to draw a picture of their family on manila folders. Dinah made circle faces for the people. Some of the people had hair. They were drawn in this order: mommy, sister, brother, brother, brother, brother, dog (Butch), and dog (Lulu May). She drew legs on the baby sister. She concentrated on the picture and picked at her fingernails. She looked at her brother's picture and smiled. She was very quiet and passive, although she did answer when I asked her the names of each person and the dog. She did not volunteer any additional information. It was difficult to understand her.

On the playground Dinah ran first to the jungle gym. She stayed for a minute and then ran to the spiral climbing apparatus. She ran there eagerly, but once there, she stood and watched. She put her hand in the top part of her dress and then sucked on her dress. She then walked away from the climbing bars without trying them.

Dinah walked slowly to the parallel bars. She climbed up and went across two bars before falling down. She got up smiling. Dinah then stood around watching. She put her hands to her mouth and went back to the jungle gym. She climbed to the top and stood there for a while before climbing down. All of this time, she hadn't said a word.

Now let us take a look at Jane's behavior on her first day of school.

Jane talked to her brother while drawing, "This is Mommy." She rummaged through the crayon box and said, "Is skin color in here? Skin color, skin color, skin color!" She had a discussion with her brother about the color of her father's eyes. Then she asked her brother and the observer, "Is it all right if you make a mistake?" When she was assured that it was O.K., she asked, "Are you sure?"

She showed her picture to her brother and told him who was in it. "Mom has short hair. John, does Mom have short hair? John, draw a beard because Dad has a beard." Then she announced that she was done. John reminded her about the dog and the fish, but Jane said, "I can't draw all that."

On the playground Jane ran to the climbing apparatus. Other children joined her, and a few boys began to climb on the same side Jane was on. She said, "The boys are on the girls' side." She climbed down and went to the other side where a few girls were climbing. As she reached the top, she looked around and announced, "I'm coming down."

Jane then went to another part of the playground where there were not any other children. She shouted, "John, look what I'm going on!" She ran to the new equipment, with arms swinging freely. "What do you do on this? Climb? Just do nothing on them?" She seemed to be talking to herself, as no one else was nearby.

Each of these little girls was making a rather good adjustment, considering the fact that they were new to a situation that was familiar to all of the other children. Dinah participated in the activities, although she did so silently. Some anxiety revealed itself in her picking at her fingernails and sucking part of her dress. She ran to the climbing apparatus on the playground but then stood and watched as other children climbed. She was bold enough to try the parallel bars, but fell. She took this cheerfully and smiled but did not return to the climbing activity.

Jane stayed close to her brother at the beginning of the session but talked to him all of the time. Her feelings of insecurity were verbalized when she asked, "Is it all right if you make a mistake? Are you sure?" She became restless and did not finish the picture, even when her brother suggested that she include the family pets. Again she verbalized her feelings, saying, "I can't draw all that." Outdoors, she seemed perfectly secure, running freely from one apparatus to another. She boldly announced that the boys were "on the girls' side" but then conceded and went to the other side herself to join other girls. She talked freely, even when there was no one around to answer her. Jane's verbal ability and her interest in language continued to reveal itself throughout the next few weeks. She "listened avidly" when stories were read to the class. She remembered details from the stories and could describe what she saw in pictures. At one point she was called upon by the teacher to explain what an igloo was. Even though the other children did not agree with her explanation, she stuck with it. She participated well in classroom games and was even asked to be a leader. On one occasion, she did not use the exact words that the children were used to, and the children teased her. She told them quietly, "I'm going here next year, and next year I'll be able to know." The poise with which she carried off her mistake was an indication of this child's self-acceptance.

Jane and Dinah were frequently observed together. When they were in the housekeeping corner, a favorite spot for both of them, they often played side-by-side, without conversing or interacting with each other. Occasionally Jane gave Dinah directions, and Dinah followed them without talking. Dinah was observed, at one time, talking on the toy telephone, but this lasted for only a few seconds. Dinah was very careful to put each object in the housekeeping corner in its correct place.

At one time Dinah was observed taking out an egg carton and breaking imaginary eggs into a pan. When the observer asked her what she was cooking, she replied, "Eggs." The observer asked, "Anything else?" and Dinah repeated, "Eggs."

The observer, who was doing a case study on Dinah, took her and two of her brothers to the zoo. There was little conversation among the children. Climbing on the railing together, the children occasionally made sounds to the animals and to each other, however. They were treated to souvenirs and promised to bring them to class for "show and tell," but they came without them the next day.

Although her use of language was very limited, Dinah is not a "dull" child. When asked questions, she answered correctly. She knew her colors, and she could also count accurately, establishing a one-to-one relationship as she did so. She could sing the A, B, C's. When asked where milk came from, she said, "from a cow," and she knew that you "had to pull on the cow to get the milk." She told the observer she knew about farms from watching television.

Her few comments while on the trip to the zoo were intelligent ones. She noticed that the flag outside the zoo was the same as the one in school. She was able to match the animals she was seeing in the cages to those pictured in a booklet she was given.

Her limited vocabulary was revealed, however, during a "touch-and-feel" game played at school. Each child was to reach into a bag, and tell what object they were feeling. Dinah said hers felt like "a watermelon." The teacher asked her to take out the object, which turned out to be a marshmallow. Dinah still called it a watermelon. The teacher told her what it was and told her she could eat it. It was, perhaps, her first experience with this candy.

Let us compare the experiential background of these two little girls. Dinah had never seen a marshmallow, but Jane knew all about "igloos." Dinah spoke very little, even with her own brothers. Jane talked frequently and expressed her feelings freely. There is no doubt that the child with verbal abilities will be more successful in the school situation.

When we examine the family structure and life-style of these two children, we understand more fully their differences in behavior. Dinah is one of eight children. Her mother works, doing cleaning on a part-time basis, sometimes during the day and sometimes at night. When she goes to work, the children take care of each other. The oldest is thirteen. The mother is proud of the academic achievements of her family. Four of her brothers are teachers.

Since she had been the eldest, she had missed out on an education, and she is, therefore, determined to have her children get good schooling.

The family lives in a small house. Dinah's father is a foreman of a building crew. He had paneled the walls in the living room of their home. Dinah did not include a drawing of her father in her family picture.

Dinah's mother has a mother in a nearby city who is very ill. Once a week she visits her mother and does her cleaning for her. She takes three children at a time on these visits. She told the interviewer that she would like to take her children places, but lack of time and money prevents her from doing it. She was very appreciative of the trip to the zoo planned by the student observer. When the interview was over, and the student observer prepared to leave, Dinah reached out with both arms to touch her. She was smiling, and the student observer felt the trip had been well worth while.

Jane's father is a surgeon, and her mother is a former teacher. She lives in a large, spacious home with a swimming pool. She has a brother who is only a year older than she, and they have a very good relationship. They have a dog, some fish, and, at the time of the interview, had just retrieved a stray bird that had fallen from its nest.

Jane's mother has a lively interest in her children. Jane sews with her mother, helps with cooking and cleaning, and loves to play at being a grown-up. Jane says she "wants to be a mommy" when she grows up. Jane's mother feels that Jane has very healthy attitudes, will try anything and will do the best she can, but will realize and accept her shortcomings. She feels that her daughter's strongest quality is "her ability to verbalize."

Jane and Dinah started school on the same day and will be in the same class the following term. They will perform the same activities, will handle the same materials, will be given the same books. Their reactions will be different, and it is little wonder. Both of these little girls are pleasant, attractive children. Both of them have exhibited a good deal of intelligence. One is strongly verbal and has had many enriching experiences. The other is a member of a large family with a working mother. There is little time for conversation with adults, and the life-style in this family does not include much talking, even as the children play together. This child's experiences, both of a first-hand and vicarious nature, have been limited.

School achievement is dependent to a large degree upon verbal abilities. Opportunities must be made to develop these abilities in children like Dinah. Her natural intelligence, which exhibits itself in the way she handles materials in play, must be given an opportunity for recognition in the school setting. Otherwise, her feelings of insecurity, which already are in evidence, will keep her from normal advancement in school learning.

If we look at children as individuals, examining their behavior and investigating their backgrounds, we cannot expect the same performance from all of them. School should be a rich and rewarding experience for both Jane and Dinah. Teachers must learn to know them and must find ways of reaching each of them in appropriate ways.

REFERENCES

BRECKENRIDGE, MARION, AND E. LEE VINCENT. *Child Development*. 4th ed. Philadelphia: W. B. Saunders Company, 1960.

FLAVELL, JOHN H. *The Developmental Psychology of Jean Piaget*. Princeton, N.J.: D. Van Nostrand Company, Inc., 1963.

FRAIBERG, SELMA H. *The Magic Years*. New York: Charles Scribner's Sons, 1959.

GESELL, ARNOLD *et al*. *The First Five Years of Life*. New York: Harper & Row, Publishers, 1940.

HARTLEY, RUTH, LAWRENCE FRANK, AND R. M. GOLDENSON. *Understanding Children's Play*. New York: Columbia University Press, 1952.

MURPHY, LOIS B. *Personality in Young Children*, vol. I. New York: Basic Books, Inc., 1956.

MUSSEN, PAUL HENRY, JOHN J. CONGER, AND JEROME KAGEN. *Child Development and Personality*. 2d ed. New York: Harper & Row, Publishers, 1963.

NAVARRA, JOHN G. *The Development of Scientific Concepts in a Young Child: A Case Study*. New York: Teachers College Press, Columbia University, 1955.

PIAGET, JEAN. *The Language and Thought of the Child*. New York: Harcourt Brace Jovanovich, Meridian Books, 1955.

READ, KATHERINE H. *The Nursery School: A Human Relations Laboratory*. 4th ed. Philadelphia: W. B. Saunders Company, 1966.

ROBISON, HELEN, AND BERNARD SPODEK. *New Directions in the Kindergarten*. New York: Teachers College Press, Columbia University, 1965.

ROWEN, BETTY. *Learning through Movement*. New York: Teachers College Press, Columbia University, 1963.

RUSSELL, DAVID. *Children's Thinking*. Boston: Ginn & Company, 1956.

WANN, KENNETH *et al*. *Fostering Intellectual Development in Young Children*. New York: Teachers College Press, Columbia University, 1962.

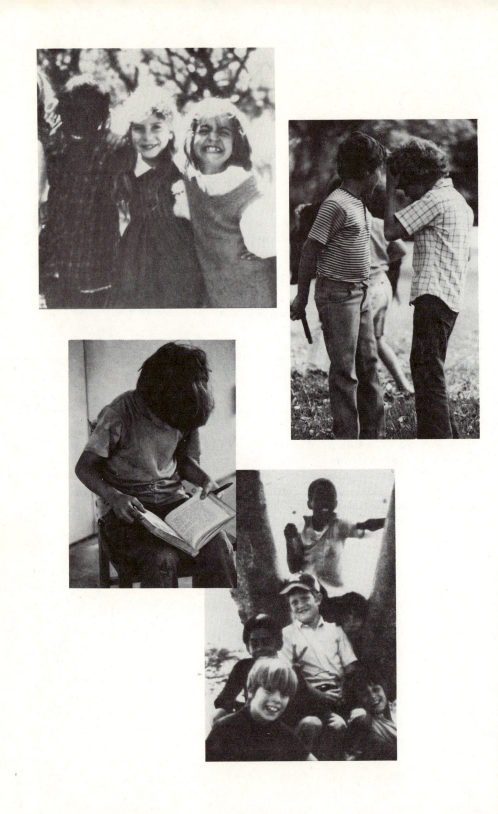

10

Knowing the school-age child

During the period from age six through age twelve, the child's life centers around his experiences within the school setting. We will call this the period of the "school-age child," referring, of course, to the years of elementary school attendance. Schooling usually begins before this time and certainly extends well beyond it. But at no time is school more significant in the child's development than during these years.

Adults seem to know less about the school-age child than about children at other levels. Parents can relate detailed stories of their experiences with toddlers and preschoolers, but, once their children pass their sixth year, adults seem to become less involved with them. There are many reasons for this. Children in this age range tend to form a society of their own. They enjoy and value the companionship of their peers. They share few of their inner thoughts with elders. They are capable and self-sufficient and demand less of their parents' time. Then, too, children show less dramatic change during this period. Personality traits are usually well-established and tend to persist throughout these years. Physical growth continues in an even progression, and skill development follows its natural course. The observed changes that take place cannot be compared to the huge differences that can be seen between infants and toddlers or between toddlers and kindergarten children.

Yet, the observant and concerned adult can learn a good deal about the school-age child. During this period children express themselves readily in language, and their memories are well-formulated. It is at this time that organized, sequential thoughts are replacing the piecemeal, episodic ones of the preschool child. If adults are asked to recall experiences from their own childhood, they will, most likely, recall an event that happened during these school years. Memory has been established, and the sequence and order of occurrences can be recalled, even many years after they happened.

Interviews with children can produce some meaningful insights. Children's writing often reveals much of their inner thoughts. Role-playing and dramatization are effective means of discovering more about the school-age child. The reader is reminded to review some of the findings in Chapter 5, where the author discusses the arts as a means for knowing the child. School-agers can be easily understood by the teacher, if she takes the time to explore the many avenues available to her.

The use of time samples may not prove as effective for viewing the school-age child as they were with younger children. After six, children do not reveal as much of themselves through gesture and movement as they did previously. As they get older, children learn to hide their feelings and to control their physical activity. Most of them are able to sit still for longer periods of time. Student observers found that ten minutes of observation often did not reveal any significant behavioral characteristics when they were watching children in the school setting. More time spent in observation was necessary before a revealing incident would occur.

Case histories done over a period of time might be more effective in studying children of this age group. Previous experiences play a significant part in determining attitudes and behaviors. A long-range picture tells more than a brief observation can reveal. Then, too, school-age children have begun to formulate specific personal characteristics that are more significant in their development than those related to their age level. A shy and withdrawn youngster will exhibit similar ways of coping with situations throughout his school experience. Leadership ability that may be observed at six is likely to be in evidence all through the school years. The unique qualities that make up the individual become more significant as the child grows older. Characteristics of a specific level of development are not as likely to be the determining factors in behavior as they were at previous stages.

The reader will be able to develop greater insight into the unique characteristics of specific school-age children when she examines the case studies reported in Chapters 12, 13, and 14. However, there are kinds of behavior exhibited frequently enough by school-agers at various levels for us to be able to report on these findings. Since changes occur less frequently and less dramatically than at previous levels, we will discuss a two-year age span at a time. It must be understood, however, that many characteristics attributed to eights and nines could be evident in the behavior of some sevens, and, similarly, descriptions of sixes and sevens might easily apply to some older children.

Six- and seven-year-olds

Beginning with the first grade, the child experiences a stress upon intellectual competence. His newly acquired ego is put to a test. Can he perform the required skills? Self-evaluation is no longer dependent upon relationships within the family unit or upon motor abilities. The preschooler develops pride as he learns to climb the jungle gym. He insists upon feeding and dressing himself and wants the adults in his life to recognize his abilities and respect them. But the six- and seven-year-old is forced to evaluate himself on the basis of other skills and attributes. Parents are no longer the only judges of his worthiness. He must prove to his teachers and to his peers that he is a worthwhile person.

It is little wonder that six-year-olds are so concerned about their ability to read and write. They come to school anxious to learn and are impatient if they do not get books, paper, and pencils the very first day. They are proud of every letter that they can identify and want to show off their new-found knowledge at every occasion. The beginning of their school career marks a radical departure from their previous way of life, and most children are deeply impressed with the important step they are taking.

Reading and writing skills

Student observers who studied six-year-olds were frequently exposed to demonstrations of the children's newly acquired reading skills. As a matter of fact, observers of this age level could not avoid it! One six-year-old who was being observed sat between the student observer and another guest in his family's living room. His first-grade reader was open on his lap. The child asked the other guest several times if she wanted to hear him read. Since she was talking, she did not answer the boy. He then asked the observer the same question. As soon as she looked in his direction, John began to read. Although he was advanced for his age, the observer noted some tension as John "squinted his eyes and shook his head" when he came to a word he couldn't pronounce.

A typical six-year-old was observed while with his parents in a shoe store.

TIME	OVERT BEHAVIOR	COMMENTS
2:20	Robbie is sitting about two feet away from the observer, on the same bench. He is kneeling on his knees, with his arms wrapped around the cushioned seat. He drops down, his feet going to the floor, and his stomach and arms sliding down the couch.	Robbie is very active—constantly moving around.
2:25	He glances over at me. He climbs back on the couch and resumes the same position as before. He walks over to me on his knees while hitting the back of the cushion with his hand. He says, "S-A-W spells saw!" I ask him how he knows, and he says, "I'm six years old and I'm in first grade! R-A-M spells ram!" He continues sliding up and down on the couch as he talks. I ask him what a ram is.	He looks at me very closely as if he is looking me over. It seemed as though I might be a good subject to tell all of his new-found knowledge! He is very proud of his spelling skills and of his age and grade.
2:28	He jumps up, turns to his mother, slaps his hands down, palm open, and says,	I believe this is an act to hide the fact that he doesn't know what a

TIME	OVERT BEHAVIOR	COMMENTS
	"She doesn't know what a ram is!" He points to me, eyes wide open, a surprised look on his face. He turns back to me and says, "T-R-E-E spells tree, and R-A-T spells rat!"	ram is! He continues to spell for me. He seems excited that I am listening.
2:30	I asked him what a rat is. He stops, thinks for a minute, raises his finger up and says, "It's like a mouse!" His father turns away from the shoes he is looking at, and says to Robbie, "Robbie! Enough! Now sit down!" I tell him I do not mind but the father says he has heard this all day today!	He is quite sure of his answer, and again, he takes pride in it. Robbie's father seems bothered by the continual display of his knowledge.

Another father, who was known to be a strict disciplinarian, insisted that his son, Stephan, age six, show the observer how well he could print his name. "His letters were well-proportioned, and he worked very hard at keeping the paper neat. When he accidentally made a mark, he would be sure to erase and reprint it over and over again, each time very carefully." This same child took great pains in unwrapping Christmas ornaments, being extremely careful not to damage anything. When the student observer offered to help him, he answered, "This is my job; I have to do it right and finish it."

We wonder if this compulsion for perfection will be harmful to this child. Most six-year-olds are not as well-controlled or as systematic. The observer commented that Stephan was the "most well-behaved and well-adjusted six-year-old I had ever seen. He always did what he was told without question, and, with all this, he seemed to be a happy person."

Parents and teachers have been concerned with the amount of discipline to impose upon young children. Langdon and Stout did a survey in which they interviewed parents of children who were considered, by their teachers and principals, to be well-adjusted.[1]

These children came from all types of family backgrounds. They were from urban, suburban, and rural settings. Some lived in large houses, some in crowded apartments, some in trailers. Some were "only" children, some had many brothers and sisters, and some came from one-parent homes. The patterns of administering discipline were equally diversified. Some parents expressed the opinion that they must be very strict; others felt that, "After all, they're just kids. You have to be patient on this discipline business." The only point upon which there seemed to be agreement was that "The most important of all is loving them and letting them know it, thinking of them as people and treating them so, appreciating what they do and trusting them and

[1] Grace Langdon and Irving W. Stout, *These Well-Adjusted Children*, pp. 33–37, 157.

telling them so, and above all letting them know that they are wanted." All of the parents interviewed expressed this thought in one form or another.

Children need to feel that they are respected as people, but sometimes the practices in our schools do not help to build this self-respect. The emphasis upon reading and writing skills in the early grades sometimes develops feelings of inadequacy in those children for whom these tasks are not easily accomplished. For many, coming from less advantaged backgrounds, the preliminary verbal and experiential groundwork has not been laid. For others problems occur owing to a lack of perceptual discrimination abilities possibly because of some innate dysfunction. Chapters 11 and 12 deal with case histories of youngsters who face these problems.

ACTIVITY 1

Arrange to tutor a child who is having difficulty beginning to read. See if you can detect the source of his difficulty. Consult with his teacher, if possible. Refer to discussions of prereading skills in curriculum textbooks. See the "Suggested Checklist to Identify Interferences in Learning Pathways" in Appendix C of this book.

Is the child able to concentrate? Does he respond to you and look forward to your visits? What kind of self-concept does he seem to have?

One student observer related an experience she had when she was asked to assist a slow learner in a first-grade classroom. The time sample below reveals the child's change in attitude as he begins to feel some degree of self-respect.

TIME	OVERT BEHAVIOR	COMMENTS
1:10	We are working with a language workbook. Paul does not talk to me. He just nods and does not get one answer right. I try to explain things, and when he sees that he is wrong, he just erases the answer. He keeps on staring at me and at the other children.	Paul acted strangely. I believe he felt uncomfortable. It was as if everyone knew why he was picked. He was slow and behind the rest. He seemed to be afraid of me, and his reaction was not talking. I think he wasn't even trying to do the work.
1:20	The teacher comes over and asks if I would like to take a reading group outside, and she asks Paul if he will join this group. Again, Paul just shakes his head.	The teacher seemed to notice the barrier between us and tried to help. When Paul shook his head, I began to think her efforts were useless.
1:22	The teacher calls the "Blue Jays" to get their books and to go with me. She asks Paul to show me where to go. He smiles and says, "O.K."	Paul's smile meant a lot, and I felt a change taking place. The teacher did all she could to help.
1:24	A group of five children walked outside and down the steps to the picnic benches. I ask Paul which way to go. He says, "This way" and points his finger.	Letting him help me seemed to break the barrier.

TIME	OVERT BEHAVIOR	COMMENTS
1:25	We all sit down, and Paul sits next to me.	I was surprised. I think Paul wanted everyone to know that I was his friend.
1:26 to 1:35	All of the children take turns reading from the books. Paul and I share one book, and he turns the pages for me. When it is his turn to read, he tries very hard to get all of the words right.	Everything seemed to go well. When a child said a word before Paul could, he seemed to get upset. He wanted to read well for me.

This teacher provided an opportunity for Paul to feel helpful to the student observer. Paul was then ready to accept her as a friend and was willing to try to do better with his reading.

There are many ways in which a teacher of young children can help to build up the healthy self-concept they all need in order to be ready to learn. Every child has an area in which he can be successful, and the teacher who knows her children as individuals can give him a chance to make a contribution. Those who are slow in learning to read may have other skills. They may be good athletes, or they may draw well. They may have some special interest that they can share with the class. Through creative movement the child, who is not achieving in other areas, has an opportunity to gain acceptance from his peers. Here is an example.

> Mark tries hard in school, but he just cannot sit still for long, and is likely to be playful when others are working. He falters with his reading, and his writing appears to be careless and sloppy. He is often scolded for misbehavior. His teacher has worked hard to get him to concentrate more, but he seems less mature than some of the other second graders, and has a shorter interest span.
>
> But Mark moves expressively. He makes noises as he goes and has the uninhibited "feel" for combining sound and movement often exhibited by a younger child. His "steam-shovel" is so realistic in terms of both sound and movement the we can almost expect a piece of the floor to come up as his arms reach like claws toward it! Children always chose him to be the airplane, or the engine of the train. His "seagull" flying over the ocean is beautiful to watch. He swoops down and curves, and the gull sounds that accompany his movements accent the changes in direction. He loves, the recognition the class gives him after such a performance.[2]

Mark's mother told his teacher that Mark had hated school in first grade, and that she had had difficulty in getting him to go each morning. His second-grade teacher gave him opportunities to succeed, and consequently, his attitudes changed. His reading and writing skills did not show immediate improvement, but Mark developed self-respect. He was an alert, though immature child, and eventually became a good student in all areas.

[2] Betty Rowen, *Learning through Movement*, pp. 59–60.

Winning the teacher's approval

As we can see, academic areas are not the only ones in which six- and seven-year-olds seek approval. The teacher has become a surrogate parent, and the primary-grade child often feels a strong need for her support. John was so eager to be complimented by his teacher that he was willing to give up his outdoor playtime to achieve this end.

TIME	OVERT BEHAVIOR	COMMENTS
10:45	Some boys are climbing on the jungle gym, when a large branch hanging on it gets in their way. They try to get it out. John then tells the other children, "I've got to clean up our playground."	John seems pleased with himself that he has such an important job to do.
10:49	John runs to tell his teacher. Goes back to the jungle gym. Picks up branches and stacks them near school building. Runs to teacher to show her. Returns and picks up more sticks. Goes to teacher again. She doesn't notice him this time. Sees me and tells me, "With the twigs you can build a fire." Returns to teacher and repeats this remark.	Seeks approval and attention often.

John is not a poor student and is capable of getting approval frequently for his good work in class. He is very fond of his teacher, however, and seems to need recognition from her often. Perhaps this is due to the presence in the group of his sister who is only one year younger. Jane, about whom we have reported in Chapter 9, is a personable and alert school beginner. John seems to be very fond of her. He frequently plays the role of "big brother," helping her find materials and reminding her of routines. Although he shows no resentment toward his sister, his need for extra attention from his teacher may be his way of expressing a degree of sibling rivalry.

Six-year-olds do not always try to get their teacher's attention in positive ways. If approval is not easily available to them, some six-year-olds try a little mischief to gain their ends! The goals are really the same. The teacher is omnipotent, and the six-year-old needs to be recognized by her. In this time sample Bruce is discussing his teacher with the student observer who is his next-door neighbor.

TIME	OVERT BEHAVIOR	COMMENTS
5:15 PM	Bruce: How can I be mean to my teacher? She's awfully mean! Observer: Your teacher, she's mean to you?	The observer is using a play-therapy technique of reflecting the child's feelings.

TIME	OVERT BEHAVIOR	COMMENTS
	Bruce: "To all of us. Sometimes she's mean to me only. What can I do to her? I know, put a tack on her seat! (Snaps his fingers in the air.) Observer: A tack can really hurt someone.	
	Bruce: I know. So that's good. A tack on her seat.	Bruce may be fantasizing. I doubt if he ever carried through this plan.
	Observer: She must make you very mad to want to hurt her so badly.	
	Bruce: No, only once in a while. One time I was rude to her though (impish grin). She came over to my desk and cut my paper in two with the scissors. I started yelling at her, "Leave it alone, you interior decorator. I don't like you. You're mean and nasty!"	Bruce is being very dramatic. He really put himself into this scene.
	Observer: You must have been mad at her.	
	Bruce: I was. She said, "no-no-no" (shakes his finger in the air). What would be better? Maybe I could throw an air conditioner at her. The door. No. I couldn't sneak a door in. A brick. I'll throw that at her!	Bruce is mocking his teacher. He is still trying to act in a serious manner, but it seems he has become a bit silly!

Obviously, Bruce is an imaginative child with a strong sense of humor. He is a "small boy with an unmistakably mischievous face," according to the student observer. It is doubtful if he ever intends to carry through these plans, but it is clear that the teacher is a central figure in his life, and he spends much time thinking about ways he can get to her!

Kindness and cruelty

Six- and seven-year-olds have very volatile feelings. They frequently have temperamental outbursts. They can be excessively kind or cruel to younger children. They are easily frustrated when something or someone interferes with their activities.

The younger sister or brother is frequently the target for the six-year-old's emotional outbursts. But he also enjoys playing with the younger child. A six-year-old girl was observed minding her baby sister at an airport. She "seemed to enjoy playing the mother role, giving the baby orders on what to do. She grabbed her arm and led her back to where the parents were sitting. When the baby fell down, Suzi fell with her, giggling as if it were a great joke." But, as the student observer reported, she soon lost interest in playing with the baby when a puppy caught her attention. Suzi petted him gently and laughed when he licked her face.

Animals are frequently the objects of a six-year-old's kindness and cruelty. The boy, Bruce, who wanted to put a tack on his teacher's seat, also liked to tease the student observer's cat. When asked to stop chasing him, he said, "I don't care whose cat it is. I'll chase him anyway." Sometimes a child will show excessive concern that the cat "has not been given his dinner" but will "pull his tail as he comes to get his milk!"

David is a six-and-a-half-year-old boy who was playing in a park when observed by a student.

TIME	OVERT BEHAVIOR	COMMENTS
2:33	David is playing with a group of boys; he sees Regina and goes over to her and sits down. Asks, "What are you doing? Making a castle? How old are you? You're three years old?"	Seems interested in younger child. Asks questions. If no answer, he makes his own.
2:35	Helps Regina bang on dirt to make a dirt hill. Big boys come and threaten to knock it down. David says nothing.	No reaction to threat of other boys.
2:37	Sees Carol and says to Regina, "She's a girl. She will help you make it like this." Goes off to play with other boys.	Aware of sex differences and feels that another girl can help Regina more.

David shows himself to be a kind and considerate boy as he plays and talks to the younger child. Yet a short time later this same boy is observed as he wanders through the park with his friends.

TIME	OVERT BEHAVIOR	COMMENTS
3:08	David has stick in hand and is banging a frog on the head. Each boy takes a turn with stick.	
3:10	David pushes frog away from tree with stick. I go over and ask him who killed it. "I got him. I poked his eyeballs out. He was a really big one."	David takes credit and is proud of this vicious act.
3:12	Father calls children to come. David runs with stick to car. Leans on it as father opens door. Lets his sister, Carol, in first, then climbs in after and closes the door.	Evidence of consideration and politeness.

Competition

When six- and seven-year-olds play together, it is very likely that they will try to outdo each other in whatever activity they pursue. If our student observer had stayed with David and his friends longer and at closer range, she might have heard them competing to see who could throw the rocks farther into the water. They were certainly competing with each other as they tried to kill the frog, and David's "I got him!" was a cry of victory. Any activity becomes a competitive game, and any available material is put to use, when small boys get together.

ACTIVITY 2

Try to organize a punchball or a kickball game with some six- and seven-year-olds. Notice any indications of competitive actions and comments. Which child assumes leadership of the group? How do the children relate to the poor performer? What is the attitude of the children toward you?

Record your observations, and be ready to discuss them in class.

Girls are frequently excluded from the rough-and-tumble play of six-year-old boys. Occasionally a girl is allowed to join, but then it is because of some special consideration that is given to her. As some six-year-olds were preparing to play punchball, a student observer offered to join in the game.

BOY ONE: Are you really going to play?
BOY TWO: She says so, but I bet she can't, really.
WAYNE: She's my cousin. Let her play.
BOY ONE: Come on, come on, come on already!
(A little girl wants to join the game.)
BOY ONE: She can't play. She's a girl!
WAYNE: But Wendy (the student observer) is a girl!
BOY TWO: She's not a girl. She's different.

Later, as Wendy took the boys for some ice cream, one remarked, "She really can play—even if she *is* a girl!" Sex differences are being noticed, and the separation of activities that begins at this age will continue for several years to come.

Girls are as aware of competition as boys. Kathy attended a swimming class in which she was the youngest member. In a meet in which all competed Kathy swam halfway and then left the pool. Her parents praised her but asked why she had stopped. Her reply was simple. "I saw I was last, so why go on?"

Competition for girls is more likely to take a verbal form and is often concentrated upon classroom activity. Emily is a seven-year-old second grader who is an *A* student. She finishes her work quickly and often comes to her teacher's desk seeking praise. She is eager to answer questions. At reading time she frequently corrects her fellow students or prompts them with the right word. Sometimes she gives up her recess period, so that she can continue working to "get ahead of everybody." When it is time for the class to be dismissed, Emily can be seen running to the front of the line and shouting, "I'm supposed to be here."

Emily's desire to be first may lead to some unpleasantness and even unkindness. When discussing her brother with the student observer, she told her, "I got all *A*'s and he got all *F*'s," and added, "I never watch TV; I work!" She gloated over the fact that her brother is not allowed to ride his bicycle until he gets better grades. When she was observed in the lunchroom, she refused to give another girl some almonds that she had asked for, saying, "No, they're mine!" She then threw them away in the garbage can.

There are many little girls like Emily in second grade. Teachers often encourage their smug behavior by praising their abilities and by giving them special privileges. Families who regard grades as the most significant factor in a child's development also encourage this kind of behavior. Emily is a bright and attractive little girl, but, in the opinion of the student observer, "Emily seems to feel that she has more rights than others." When competition is encouraged at the expense of respect for others, then the natural tendency of six- and seven-year-olds to outdo each other develops beyond proportion.

Eight- and nine-year-olds

Competition continues to be important for eight- and nine-year olds, but there is a significant difference between the sexes as to where it is important to succeed. Girls may still value high achievement in school. The girl chosen by others to be the leader in a club is likely to be a good student. Boys, on the other hand, respect the good athlete or even the class clown. It is often considered undesirable to do too well in school. Eight- and nine-year-old boys like to brag to each other about how they did not do their homework and got away with it! This conversation was overheard by a student observer, as four nine-year-old boys rode on bicycles near her home.

TIME	OVERT BEHAVIOR	COMMENTS
3:35	Steve was riding by with no hands on the handlebars. Mike came out of his house and said, "Guess what I made in spelling?" I made an *A*." Steve laughed and said, "I had everything wrong. I didn't study. I got *D*." All of the boys laughed.	They rode their bicycles with much skill, showing off to each other. They were amused that Steve got a *D*. Girls would not brag about this.
3:40	They rode up and down the street, calling out to each other. They asked Mike to spell some of the words. Mike answered, then started riding fast, standing up on his seat.	I missed some of the conversation. The boys respected Mike for doing well, but Mike did not want to appear too smart. He started showing off some physical accomplishments.
3:47	One of the boys said, "Boy, you're going to break your neck!" Another said, "It's better if he breaks his neck than if he breaks that new bike. His mom would kill him!" They all laughed.	The warning was accompanied by admiration.
3:50	They gathered in a group and Mike said, "Let's go to the club." Some other boys were coming down the street, and Mike added, "Wait till they go by. We don't want them to go."	They show a clannishness. The club is just for their own group.

Mike was obviously the leader in this group, and the boys respected his achievement in school. But Mike did not want to dwell on this and quickly shifted attention to the stunts he could do on his bike. Steve, on the other hand, bragged about his poor achievement in spelling, and this attitude also seemed to get approval from the group. There was a good feeling of comradery among the boys, as if they would support each other under any circumstances. No doubt they play together often and are members of a special "in" group with its own clubhouse. The society of children, with its own codes and mores, is very much in evidence in the previous time sample.

ACTIVITY 3
Arrange to do a sociogram in a third- or fourth-grade classroom. Ask the children to choose three members of the class they want to work with and chart their responses. Check with the teacher about the children who were most popular and about those who received the least recognition from their peers. Did the girls with high academic achievement receive many votes? Were the popular boys all good students? (See Figure 5 for example of a sociogram.)

Skill development

The middle years are the time to acquire skills. Children learn to ride a two-wheeler, to skate, to dive and swim, to jump rope, to play ball. All of these things are special accomplishments, which help to develop a self-concept and to establish prestige in peer relationships. Both boys and girls value these skills highly at this stage.

When they are in school, the emphasis is strongly upon reading, writing, and arithmetic skills. Free exploration and creativity are not as much in evidence as they had been at a previous level. Eight-year-olds in third grade want to be told the right way to do things. They wait for instructions before beginning work in a new medium. Give a five-year-old a lump of clay, and he will roll it, pound it, poke his fingers into it. When clay was given to one third-grade class, the children asked, "What are we supposed to make with it?"

A student observer, who had just finished her student-teaching term, told about a project she had prepared for a third-grade class. She wanted them to draw a map of the classroom and gave out large drawing paper for them to use. She was deluged with questions, "How should we hold the paper?" "How should I make the windows?" "Where should I put the teacher's desk?" When the class was told to look around the room and then proceed to draw what they saw, only a few could begin on their own.

We wonder if this limitation is the result of the treatment children have had in school up to this stage, or if it is generally characteristic of the age level. John Holt claims that children learn to conform to what is expected of them in school.[3] They learn to anticipate the desired response and to meet teachers' expectations. This writer tends to agree with Holt's point of view. The third-

[3] John Holt, *How Children Fail.*

grade class who were asked to make a map of their room had not been expected to make decisions on their own prior to this. Their teacher always set out procedures for them to follow, and there had been little opportunity for student initiative.

For whatever reasons eight- and nine-year-olds in our culture are strongly oriented toward skill development. They like to see how well they can perform a task, whether it is writing, doing arithmetic, or making an ashtray out of clay. Their drawings are realistic, with great attention to detail (see Figure 6). The abstract use of space and color found in kindergarten children's art cannot usually be seen again until children are well into their teens, unless, of course, they are instructed to work in abstraction by an art teacher.

ACTIVITY 4

Collect the artwork of an eight- or nine-year-old for a period of several months, or ask the classroom teacher or the art teacher if you might borrow such a folder for a few days. When several students in the child-development class have been able to secure such folders, they should be brought to class and compared. What do they indicate to you about the child who has done the artwork? How observant is he? What are his major interests? Guess at these questions, and then verify with someone who knows the child.

Even in movement and dance children seek to acquire specific skills. It is at this age that little girls all want to take ballet lessons. They want to learn formal positions and steps. While previously these same children enjoyed making up their own dances, they now prefer to learn routines and to imitate ballerinas by wearing tutus and toe shoes.

In middle-class America children of eight and nine are so busy learning skills that there is little time for free choice of activities. Piano lessons, ballet, swimming, Little League, scouts, religious instruction—all compete for their time. Even birthday parties are frequently organized into treasure hunts, races, and games. At one eight-year-old's party a little boy was heard to ask, "When all this is over, can we play?"

Hobbies and collections play an important part in the life of eight- and nine-year-olds. Boys will save anything from stones, to coins, to bottle tops. Girls make scrapbooks and collect dolls and doll clothes. Skills are sometimes involved, such as sewing, weaving, assembling models, or building electric train sets.

Minor skills seem to rate as highly as major ones. It is an accomplishment if a boy can cross his eyes, or perform some "double-jointed" stunt. Girls are highly respected if they can play hopscotch well. This is the age for chicken fights and Indian hand wrestling. It is a time for memorized jingles, secret codes, and passwords. All of these tricks and skills help the child become a part of an inner circle where he can be accepted by the people who matter the most—the members of his own sex and age group.

Boys work hard to become proficient at games. Baseball and football are important activities. The good athlete is usually popular. Others who do

Figure 6   Drawing by an eight-year-old boy.

not have as much skill try to "fake it"—to appear to be knowledgeable and competent so that their teammates will respect them. In this time sample eight-year-old Tony is making this effort while playing kickball with older boys.

TIME	OVERT BEHAVIOR	COMMENTS
1:03	As the pitcher (a boy about twelve) pitches the ball, Tony (playing second base) bends over at the waist, puts his hands on his knees, awaiting the kick. A look of concentration is on his face.	Tony's mother told me later that Tony is a "big baseball fan" and likes to look like a baseball player when he plays.
1:04	After the ball is kicked, it goes toward Tony, but Tony overruns the ball, and it bounces over his head. As his teammates scream to "get the ball," Tony runs around in circles.	Tony has not yet developed the skills of the older boys. He is flustered and excited and is further confused by the shouts of teammates.
1:06	When he finally gets the ball, it is too late. His teammates yell that he is "stupid" and "no good." Tony throws the ball down and walks over to second base with his head down. He sits down on the base, arms and legs folded, head down.	Tony shows embarrassment for not being able to perform well.
1:08	The other children call a warning that he'd better get up or he won't be able to play. Tony slowly stands up, kicking the base with his right foot.	He is disgusted with himself but wants to stay in the game.
1:15	Tony's team is up. Each time one of his teammates is ready to kick, Tony goes up to him, and, in an excited and secretive manner, tells him where to stand, how to kick, and so on. One boy says, "Tony, what makes you think you're so great?"	Tony acts like he is the captain. He "bosses" other children around, and they seem to resent this.
1:18	Finally Tony is ready to kick. He stands about two yards back of the base one foot in back of the other, feet apart, head up, eyes squinting (There was no sun out!)	Tony tries to look professional.
1:19	The ball is pitched, and Tony kicks a base hit.	Good thing for Tony!

Eight-year-old Tony was actually trying too hard to be accepted. In his eagerness to achieve and to establish himself with the older boys, he made numerous errors. His attempt to give directions to others was possibly a cover for his own feelings of inadequacy, but it was resented by his teammates.

Fortunately, Tony made a base hit. When his skills improve, Tony will have an easier time being "one of the boys!"

In any eight- or nine-year-old group, there is usually a "wise guy." The boy who is smaller than the others, but who always has a ready quip, can maintain his position with his peers. Skippy, the eight-year-old who wrote the story about "The Owl That Went to Medical School" (see Chapter 5) was such a boy. His story revealed his flippant attitudes about school and his ability to use a pun effectively. These are qualities that made him popular with his classmates. They teased him for his swaggering manner, but they enjoyed and respected his wit and humor.

Peer relationships

Those adults who look back nostalgically upon the "joys of childhood" might care to reexamine their experiences during those years.

ACTIVITY 5
Recall some experiences of your own that took place when you were in elementary school. Did you get along well with your classmates? Who was your "best friend"? How did you feel about a child who was "left out"? Were you a good student? What were the things you valued most? Discuss these feelings in class, and compare them to children you have observed and to those discussed in this chapter.

Many of the direct observations done on children of this age reveal an anxiety about peer acceptance that is painful to contemplate. We have seen some of the attempts to deal with this problem in the time samples above. Athletic prowess is one means for achieving the desired goal of acceptance. Wit and humor provide another avenue. But the struggle is a difficult one. Eight- and nine-year-olds generally do not let their feelings show. If they are hurt, they try to hide it under a veneer of bravado. Even the most outstanding leaders may be protecting themselves with a ready smile which may cover loneliness or insecurity. A case study of a gifted nine-year-old which reveals this pattern will be reported in Chapter 14.

Children ban together in small groups which provide them with the necessary security of belonging. Members conform by following prescribed codes of dress and speech. They have secret passwords and special meeting places. Strangers are excluded. The outsider is sometimes subjected to. cruel treatment.

A nine-year-old girl, who had recently moved to the community, had the following conversation with a student observer.

OBSERVER: Ellen, how was school today?
ELLEN: Oh, it was all right. I don't like it a lot. Not as much as I did in North Carolina.
OBSERVER: How come?
ELLEN: No one is friendly down here. Linda and Diane won't speak to me. I told Diane that I thought her dress was very pretty, and she pushed me out of the way. That made me so mad.

OBSERVER: That wasn't nice of them.

ELLEN: No one is nice, except for Debbie. At least she talks to me. I'm tired of trying to be nice to all of them. From now on, if anyone pushes me I'll push them back! I have some friends in North Caroiina. We had delicious water there. I hate this water (making a disgusted face). Isn't there anyplace to get spring water here?

OBSERVER: Perhaps from Mineral Springs.

ELLEN: Oh, we'll go down there. Back in North Carolina we had a river that was real swift. And we had springs, and springs, and springs (gesticulating); and we had horses. And we had a pond where we could catch our own fish. A great amount of fish.

OBSERVER: Well, maybe you'll go back for a visit sometime.

Ellen seemed to the observer to be very homesick, and it is not surprising! She missed her friends in North Carolina and was not doing too well in finding a group that would accept her in her new school. But rather than admit to this disappointment, Ellen shifted the topic and began talking about the water and the landscape.

Nine-year-olds will use any device to protect themselves from exposure or to insure inclusion in the group. Stealing is not uncommon at this age and is often regarded lightly as a prank.

A boy who had difficulty remembering his task tried to protect himself with a fib, when he was questioned at a Cub Scout meeting. The following observation reveals evidence of anxiety in his gestures and manner.

Danny is seated at the table. Cupcakes and cokes are being passed out. He holds the bottle with two hands and drinks in quick gulps. He wipes his head, which is wet with perspiration, with his left hand. The other boys are talking loudly and his eyes dart from face to face.

The den mother speaks to Danny, scolding him for not bringing his script. (They are about to rehearse for "Skit Night.") She reminds him that she had called on the phone and he had said he would bring it. Danny stares ahead of him and says she didn't speak to him. It must have been someone else. She insists that she spoke to him. Danny frowns slightly, nods his head, and says softly, "I remember now. I didn't remember before."

The observer comments that Danny is a quiet, mild-mannered, introspective child. He is a dreamer, his thoughts wander, and he is forgetful. He is anxious and feels guilty about things he should have remembered. He tries to evade the issue, or to tell a fib, in order to save face with his peers. He has difficulty becoming part of the group.

Eight- and nine-year-olds like to have best friends, and these places of honor are reserved and highly valued. Girls may be heard asking each other "Will you be my best friend?"; boys rely heavily on a buddy to do things with. Here is a conversation a student observer had with her nine-year-old cousin.

SUE: My girl friend in school has the same glasses as you, Norma. Only instead of being pointed here they are straight.

OBSERVER: Well, Sue, then they are not the same ones.

SUE: No, but they look like them. My girl friend, no, not my girl friend—my friend—my friend picked them up yesterday from the doctor, and she wore them today.

OBSERVER: What do you mean—not your girl friend, but your friend? Is there a difference?

SUE: Yeah, my friend. 'Cause Carolyn is my girl friend.

OBSERVER: But what's the difference between Anna, your friend, and Carolyn, your girl friend?

SUE: Well, Carolyn is my best friend, so she's my girl friend. Anna isn't my best friend, so she's just a friend.

Heroes and villains

While being fiercely loyal to one's best friend, school-age children tend to reject family and adults in general. The grownups belong in a different camp, and there seems to be undeclared warfare going on most of the time! In a sense the child is asserting his independence from the adults who have had so much meaning and control in his life. The bravado and self-assertion may be covering up doubts and anxieties, and the solidarity of the peer group is protection against the power of "the enemy," that is, the significant adults in the child's world.

In spite of the resentment felt toward adults the nine-year-old knows that parents behave as they do for his own good. Much of the resistance is a kind of role playing, and the child would be disappointed, at times, if he were allowed to win in such a controversy. Boys are likely to be taciturn at this age, refusing to confide in adults and acting sullen and insolent when questioned by them. One student observer visited the home of an eight-year-old boy at Christmas time. She "began to question Tommy about some of the presents under the tree. He was reluctant to discuss them. He seemed more interested in taking them to another room to play. He gave me a few quick answers which barely satisfied the questions. After a few minutes, he and his friend, Joe, each grabbed a handful of toys and left the room."

Sometimes, however, an older child or a young adult becomes the object of hero worship. Eight- and nine-year-olds love to have someone to look up to. Since parents and members of the adult generation are rejected, the school-age child often finds a hero in a college-age cousin or neighbor. Baseball players and rock singers may be worshipped from afar. Fan clubs are formed by girls, and boys save baseball cards. All of this is evidence that this age group needs a model for adulation.

Tommy, who rejected the attention of our student observer when she questioned him about his presents, welcomed the assistance of his older cousin, Billy, age thirteen.

TIME	OVERT BEHAVIOR
11:20	Billy has volunteered to help Tommy assemble his new train set. An important screw appears to be missing. Tommy, his friend, Joe, and his sister, Julie, search around the floor of the basement where they are working.
11:25	Tommy leaves the search to go upstairs to ask his other sister if she knows the whereabouts of the screw. Returns downstairs, looks about quickly and says, "Joe threw things all over."
11:35	Tommy finds the screw and yells, "I found it!" Billy says, "We need scissors." Tommy says, "O.K." and runs upstairs, returning in a few minutes with scissors. He stands at the side of the table watching.
11:45	Billy asks if there is an electric outlet nearby. Tommy says, "There isn't" and asks, "You want an extension cord?" He spots one just at the same time his sister does. Tommy runs to try to get it first. He arrives at the same time as Julie. There is a short tug of war. Julie assures Tommy that she would plug it in for him, and Tommy lets go. Julie tries to plug it in and Tommy offers some suggestions. It is seen that it is a three-prong plug and won't go in.
11:55	Billy interrupts, asking Tommy for a screw driver. Tommy answers, "O.K." and runs upstairs. He returns and presents the screw driver to Billy. He stands and watches Billy work. He says, "Some trains come with lights." He walks to the other side of the table, jumps up on the table, crawls to Billy, watches a few seconds, turns around, crawls to the table edge, and jumps off. He says, "Where is that brown thing?" He seems to remember another extension cord. He finds "the brown thing" and plugs it in quite confidently.
12:05	All of the trains are now working. Billy asks Tommy if the trains belong to his brother. Tommy answers quickly, "It's all mine. I got it for Christmas."

We can see how anxious Tommy was to help his older cousin, Billy, as he assembled the train set. He ran upstairs several times to retrieve objects for him. He stayed close to Billy to watch eagerly awaiting directions. He blamed his friend, Joe, for the loss of the screw, and fought with his eleven-year-old sister, Julie, about who was to put in the plug. But he never disputed a thing that Billy said. Although Tommy was usually a leader in any group he played in, according to the student observer's case study, he was a very willing follower when his older cousin, Billy, was around.

Cleavage between the sexes

Boys and girls of six and seven have begun to prefer to play with their own sex mates, but by eight or nine this cleavage of the sexes is complete. Boys go through a period when girls are thoroughly rejected. Part of this attitude, like the rejection of adults, is a kind of role playing. Boys are expected to dislike girls, and this is a necessary step to be taken to assert one's maleness. Older heroes, like cousin Billy in the observation above, evoke feelings of puzzlement and outrage in their younger disciples when they begin to show an interest in girls.

Boys, who readily worship older cousins of the same sex, are suspicious of older girl cousins who happen to show them some attention. One student observer, visiting her eight-year-old cousin, Lee, asked him if she could play with his trucks. He said, "No, it's not a girl's game. Girls don't play with trucks." The student observer commented, "He was very much annoyed with me for wanting to play with his trucks but soon gave in. He seemed to be annoyed just having me around." When he finally agreed to let his big cousin have a truck, he began running into it with his truck and laughing every time. If the student observer made sounds like trucks moving, Lee made louder sounds. It seemed that he didn't want to be outdone at this activity, especially by a girl!

One student observer heard a nine-year-old boy calling his friends together for a stickball game. When he found out that some girls intended to play with them, he called the game off.

Sisters are objects for teasing by eight- and nine-year-old boys. One student observer recorded a nine-year-old threatening to throw water on his sister's head, but he never got around to doing it. Much of the teasing is only a bluff, for a few minutes later, this boy and his sister were climbing trees together. Boys will defend their sisters against outside attack, no matter how much they might abuse them themselves!

Girls, at this stage, protest that they hate boys, but they will have romantic visions of domesticity and will worship older boys from afar. They have secret clubs and meeting places where boys are not allowed to come. But an occasional invasion by a group of boys is a cause for much excitement and is sometimes eagerly anticipated.

Much of this feeling is exaggerated in order to make the proper impression upon peers of the same sex. Boys may like to paint, play piano, or dance, but they will never admit this when other boys are around. A girl may be very proud of her brother's achievements, but, with her friends, he is always the object of ridicule.

That these feelings come to the fore at age eight is illustrated clearly by an incident that occurred when this author was preparing to show the film of the action study dealing with the development of aesthetic concepts, reported in Chapter 5.[4] All second graders, boys as well as girls, participated eagerly in the movement activities presented to the group. In a scarf dance done to Fritz Kreisler's *Caprice Viennois*, it was the boys who chose to move with the scarves to the swaying theme, while the girls preferred to move on the running theme.

Yet, six months later when the film was ready for viewing, the author was requested by the principal not to show it to the entire school. Boys, who

[4] Betty Rowen, *An Exploration of the Uses of Rhythmic Movement to Develop Aesthetic Concepts in the Primary Grades.*

had been seven-year-olds when they performed the scarf dance, were now eight-year-olds. They were no longer all in the same class, but had been distributed to three third-grade classes. George, who had a small solo part at the entrance of one theme in the music, was worried that his present class-mates would laugh if they saw him moving with the scarf. Other boys agreed that they did not want the film shown in their classes. A special showing was arranged for those children who had participated, and all of the group, boys as well as girls, enjoyed watching their performance in the picture.

Ten- through twelve-year-olds

At the beginning of the preteen period the most startling changes that occur are in the attitudes toward the opposite sex. Girls begin to call boys on the telephone, and talk about boys is their main occupation when they gather together among themselves. Boys pretend indifference, but they are flattered by attention from girls, particularly if the ones who call them are pretty and popular. Going steady is the thing to do at eleven or twelve. There are frequent exchanges of pins and emblems, but relationships are superficial and usually of very short duration. After a week, a boy might "break it up" with one girl friend and might start going steady with another girl in the same day!

Teasing girls is still a popular pastime. Twelve-year-old Willie called to a student observer, who is an attractive, well-built young lady, "If you wasn't so fat, I would give you a ride on my bicycle, but you might break it down!" A little later, he said, "I didn't really mean that" and winked his eye with a sly grin. This young man was really practicing his wiles on his next-door neighbor, even if she was an older college girl!

Willie is still resistant to parental authority. When his mother began to tell him about cleaning his room, he said, "That's all you think about is cleaning this and cleaning that. Boy, I'm glad I'm a man!" He went toward his room a little reluctantly. After a short while, he emerged, asking if his girl friend had called. Later, when asked to go to the store, he said, "I can't go right now, I'm expecting a phone call."

Willie was described by his observer as "very small for his age." It is possible that the smaller boys, who have difficulty holding their own on the athletic field, are the first to succumb to the flattering attentions shown to them by the opposite sex. This was true, also, for an eleven-year-old named Jeff, who was interviewed by a student observer. Here are some answers to the questions that were put to him:

Q: What is the one thing you enjoy doing most of all?
A: Kissing girls if I can. And the other thing is building my fort.
Q: What do you dislike doing most of all?
A: Getting in a fight with my girl friend. I can't stand hurting girls' feelings. If a girl cries, I feel really bad.
Q: Do you like being a boy?
A: Yes! I get to pick my girl friend. I don't have to worry if I'm pretty. Girls have to wear too much stuff.

ACTIVITY 6

Interviews and questionnaires are effective ways of getting to know children in this age group. Devise a questionnaire, using as a model the example given above, or the sentence-completion questions discussed in Chapter 14, or any personality test you can find and adapt for your own purposes. Administer your questionnaire to several children within the same age group. Discuss your findings in class.

Certainly Jeff is quite preoccupied with girls, but it is possible that this intense concern is a substitution for other areas in which he is not so successful. His favorite activity, aside from kissing girls, is "building my fort." Nothing is said about the usual preferences of baseball or other sports. Jeff's fort is something he has had in his backyard for several years, and he loves to take it down and then rebuild it.

Friendship means a great deal to Jeff. He told his interviewer, "A friend is a person you can depend on, not just use." When asked whom he would like to be left alone with in the whole world, he at first said his girl friend, but then decided he couldn't very well leave out his best friends, Dave and Tim. Loyalties to the peer group continue to be of paramount importance to eleven-year-olds. Relationships with adults are still somewhat suspect. Jeff considers his father to be "old fashioned," and his mother is "a lady." When his interviewer first approached him, Jeff needed reassurance that "his teachers and his friends would not have access to the paper," before he was willing to participate. At the end of the time he thanked the student observer for listening to him and for trying to understand him. He said he was glad that he "finally had someone to talk to." The student observer commented that she was glad she had attempted to "break the communication gap" and that she wished that more teachers would try to do this.

Becoming a woman

In the years between ten and twelve girls far excel boys in their rate of physical growth. Many sixth- and seventh-grade girls have entered puberty. They tower above their male classmates and frequently have all the outward characteristics of womanhood. In some communities girls of this age are already being treated as adults by the opposite sex. How strange, therefore, for these same girls to be treated like children in the school setting, where they are given little opportunity to make decisions or to assume responsibilities!

But, for many girls, their physical growth greatly surpasses their emotional maturity. It is not unusual to see a full-bosomed young woman intensely involved in playing tag or jumping rope. Inside the body of a woman a little girls still exists. When, at twelve, the young lady begins to use that body seductively, she is often not even aware that she is doing so. Here is a detailed bit of observation of a twelve-year-old as she mingles with her peers at a rehearsal of a school play.

TIME	OVERT BEHAVIOR
3:15	Judy sits down on a wooden folding chair. Her right leg is crossed over her left, and she leans forward with her chin resting on her right fist. She is watching the activity on the stage. A girl comes over, sits alongside of Judy, and begins to talk to her. Judy is paying close attention to the girl, a half-smile on her lips. A boy walks over to her and stands in front of her, speaking to her. She tilts her head to the right, looks up at him, smiles, and asks him a question. As he talks to her, she smiles and nods. Her chin is resting on her right fist. She grins broadly at something that he says to her.
3:20	Judy tilts her head slightly to the right, and looks directly into the boy's face as she listens intently. She begins to talk, and as she speaks, she is smiling. She jumps up quickly for her entrance on stage, and, as she does, she hands the boy something, asking him to hold it for her. He makes a move to give it back to her, but she avoids his arm. She is laughing. The boy shrugs, and walks away, holding the object.

There is no doubt that Judy is making use of her femininity in the way she uses her body. Whether this twelve-year-old is conscious of her flirtatious manner is not known. Certainly the trick of asking the boy to "hold something for her" is one way to guarantee a reopening of the conversation after she has completed her part on the stage.

We do know, from this astute observation, that Judy is an attractive, outgoing girl, and that she is not lacking in self-confidence. She seems to be completely at ease in a social situation and relates well to girls as well as boys. It might be interesting for the reader to compare this description of Judy with the one of Laura, done by the same observer in the same setting and reported upon in Chapter 4. The most striking difference between these two twelve-year-old girls lies in their varying degrees of self-confidence.

Both twelve-year-olds make use of their bodies to express their feelings. Laura uses random movements (for example, the "turning of her foot in a circular motion") to overcome boredom or to keep time with some music that is playing. Judy registers feelings freely and is more expansive in her body movement. Both girls are exhibiting qualities of femininity, whether they are aware of it or not. It is interesting to see that so much can be observed, both in similarities and differences between these girls, during only brief periods of detailed observation.

ACTIVITY 7
Role-play a situation in which a twelve-year-old girl begins to relate to the opposite sex. The scene might be in a classroom, on the beach, or at a movie. Let other members of the class play the roles of observers, reacting to the twelve-year-old's actions. Discuss what you have observed during several scenes of role playing. How much did you infer from body movement? From facial expression?

Assuming responsibilities

Eleven- and twelve-year-olds seem quite willing and able to assume some adult responsibilities. Twelve-year-old Frances was frequently left in charge of her three-year-old brother. While being observed on a two-seated backyard swing, she showed "her mature quality in handling her younger brother by slowing the swing down and allowing her brother to jump off without harm to himself." Frances was also frequently seen doing some family mending, knitting, or doing a thousand-piece jigsaw puzzle. Fine hand coordination has developed by this age, and girls, in particular, enjoy detailed and intricate handwork.

Many occupations of preteen girls seem to be a preparation for later domestic roles. Boys, also, seem to enjoy woodworking and may assume some responsibility for fixing things around the house. Many boys this age have newspaper routes and like the idea of earning their own money.

Willie, the twelve-year-old discussed previously, had a newspaper route. Here is some of the conversation, recorded by a student observer, between Willie, his mother, the observer, and his older brother.

Willie's older brother, George, asks Willie to give him a dollar. Willie quickly tells him, "You mean *lend* you a dollar with twenty-five cents interest!"

George says, "You are going to be a rich man one day if you keep that up."
Willie replies, "That's my goal!"
Willie then tells his mother that he thinks he wants to be a paper boy all his life. She laughs and says, "Every week you want to be something else! I wonder what you will want to be next week. An airplane pilot?"
Willie answers, "I never thought of that. That's neat. Thanks a lot." He leaves the kitchen.

It is at this stage that many boys and girls begin thinking about what they want to do when they are grown up. Jeff, who was interviewed by a student observer, answered her question about what he'd like to do after college quite realistically. He said he wanted to be a "dentist or a jockey. But I know I probably won't be a jockey."

Boys often dream of being professional baseball players, and girls think about being actresses or ballerinas. But many have already begun to realize that some of their ideas are unlikely to happen. They like to fantasize, however, and frequently are irritated when their dreams are interrupted.

A ten-year-old boy, who shared a crowded apartment with his mother and several brothers and sisters, insisted that "everybody get out of the room" when he wanted to watch television. After he was alone, he watched for a short while, then got a book with pictures of football stars in it. He "stared into space and talked to himself while looking at the pictures in the book." The student observer, who was watching from another room, recognized that this boy wanted to be alone to daydream and that he was frequently a moody child.

Moods and temperament are common at this age and sometimes affect a child's schoolwork. These emotional ups and downs may be of temporary duration, or they may stem from some deep-seated problems that require further investigation. Sally, whose temper tantrums sometimes disturbed her fifth-grade class, had a problem with a younger, retarded sister at home. Sally was easily frustrated in school and sometimes seemed to be imitating the behavior of her sister who received so much more attention than Sally did. Over the period of the term her classmates began to accept Sally's disorderly behavior. It is possible that they were reflecting the attitude of the teacher, which was that Sally needed help and encouragement. The children would ignore her violent outbursts, even when they might be directed at one of them. But they were quick to call it to the teacher's attention when Sally deserved praise. Sally was a capable artist. Her classmates always asked to see her drawings and wanted the teacher to display them.

One student observer did a case study on a sixth-grade boy who had always done well in school but was now failing in one subject. Here is a part of her report.

James is quite popular among his classmates, including girls, who occasionally develop crushes on him and call him at home. His teachers have always liked him, and many have not hesitated to show it. James has proven himself to be an able student.

He is an avid reader and reads on the seventh-grade level (although he is only in sixth grade). His selection of books is primarily historical biographies, and he also chooses some books on the natural sciences. He has entered some scholastic competitions, and once he won first prize for a science project.

James' conduct record is not as outstanding as his scholastic record. However, he is not a discipline problem. He talks a lot and has received his share of demerits for doing so. On occasion he has received detentions for being fresh to some of the school monitors.

This year, however, James is not performing up to his usual level. He received a *D* in history for the first grading period, and the teacher has sent a note home with a threat that James would fail if he didn't improve. History is the only subject he is doing poorly in, however.

When the student observer interviewed James, he told her that he used to like history second to mathematics, but now he dislikes it. He said that he could not do well when he hates the teacher. He admitted that he had not been doing the work.

Perhaps James has good reason for his rebellion, as the teacher was known to be punitive, to use abusive disciplinary tactics, and to employ ridicule upon occasion. James was a student who frequently asked questions and sometimes talked out of turn. He seemed to need approval from adults, particularly since his mother had recently returned to work and was no longer giving him as much attention as she had previously. The student observer felt that James was developing feelings of inadequacy that might affect his work in his other classes. She hoped that James would be able to "surmount this obstacle soon, before any serious damage is done to his self-concept."

It is doubtful if this single situation with one teacher will have a permanent effect, but, the rebelliousness of an eleven-year-old boy could easily develop into a generalized condition that could influence other areas of his life as well as his future school work. It may take more maturity than a boy of eleven can possibly have to see that teachers are people who have their likes and dislikes as well as their own personal limitations. James should be made to realize that one teacher's opinion of him need not keep him from fulfilling his potential as a good history student.

We are reminded of the classic study by Lewin, Lippitt, and White which was discussed in a previous chapter.[5] In this study, eleven-year-old boys were subjected to three types of group atmospheres—autocratic, democratic, and laissez-faire. Rebellious feelings were expressed most frequently when the boys were in the group that was exposed to the autocratic treatment.

There seems to be much evidence to establish the view that dominating or hostile teachers will affect pupil adjustment adversely, while nonpunitive, interested teachers will facilitate behavior that is spontaneous, productive, and integrated. The classroom atmosphere in the fifth-grade class where Sally was given encouragement and support by her peers is further testimony to this fact. Children in the preteen years are highly sensitive to the climate created in a classroom and to specific teacher personalities. One needs only to walk through the corridors of a junior high school to observe this. The same class of students might be found working cooperatively with each other and with the teacher in one room, while in another room a period later, they might be throwing books at each other and climbing on the desks!

ACTIVITY 8
Visit a fifth- or sixth-grade classroom. Try to assess the atmosphere of the class. Use the Flanders Scale (see Appendix B), or an adaptation of it, to measure the amount of teacher talk and of pupil talk within a limited period of time.

Bring your findings to class and compare them with observations of classroom atmosphere done by other students in the child-development class.

Teachers and prospective teachers in the elementary schools and junior high schools might do well to study the children they will be teaching to determine, not only their personal characteristics, but also the level of development at which they are operating. There is no one environmental factor that can predict how school-age children will behave or what they are ready to learn. The children who were reported upon in this chapter came from various backgrounds. Several were black; one was Cuban. Some attended parochial school; some were observed in private school settings, others in public schools. One family (both the boy and the girl were studied) had just arrived in this area from a rural setting in North Carolina. Some were seen in crowded inner-

---

[5] Kurt Lewin, R. Lippitt, and R. K. White, "Patterns of Aggressive Behavior in Experimentally Created Social Climates," *Journal of Social Psychology*, X (1939), pp. 271–299.

city apartments, some in suburban homes with swimming pools. Yet, in spite of these many differences, the children discussed in this chapter showed many of the same decided characteristics of their age group, while still remaining very much themselves.

REFERENCES

ALMY, MILLIE. *Child Development*. New York: Holt, Rinehart and Winston, Inc., 1955.

BINTER, ALFRED R., AND SHERMAN H. FREY. *The Psychology of the Elementary School Child*. Chicago: Rand McNally & Company, 1972.

BRECKENRIDGE, MARION, AND E. LEE VINCENT. *Child Development*. 4th ed. Philadelphia: W. B. Saunders Company, 1960.

GORDON, IRA J. *Human Development: From Birth through Adolescence*. 2d ed. New York: Harper & Row, Publishers, 1969.

HOLT, JOHN. *How Children Fail*. New York: Pitman Publishing Corporation, 1964.

JERSILD, ARTHUR. *Child Psychology*. 5th ed. Englewood Cliffs, N.J.: Prentice-Hall, Inc., 1960.

LANGDON, GRACE, AND IRVING W. STOUT. *These Well-Adjusted Children*. New York: The John Day Company, Inc., 1951.

MCCANDLESS, BOYD. *Children: Behavior and Development*. 2d ed. New York: Holt, Rinehart and Winston, Inc., 1967.

MILLARD, CECIL V., AND JOHN W. M. ROTHNEY. *The Elementary School Child: A Book of Cases*. New York: Holt, Rinehart and Winston, Inc., 1957.

MUSSEN, PAUL HENRY, JOHN J. CONGER, AND JEROME KAGEN. *Child Development and Personality*. 2d ed. New York: Harper & Row, Publishers, 1963.

ROWEN, BETTY. *An Exploration of the Uses of Rhythmic Movement to Develop Aesthetic Concepts in the Primary Grades*. Cooperative Research Report, No. ED 020770, USOE. Washington, D.C.: Government Printing Office, 1966.

ROWEN, BETTY. *Learning through Movement*. New York: Teachers College Press, Columbia University, 1963.

STONE, JOSEPH, AND JOSEPH CHURCH. *Childhood and Adolescence*. 2d ed. New York: Random House, Inc., 1968.

STOTT, LELAND H. *Child Development: An Individual Longitudinal Approach*. New York: Holt, Rinehart and Winston, Inc., 1967.

STRANG, RUTH. *An Introduction to Child Study*. 4th ed. New York: Crowell-Collier and Macmillan, Inc., 1959.

PART 111

A CASE-STUDY APPROACH TO DEVELOPMENTAL PROBLEMS

11

Environmental deprivation

In Part III of this book we will look at some specific problems that occur in the process of child growth and development. Case studies prepared by students as term papers in child development courses will be used as the starting place for investigation of these problems.

None of the children described in the following chapters can be considered abnormal. Yet each of them seems to personify some common area of developmental difficulty so aptly that we have been able to use the case studies of these children to illustrate various types of developmental problems. It becomes evident that observation of normal children frequently reveals problems that might, in more severe cases, lead to behavior that deviates from the normal.

The study of abnormality is not the focus of this book. Thus we have not included exercises and activities in Part III which require study of exceptional children. Students in undergraduate courses in child development are not expected to be able to diagnose learning disability or to become knowledgeable about all aspects of emotional disturbance. The special skills required to deal with these problems must be developed through more intensive study in courses designed for this purpose. However, it is recommended that our readers try to avail themselves of opportunities to visit classes for exceptional children, if such arrangements can be made. Insights gained through observation of deviance are frequently helpful in understanding the range of normal behavior.

Case studies have frequently been used by psychologists to study children with special problems. When applied to the so-called "average" child, this method can be equally beneficial. The case-study approach is an attempt to delve into the background and previous experiences of the child in order to gain an understanding of present behavior patterns. Cumulative records and interviews with parents and teachers can be used in conjunction with direct observation of the child. As a matter of fact any of the methods described in Chapter 4, or a combination of several of them, can be used effectively in developing the case study. Insight gained through observation during earlier assignments will be helpful when students examine individual children over a period of time. The case studies are thus collections of various types of observational data, revealing a longitudinal view of a specific child. The manner of presentation of each case study is left to the discretion of the student writer.

Although the child in each case study, reported in the following chapters, is unique unto himself, his behavior has characteristics that are common to those described by researchers. The discussion following each study, therefore, will deal with some of the relevant writing on the problem described, and comparisons will be made with findings of authorities in the field. As in Part II, these references to the research on each topic are not all-inclusive, and the reader is encouraged to seek further knowledge through various sources.

The case study relating to each problem area will thus be followed by both an analysis of the reported behavior and by a comparison with relevant literature in the field. Questions will occasionally be raised for the reader to consider. Some general questions which might be asked while reading the case studies that follow, are:

Are the inferences truly based upon the data collected?
Have I noticed similar behavior during my observations?
Are there other implications that have not been mentioned?
Does the literature that I have read on this topic support this diagnosis?
What are the strong and weak points about each environment?
How might the teacher in the classroom deal with this child?
What recommendations can be made to the parents?

The reader is also encouraged to develop case-study material of her own. Data from such sources might be incorporated into the discussion following the reading of those presented here. In addition to the selected case history at the beginning of each chapter, some parts of other student reports are included in the discussion where the data collected have bearing upon the topic. Student readers should feel free to introduce other findings into the discussion wherever possible. Selections from fiction often have bearing upon a particular topic, as do case studies done by psychologists and therapists. Case-study methods are being used more extensively in research.[1] There is reason to believe that in-depth knowledge of individual children will help break down the stereotypes which have been set up by the application of behavioral norms.

The term "disadvantaged" evokes one such stereotyped image, and, although we will be discussing "deprivation" in this chapter, we want to avoid isolating segments of the population upon which to pin these labels. The children described in previous chapters of this book have come from many different backgrounds. Observations had been done on inner-city black children as well as upon children in suburban settings with backyard swimming pools. We do not study "disadvantaged" children in any special way. If the

---

[1] See the work of Robert Coles, Kenneth Keniston, R. J. Lifton, and others.

student observer learns to listen and respond to the child, she will be able to reach him regardless of differences in life-style.

It will be noted that, at several points in this book, children from poverty backgrounds were discussed. In the section on puppets in Chapter 5, a language-arts coordinator used puppet shows to stimulate verbal expression with a group of children with limited language ability. It was seen that the children's artistic expression was at a higher level than their verbal expression (see Figure 2 for children's drawings of puppet characters). This ability to conceptualize spatially and artistically is a recognized characteristic of so-called "disadvantaged" children.[2] A capable teacher or a sensitive observer can draw upon this strength in order to find out more about the individual child.

At the end of Chapter 9 we described two children who were beginning school, Dinah and Jane. The experiential backgrounds of these two little girls were quite different, and their behavior during their first days of school is contrasted. The child with many enriching experiences prior to her entrance into school was highly verbal and much more self-assured than her classmate. This information is presented as a study of two individuals, however, not as a description of a class of people.

Similarly, we will look at environmental deprivation in this chapter, not as a pattern reserved exclusively for children of low socioeconomic groups, but as a phenomenon likely to occur whenever a given set of circumstances presents itself.

Environmental deprivation

In recent years the problem of environmental deprivation has received much attention. With the advent of the war on poverty in the 1960s efforts have been made to discover why children raised in lower-economic-level homes are often less competent in academic areas than middle-class children. The child who has been designated as "deprived" or "disadvantaged" differs from other children in language development, self-concept, cognitive, and social skills. He has few academic interests and is not motivated to learn. He has difficulty focusing his mind and listening to directions. He is frustrated at every turn in the school setting. His feelings of inadequacy are quickly confirmed as he moves from kindergarten into the grades.

Various programs have been initiated to overcome the deficits that children of poverty seem to have at the time of their entrance into school. Head Start programs attempt to reach the child before the usual age for school entrance and to provide him with experiences that have been lacking in his background. Such programs have tried to develop the child's ability to listen, to discriminate sounds and shapes, to express ideas, to manipulate materials, and so on. Most of all, these programs have tried to build the self-concept of these children so that they are mentally and emotionally ready for learning.

[2] Arnold B. Cheyney, *Teaching Culturally Disadvantaged in the Elementary School,* p. 49.

In addition to the intervention programs, which attempt to make up for the gaps in young children's experiences, there are further studies as to what causes such gaps in the early development of poverty children. Hunt summarizes the evidence that suggests that being reared in poverty deprives a child of opportunities to develop the linguistic and conceptual skills necessary for achievement in school.

The children in poor families have typically encountered many fewer kinds of objects than children of middle-class background. Often as infants the children of poverty in crowded circumstances are submitted to a continuing vocal racket to which they become habituated. This habituation may account for the inadequacies of auditory discrimination. . . . Too often the verbal interaction of children of the poor with their elders is limited to commands to cease whatever the child is doing; seldom two- and three-year-olds are asked questions which demand that they formulate matters verbally in response. . . . Seldom are the reasons for actions explained; seldom is ingenuity rewarded, except for that ingenuity in avoiding punishment that comes from getting caught at something prohibited. . . .

On the motivational side, moreover, children have little opportunity to take initiative, to give up present gratifications for future goals, or to take pride in problem-solving achievement.[3]

Further investigation is deemed necessary to determine the key factors in the background of children of poverty which might be accountable for their learning deficiencies. However, sufficient evidence exists to establish the belief that intelligence and ability to succeed at academic tasks is not purely genetically determined but is a product of interaction of the organism with its environment.

Hunt and others maintain that children of poverty exhibit some of the same characteristics as institutionalized children raised in sterile environments.[4] Because of their relevance to present-day problems of the disadvantaged, much attention has been given to studies of environmental deprivation reported by psychologists in the late 1930s. Some of these research findings will be discussed later in this chapter. It is postulated that children who enter school lacking in learning abilities may have been deprived in infancy of the necessary stimulation and interaction with adults that is deemed essential for the development of language and concept formation.

How does it happen that young children suffer from such deprivation? Poverty parents, as well as middle-class parents, usually love their children. What kind of attention is lacking, and how does this affect the very young child?

The following case study of an eighteen-month-old baby seems to illus-

---

[3] J. McV. Hunt, "Political and Social Implications of the Role of Experience in the Development of Competence," *The Challenge of Incompetence and Poverty* (Urbana, Ill.: University of Illinois Press, 1969), pp. 135–136.

[4] J. McV. Hunt, "The Psychological Basis for Using Preschool Enrichment as an Antidote for Cultural Deprivation," *Preschool Education Today*, ed. Fred M. Hechinger (New York: Doubleday & Company, Inc., 1966).

trate some of the elements in the environment that cause deprivation and to reveal many of the behavior characteristics of the deprived child. This case study is particularly interesting, since the home does not provide the typical poverty setting and the child is not of a minority group. When she did her observations, the student was not aware of the similarity of her descriptions to those in the literature on deprivation. The fact that these symptoms appear in so young a child is evidence that attention must be given to problems of environmental deprivation at much earlier levels than had previously been considered by government agencies.

A CASE STUDY OF BILLY, EIGHTEEN MONTHS OLD

FAMILY BACKGROUND

The family consists of father and husband, John, age 28 years; mother and wife, Sally, age 26 years; David, age five years; Dwayne, age three years; Billy, age eighteen months; and Marie and Martha (twin girls), age six months.

John is from a wealthy southern family. He is the oldest of five sons and says he will inherit a large sum of money one day, especially since he is the oldest. He cannot seem to adjust to living an average life. He has brought his need for quantity and quality with him. He spends money all the time—even money he doesn't have! When I first met him and came to his house, he was immediately on the defensive about his old furniture. Throughout my two weeks in his home I noticed John maintained his defensive attitude about his lack of material things.

John graduated from a military high school and went immediately into the army. He and his wife met while he was on leave. They saw each other as much as possible over a two-year period and were married shortly after his military release. He never attended college, but he has been extremely successful in any type of work requiring mechanics—especially automobiles.

While I was staying in his home, John was very busy trying to make good in a garage he had opened recently. He and a friend worked day and night. John was home very little. Most of the time his children never saw him, and when they did, it was for five minutes. The only words I ever heard him speak to his children were, "Sit down over there" or "Shut up." He never invited them to sit by him or asked what they did. He did nothing aside from ordering or scolding them. His attitude was very military. This may be a result of his own up-bringing—especially his high school and military years.

Many times I heard John say he wished he did not have so many children. His own children were scared to death of him—it could be seen in their nervous gestures whenever he came home. John was not a very responsible person. Many times he used the grocery money to buy parts to a car, or the like. My friend and I were put in the position of lending him money.

Sally is from a small country town. She is the youngest of a family of thirteen children. Her father died when she was five years old, therefore, she was raised predominantly by her elderly mother and her brothers and sisters. The child closest in age to herself was a retarded brother who was mistreated, made fun of, and thought crazy.

Sally's ambition was to get married and have children—which she is definitely doing! She never completed her senior year in high school because at the time it didn't seem to matter. However, she is now sorry she did not. She does not speak correct English and doesn't write very well either. She feels this may jeopardize her children and tries hard to speak as correctly as possible.

She is more patient than many mothers I have seen, but once she becomes angry almost anything goes. She is more honest and blunt than the average person and says exactly what she means.

David is a five year old who is extremely immature for his age and is also very nervous. He is not especially cute looking. David is extremely fond of throwing tantrums when he wants something, although they are ignored. His mother said he used to cry whenever he wanted something and he used to get it; now she does not want to spoil him. He has no friends other than his brother because he is not allowed outside without his mother. He does not get out because his mother is indoors watching the other children. He is always seeking attention and never receiving it. His favorite words are "See" and "Look at me." If you don't look, he screams louder! He has a poor vocabulary, and he pronounces the words he knows poorly. David is to start kindergarten in the fall.

Dwayne is a beautiful child and has received more attention than the other children. He also appears to be much smarter. Many times I have noticed him sitting, thinking, and figuring little problems out. He asks whatever he wants to know and is very warm and outgoing. He also throws tantrums—he throws himself on the floor and pouts until he sees it won't work—then he's all smiles again. Dwayne does not seem to have suffered from his father's lack of attention as much as David has. Possibly this is because he has a male image to look at, even if it is his older brother. Also, a friend once lived with their family and he paid an enormous amount of attention to Dwayne, frequently taking him places.

The two boys play together because there is no one else. They seem to get along fine when no one is around. There is a lot of copying what the other boy does and naturally much tattling also. Both boys are very active and love trucks and games like most little boys their age.

The twin daughters of John and Sally have an effect upon Billy's life because they must be cared for and therefore receive more attention than Billy. All day they remain in a playpen used as a crib filled with blankets. At least they have each other for company!

Sally almost lost her life with the birth of the twins. She had them at home without warning. She remained in the hospital for two weeks after their birth. They were premature and did not come home until a month after their birth.

When all the children are downstairs after dinner, the twins receive the most attention because they are changed and held until they are through eating their dinner.

Billy, the middle child, is a mere observer of all.

Billy was born during difficult times for his parents and was a "mistake"! His parents had not planned to have any more children until John was established financially. At the time John was seeking work. The family, then made up of five members, was living in a three-room apartment with two male friends of John's.

Ever since Billy was about three months old he has been sickly. He is extremely susceptible to colds and viruses. He was in the hospital for a month or more with pneumonia at approximately the age of six months. Then he was in and out of hospitals for fevers. His parents rushed him to a doctor at the sign of any unusual symptom because of his early medical history. When Billy came home from the hospital after pneumonia, his mother became ill and had to be hospitalized for two weeks. Therefore, Billy received very little attention from his mother during his first year of life.

OBSERVATIONS

I observed the entire family of seven members (including the twin girls) for a period of two weeks while I was a guest in their home. Billy caught my immediate attention because of his beautiful face and his gentle, shy, and timid nature. Also, I wanted to get to know him better because he is the middle child in a family of five children as I myself am. Much of what I saw in Billy made me wonder what I was like when I was his age. What did I think? What did I feel? What did I do? I thought perhaps I could find some answers in Billy.

During my two-week visit Billy was kept in his room *most* of the time—inside his crib filled with quilts, blankets, and pillows. His mother "visited" him to give him his bottle of milk or water and once in a while she changed him! His room smelled of dirty diapers. Billy spent much time babbling to himself. Many times during the day he could be heard banging the bars on his crib back and forth, hoping to get some attention. This was usually ignored unless the babies were sleeping. In such a case he was spanked! Billy banged the bars on the crib during the night also. I cannot remember one night when he slept through the whole night. This was partly because he hardly ever left his crib except for dinner and a little while afterward. At night when he began banging his father would get up and scream or hit him; other times he was left alone until he stopped. Only once did his mother go upstairs and bring Billy down to sit with us for awhile. I had suggested it to her many times before. On this occasion Billy sat and did not move. He appeared frightened and was not sure what to expect. I can easily understand this reaction since the experience of being with his mother and not having the other children around was somewhat new to him. Then suddenly Billy began to cry, a fearful insecure cry. His mother placed him on her lap and rocked him until he knew he was okay. He remained curled in her arms and would not move. He did not smile once, not even a little. In fact, he never smiled. Then when it was time for bed, he cried but did not continue the banging. Soon all was silent.

Billy was always brought downstairs about five o'clock for dinner. The three boys sat on stools facing a counter in the kitchen. David and Dwayne always wanted more and argued about who had more or less. Billy never even mumbled. He sat on the stool and watched and listened. Usually he got food all over him, because he did feed himself. He loved toast—that was the one thing he always finished. After dinner the twins were also brought downstairs and there was mass diaper changing on the four youngest . . . including Dwayne who was spanked whenever he wet his pants. The children were bathed at least three times a week.

One day I took Billy, Dwayne, and David outside for a walk. Billy did not want to walk. It took quite a bit of patience before I could get him to try walking! At first he held both of my hands tightly and finally he walked slowly while holding one hand. He would take a few steps and then stop and stare at the other children. He had such a confused look on his face. Again he never smiled once. A few times he stopped and clung to me.

When we came back to the house I tried playing with Billy on the front lawn. Billy mistook the fun of rolling in the grass for something else and began crying. Then I tried rolling trucks to him but he merely stared at me with that confused look about him. Billy was hardly ever outside. His mother had the other children to worry about. Also, she could not take the children to visit various places because she could not drive.

One day when Sally went grocery shopping, I was left to baby-sit. All the children were supposed to be taking naps, however, I knew Billy was up. I brought Billy downstairs to play with him. We rolled a truck back and forth—he even laughed once or twice. Then I decided to see if he would walk by himself. He had not done this for anyone in his family. At first he did not respond to my talking and holding out my hands. Finally he stood up while holding my hands and proceeded to walk toward me. He did not appear to have much confidence in what he was doing. Gradually I began moving my hands so that he was holding less and less. Actually he was walking without assistance except for the security of knowing my hands were there. When he was holding only one finger, Billy reverted back to his sitting and pouting. After an hour or more of playing and trying to get him to walk, I succeeded. Billy seemed to be happy with himself and the praise I gave him. He tried talking—something he never did except when he was alone. Perhaps these were among Billy's most satisfying moments.

Later, however, when his mother came home, Billy refused to walk alone. She tried working with him because I was so enthusiastic, but without results. She was very much surprised that he had responded to me.

INFERENCES

Being the middle child, Billy was neither here nor there. By this, I mean that he did some things that his older brothers did—as when he ate dinner—but, he was kept in his room all day as if he was a baby who did not and could not care. His room consisted of a set of drawers, a bunk bed, and a crib. He definitely suffered from lack of stimulation and attention. He was small for his age—about the height of an eleven- or twelve-month-old child. This is partly due to his poor health. Billy played with his brothers occasionally; usually he was a bystander and observer.

He was afraid of his mother because she had a way of showing affection to him that would scare me too. She would slap his face or pinch it making him cry nine times out of ten. Billy rarely knew what to expect; for that matter neither did I! I don't think he really knew he had a father, nor did the other boys because the man whom they saw once in awhile was either scolding or slapping them.

Billy's mother was tired of babies. She has had dirty diapers "up to her eyeballs," as she said often to me. She goes through her everyday routine of caring for five young children and getting nothing from it. This is what she thought she wanted.

Billy will probably be a slow learner since he has had little opportunity for much else. I am hoping Sally will find more time for him when David enters kindergarten.

In conclusion, I found Billy to be extremely introverted for a child his age. He is shy, timid, and very gentle. He has many fears of the unknown and does not explore as readily as children his age do—nor has he ever (according to his mother). He seems insecure and has a definite lack of confidence in what he can do. Billy seeks attention but does not know if he should fear the attention he gets. Most of the attention has not been beneficial. He never seemed to be held and loved by anyone in the family. I feel this child will have many adjustment problems both emotionally and socially and that they will become worse if he is not cared for soon. Lack of stimulation has been a major factor as well as lack of loving attention.

ANALYSIS OF THE CASE STUDY

This case study was based upon the student's own experiences when she was a boarder in the family dwelling. She was particularly sensitive to the plight of Billy, since she herself was a middle child in a large family. It is doubtful if her home life resembled Billy's in any other way, but her concern for this child was based, in part, upon her feeling of identifying with him. Such empathy increased her insight. Her personal style of writing presents a rather touching picture.

The description of Billy very strongly resembles that of neglected children reported in the literature on deprivation. Billy is apathetic, timid, and withdrawn. He has a history of poor health, although there is nothing in the records to make us believe there is any physical disability involved. He "could be heard banging the bars of his crib" and no doubt exhibited the rocking pattern often observed in retarded children. Skeels describes two baby girls observed at an orphanage prior to the initiation of an intervention program in these terms:

Early in the service aspects of the program, two baby girls, neglected by their feeble-minded mothers, ignored by their inadequate relatives, malnourished and frail, were legally committed to the orphanage. The youngsters were pitiful little creatures. They were tearful, had runny noses, and sparse, stringy, and colorless hair; they were emaciated, undersized, and lacked muscle tonus or responsiveness. Sad and inactive, the two spent their days rocking and whining.

The psychological examinations showed developmental levels of 6 and 7 months, respectively, for the two girls, although they were then 13 and 16 months old chronologically. This serious delay in mental growth was confirmed by observations of their behavior in the nursery and by reports of the superintendent of nurses, as well as by the pediatrician's examination. There was no evidence of physiological or organic defect, or of birth injury or glandular dysfunction.[5]

We might compare the descriptions of the behavior and physical appearance of these two little girls to that of Billy. Although we do not have medical records or psychological tests available to us, we can rather safely assume that Billy, like the little girls described above, was suffering from neglect and environmental deprivation. His withdrawal and his meager attempts to explore his environment seem to be the direct result of the lack of attention he had received prior to the period of observation. The student's efforts to get him to play with the trucks were regarded suspiciously by him. When she tried to encourage him to stand up and walk, she met with some success, but he refused to make these attempts with his mother. Compare these observations to the descriptions of babies of this age and younger that are in Chapters 7 and 8. Most babies are walking at one year of age, and their curiosity about things around them cannot be contained. The mother, rather than inhibiting attempts at exploration, is used as a source of reassurance before the baby ventures forth for further investigation.

The pattern of emotional insecurity is clearly seen in the behavior of this eighteen-month-old. Even when his mother, at the student's insistence, brought Billy downstairs to give him her undivided attention, he remained fearful. Rocking reassured him, but there was no evidence of the smiling and in-

[5] Harold M. Skeels, *Adult Status of Children with Contrasting Early Life Experiences*, p. 5.

vestigating behavior so typical at this age. Fraiberg claims that babies deprived of maternal care are not attracted to objects and do not find pleasure and excitement in discovery.[6] "It appears, then, that the miraculous achievement of the normal infant, the movement away from body-centeredness to object relationships, is not just the product of biological maturation but the achievement of the human family through ties of love."[7] Mother is the link to the external world. When she is present, the baby feels free to explore his environment. When the baby is deprived of this attachment, he is "confused, disoriented, as if he had lost his connection with his new found world and with it his own newly discovered self feelings."[8]

Fraiberg, as a psychoanalyst, attributes this behavior to a need for a love relationship with the mother. There is evidence, however, that the biological mother need not be the sole provider, and that security and interest in the world is equally evident in babies raised without strong maternal ties. This author recently had occasion to visit the children's houses on an Israeli kibbutz. Infants as young as six months old were observed living in small cottages under the care of trained caretakers or "metapelets." There were no more than five children in each cottage, and they were well-provided with stimulating toys, attention, and love. All of the children observed appeared to be bright-eyed, eager to explore, and happy. Nine-month-olds were creeping and standing up by themselves. Eighteen-month-olds were climbing on outdoor apparatus, waving bye-bye, and grinning at the visitors. One or two less outgoing children sought the security of the metapelet's arms as we approached them, much as children this age seek the reassurance of their mother when meeting strangers. These children see their biological mothers only for two hours a day during visiting time. They have been cared for by trained personnel practically since birth. They seemed to be healthy, secure, and normally curious about the world. There was no evidence of deprivation and no symptoms of retarded behavior of the kind exhibited by neglected children.

Many readers might question the mental ability or innate intellectual potential of a child such as Billy. Of course, we have no proof that he was born without a deficiency. But there is sufficient evidence that children with similar patterns of behavior at this age have overcome their handicaps when placed in more stimulating and more loving environments.

There is every likelihood that, without a significant change in his style of living, Billy will be a slow learner and possibly a retarded child. At eighteen months he is already the victim of environmental deprivation. Without opportunities for manipulation of objects, he will no doubt be lacking in perceptual skills when he reaches school age. With limited experiences in muscular control, he may not have the physical coordination required for the development of later skills. Most of all his lack of confidence and sense of self will affect his motivation to learn.

[6] Selma H. Fraiberg, *The Magic Years*, pp. 47–56.
[7] Fraiberg, *The Magic Years*, pp. 55–56.
[8] Fraiberg, *The Magic Years*, p. 48.

Many children from "culturally deprived" or "disadvantaged" backgrounds have these kinds of deficiencies when they reach school age. Evidence seems to point to the fact that lack of stimulation and adult attention during infancy is at the base of their problem, rather than simply factors of economic need or of ethnic origin. Billy is not a typical disadvantaged child. His father came from a wealthy family and had high expectations of material success at some future time. His mother, though from a less advantaged background, was interested in her role of motherhood. She "tries hard to speak as correctly as possible" so as not to jeopardize her children's chance of success in life. The family is not a member of a minority ethnic group; nor do they live in a congested slum area.

Yet, eighteen-month-old Billy, caught between demanding older brothers and twin infant sisters, is suffering from neglect. His lack of intellectual stimulation due to the absence of toys and adult companionship has already resulted in a slowing down of the explorative impulses which are so necessary to the development of thought processes. Even more significantly, he has not developed the sense of trust, usually associated with the mother-child relationship, which is so essential for healthy growth in the social domain.

Many students now preparing for teaching will be working with disadvantaged children who have had experiences similar to Billy's. Limitations in learning abilities might stem from the same pattern of neglect. Overworked mothers, harassed by the care of many children, do not have time and energy to provide the stimulation and the attention necessary for healthy development of infant cognition and social abilities. Moreover, they do not see that playing with their children is essential to their growth. Teachers must take a more active role in making parents aware of these factors. Teachers also need to look at the possible causes for learning deficiencies. They must understand these causes in order to reach the child at the level at which he is operating. When confronted with an apathetic, slow learner, whether from an economically disadvantaged home or not, we might do well to remember Billy.

Comparison to research studies

Let us return to the two little girls in the orphanage with whom we compared Billy earlier in this chapter. Quite by accident they became the inspiration for a classic research study which has had an impact upon the thinking of psychologists about heredity and environment and has had a significant effect upon the standard practices in institutions for dependent children.

In 1932 Dr. Harold M. Skeels became the first psychologist to be employed by the Iowa Board of Control of State Institutions. It was on a tour of duty to a state-operated orphanage that he saw the two infant girls described above. The two children were considered unplaceable for adoption and were transferred to a school for the mentally retarded. Six months after the transfer had taken place, Dr. Skeel's duties took him to visit the wards of that institution, where he noticed two outstanding little girls. "They were alert, smiling, running about, responding to the playful attention of adults, and generally behaving and looking like any other toddlers."[9] It was difficult for the psychologist to recognize them as the same little girls he had observed at the orphanage. He tested them again and found that the results indicated that the two were approaching normal mental development for their age. Twelve months later they were reexamined and again at forty and forty-three months old. Their development remained well within the range of normal. They were eventually transferred back to the orphanage and shortly thereafter were placed in homes for adoption.

What had occurred that had so dramatically changed the life-style of these two children? When they arrived at the school for the mentally retarded, they had been placed on one of the wards of older girls and women. These mental defectives ranged in chronological age from eighteen to fifty and had a mental age of five to nine years. The two little girls were the only children of preschool age on the ward. An older girl had "adopted" each of the two girls, and other older girls "served as adoring aunts." They were shown affection and were taken on shopping excursions. Toys were purchased for them, and they had play materials in great abundance. The nurses and attendants also helped to provide a homelike atmosphere, abundant in affection and rich in experiences suitable for preschool children.

These remarkable changes in behavior of two "feeble-minded" babies led to a planned program of intervention for orphaned infants. A study was undertaken by Skeels and Dye in which thirteen such infants were placed in similar settings on the wards at the school for the mentally retarded.[10] These thirteen were matched, as far as was possible, with twelve infants of similar mentality and background who remained in the sterile environment of the orphanage.

The length of the experimental period varied from 5.7 months to 52.1 months, due to the fact that when a child showed normal development, the visit to the school for the mentally retarded was terminated. Every child showed a gain of from seven to fifty-eight points, according to the Kuhlmann-Binet Intelligence Tests. Three made gains of forty-five points or more, and all but two gained more than fifteen points. The children who were initially at the lower levels tended to make the greatest gains.

The mental development of the contrast group who remained at the orphanage was quite the opposite. All children, except one, showed losses of from nine to forty-five points. Ten of the twelve children lost fifteen or more points in IQ over the period of the study. The greatest losses were associated with the children at the highest levels initially.

[9] Skeels, *Status of Children*, p. 6.
[10] Harold M. Skeels and H. B. Dye, as reported in Skeels, *Status of Children*, pp. 6–21.

Follow-up study

Years later a follow-up study was done which investigated the adult status of these children with contrasting early life experiences.[11] All subjects were located and information obtained on them after a period of twenty-one years. The two groups had maintained their divergent patterns of competency into adulthood. All thirteen of the experimental group were self-supporting, and none were wards of any institution. In the contrast group four were wards of institutions, four worked as dishwashers, and only one earned an adequate salary and was self-sustaining. The study makes it clearly evident that prediction of later intelligence cannot be based on the child's first observed developmental status, but account must be taken of the environmental encounters which constitute the conditions for growth.

These studies have been cited by Hunt and others as dramatic evidence of the effect of experience upon intelligence. In the years between the original and the follow-up study on the adult status of the subjects, much has happened to change the thinking of psychologists and educators concerning the nature-nurture controversy.

When it was first published in 1938, the initial findings of Skeels's study were ridiculed by several knowledgeable psychologists and were not generally accepted. Belief in fixed intelligence was popular at that time, and the idea of compensatory education at the preschool level did not exist.

It was about this time, however, that evidence on the effects of environment on intelligence began to accumulate. Skeels and his associates did another study in which twenty children living in an orphanage were provided with nursery school for a few hours a day, while a matched group of twenty youngsters did not have these experiences.[12] Both groups were exposed to the same environmental influences except for the school hours. They lived in cottages together, ate the same foods, were attended by the same staff. The experiment lasted for three years. At the end of that time the group that had had preschool experience showed trends toward normal development, while the control group moved in the direction of feeblemindedness. Those of the preschool group who were placed in foster homes after this experience developed in intellectual growth more than control group placements.

Other researchers began to investigate the problem of deprivation. Spitz compared babies reared in institutions with babies raised normally with their families and concluded that being reared in institutions seems to have serious consequences for later emotional and intellectual development. Goldfarb found that children brought up in institutions for three years and then placed in foster homes were inferior in conceptualization and school achievement to

---

[11] Skeels, pp. 27–65.

[12] Harold M. Skeels, Ruth Updegraff, Beth L. Wellman, and H. M. Williams, "A Study of Environmental Stimulation: An Orphanage Preschool Project," *University of Iowa Studies in Child Welfare*, 1938, 15, No. 4.

similar children placed in foster homes from early infancy.[13] Fourteen years later the children who were institutionalized longer were retarded in a number of areas and displayed various ill effects from their early institutionalization. These investigators attributed the loss mainly to the absence of a close mother-child relationship.

Other investigators claim that it is mainly lack of sensory stimulation that seems to make the difference. Dennis and Najarian found that children institutionalized shortly after birth showed some signs of retardation but no evidence of emotional damage.[14] Studies of children raised in kibbutzim in Israel show that children can be institutionalized and still be well adjusted and basically capable of meeting the demands of living. Fortunately, institutional life for children has been improving, and much of the results of these studies is dependent upon the environment of the institution under consideration.

Casler points out that, at both the animal and the human level, the damage is more likely to stem from sensory deprivation than from absence of the mother or the nature of institutional life in itself.[15]

Animal studies provide evidence similar to that gathered about deprived infants. Hoffman found that rats confined to small cages do less well than rats who were given more freedom. Thompson and Heron did similar experiments with dogs and found the adult problem-solving ability of Scotty pups raised as pets to be considerably higher than their littermates reared in isolation in laboratory cages for the same period.[16] Other well-known animal experiments, such as Harlow's work with rhesus monkeys and Kuo's study of pecking responses in chicks, support the point of view that deprivation of one kind or another in early infancy affects the emotional and intellectual development of the animals in later life.

It is, of course, more difficult to obtain evidence concerning infant deprivation than it is to perform experiments upon animals. No researcher would purposely deprive a human being of a rich and stimulating environment in his early years, simply to be able to set up a controlled experiment. We cannot put infants in cages, or work with them in laboratory settings, as has been done with these animal subjects. But occasionally a clinical record provides evidence that nearly matches the controlled situation.

The study of identical twins reared apart from each other provides evidence of this nature. In one study by Newman, Freeman, and Holzinger[17] nineteen such sets of twins were reported on. The findings strongly suggest that

[13] Rene A. Spitz, and William Goldfarb, as reported by George J. Mouly, *Psychology for Effective Teaching*, cited in 2d ed. (New York: Holt, Rinehart and Winston, Inc., 1968), pp. 95–98.

[14] W. Dennis and P. Najarian, as cited in Mouly, p. 97.

[15] Lawrence Casler, *Maternal Deprivation*.

[16] C. S. Hoffman, W. R. Thompson, and W. Heron, as cited in Casler.

[17] H. F. Newman, F. N. Freeman, and K. J. Holzinger, as cited by Boyd R. McCandless in *Children: Behavior and Development*, 2d ed. (New York: Holt, Rinehart and Winston, Inc., 1967), p. 345.

the more widely different the environments in which they grew up, the more divergent their IQ's were likely to be. A difference of twenty-four points on the Stanford-Binet was reported for one set of twin girls, where one had spent much of her life in an isolated mountain setting and had dropped out of school at an early age, and where the other girl had been adopted into a home where there was much emphasis upon education.

A case study[18] at the University of Miami's Mailman Center for Child Development reveals some dramatic effects of changed environments. Two baby brothers, ages nine months and three years, were brought to the center for examination and possible placement for adoption. The children showed all of the symptoms of neglect, malnutrition, and deprivation. They were listless and apathetic. They did not respond to toys placed before them, nor did they show any facial expression when adults approached them. They had distended abdomens and spindly arms and legs. All of these characteristics are clearly shown on films taken of the children at their time of arrival at the center.

Both boys were placed in a foster home where care, affection, and ample stimulation were provided. Films were again taken of the older boy after a period of four months had elapsed. His physical appearance had changed so radically that it would be hard to recognize him as the same child. His arms and legs had filled out, and he appeared to have good muscle tone. His face showed animation, and he smiled at the approach of an adult. He enjoyed playing with blocks and toy trucks. This boy has been observed for a period of five years, and, although he has made considerable strides, and tests as normal in many areas, his scores exhibit a "scatter pattern" with some deficiencies still existing. His baby brother, who had been placed in the foster home at a much earlier age, tested within the normal range in all areas shortly afterward, and was therefore placed for adoption. No further record is available for this younger boy.

Although none of this evidence is conclusive, there seems to be every indication that, where a healthy environment is provided soon enough, effects of environmental deprivation can be overcome.

Gordon's infant stimulation program

Ira J. Gordon, at the University of Florida at Gainesville, has set up a project to investigate a way in which early intervention into the lives of babies might break the poverty cycle.[19] Women from disadvantaged areas were trained to teach mothers how to stimulate their infants. The stimulation procedure consisted of a series of games designed to increase perceptual and motor abilities. Many of these games are of the kind usually played by middle-class mothers with their infants, such as "This little piggie went to market" or

---

[18] *Case Study of Ralph* (Mailman Center for Child Development, University of Miami, Miami, Florida).

[19] Ira J. Gordon, *Early Child Stimulation through Parent Education.*

"Pat-a-cake." Others were specifically designed to achieve certain goals as defined by the psychologist, Piaget. For example, playing a game in which the baby is to find an object hidden under a towel establishes for him the idea that objects exist even when out of sight.

Paraprofessionals trained as parent educators visited the homes and instructed mothers in the use of the games. This instruction took place once a week, and it was the mother who was to interact with the baby through the use of these games. The program began with infants as young as three months. It had been in operation for two years, at the time of the report, and experimental and control groups had been established, with some groups of mothers and babies remaining in the experimental group for only one of the two years. The first objective was to enhance the development of the babies, while other objectives were to determine the effectiveness of the method of working with mothers and the use of paraprofessionals. We will report here only on the results pertaining to the first objective.

At the end of the first year children whose mothers had been involved in the project were superior to control children on both the Griffiths Mental Development Scales and on the series material designed originally as teaching materials for the project. At the end of the second year, children whose mothers had been in the project from the beginning or those whose mothers entered the program of parent education when their child was one year of age were also superior. The children who had only the first nine months of the program (from three months old to twelve months old) were not superior to the control children.[20]

Thus, generally speaking, the program was effective in improving abilities of babies, especially those between one and two years of age. The Gordon program has been widely discussed as an innovative intervention study and has served as a model for other programs involving parent-child interaction.

A comparison study of an advantaged child

A case study was done by an undergraduate student in which she used the exercises[21] devised for the Gordon project with her fifteen-month-old nephew, Mark. Far from being deprived of stimulation and adult attention, this baby seemed to have received both in great quantity. The living room of the home was turned into a play area for Mark, and he was given free reign during his waking hours. According to the student's report, there was a slide, a rocking horse, a car, and a bike. "There isn't much living room furniture and the floor is carpeted, so his mother lets him play there."

It is interesting to contrast this child's behavior with that of Billy, who was actually three months older than Mark. In terms of motor coordination, Mark seems to be extremely precocious. His attitudes toward exploration and

[20] Gordon, p. 201.
[21] Ira J. Gordon and J. R. Lally, *Intellectual Stimulation for Infants and Toddlers.*

his efforts to develop new skills can be seen in the following anecdotal record from the student's case study.

Mark went over to his slide which is a new gift that he received from his parents for the holidays. It is one of those new toys, made of wood, with parts that can be assembled in different ways. It is approximately three feet high and has three steps to climb up. Mark liked it from the very beginning and had no trouble using it. His mother had to show him how to climb at first, and now he is very good at it. He climbs up, stands up, and then slides down. When he reaches the bottom he laughs as he falls over.

Later he began going up his slide backward. He climbed up the down part of it. He would look at his mother when he did this and then proceed. I think he liked it better this way because it was much harder for him to get up.

Most children who feel secure in their environment like to explore and get great satisfaction from new physical accomplishments. Mark is no exception. But contrast his behavior to eighteen-month-old Billy, who hesitated to venture forth in the effort of walking, although he was probably physically capable of performing the task. Billy did not have a room full of climbing apparatus to experiment with. What is even more important is that Billy did not have a mother who gave him reassurance and support. He was therefore not willing to take a risk. Even brave little Mark looked to his mother for reassurance before he tried "to climb up the down part."

The student observer decided to experiment with some of Gordon's games on her nephew. The first one, selected from the beginning of the book, offered little challenge.

Position:
   1. Baby's position: sitting with a flat surface in front of him.
   2. Mother's position: beside the baby supporting him.
Action:
   1. Hold a favorite toy out to the baby.
   2. When he reaches for it, place it in front of him and cover it quickly.
   3. Say, "Where is the toy?" "Find the toy."
   4. Repeat actions 1 and 2 but cover the toy completely.
Aim of the game:
   The baby gets the toy after it is completely covered.
Purpose:
   To help the baby realize the permanence of objects.[22]

Mark sat on the living room rug and was quiet as we prepared for this activity. I explained the instructions to his mother and sat back ready to observe. The toy used was a set of plastic keys that Mark has had for a long time. From the beginning Mark seemed to know that we were playing a game. He saw the keys and grabbed for them, at which time his mother hid them. He went right over to the blanket and took out the toy and laughed. I asked his mother to repeat this activity and Mark did the same thing.

[22] Ira Gordon and J. R. Lally, p. 15.

This activity was not new to Mark, and, although he enjoyed it, it offered little challenge. The student observer decided to move ahead to Series Four in the book of stimulation games. One game involved unscrewing the lid from a small jar filled with small objects. This was a new activity to Mark. He was able to unscrew the lid after being shown how to do it twice. The effort required for this movement was evident. His whole body moved with each turn of the wrist. Putting the lid on was easier for him, and he did this on the first try. The student observer reported that each time that he put the lid on, he took it off again. He obviously enjoyed this new game.

The student observer proceeded to introduce another game to mother and child immediately after this one.

Position:
1. Child's position: sitting on the floor or at the table.

Action:
1. Place a small container, with a hole in its screw-on lid, on the floor.
2. Drop buttons (or pennies) through the slot while the child is watching. Say, "Watch the buttons go in." "See how Mommy does it?"
3. Empty the jar and put the lid back on.
4. Put the jar and buttons in front of the child.
5. If he does not put any buttons in the jar, put some in for him and say, "Let's put the buttons in the jar."
6. Empty the jar and let the child try again.

Note:
Do not make the slot too small. It should be easy for the buttons to go in the slot.

Aim of the game:
The child puts buttons through the slot by himself.

Purpose:
To help the child gain skills in using his small muscles.[23]

In this activity Mark's mother chose to use pennies. While she was showing him how to put the pennies in the slot, Mark picked up some and put them in his mouth. His mother took them out and continued. Then she pushed the entire pile over to Mark to signify that it was his turn. He put the pennies in. Sometimes he would try to get more than one penny in at a time and sometimes his fingers would go in the slot with the penny. When it was all filled Mark unscrewed the lid, as he had done so well in the previous activity, and spilled the pennies out.

Not only had Mark performed this activity with ease, but he had applied knowledge gained from a previous activity to this one in order to continue with the game! The student observer remarked that Mark had a toy that is somewhat similar. It was a mailbox with slots of different shapes. It is no wonder that he did well at a task less difficult than one he faced when he played with one of his familiar toys. The application of the newly acquired skill of unscrewing was his own highly intelligent contribution to the game.

[23] Ira Gordon and J. R. Lally, p. 40.

Mark is a child who has been given every opportunity to explore his environment. His new accomplishments are duly rewarded. It is not surprising, therefore, that problem-solving abilities are well developed in this fifteen-month-old. The student observer reports on a discussion with the child's mother.

Mark's mother feels that Mark is a healthy, normal child with a pleasant personality. She thinks that the age that he started to walk is normal, and she is not the least bit worried that he has not started talking yet. She feels that when he is ready to talk he will and, when that time comes, she will be happy.

She also said that lots of mothers would have spoken to their doctors by now if their child had not talked. She isn't like that at all. Many times her mother-in-law tells everyone what a genius Mark is, but Mark's mother just has to laugh to herself. She will rarely brag about Mark but does commend him when he does something that is commendable.

With such a healthy attitude on the part of the mother, it is little wonder that Mark is an alert child with a pleasing personality. No doubt he will do well in school and will be able to cope with problems in life just as he was able to cope with the problems of the stimulation games. It is the feeling of this author that, if a child who is normal at birth is provided with affection, stimulation, and reinforcement in infancy and early childhood, he will enter school with motivation and ability to perform adequately in academic areas. Environmental deprivation, whether caused by poverty, neglect, or the indifference of society, need not keep any child from the equal opportunity that is his natural birthright.

REFERENCES

BLOOM, BENJAMIN.   *Stability and Change in Human Characteristics.* New York: John Wiley & Sons, Inc., 1964.

CASLER, LAWRENCE.   *Maternal Deprivation: A Critical Review of the Literature.* Monographs of the Society for Research in Child Development, serial no. 80, vol. XXVI, no. 2, 1961.

CHEYNEY, ARNOLD B.   *Teaching Culturally Disadvantaged in the Elementary School.* Columbus, Ohio: Charles E. Merrill Books, Inc., 1967.

FRAIBERG, SELMA H.   *The Magic Years.* New York: Charles Scribner's Sons, 1959.

GORDON, IRA J.   *Early Child Stimulation through Parent Education.* Final Report to the Children's Bureau, Department of Health, Education, and Welfare, PHS-R-306. Gainesville, Fla.: The Institute for the Development of Human Resources, 1969.

GORDON, IRA J., AND J. R. LALLY.   *Baby Learning through Baby Play.* New York: St. Martin's Press, Inc., 1972.

GORDON, IRA J., AND J. R. LALLY. *Intellectual Stimulation for Infants and Toddlers.* Gainesville, Fla.: The Institute for the Development of Human Resources, 1969.

HECHINGER, FRED M., ed. *Preschool Education Today.* Garden City, N.Y.: Doubleday & Company, Inc., 1966.

HUNT, J. MCVICKER. *The Challenge of Incompetence and Poverty.* Urbana, Ill.: University of Illinois Press, 1969.

MCCANDLESS, BOYD. *Children: Behavior and Development,* 2d ed. New York: Holt, Rinehart and Winston, 1967.

MOULY, GEORGE J. *Psychology for Effective Teaching,* 2d ed. New York: Holt, Rinehart and Winston, 1968.

RIESSMAN, FRANK. *The Culturally Deprived Child.* New York: Harper & Row, Publishers, 1962.

SKEELS, HAROLD M. *Adult Status of Children with Contrasting Early Life Experiences.* Monographs of the Society for Research in Child Development, serial no. 105, vol. XXXI, no. 3, 1966.

SKEELS, HAROLD M., RUTH UPDEGRAFF, BETH WELLMAN, AND HAROLD M. WILLIAMS. *Study of Environmental Stimulation.* University of Iowa Studies, series no. 363, vol. XV, no. 4, 1938.

12

Learning disability

In the previous chapter we presented a picture of a kind of deprivation that might prevent children from being able to achieve in academic areas. We concluded that, given adequate stimulation and affection, a "normal" child would enter school with sufficient motivation and ability to perform. But what about the child who is not disadvantaged, the child who has had every opportunity to interact with adults, who has had toys and manipulative tools to play with, but who is, nevertheless, having difficulties with learning?

Until recent years children who had problems in learning and adjustment were categorized as being mentally retarded, sensorily impaired, or emotionally disturbed. Special classes were established to teach these children. It was discovered, however, that many so-called "mentally retarded" children had some areas in which they performed at high levels. Others overcame retardation when proper stimulation was provided. It is therefore likely that the classification of "mental retardation" was not always an appropriate designation. It has been said that 75 percent of the "mentally retarded" are suffering, basically, from nutritional or environmental deprivation of some kind.

The sensorially impaired, children with visual or auditory handicaps, are also suffering from deprivation. The "input" from the environment is certainly different for a child who has difficulty seeing or hearing. Special educational programs must be designed to meet the needs of these children.

But, in this chapter, we are concerned with children who have no obvious physical defect, who have not been deprived of stimulation, and who do not have intellectual limitations. There are many children of average or superior intelligence who still have difficulty in learning to read and write. They have been called "underachievers," and, for many years, were frequently referred to psychologists who investigated the possibilities of emotional problems as the cause of their failures. These children have been described as "lacking in motivation," but the study of animals and young babies has established the fact that the desire to achieve competence is a basic drive.[1]

[1] Robert White, "Motivation Reconsidered."

Nonlearners have been considered to be "immature," but the reasons for immaturity were not investigated. If the maturational lag persists, other problems of adjustment set in which are difficult to overcome.

Defining terms

Recently, the designation of "learning disability" has come into vogue. This category usually refers to children who have learning problems due to an inherent neurological weakness, and it is this meaning that is applicable to the use of the term in this chapter. The learning-disabled child has difficulty organizing his inner self and the world around him. The circuits in his personal computer, for some reason, do not receive and process the symbolic data channeled to them from his eyes and ears. There are various forms that this distortion of messages takes. For example:

1. A child who has problems in visual organization may pay attention to everything he sees in the room instead of the lesson on the blackboard. He is easily distracted by visual stimuli, hence, *distractible*.
2. A child may not be able to separate the stimuli presented to him from its background. He is unable to zero in on the particular word he is supposed to be reading, and is distracted by the colors on the page, the other letters, etc. This is called a visual *figure-ground* problem.
3. A child may not organize visual impressions into a meaningful whole and may fixate on one letter, or a part of it, without seeing its relationship to the entire word. He lacks global perception and does not perceive the *gestalt*, or whole.
4. A child may be faulty in his ability to categorize and generalize concepts. He may not be able to make the connections between one dog that he sees, and others in the category, or he may not relate the spoken word to the thing itself, or to the picture of it or to the written word.
5. He may have difficulty in remembering things in proper sequence. He may remember letters in a word, but not the order in which they appear. This is a problem in *visual sequential memory*.
6. A child may perceive a visual configuration properly but may not be able to reproduce it. This may be one kind of *visual-motor* problem.
7. Children may have similar problems in the auditory channel. They may not be able to separate auditory stimuli from all of the sounds in the environment, or they may perceive words as a series of unconnected sounds with no awareness of the gestalt or configuration.
8. A child may misperceive some of the sounds he hears, confusing p and b, or g and c. He thus has a problem with *auditory* perception.
9. In a manner similar to the visual problems, a child may not be

able to categorize oral language, or to put sounds he has heard in sequential order. He may forget names of words, and thus have problems of *auditory memory*.

10. A child may have difficulty with *spatial orientation*. He may lack ability to recognize symbol size and placement in relation to each other.

11. *Perceptual-motor problems* which affect reading and writing may result from poor hand-eye coordination, left-right confusion and other deficiencies in body awareness.[2]

It can be seen, from these brief descriptions, that "learning disability" is a term that may be applied to a variety of behaviors. The field of research is new, and the terminology is in a state of flux. These characteristic behaviors have been attributed to "brain damage," but this term has come into disuse and has been replaced by the currently more acceptable term, "minimal cerebral dysfunction." One well-known authority, writing in 1966, listed seventeen terms used to describe the problem, and called his article an "essay on confusion."[3] "Dyslexia" is a term frequently found in the literature, but this term refers only to disturbances relating to reading. It is inappropriate when applied to children whose disturbance is related to spoken or written word usage. The problem of a unified terminology seems to defy consensus, possibly because people of various disciplines are involved. Each term has meaning to certain professions or segments within those professions. Identification of the cause and the eventual prevention of neurological learning disorders is the responsibility of the medical profession. Methods of diagnosis are within the province of the field of psychology. Remedies and curriculum approaches must be found in the field of education.

Diagnosis and treatment

Regardless of what name is used the condition itself is an elusive one. To all outward appearances, the child with a learning disability usually seems to be healthy and alert. There is no one specific tool or measurement that will locate the source of the difficulty. One writer in the field draws an analogy between the manner in which an educational problem is handled and the way a physical disturbance is dealt with.

An educational problem

Complaint: Failing in school.
Recommendation: An IQ test.
Results: An IQ of 120.
Recommendation: Psychological counseling and a home visit because this child is a day dreamer, lazy, comes from a poor home environment, is uncooperative, etc.
Treatment: Repeat present grade placement.

[2] Adapted from Doreen Kronich, *They Too Can Succeed*, pp. 1–4.
[3] William M. Cruickshank, *The Teacher of Brain-Injured Children*, p. 11.

A medical problem

Complaint: A child is not feeling well.

Recommendation: The physician takes the child's temperature.

Results: Normal temperature.

Recommendation: The physician does not dismiss the child or say he is malingering. Rather, recommendations are made for further tests to help determine the problem.

Treatment: It is related to the basic problems uncovered through specific type tests.[4]

Fortunately, tools for the assessment of particular types of problems are being developed. Dr. Mark Ozer, of the George Washington School of Medicine and Children's Hospital of the District of Columbia, has developed a fifteen-minute test for use during a child's regular, prekindergarten medical examination at age four or five.[5] The test is designed to determine the child's ability to discriminate sounds and symbols, to process auditory and visual clues, and to follow directions. It is hoped that, from tests such as these, recommendations can be made to the schools concerning the learning conditions under which a child will be most successful.

School psychologists now offer a variety of tests to children which help to screen out learning problems. These tests attempt to detect poor visual-motor coordination, difficulty with memory for design, ability to perceive figure-ground relationships, and so on. Remedial programs have been designed, and special classes have been set up for children with learning disabilities. To date, however, only children with severe learning problems have been referred to these classes. There are not enough of these classes to accommodate the many children who have learning problems of a minimal nature. Estimates have been made that approximately 10 percent of all children of normal intelligence or above have some form of learning disability. The most difficult cases to identify are those of exceptionally bright children who suffer from only a mild handicap. Despite the fact that their academic progress is impeded, and they face emotional problems, the disability is concealed because these children manage to "get by" in school.

Efforts must be made to diagnose learning styles and to discover areas of strengths and weaknesses so that each child will be able to reach his true potential. The Wechsler Intelligence Scale for Children (WISC) has been used as a measuring device to analyze the child's pattern and to help plan meaningful remedial programs for the learning-disabled child.[6] Such testing reveals "the open pathway," that is, the child's strength which can be used for effective intake of stimuli. This kind of diagnosis and treatment is time-consuming and requires much individualized instruction. Some private clinics have come into existence which take this approach, but the problem is wide-

---

[4] Tina E. Bangs, *Language and Learning Disorders of the Pre-Academic Child*, p. 26.

[5] As reported by Maya Pines, "Hidden Threats to Your Child's Learning Ability."

[6] I. H. Wills and Norma Banas, "The Vulnerable Child."

spread. Teachers must be alerted to the many symptoms which can be detected in the classroom, and public schools must provide resource personnel for diagnosis and counseling. A checklist can be provided for the classroom teacher which will help her to identify learning disabilities. (See Appendix C.)

It is not our concern in this book to provide prescriptions for the treatment of learning disability. It is simply our purpose to make the teacher and prospective teacher aware of this problem, so that she can be alert to the symptoms of it in the children that she teaches. It is strongly recommended that teachers, especially those who work with young children, read the literature and take courses which will help them to recognize cases of learning disability. Early diagnosis is essential if these problems in learning are to be overcome. The longer the symptoms go unrecognized, the more likely it is that emotional and psychological effects will result, which further deter the learning abilities of the child. If the teacher spots the symptoms, then effective diagnosis and treatment can be provided. It is she who sees the child daily and can view him in many kinds of situations. She may require help in the selection and administration of special tests, but it is her observations of the child that are needed to complete the picture.

The case study presented below was done by a student-observer who had served as an apprentice teacher in a first-grade classroom. The child studied is a "normal" child, who has no apparent physical handicaps, and who appears to be bright and responsive. He comes from a good home environment and has a rich experiential background. There are several explanations about the possible causes of his learning difficulties. The fact that there are divergent opinions about this case is one of the reasons for its inclusion here.

A CASE STUDY OF PETER, SIX YEARS AND SIX MONTHS OLD

Peter's family consists of his father, who is an automobile salesman, his mother, a nurse, and a three-year-old brother. They live in an apartment in a middle-class neighborhood.

OBSERVATION

I taught Peter in the first grade during my Junior Block experience last spring. Consequently, I have had direct contact with him. Peter caught my eye as a cute little boy who was friendly and kind, as he would always greet me when I came into the classroom. I noticed, however, that every time a lesson would begin or the teacher was talking to the class, Peter would, without fail, speak out of turn and pay no attention to the person speaking. He not only did this with the teacher but with other children as well.

When the class had seatwork assignments, I observed the children and assisted some of them. Peter was slow to follow directions and often forgot what he was directed to do. Like many children his age, he had trouble writing the alphabet. However, Peter seemed to have a greater inability to form letters. I offered my help finding that he always wanted me to review his directions. I would hold his hand moving it in the direction of the letter form, in order that he get the kinesthetic (the communication between muscle and mind) sense of the form. Then I would let him try to form the letters on his own. He wanted me to stand over him; yet he refused to follow my directions or advice.

Several afternoons after school were spent together working on his writing. After his constant refusal to let me show him how the letters looked and felt, the teacher and I decided that we had a definite problem. Peter just would not do things any way except his own way. He made a point to tell us that he wanted to do it his way.

The children in the classroom sensed that Peter caused a disturbance and had to be reprimanded. Consequently, they were not as friendly toward him. During recess he would often stand near the girls jumping rope, but he would never engage in rough play like other boys his age. One hardly ever saw Peter chasing a girl in the class, though this was a favorite pastime for most of the little boys. One time he tried to jump rope with the girls but he got tangled in the rope, and this resulted in banishment by the girls.

Peter's lack of coordination became evident in his other recess activities such as jumping, running, and even walking. His movements were jerky and clumsy, much like those of a two-year-old. One would often see Peter bumping into things. Once, on the way to the lunchroom, Peter walked in the opposite direction from his classmates and went head-on into a pole.

Peter's mother was very concerned about his slow reading ability and his incomplete seat work. Consequently, she took him to New York for a test, the results of which will be discussed later. During this time Peter's teacher kept in contact with his mother as she was concerned about his development.

A time sample will show how he reacts in a typical classroom setting.

TIME	OVERT BEHAVIOR
9:00	Teacher is asking about the month in relation to the bulletin board. Peter changes seats with another child due to his incomplete work and talking. The seat is apart from the others.
9:02	Peter sits on his knees. He stands up, then sits down while teacher asks, "What does the leprechaun stand for?"
9:04	He yawns, then puts his little finger in his mouth. The teacher asks, "Who can read the first name on the board?" Peter walks up to me and asks, "You know how many stars I have by my name? Six!" He is sent back to his seat by the teacher.
9:07	He appears to be daydreaming while sitting on his knees. He puts his thumb in his mouth while resting on his elbows.
9:12	His head is on the desk while he reads in unison with the class as the directions for work are given.
9:13	Teacher asks Peter what the third direction says. "Color pictures with a . . . short . . . A sound." He is rewarded with a "very good."
9:15	His stomach is on the desk top, with a finger in his mouth.

TIME	OVERT BEHAVIOR
9:20	He starts writing his name when handed a paper. He holds his pencil very tightly. After he tries to write his name on five papers, he puts his thumb in his mouth.
9:30	He starts writing a sentence which is written on the board. He has trouble with spatial relationships here as many large letters are found in the middle of his words. He starts watching the other children.
9:40	Peter gets a drink from the water fountain. He plays with the water. Then he says out loud, "Mrs. Miller, I found this star by the sink!" He goes over to another child and talks.
9:43	He goes back to his seat resting one leg on it.
9:44	His teacher comes over to his seat and says she finds some of his papers missing. He goes to get them.

At this point the music teacher comes in.

9:45	Teacher sings, "Put your finger in the air." Peter does the same and giggles. While singing the song he turns toward me and smiles.
9:48	Peter is sitting on his knees. He stands by his seat, covering his face with his hands. (The other children are sitting quietly.)
9:50	Flute music is playing. He stands by his seat. Then he pushes himself up on his desk top making a "Wo, wo, wo" sound. The teacher gives him a look but says nothing.
9:55	He raises his hand, although this seems to have nothing to do with the lesson. He then bites his palm. The teacher asks the children to stand up and do what she says to the music. Peter responds to the request with uncoordinated movements. He remains standing when other children sit down.
10:00	He then returns to his desk with his stomach resting on top of it. The music teacher leaves after a final song. During the song Peter does not sing much.

Another time in which I observed Peter was when I took him to the zoo. He greeted me enthusiastically and never stopped talking on our way there. Among his many questions were: "Why are you taking me to the zoo?" "Are you teaching school?" "Where do you live?" and "Do you know that I received ten stars for good conduct?"

At the zoo he wanted to buy his brother and himself a toy with fifteen cents. (He later bought a toy with my help.) The map of the area caught his eye. He read, "Duck, snake, and what does that say?" while pointing to the word, *alligator*. From the map we walked over to the snakes. He profoundly stated that he did not like snakes. He then spotted the birds saying that he knew which ones were girls and boys. On seeing the turkey he leaned over the rail and gobbled several times. Peter turned to me saying that he had decided he would rather have barbecued potato chips instead of cookies for a snack.

At times Peter was rude toward other people, often pushing to get to the animals so he could feed them. I tried not to interfere until he got out of hand, at which time I called him to see another animal. Drinking cokes and eating peanuts proved disastrous because they landed on his clothes. After a few wipes here and there I offered to help him crack open the nuts. He accepted my offer.

Peter hopped and skipped clumsily over to the camel's cage proclaiming that he did not know there were such things as camels. Upon seeing one of the zoo keepers, he asked if he could see the man from the zoo who is on television. After the keeper replied that he was not around the zoo, Peter concluded that the man must be at his office and suggested that we go there. I said that the man is probably very busy and could not have any visitors. (I did not want to make any false promises that we would visit him.)

When Peter saw some Cub Scouts he proudly said that someday he would become one. He really wanted to be with other boys.

We then went to the train station. Peter had trouble sitting still during our ten-minute wait so we viewed an old cabin car on display. Joy filled him all the time we were on the train ride around Crandon Park. His biggest problem was keeping his toy monkey, train, and tickets together on his lap.

As we got out of our seats Peter bumped into the side of it and started to cry. With a little comforting the tears ceased as we walked toward my car.

The trip on the way home was most revealing. He said that he had trouble putting his shoes on the right feet. He then asked, "Why is it easier to put on socks?" I asked him his opinion at which time he surmised the correct answer.

I asked how he liked school. He said, "I like it except no one likes me." I said that surely everyone likes him and reassured him that I did. He replied that the children said he was bad and laughed at him. "I have trouble staying in my seat," he said. "You know why I can't sit very long? Because my bottom hurts on those seats." (That is a pretty good reason, come to think about it.) Nothing else was said about the matter.

When I visited Peter again at his home, he was playing in the swimming pool with his friend John who is the same age. Peter can swim well for his age and enjoys going under water. During this visit he read very well to me from his Dr. Suess books. (Perhaps he had memorized the words.) I asked him to draw me a picture about his trip to the zoo. He said that he could not because he did not have anything to trace. With a few suggestions and encouragement he managed to draw several animals.

INTERVIEWS

Peter's teacher said that he had improved considerably in his handwriting and reading skills. He was now in a reading group in his own classroom. She said that he still is uncooperative in listening and finishing his work. She strongly feels he definitely has a learning disability.

Peter's mother was surprised to find out about her child's trouble in school. However, she did take him to New York City for testing. She realized, by watching her three-year-old, that Peter is uncoordinated for his age.

Peter was interviewed by the school psychologist in January of his first-grade year. Previously he had a psychological examination in New York City. According to the school psychologist Peter has average mental ability with verbal functioning above non-verbal skills. "Relative deficits in the latter involved reversal tendencies in writing and reading, as well as difficulties in fine motor coordination." The psychologist believes this was a result of delayed development. When Peter was observed in January, he was given the Bender Visual Motor Gestalt Test and the Graham-Kendall Memory for Designs Test. These, according to the psychologist, tend to make one believe that Peter is handicapped by a specific learning disability in the visual-motor-perceptual area.

Consequently several suggestions were made to the teacher to aid Peter. Training in "psychophysical integration of fine and gross motor activities" through writing skills was suggested. The initial gross motor training could be used in the physical-education program or informally conducted in the classroom. According to the tests Peter needs to acquire a "consistent right- or left-sided approach in the use of eyes, hands, and feet in kicking ball, cutting paper, or sighting with a telescope."

SUMMARY

Motor skills: Peter is average size for a six-and-a-half-year-old boy. He has developed slowly in fine and gross motor activities. He should have training in the basic skills of hopping, skipping, and catching and kicking balls.

Mental ability: Peter has average mental ability with fine use of language. He expresses himself well with adults and children. He enjoys reading when he knows the words. As for all children, Peter needs to be rewarded for his achievements.

Emotional aspects: Peter is a kind person and thoughtful of others. He is affectionate with his mother; however, his father pays little attention to him. I cannot stress his need for approval and love enough, in order that he may develop into a well-adjusted person both physically and mentally.

ANALYSIS OF THE CASE STUDY

Peter appears to be a healthy, normal youngster in many ways, yet he is having difficulty in the school situation. The student teacher sensed this and decided to do a case study about him.

Peter's main problem seems to be one of coordination. Many little boys in the five to seven age range have difficulty in controlling fine muscles and cannot relate eye and hand coordinations. Girls seem to mature faster in these areas, possibly due to more sedentary activities with crayons and cutouts prior to school. Peter's restlessness is partly due to his inability to perform the tasks required of him. His condition is aggravated by his lack of success and his subsequent loss of prestige among his peer group.

Peter is a child who is accustomed to praise and recognition. His mother is concerned about him and evidently is willing to spend time and money on tests and treatment to help him. The attention he gets at home is not matched in the school setting, where he has little chance to excel. Inattentive and restless behavior gets him some of the recognition he requires.

How severe the perceptual-motor problem is cannot be determined from the evidence presented in the case study. There is room for divergency of opinion as to whether the condition requires remediation outside of the school and the home setting.

A clinician who works with learning disabilities states that the problem, as revealed from the information included in the case study, "does not appear to be of a dyslexic nature, since the child is learning to recognize and copy symbols. However, there may be possible figure-ground deficit, with directionality and control problems due to a motor lag. This might result in perceptual errors for many years to come, even though the child learns to read and memorize words. A full developmental screening covering visual and motor functions would be warranted."

Another clinician states that the "hyperactive, distractible syndrome" exhibited in Peter's behavior presents a fairly common picture. "The fact that Peter was having trouble copying symbols and learning the letters of the alphabet suggests that there may be a visual-perceptual interference. There is also a developmental lag in the eye-hand coordination, as well as general lack of body awareness."

Both of these specialists agree that "teaching a child like Peter can be much more effective if the learning pathways are understood and the interferences identified." They claim that the developmental gap will not close by itself. Left unattended, these deficits will put Peter at a disadvantage in school. Though his skills may improve, he will not have them when he needs them. Further testing and remediation is required, according to these clinicians, whether we consider Peter's case to be one of learning disability or of maturational lag.

This is a particularly significant case study for prospective teachers to examine. The study raises some pertinent questions about current school practices. Is the curriculum of the early grades designed in such a way that it undermines the ego concept of little boys who are not ready for the skills of reading and writing that are stressed so much of the time? Are there other ways for these children to achieve a measure of success in the school setting?

Peter is a particularly verbal child, capable of astute observations, as revealed in his comments at the zoo. Opportunities must be provided within the classroom setting for this ability to be recognized. No doubt he could easily assume a leadership role in research related to social studies, if such projects included investigations concerned with places and people in the community as well as reading matter. He could excel at dramatization were the focus on reading supplemented with opportunities to act out the story.

Of course, it would be beneficial if Peter's teacher were knowledgeable enough to provide materials for perceptual-motor training within the classroom setting. Ideally, in classes where children are allowed to progress at their own rate, such material is available, and special help is provided. Consultation with specialists in learning disability might be provided for the teacher, so that she could work effectively with the child within the classroom setting. Coordination could be helped during the physical-education program where specific motor skills could be emphasized. Peter needs to feel that he is an integral part of his class, not someone who, because of special deficiencies, cannot participate with the others.

His family, especially his father, might be advised to help him with coordination by playing games at home. Equipment such as balance boards and trampolines have been known to be an aid to perceptual-motor difficulties. Above all, attention should be given to opportunities for praise and recognition. A disability in the area of motor coordination should not be the cause of permanent personality damage which blocks a child's ability to function in school and in life.

Hyperactivity

Hyperactivity, such as Peter exhibited, is frequently evidenced in the behavior of children with learning disabilities. As a matter of fact, the classic description of the brain-injured child was proposed in 1957, and is known as the "Strauss Syndrome."[7] Such behavior was described as being "disinhibited, perseverative and distractible," and these characteristics were considered, at one time, to be a means of identifying children with learning disabilities.

Later investigations have established the fact that this description applies to only a segment of the total group having neurological disorders of learning. However, the combination of behavior patterns occurs together frequently and includes such characteristics as:

1. Hyperactivity of the type that is typical of the normal behavior of a younger child.
2. Easy distractibility or short attention span.
3. Immature emotional development with uninhibited behavior, manifested by low frustration level, aggressiveness, and impulsivity.
4. High incidence of specific learning disabilities such as perceptual-motor impairments.
5. Lesser signs of neurophysiological immaturity, such as clumsiness or infantile speech articulation.
6. Vulnerability to concomitant emotional overlay such as feelings of rejection, anxiety, or hostility.[8]

This combination of characteristics was noted in an eight-and-a-half-year-old boy who was attending a special class for learning disability. Bob was selected by a graduate student as a subject for a case study because he

[7] As described by Doris J. Johnson and Helmer R. Myklebust, *Learning Disabilities*, p. 6.

[8] Adapted from Elena Boder, "A Neuropediatric Approach to the Diagnosis and Management of School Behavioral and Learning Disorders," p. 27.

appeared to be such an attractive, alert boy. He had been with the learning-disability class for three months, having been referred by the psychologist in a public elementary school. At the time of the study Bob was reading on a beginning first-grade level, although his score on the Wechsler Intelligence Scale for Children was 116.

Bob is the only child of middle-class parents. His father "enjoys a good relationship with his son, and shares his interest in softball." His mother is a full-time housewife who is "very much concerned with her child's growth and development." She tries to help Bob with his reading but states that this experience has been frustrating, because Bob is "stubborn," and she "sometimes feels that he is a spoiled child." The family is considered to be a stable unit, and the medical record reveals nothing unusual.

At the time of referral the statement of the problem was put in terms of hyperactivity. Bob was unable to sit still for long periods of time, and his attention span was short. He was described by his mother as "always known to be overactive and constantly requiring attention as a toddler and in pre-school." When he was placed in public kindergarten, considerable inattention and hyperactivity were noted, and he was recommended to remain on a half-day program in first grade. During the testing program at the time of his admission to the learning-disability class, the psychologist commented that "Bob's ability to listen and concentrate was markedly reduced during the second half of testing. . . . At the completion of the test, Bob immediately became very active, tumbling from wall to wall on the floor."

The graduate student who did the case study observed Bob in two contrasting situations involving physical activity. One class was a highly structured physical-education program particularly designed for learning-disabled children. The second class was an experimental one in creative movement, which was developed for the sole purpose of determining whether this freer atmosphere would have a detrimental effect upon the behavior of such children. One observation from each of these settings will be included here. The following is an observation of a structured physical-education class.

Bob and his friend, Tommy, were playing with large yellow balls before the class began. Bob kicked off his shoes and continued to bounce. When the teacher asked Bob to grab his shoes and line up, he did as he was told. The children began running around the room. Bob ran very fast and would occasionally push himself off the wall with his right hand. He began to get wild when the teacher told the children to go faster. Bob got a burst of energy and ran faster. Then the children were told to walk. Bob put his hands on his hips and, as he walked, he occasionally looked around for Tommy. If he found Tommy to be close behind, he ran to keep a little ahead.

The following is an observation in an unstructured-movement class.

Bob did well as he tiptoed along a line on the floor in time to the drum. His arms moved rhythmically, alternating with his foot pattern. While the teacher was talking, explaining the next activity, Bob yelled that he was going to hop on Tommy's back. Then Bob came back to the group and pranced in time to the music. His knees were high and he was concentrating on doing the activity well. A little later Bob left the group as the teacher began talking about a tightrope walker at a circus. She asked the class if they had ever seen a tightrope walker. Bob, from the other side of the room, yelled, "No." He came back to the group when the children began to do a tightrope walk.

Bob was capable of many creative responses. At another session it was noted that he made suggestions and suitable movements to show a snail coming out of a shell. He played the role of Peter in a dramatization of *Peter and the Wolf*, and his movements were appropriate and imaginative. However, in all of the unstructured-movement classes, Bob alternated between active participation and disruptive activity. His hyperactivity was more evident in the unstructured-movement class than it was in the structured class. (See the sample of a coded behavior record of this class in Chapter 4.)

The teacher of the special class felt that Bob's hyperactive behavior is of a compulsive nature and is not purposeful misbehavior. It is believed that hyperactivity is a reaction to the child's inability to choose a suitable focus for his attention, and it is this behavior that he cannot control. This was particularly evident in the case of Bob, since he was known to be very anxious to please the teacher. He took every opportunity to be helpful to her, holding open the door, requesting to carry her drum, and generally seeking attention and approval whenever he could.

The teacher of the learning-disability class commented that "Bob is able to control his behavior adequately during the first hour of school. However, as the day gets longer, he becomes more restless, and his hyperactivity gets him into trouble. His response to correction is quite immature. He usually pouts and stomps off to his seat. In group activity he strives to achieve at all times, occasionally at the expense of his peers. He is rough with others, becoming aggressive and often fighting for position in line."

Bob was put on medication, and he was frequently heard to ask for his pills. His reading problems were being handled by the use of teaching methods that emphasized linguistics. He is considered to be an auditory learner with weaknesses in visual discrimination. (His response to the rhythm of the drumbeat was further evidence of his strength in the auditory channel.) Both his hyperactivity and his reading disability are considered by the specialists who work with him to be evidence of minimal cerebral dysfunction.

Bob is a child who exhibits many of the characteristic behavior patterns usually associated with learning disability. His personable manner, his attractive appearance, and his high intelligence make him appear to be a boy who should get along well in a school setting. It is frustrating and annoying to teachers to find that children like Bob cannot be controlled in the classroom and do not make satisfactory progress in their work. When the reasons for such behavior are not understood, the child is likely to be excessively penalized for "causing trouble" and "being lazy." He becomes upset emotionally as a result of repeated failure to achieve, and he is likely to misbehave and to exhibit wide gaps in his developmental patterns. The situation compounds itself as the child grows older. Early detection and treatment can prevent failure for children like Bob.

Other characteristics of learning-disabled children

Not all children with learning disabilities are hyperactive. Some are dreamers. The child who seems to be in a world of his own, who is forgetful, who can be observed staring vacantly into space, and who is inattentive during class instruction; this child, too, may have a learning disability.

Such a child might be the one who never participates actively with the group. He can be observed on the sidelines, watching what others do. Fear of failure may be the cause for this withdrawal, or it might simply be an inability to focus on what is happening at the moment.

In earlier sections of this book we have seen glimpses of eight-year-old Kathy whose beautiful story, "In the Field," was reproduced in Chapter 5. Kathy was a daydreamer and an "underachiever" who never finished her work in class and frequently forgot assignments. She was a "loner" in the classroom and on the playground. The school principal noticed that "she always walked alone, following the class as it left the building, often gazing at the ceiling as she walked along." He suggested that she be referred to the school psychologist for examination.

The teacher, in this instance, decided to meet with Kathy's mother first. The interview with the mother assured the teacher that Kathy had a loving and accepting family. Kathy was not referred, since both her mother and her teacher felt that "the discomfort of lengthy psychological tests and involved questioning would certainly have made Kathy more self-conscious."

The observations on this child were made in the early 1960s. The teacher's decision might have been different today in the light of more recent evidence. It is very likely that Kathy had a learning disability. Her writing (which can be seen in Figure 3, Chapter 5) revealed frequent omissions and insertions of letters. Even after her paper had been corrected by the teacher, the rewritten copy (which is the one shown in Figure 3) contained as many, though different, incorrect spellings as the first copy did.

Kathy's sensitivity, as revealed in her writing, may also be an indication of a learning disability. Many children who have problems of this kind are known to be withdrawn, delicate, and capable of deep feelings and empathy. They often relate well to very young children and to docile animals. Her mother said that Kathy could spend hours sitting by the window, watching the birds as they came to the feeding station in the backyard. Or she could play with her baby sister, making a bobby pin and some tissue into a fairy that danced. Understanding and recognition of her gentle, beautiful qualities can help Kathy to grow up to become the sensitive, self-respecting adult she deserves to be.

Sensitive children with problems of learning and remembering often use protective devices to defend their delicate egos. This is understandable in the light of the frequent frustrations and rejections they must experience. In Chapter 10 we met nine-year-old Danny, who had forgotten to bring his script to a rehearsal for a play that his Cub Scout group was preparing. He denied that the Den Mother had called him the night before to remind him, but later he admitted it. His anxiety and his daydreaming are evidenced throughout the brief but detailed observation of him.

It was later firmly established that Danny was a child who had a learning disability. Much of his behavior in school and in his relationships with his family and his peers could be attributed to problems of memory and concentration over which he had no control. Danny was an "average" student, but teachers always claimed that he was not performing as well as he might. He was forgetful about class assignments, and his work was considered "sloppy" and "carelessly done." His reading was marked by poor phrasing, disregard for punctuation, and habitual insertions and omissions. Although he seemed eager to achieve, he was easily distracted. He had difficulty in organizing and outlining material.

At this point, it might be interesting for the reader to go back and reread the observation of Danny, presented in Chapter 10. If his lapses of memory were due to some malfunction in brain circuits, then certainly Danny should not be subjected to scolding and to embarrassment. Yet children like Danny are constantly being put in this position, due to no fault of their own, and to no intentional mistreatment by the adults they come in contact with. It is little wonder that this frustration leads to emotional problems which subsequently increase the likelihood of poor performance and poor adjustment.

Danny and others like him manage to "get by" in school because of superior intelligence and ability to perform well in some areas. Usually their work is considered to be erratic, and teachers do not understand how such apparently bright children can make so many foolish errors.

Carol is a capable student who is doing well in school, in spite of a learning disability. She and her family are aware of her problem, and she has received some remedial instruction. Her teachers do not always know of her difficulties, however. Their report card comments reveal Carol's inconsistencies.

1. Carol does well in school and has good attitudes. She is imaginative and creative. She has ability with words, but she does need structuring as she becomes rambling and repetitious. Her spelling errors are *peculiar*, such as, "the" for "them," and so on. She often leaves off "ed" and "ing" endings. She can correct these errors immediately if they are pointed out to her.
2. Carol needs to learn to proofread her work . . . she makes three or four errors on a page.
3. When she is reading, she is difficult to understand; she sort of chops off her words, or her rhythm is choppy—or something!

4. It is difficult for the class to understand what Carol is saying when she reads aloud.

5. No homework Tuesday, but handed it in Wednesday. Sometimes forgets capitals and periods.

6. Analysis of written letter: omits words; does not mark sentence endings; omits endings of words.

There is nothing in this series of teachers' reports that is unusual. Carol is a good student and has been placed in an accelerated class. However, it is interesting to see how many of the comments reflect a condition that is caused by her learning disability. It is likely that, if the situation were not known and understood by Carol and her mother, these consistent criticisms would cause some uncomfortable moments for them.

The emotional overtones of learning disability

We have mentioned, several times in this chapter, that emotional problems are likely to accompany learning disabilities. Once emotional complications set in, it is sometimes difficult to determine whether the emotion blocks the learning, or if the learning problem causes the emotional reactions.

In the observation below, a six-year-old begins to reveal his frustration when he is confronted with a problem of visual discrimination which he cannot handle. Roger was selected for observation because he was said to be free from any emotional disturbance. It was early in the school year, and Roger had not had time to feel defeated due to his problems in reading. His mother brought him to a clinic for part-time instruction as a precautionary measure. She was sensitive to the problem of a learning disability, since another member of the family was being treated. Roger's only learning difficulty was in distinguishing the letters *p*, *b*, and *d*.

When he was first seen by the observer, Roger was playing with plastic construction cubes during a break between instructional sessions. Roger's conversation is recorded below, with the observer's comments in parentheses.

I'm making a car. I need some back wheels. I won't be able to finish unless Adam comes over here. (Adam joins him and picks up a small plastic block.) Let me see that; no wonder I can't make this go! (Roger has assumed a leadership role and is doing a good job in constructing a car with the small plastic parts.) I can't make this car go. This car is already dead. (He sings as he tries to make the wheels roll. A teacher interrupts him to tell him it is time for instruction. He ignores the teacher and continues playing with the car. When she finally gets his attention, he looks up.) Not those again! (The teacher has set up flash cards with words which are to be sorted out by sounds. The first two words are *pad* and *dad*.) They are both the same! Wait. I'm going to do this and fast. (Roger sorts out a number of the cards correctly. He identifies *sad* and reads it as he puts it in place.) What is this? (Picks up card with *pad*. Teacher does not respond immediately.) I'm asking YOU. "What is this?" (Roger has gotten very angry.)

Roger may have been annoyed that his play was interrupted in order to work on word recognition, but it is evident that the anger manifested itself only when he was confronted with the letters which he could not distinguish. Initially he perceived *pad* and *dad* as "both the same," but he was corrected. In his second confrontation with the word *pad*, Roger was not going to allow room for error!

Roger's problem is a perceptual-motor one. He has difficulty putting jigsaw puzzles together, because he lacks a sense of directionality. With help in this area, he will learn to read well, and he has already mastered the skill of blending sounds. But when a person is confronted with a situation in which he sees things differently from everyone else, it is likely to make him angry. Roger is no exception. When there is a distortion of reality, it creates emotional disturbance. This is true whether we are considering the hallucinations that accompany mental illness, or the very simple problem of distinguishing the difference between *p* and *d*.

The investigation of the problems of learning disability has resulted in new insights about how any child achieves success in learning. It is not only the child with learning disabilities who has areas of strengths and weaknesses. Each boy and girl can be reached more effectively if the teacher is aware of how the child perceives. It is helpful to a teacher of reading to know that Johnny learns best by recognizing sounds, or that Suzy does not know differences in shapes. It is important that all children be given the opportunity to learn in a style that is best fitted to their abilities.

A main task of the classroom teacher is to identify problems in learning whether they are emotionally, environmentally, or neurologically based. There is no single theory that will explain all behavior. But the teacher might find it useful to investigate further when a child is "underachieving" or "hyperactive." If she can recognize some of the symptoms indicative of learning disability, she will be less likely to make value judgments that are damaging to the child's ego. Whether the condition warrants referral or placement in a special class is a decision that must be made for each case individually. But, in order for him to achieve a degree of success in school, the child with learning problems needs his teacher's understanding and guidance.

REFERENCES

BANGS, TINA E. *Language and Learning Disorders of the Pre-Academic Child.* New York: Appleton-Century-Crofts, 1968.

BODER, ELENA. "A Neuropediatric Approach to the Diagnosis and Management of School Behavioral and Learning Disorders." *Learning Disorders*, vol. II. Edited by Jerome Hellmuth. Seattle, Wash.: Bernie Straub and Jerome Hellmuth Copublishers, 1966.

CRUICKSHANK, WILLIAM M. *The Teacher of Brain-Injured Children.* Syracuse University Special Education and Rehabilitation Monograph, series 7. Syracuse, N.Y.: Syracuse University Press, 1966.

DELACATO, CARL M. *The Diagnosis and Treatment of Speech and Reading Problems.* Springfield, Ill.: Charles C Thomas, Publisher, 1963.

ELLINGSON, CARETH, AND JAMES CASS. "New Hope for Non-Readers," *Saturday Review* (April 16, 1966).

FINE, BENJAMIN. *Underachievers.* New York: E. P. Dutton & Co., Inc., 1967.

HALL, MARION D. "Family Relationships of Latency-Age Boys with Emotionally-Based Learning Inhibitions." *Learning Disorders*, vol. II. Edited by Jerome Hellmuth. Seattle, Wash.: Bernie Straub and Jerome Hellmuth Copublishers, 1966.

JOHNSON, DORIS J., AND HELMER R. MYKLEBUST. *Learning Disabilities: Educational Principles and Practices.* New York: Grune & Stratton, Inc., 1967.

KEPHART, NEWELL C. *The Slow Learner in the Classroom.* Columbus, Ohio: Charles E. Merrill Books, Inc., 1960.

KRONICK, DOREEN. *They Too Can Succeed: A Practical Guide for Parents of Learning-Disabled Children.* San Rafael, Calif.: Academic Therapy Publications, 1969.

MANN, PHILIP. "Learning Disabilities: A Critical Need for Trained Teachers." *Journal of Learning Disabilities*, II (1969).

PINES, MAYA. "Hidden Threats to Your Child's Learning Ability." *Reader's Digest* (February 1971).

RABINOVITCH, RALPH D. "Dyslexia: Psychiatric Considerations." *Reading Disability.* Edited by John Money. Baltimore: The Johns Hopkins Press, 1962.

WHITE, ROBERT. "Motivation Reconsidered: The Concept of Competence." *Psychological Review*, LXVI (1959).

WILLS, I. H., AND NORMA BANAS. "The Vulnerable Child: Prescriptive Teaching from WISC Patterns." *Academic Therapy*, VII (Fall 1971).

13

Emotional disturbance

Emotional disturbance is frequently the concomitant of a learning disability or of environmental deprivation, as we have seen in previous chapters. But emotional problems, per se, are sometimes the source of difficulties that occur in the classroom. Teachers must be prepared to recognize these emotional problems and to deal with them effectively. In some cases the teacher should refer the child for consultation outside the classroom. But, under any circumstances, she must be able to spot children who need help and must be able to recognize symptoms of disturbance as they occur in the behavior of her students.

The principles that govern normal and abnormal behavior are alike in many ways. Each of us has had, to some degree, the kinds of experiences that are common to psychotics. Our nightmares are one such example. When we lose our temper, we are experiencing the feeling of uncontrollable rage that the child who lacks impulse control experiences. We are all familiar with some neurotic symptoms, such as a compulsive desire for order and neatness, a fear of heights, and so on. We have all experienced momentary physical discomfort due to emotions, such as shortness of breath, loss of memory, and so on. Freud established the fact that the normal individual, when he is in a state that weakens the ego, such as toxicity or dreaming, will think very much like the person who is mentally ill. Under sufficient stress normal individuals also develop neurotic symptoms. "The difference between the mentally ill and the normal is a difference of degree, not of kind. This precept is particularly important in the study of emotional disturbances of childhood."[1]

Every thought, feeling, and action has a cause. When a child who is usually a good student begins to show evidence of inattention or becomes a discipline problem, there is always a reason for this change in behavior. Teachers who are observant notice these changes. Sometimes only a brief talk with the child will reveal the source of the difficulty. Sometimes further investigation is necessary.

[1] Jane W. Kessler, *Psychopathology of Childhood*, p. 9.

An understanding of how emotional disturbance manifests itself is helpful to any teacher. An awareness of the ways in which children use defense mechanisms gives her understanding of many types of classroom behavior. If she is sensitive to clues, the teacher can frequently detect anxieties as children project their feelings into play situations or reveal themselves through expressive drawings. Sometimes feelings resulting from family conflicts are transferred to situations in the classroom. The child under stress may react to his teacher as he might like to react to his mother. Examples of these and other patterns of emotional disturbance that are frequently seen in the classroom will be discussed in this chapter.

We are not suggesting here that the classroom teacher become a psychologist or psychoanalyst. She need not, and should not, deal in depth with emotional disturbances that have their origin in family conflict. She is not qualified to interpret behavior that reflects subconscious impulses. But one need not be trained in these areas to recognize many of the symptoms of disturbance. We speak, in everyday parlance, of a "guilt complex" or of "sibling rivalry," and everyone knows what we mean. Freudian terminology is part of the vernacular, and we discuss these things without awareness that we are dealing with psychological matters.

Long before Freud and the advent of psychoanalysis literary artists were aware of subconscious motives for behavior. Lady Macbeth seemed to be compulsively involved in the act of washing her hands in an attempt to rid herself of feelings of guilt. Greek tragedy dealt with conflicts in feeling between mother and son, from which Freud borrowed the term "Oedipus complex." Good writers have always been skilled in conveying the feelings and the motives of their characters, and their descriptions often have greater impact on us than any clinical, psychological descriptions.

Teachers might use the insights gained from literature, from psychology, and from experience in living to help them to interpret classroom behavior. Emotional disorder, of a temporary or of a mild nature, is as much a part of everyone's life as is the common cold. We need not be psychologists in order to be able to piece together bits of evidence as they unfold before our eyes in the classroom. The application of keen powers of observation, and insight based upon life experience, can sometimes reveal a great deal about a child with a problem.

The following case study was done by a young man who had returned to college on a part-time basis, having served several years in the army. He was married and held an executive position in industry. The maturity of his insight is seen in his writing. His case study consists of a series of anecdotal records in which the observer's knowledge of the child gleaned from previous visits is applied to the interpretation of the succeeding observed behavior. In this series of anecdotal records the problem confronting young Wilma is clearly revealed. It is a deeply disturbing problem, although it may not be of permanent duration. Here is a picture of a bright little girl who usually seemed to function well, but whose behavior reveals the devastating effects of emotional trauma.

A CASE STUDY OF WILMA ADAMS, FIVE YEARS OLD

FIRST OBSERVATION

The Village Preschool, a privately owned and operated institution, is located in a residential area in a small city. In existence for fourteen years, the school functions on a general preparatory level and is comprised of four grade levels—junior and senior nursery and junior and senior kindergarten. The latter two groups include an age range of approximately four years and seven months to six years. They are combined as one in the classroom, with certain areas of the curriculum divided on the basis of achievement. Wilma Adams is a member of the junior kindergarten.

My first hour of observation began as the kindergarten children returned to the classroom following an extended period of active free play. The room itself, occupying one half of the long and low school building, is arranged specifically to resemble the elementary school.

I seated myself, and the teacher proceeded to explain the nature of the activity to follow. It would deal with free creative expression, using paper and watercolors. The children were told they could use these materials to do as they wished. This was an excellent beginning for me, as it created a situation in which I was able to study the children closely because, through their creative processes, they express themselves naturally.

As the appropriate materials were distributed, my attention was drawn to Wilma. Light haired and fair skinned with very pretty features, she would be considered a beautiful child. Although she appeared to be somewhat taller than the other girls, her movements seemed to have little awkwardness. She was well-dressed and immaculately clean. She sat between a boy and another girl and contributed casually to a conversation being conducted by the two. The greater part of her attention however was devoted to the approach of her teacher with paper and paints. She appeared eager and intense.

Wilma went immediately to work. For several minutes she remained quiet as she carefully selected colors and experimented with different amounts of water. She appeared to be concentrating deeply and was quick to realize the many effects of water on the paint. She began mixing colors and, as her picture took on the shape of a design, she voiced her various discoveries to the other children. This soon led to a consistent commentary about her work to the other children around her. Her sentences were complete and comprised of a rather large vocabulary. Words such as *lovely* and *terribly* were used in describing her work. These descriptions were seemingly effortless. Her picture was a river into which a rainbow had fallen. It had "fallen terribly far." It had "crashed the water and spread its colors all about." This comment announced that Wilma was finished and drew her teacher's attention to her work.

As the teacher approached, Wilma got up and held her around the waist. She seemed concerned about the teacher's approval. The teacher responded with a smile, hugged her, and enthusiastically praised her work. She prodded Wilma into a description by asking her to talk about it. Wilma appeared to be quite fond of her teacher and throughout their conversation held her hand. Papers were then collected, with several children assisting (Wilma remaining by her teacher), and all were directed outdoors.

While the class was on the playground, Wilma's teacher took some time to tell me what she could about the child.

Wilma had become five years old in the beginning of May and had entered the school just after that. Upon her enrollment her mother told the principal (with much difficulty) that Wilma's father had been drowned only six months before. She said that this was not to be discussed with Wilma at any time, and that she was not to be questioned about her extreme fear of water. Wilma had only once mentioned that she had no father, and this was to the principal, a man, whom she asked to be her daddy. She also constantly asked when she would have swimming lessons. This was answered, as it was for the other children, that the lessons would begin in late July. Wilma seemed to show no abnormal reaction to this. She did, however, constantly seek physical affection and would often appear troubled when playing alone. Her arrival in the morning and her adjustment in her first few days were without incident until her second week when her mother arrived holding her. Wilma seemed fine until it was evident that her mother did not want to leave her. Mrs. Adams became tearful and desperate and could not let her loose. Wilma was taken from her, and Mrs. Adams was taken to her car. Each morning when she was met at the gate, Wilma was greeted, and her mother was signaled to leave. This appeared to be quite difficult for her. The teacher felt that the mother relied heavily on Wilma for comfort, and Wilma in turn was aware of this. My next period of observation will be conducted at the time Wilma arrives at school so as to view the events described to me by the teacher.

SECOND OBSERVATION

Wilma Adams arrived at school each day between 8:30 and 9 o'clock. As pointed out to me by her teacher during my first visit, this seemed to be a very difficult time for both Wilma and her mother. On the day in which I was present to observe Wilma's arrival, I had a full opportunity to see the difficulty, and, on this particular day, I was able to observe the unpredictability of the situation.

At 8:30 Mrs. Adams arrived with Wilma. After having parked her car and opened the door for Wilma, she took her in her arms and walked to the playground gate. The kindergarten teacher held the gate and greeted Wilma, gesturing for her to come in. Wilma, after having watched her mother for a moment commented that she would "really rather not come to school today." This was said with no great emphasis, nor followed by any direct action such as tears, until she looked at her mother once again, this time just glancing quickly. Mrs. Adams had openly winced at hearing this and tightened her hold on Wilma. Wilma repeated her reluctance once more, then began to cry, watching for her mother's reaction. As Mrs. Adams became visibly shaken and began clinging to her, Wilma increased her tears until she was screaming.

Her teacher said that she should stop, for she knew how enjoyable school was and how much everyone liked her. As she attempted to take her from her mother, Wilma began kicking violently, her screams becoming louder. At this point Mrs. Adams had become tearful and desperately repeated that she could not let her go or leave her that way. She would retreat a few steps as the teacher more emphatically tried to take Wilma. Mrs. Adams, at one point, agreed to the teacher's logic that, if given in to once, this would happen every morning. At another point Mrs. Adams gave in totally to Wilma as she increased her tantrum. The situation was ended as the principal appeared and pulled Wilma away. She was carried away screaming to the classroom while Wilma's teacher tried to calm and reason with Mrs. Adams. Finally, Mrs. Adams returned to her car after having been coaxed and reasoned with. With her departure Wilma's tears stopped abruptly.

This incident was ignored until it was certain that Wilma had gained complete control of herself once again. She was treated gently, but told that when she felt she was ready, she could have a talk with the teacher. Wilma went to the playground and played relatively alone. At one point she announced that she would be ready "perhaps later" to talk. Soon after this she approached her teacher who pointed out that her behavior was not right for someone her age. Wilma simply listened and said she would try to be happy to come to school from then on. Her only comment was a proposal that if her teacher would be her mother, "there wouldn't be so much to do and I could be the baby."

Wilma's teacher, in commenting on the incident later, felt it was quite evident that much of Wilma's behavior was triggered by her mother's emotions. Here I recalled Wilma's behavior that morning with her repeated looks at her mother as if she were testing her. Wilma's teacher also pointed out that, in the course of my observations, I would find that Wilma displayed a very different personality during the day than the one I had seen that morning.

THIRD OBSERVATION

My third period of observation began as the kindergarten children were taken out to the playground for a long period of free play. Wilma was one of the first out and ran eagerly for the swings. She was smiling and seemed quite happy. Her teacher pointed out that Wilma was far less tense when she left her mother in the morning. It was Mrs. Adams who still appeared to be having difficulty.

As Wilma swung, she appeared quite content but drawn within herself. At one point she would swing high, and dropping her head back, would sing to herself softly. Her words were not then audible. At another point she would slow down to almost a standstill. While she twirled slowly, dangling her feet, she would whisper to herself. Neither was this audible. She would also stop completely, and then, bowing her chin to her chest, she would examine her fingers. At this time she seemed most absorbed within herself.

As Wilma continued to swing, she occasionally would call to her classmates nearby to join her on the other swing. When there was no immediate response, she seemed unaffected and stopped for a time. When she called to them again and was once more ignored she began to show some reaction. Eventually, she left her swing and approached two of the children whom she'd called to. These two, a boy and a girl, were much smaller than Wilma. I learned that they were in the senior nursery, and, being quite advanced for their age, were closely accepted by most of the older children. It was also considered an "honor" to be befriended by the little girl. Wilma asked the two why they would not swing with her. Very earnestly she asked if they were her friends. When the younger girl pointed out that she and the boy were friends only with each other, Wilma protested. As they walked away from her, she remained still watching them and biting her lip. After remaining that way for several seconds, she looked around her and headed in the direction of her teacher.

Wilma approached her teacher rapidly. Upon reaching her, Wilma held her around the legs and rested her head against the teacher's side. She began to suck her thumb but made no mention of what had upset her. The teacher raised Wilma's head, and letting her continue to hold on, made a kind, brief comment. To this Wilma made no reply. Instead she smiled happily and ran back toward the swings. The incident seemed forgotten. Wilma resumed her swinging, appearing as contented as before. She stayed on the swings for the remainder of the period except for brief intervals when she would run to the teacher and hug her as she had done before. She appeared to have found the friend she had been looking for that day.

FOURTH OBSERVATION

Several weeks had passed since Wilma Adams first enrolled at the school. In this time her teacher felt she had shown a superior ability in many areas. Wilma's creative work was one of these areas. The teacher noted that in all of her artwork and in her colorful use of imagination in free play, Wilma displayed a great deal of creativity.

My fourth period of observation took place when all of the children were confined to the school building because of rain. Most of their morning's activities consisted of work with creative materials.

The kindergarten children were each given several constructional toys called "Snowflakes." They consisted of the points and edges of a snowflake and were made of a flexible plastic. These toys could be fitted together to form any flat or three-dimensional design or specific object. The children were told they could work with these toys as they wished and could speak softly. The teacher left them much to themselves.

Wilma sat quietly for a few moments and watched her classmates. They were constructing various forms and commenting on them to one another. After a time she appeared uneasy and frustrated. She went to her teacher and asked her to make her something, as she did not know how. The teacher showed Wilma how the toys could be fitted together at different points and encouraged her to make something "special for the teacher." At this point Wilma's attitude changed and she began to work intensely. As she worked and discovered the numerous things she could do with her toys, she joined in the conversation going on about her. The voice that had been a whine just a minute before was now happy and filled with enthusiasm. She had found that a chain of the "Snowflakes" was flexible enough to form a circle and she had made herself a crown. Wearing this on her head she stated that she was a "lovely queen from across the sea." Next she said that she would make a boat for teacher. It would be a small boat and it "wouldn't ever sink." When Wilma had finished she had produced a very good likeness of a sailboat.

After Wilma showed the teacher her boat, she continued to play with her toys but seemed to be no longer constructing anything specific. She seemed instead to be experimenting with the fit of the facets on the flakes.

As Wilma continued in this way, I asked her teacher to comment on Wilma's performance. The teacher pointed out that she had grasped the principle of the "Snowflakes" rapidly and had shown good coordination. One of the objectives of the toys was to evoke an experimental attitude, and Wilma had shown a full desire to experiment.

One aspect of Wilma's play with the "Snowflakes" which her teacher noted specifically was Wilma's mention of the sea and a boat. This was the first time that Wilma had made any reference to these two things which could naturally have a connection with her father's drowning. The teacher attached much significance to this, though still unsure what its real meaning could be. She noted that comments such as these on Wilma's part must from then on be watched more closely.

FIFTH OBSERVATION

After several days of rain in which the children at the Village Preschool were confined completely to the school building, the good weather had returned and the program of extensive outdoor play had resumed. Because of the long period of rainy weather when they had had to restrain much of their energy in one way or another, all of the children were on the playground when I conducted my fifth hour of observation.

Wilma conducted herself in ways very similar to those which I had noted in my third observation. She went to the swing and began using it several different ways—to swing high and look at things upside down, to spin slowly at first and then gain in speed, to just sit and move only slightly. As Wilma continued to swing she was eventually joined by two of the younger children. These two were the same boy and girl whom I had previously seen reject Wilma's advances. Wilma greeted them only casually and did not seem too enthusiastic about their presence. She did however accept an invitation to play with them and, leaving the swings, the three ran to the other end of the playground. There other members of the senior nursery were engaged in some sort of game which seemed mostly comprised of running and screaming. Wilma joined in only to the extent of running along slowly on the outskirts of the group. She appeared much larger in size and displayed none of the awkwardness that many of the others did. She seemed more interested in watching them participating. After only a few minutes, she withdrew from the group completely and returned to the swings. She took the same swing as before.

I asked Wilma's teacher how the relationship between Wilma and the two senior nursery children now stood. She pointed out that while there did not seem to be any more rejection occurring, the three were quite prone to fighting. When they played, Wilma seemed to have an equal part in provoking these disturbances if she found something not to her liking. On a few occasions she had struck out at the other children, but this had ended after she had been told this should not happen. Wilma did not play with any of the children for very long periods of time. She seemed most content when playing alone. She definitely showed the process of withdrawal inside herself each time she detached herself from the other children.

SIXTH OBSERVATION

In my sixth hour of observation I observed a directed art lesson for the kindergarten. The senior nursery children were to have one also. Their papers would serve well for comparison purposes.

The drawing which the teacher posted on the board was that of a mother with a shopping bag in one arm and a child held by the other hand. A discussion began as to what the picture entailed. Wilma was silent for the first few minutes of it, watching her other classmates and looking as if she was listening closely to their comments. Eventually she spoke and pointed out that the lady in the picture was not "terribly much like my mother" nor was the little girl like her sister. She stated that her mother was "really much lovelier than anyone" and her "baby sister was much fatter." The latter part of this statement, made quite emphatically by Wilma, amused the other children. When Wilma found their laughter to be genuine and not directed at her, she seemed very pleased with herself. She did not, however, become carried away and attempt to overdo it.

After the class had settled, the teacher moved on in the lesson and asked the children what colors they thought would be appropriate for the picture. Many different ideas were suggested. The colors that Wilma contributed were all bright and coordinated well.

The teacher began the actual coloring of the picture. She would select a color, ask the children what it was, and then apply it to a specific area. While she colored, she continued the discussion of the picture. Wilma remained silent and observed her closely. When the one color was completed, the class was told that they could begin by doing just as the teacher had. Wilma did not get to work right away but instead continued to study the picture. She seemed to be staring at it while her mind concentrated on something else. When she finally averted her gaze, it seemed to take her several seconds to bring her attention back to her paper. Finally, she began to work and did so with her usual intensity. Although she had not started to color with the others, she finished with them. She had worked rapidly but her paper appeared neat.

The teacher continued the lesson by moving on to the next color. Wilma's mind did not appear to wander again, and her attention appeared to be completely on her paper. As she colored she showed no awkwardness in handling the crayon. Her strokes were soft where some others tended to bear down.

While Wilma finished her paper she made one comment concerning it. She pointed out that the mother was "alone with her baby at the supermarket," and that probably meant she was "alone at home always too with her baby." She commented further that the little girl was "probably terribly busy keeping her mother from getting lonely."

Afterward I asked the teacher about this particular art lesson. She agreed with me that by her standards this lesson was very poor and stifling in the creative sense, but the school's owner believed otherwise.

SEVENTH OBSERVATION

Wilma Adams did not arrive at school at her usual time on the day of my seventh observation. She came shortly after I did, and I had the opportunity once again to see her with her mother.

A good amount of time had passed since the incident which I described in my second observation, where both Wilma and her mother became quite upset at having to leave each other in the morning. Wilma's teacher had pointed out that there had never been a recurrence of this incident. Shortly after it Mrs. Adams had stopped carrying Wilma from the car. Eventually she had also stopped following her into the school yard, but would leave her at the gate if a teacher was near. As of late, the teacher commented, there were mornings when Wilma seemed to barely acknowledge her mother as she said good-bye.

Mrs. Adams drove into the school yard and parked her car. Before she had even gotten out of the car, Wilma was halfway to the gate. Mrs. Adams hurried to catch up with her and, when she did, Wilma paused only for a minute to kiss her good-bye. Mrs. Adams's face had traces of the same urgent look I had seen there before. The hug she gave Wilma seemed to convey some of this urgency, but Wilma appeared unaffected. She ran off to the swings and, as her mother drove off, turned and called "Good-bye, silly Mommy."

The kindergarten children were soon afterward brought inside for opening exercises. These exercises consisted of the Pledge of Allegiance and some songs. Wilma's recitation was clear and correct, where many of the others her age seemed to have difficulty with pronunciation and accuracy.

The children also recited their alphabet with the teacher. Again, where the other junior kindergarteners had some problems, Wilma had none.

After completion of the exercises, the children were given crayons and paper. They were told that they could color as they wished and could talk softly. Wilma began coloring and did not join in any of the conversation. Her silence seemed heavier than usual, and her face appeared troubled. When Wilma's teacher approached her and commented on her picture, Wilma did not give her customary response. Instead of smiling and hugging her teacher she just looked up into her face, her expression unchanged. The teacher asked if "there was something wrong today." When there was no immediate reply, the matter was not pursued. The teacher told me later that she felt that Wilma would come to her if and when she chose to.

Wilma's sullen attitude continued as she finished her paper. She seemed to be coloring only in blue and green and to be working much less rapidly than she usually did. She appeared instead to be taking great pains with her picture, as if she were seriously pondering its contents. Her head was close to the paper and she showed none of her usual good posture or movements. The intensity she displayed was not of the eager nature with which she usually worked.

After the papers were collected and the children were sent out to the playground, I asked to see Wilma's picture. Set in among many large blue and green waves was a drawing of a sailboat with no one aboard.

EIGHTH OBSERVATION

When I arrived for my final hour of observation all of the children were on the playground. One of the teachers informed me that they would be playing for the duration of my observation period. I was told that Wilma was present and automatically looked toward the swings to find her. I was somewhat surprised when I saw that she was not there, and I realized that each of the times I had watched her on the playground I had very rarely seen her anywhere else. Eventually I found her, and she appeared to be involved in a situation that would prove far more intriguing than her swinging.

The principal of the school, a man, was also on the playground doing some yard work. Wilma was running around him wildly, purposely getting in the way of his rake and upsetting the piles of leaves he had gathered. Her teacher informed me that at several points during the day the principal would involve himself with the children. The male and father figure he provided for the many who needed it was vital. This situation with Wilma was a regular recurrence and proved to be the one time that she seemed to lose some of her self-control. I had never had the opportunity to see this.

Wilma continued her rough-housing. At several points the principal would reach out and pick her up off the ground, setting her down away from his work area. This seemed to delight her. It also served to excite her further, and she returned to her antics more enthusiastically. Eventually the teacher asked Wilma to join the others on the playground. Wilma ignored this request, and, as she ran even more wildly, her laughter increased to screams. The teacher then told Wilma to do as she had said, and Wilma, very reluctantly and with a pout, walked off slowly toward the swings.

Wilma's teacher commented that this play with the principal usually began quietly enough with Wilma running to him for a hug when he first appeared. At that time she seemed to resent anyone else desiring the same. Wilma appeared very fond of him and at one point had asked him to be her "nursery-school daddy." If allowed to, she would hang on his legs or swing on his arm until she had to be commanded to let go. It was actually the one time that Wilma became quite unruly and disobedient.

As I spoke with the teacher, Wilma was swinging quietly watching us. When her teacher's attention was diverted elsewhere, Wilma left the swing slowly, and watching her teacher the whole time, made her way back to the principal. The whole process began again as she hugged him about the legs. She was soon discovered and went back to the playground. Very obviously withdrawing into herself, she returned to her swing and remained there. Her face assumed a blank expression and she barely moved on the swing at all until the kindergarten class was called inside.

CONCLUSIONS

At the conclusion of many hours of observation I found myself left with the impression that Wilma Adams was an extraordinary child in many ways. For a child five years old, and in relation to the others her age that I saw, she seemed quite advanced in a great number of aspects.

Wilma's maturity was first evident in her physical aspects. In relation to the other children in the junior kindergarten who are close in age, that is, five years and one month to five years and five months, she appeared to be approximately two to three inches taller. Where most of the others in this age range still retained some of their baby-fat, Wilma seemed to have lost it all. She was slim and her bone structure appeared well-defined. She carried herself well, and there was very little awkwardness in any of her movements. On the playground she displayed good control of her large muscles. On the swing she showed adequate strength in her arms and legs, while propelling the swings for a long time. When she handled small objects such as a pencil or crayon, her use of small muscles also appeared well-controlled. All of her eye-hand movements appeared well-coordinated.

The most unique feature of Wilma's physical aspects was her face.

In the same way that she had lost the baby look in her limbs so had she in her face. The obvious beauty that she would have later was now quite evident, making her more beautiful than cute, as the other little girls were. Her facial expressions were largely determined by her eyes, deep set and dark blue. She appeared to do a great deal of communicating with them. Her usual expression was one bordering on a smile. However, at some points, with the use of her eyes, she could assume a deeply withdrawn and saddened appearance. Wilma's over all physical grooming and dress, which were usually faultless, completed her total physical attractiveness.

While Wilma's physical maturity seemed advanced in all areas, there were only a few apparent areas in her emotional makeup that were advanced for a child her age. Wilma's relationship with her mother provided the best illustration of this.

In two of my observations I gave accounts of Wilma's arrival in the morning with her mother. This specific situation proved to be one which revealed a number of emotions existing between the two. One example of Wilma's advanced maturity was found in the fact that many of the more turbulent emotions were displayed by her mother. Wilma's reluctance to leave her in the morning was greatly influenced by these emotions. Wilma possessed enough insight to be aware that any emotional reaction on her part would evoke one on the part of her mother. As indicated in my second observation this was all quite obvious in Wilma's swift glances at her mother as if she were looking for a cue. When Wilma found the look of urgent expectation on her mother's face, she seemed to cater purposely to this with the expected emotional reactions. This again was obvious in the abrupt end to Wilma's hysterics when her mother left. Wilma obviously possessed the ability to influence greatly or even control her mother emotionally. It had been intimated by an aunt who came for Wilma each day that Wilma was actually the only one who could calm her mother when she was reacting to the death of her husband. Wilma obviously felt the effects of this and considered it a burden. This was evidenced in several comments that she made pertaining to her desire to change her place and "be the baby."

With the passage of time and perhaps the influence of school, Wilma seemed to gain further insight into her mother. The casual acknowledgment of her as she said good-bye in the morning seemed to be an effort on Wilma's part to avoid any emotional communication. Wilma appeared to still sense the same urgency in her mother but no longer felt she needed to manipulate it. The morning that I heard her say "Good-bye silly Mommy" after her mother had begun to drive away, I somehow sensed a form of wisdom in the child's voice.

Wilma's apparent dominance in her emotional relationship with her mother gives an adequate example of an advanced maturity. However, I observed that she was not so emotionally mature in most other areas. One example of this was her apparent feelings of insecurity as evidenced by her constant need for approval and her overly enthusiastic response to it. The encouragement that usually accompanied this approval was vital to her. Wilma also showed a great desire for physical affection. This desire was so strong that she would interrupt her play in order to seek out her teacher for some form of affectional contact. Most of the time when Wilma was not on her swing (the attachment to this also shows some insecurity), she was clinging to her teacher in one form or another. Wilma's change in character when involved with the principal also was significant in considering her insecurity. When I observed Wilma with a male figure, and noted her wild behavioral display, I could realize how much she was affected by her father's death. Insecurity was only one of the emotional factors that was revealed. The almost complete loss of her self-control, a part of her nature usually quite dominant, illustrated the emotional buildup caused by her lack of and obvious desire for a male image.

It is difficult to define the full effects of Wilma's emotional problem on her relationship with her peer group. In the time that I observed her, both on the playground and in the classroom, her contact with the other children had not been that extensive. I had seen her seek out the friendship of children younger than she, and had observed the rejection of her efforts. Her immediate response of a pout had seemed not out of the ordinary for this type of occurrence, but her continual need for reassurance and physical worth from the teacher did seem significant. Wilma's constant presence on the one swing, and the nature of her swinging, obviously affected the children in some way for she was very rarely joined on the two swings next to her. None of the children went out of their way to include her in their play, but, on the few occasions that she appeared to be attempting to include herself, she was not shunned. In actuality there was no vivid response to her in one way or another. Wilma did not have the one special friend that most of the others her age did. She seemed to prefer to be alone and her frequent withdrawal into herself gave proof of this.

In the classroom Wilma was a bit more animated with her peers. She did not participate to any full extent in general conversations but would contribute something at different times. Usually Wilma appeared as if she were first feeling out the situation, and when she was sure of her surroundings, she would open up a bit. This seemed to denote another example of Wilma's insecurity which entered into so much of her nature. It is important to note here that while Wilma did not really relate to her peers in the truly friendly sense, she never appeared to lack self-confidence in their presence. Wilma's general state of oneness was apparently a result of her own choosing and her classmates seemed to respect her for this.

In the physical and mental sense Wilma appeared to be an outstanding child. In the social and emotional sense she was lacking. Considering her physical attractiveness and her intellect which enabled her to communicate so well, attention should definitely be paid to the rounding out of her desire and ability to relate to others. To provide her the security she needs, the roles (of herself and her mother) should be far more clearly defined and definitely rearranged. Wilma's rapid growth emotionally, in the sense that she must be adept enough to ease her mother, should be slowed and replaced with the building of a more sound sense of security. If her role as the child, the protected and the loved was clear to her, Wilma would soon lose her strong desire for constant reassurance through physical contact. The strength of the drives which lead her in these directions would be redirected toward forming the groundwork for an ability to relate to her peers.

Wilma Adams displayed the basic qualities for the making of a totally outstanding child. It appeared that the loss of her father and the subsequent effect on her mother greatly hindered this. Wilma, however, seemed to be handling her reactions to the loss reasonably adequately. Her obvious superior creative ability enabled her to do much of this. She could express her feelings in any number of ways until she was ready to voice them. The presence of a male figure at the school was vital to her retaining her conception of that image.

So at this point we can only hope that Wilma's mother has the strength and the ability to recover from her grief quickly, so as to concentrate on the raising of her child, who so much needs a strong parent. Wilma will grow up to be a beautiful young lady, but the help and support of her mother must come quickly.

ANALYSIS OF THE CASE STUDY

In this case study the student observer was able to express, in a rather dramatic prose style, the emotional life of a child as revealed to him through his direct observations of her. There is little to be added to a picture so skillfully presented.

We can, however, draw parallels between the behavior of Wilma and that of other children her age. For example, many nursery and kindergarten children have difficulty adjusting to the separation from mother during the early part of a school term. In Wilma's case her initial reaction (second observation) was decidedly a response to her mother's anxiety. Wilma behaved in the way she felt her mother desired her to respond, that is, with tears. As she began to enjoy school more, and as she began to understand, at least subconsciously, her mother's need for the attachment to her, Wilma refused to play the game of creating a scene at departure. Her comment, "Good-bye, silly Mommy," (seventh observation) is evidence of a mature insight well beyond her five years of age.

Problems of adjustment during the first few days of school are often triggered by just such emotional dependency on the part of the adult that Wilma's mother displayed. When the child is separated from the parent, sometimes by force, the situation resolves itself. Teachers should be aware of the emotional needs of mothers who so frequently convey their own anxiety to their children.

Although mature beyond her years in many ways, Wilma also showed evidence of immaturity. Her need for the affection of her teacher far outweighed her need for identity with her peers. Her coordination and skills in handling materials in the classroom revealed her advanced abilities, yet she constantly sought adult approval to reassure herself. A more secure child her age would be more intent upon finding satisfying peer relationships. Wilma's desire for adult commendation is one indication of her deeply felt emotional needs.

Regressive behavior

In some children there is a close connection between high achievement in some areas and regressive behavior in others. Children cannot mature all at once. Wilma's adult behavior in her relationship with her mother created a more intense need for infantile gratifications at other times. She longed to "be the baby" in the family, in place of her sister. Perhaps she found some satisfaction through her constant swinging on the playground. It is very likely that the swinging was gratifying to her in a way that rocking would soothe an infant. Her babbling and singing to herself while swinging was evidence of her primitive enjoyment. When Wilma left the swings, it was frequently to hug her teacher, "holding her around the legs and resting her head against her teacher's side."

Of course, enjoyment of swinging is not always an indication of regressive behavior. We must constantly be reminded to view behavior in the light of all of the evidence available. For Wilma, who showed maturity in her physical development, in her conceptual understanding, and in her fine muscle coordination, swinging appeared to provide both infantile gratification and an escape from the challenge of developing closer peer relationships. The return to primitive pleasures is frequently used as a means of avoiding social interaction for which the child is not ready.

We see frequent evidence of this in the classroom when we observe young children resorting to thumb sucking or other forms of oral gratification. These patterns usually occur when their social advances have been rejected. Thumb sucking, biting the lips, or seeking an object to place in the mouth, are frequently signs of withdrawal. The child retreats to some solitary form of gratification when he feels defeated in his efforts to cope with circumstances in the outside world.

A ten-year-old boy, who was observed at a summer sleep-away camp, awoke every morning in a rather grumpy mood. Soon after awakening he frequently began an argument with someone. He would then declare that he had not finished sleeping yet, and would return to his bed. He would pretend to sleep, sucking his thumb vigorously as he did so. He then got up, appearing less aggressive, and got dressed without further ado.

Bedtime is often the occasion for regressive behavior to manifest itself. A four-year-old who attended nursery school was an extremely mature little girl. She could draw, cut, and paste like a six-year-old. She was imaginative and a leader in group activities in her class. In every way she appeared to behave like an older child, and her teacher was considering placing her in the five-year-old kindergarten group. One day her mother requested a conference with the teacher and complained that her daughter insisted upon taking her bottle to bed with her each night. No amount of reasoning could convince the child that she was now "a big girl" and did not need a bottle. The teacher advised the mother to allow the child this one form of infantile gratification, especially since she was so grown-up in so many other ways. A decision was made not to place the girl with an older group. The teacher and the mother agreed to try not to expect too much of her in her everyday performance. Within a short time she gave up the bottle of her own accord.

Transference relationships

The case study of Wilma Adams clearly reveals the transference to her teacher and to the school principal of feelings originating in her relationships with her mother and her father. Her desire for affection and for physical contact with her teacher reflects a need that was unfulfilled in her relationship with her mother. Wilma's aunt had intimated to the teacher that "Wilma was actually the only one who could calm her mother when she was reacting to the death of her husband." The need to assume an adult role with her mother left Wilma with unfulfilled desires to be cuddled and babied. Her excitement when she saw the principal on the playground, and her persistent attempts to seek his attention, show Wilma's need for a relationship with a man who could replace her father. Her desire to interact with the male principal was so strong that it caused unruly and disobedient behavior in a usually well-mannered little girl.

Transference provides a release of feelings and can thus be helpful to a child with emotional problems. Teachers who understand this can use the transference relationship to satisfy some of the child's needs. But it is important for the teacher to try to wean the child away from neurotic dependency and to gradually establish a relationship in which the teacher herself comes to be recognized as a person in her own right. In psychotherapy transference of feelings to the therapist is often used effectively to help the child develop self-awareness. Without such a relationship the therapist's advice and suggestions count for little. The child must first care about the person with whom he is interacting before behavior can be changed.

Bettelheim relates a story about Tom, a twelve-year-old boy who attended a school for emotionally disturbed children.[2] Tom's parents were married when the father was already advanced in age. Tom's mother, who was much younger, became his play companion when Tom was alone with her, and she often behaved in ways that appeared to the boy to be seductive. Disturbances arising from this complex family situation revealed itself during Tom's first few weeks at the school. It began with his severe disappointment in his mother when a letter he believed she had promised him did not come.

Tom transferred his feelings of desertion and neglect to his female

[2] Bruno Bettelheim, *Love Is Not Enough*, pp. 73–74, 80–81.

counselor, whom he accused of "wanting him to go hungry, of wanting him to feel bad, or of never giving him what he wanted." His resentment of his mother, who had deprived him emotionally, was displaced to the counselor. The counselor knew that to point out how unrealistic Tom's accusations were would do no good, since he was reacting to past, not current, events. She took Tom on shopping trips and tried in various ways to establish friendly contact with him. After a period of rejection Tom began to behave in a more positive way toward his counselor and was able to accept gifts and services from her. He could recognize her as a person, instead of thinking of her as a symbol of what he remembered as his mother's worst features.

The classroom teacher need not assume the role of a counselor or therapist, but recognition of the mechanism of transference can help her understand the behavior of some of her children. A child who displays an attachment of this sort to a teacher is usually very sensitive to criticism and easily feels rejected. Awareness of this sensitivity can prevent the teacher from inflicting pain upon a child unknowingly.

It is not only the emotionally disturbed child who is likely to transfer feelings to a teacher. Anyone who has taught nursery school, kindergarten, or first grade knows how frequently young children will refer to the teacher as "Mommy." It is natural for the child to replace the central figure in the school setting with an image of the key person in his home life. For this reason it is deemed desirable for the young child entering school for the first time to be placed in a small group with a single adult to whom he can relate easily. After a while the child will feel comfortable in the school setting and can join larger groups and relate to several adults at the same time without difficulty.

Infantile trauma

Early experiences have persistent effects on children's behavior. The trauma in Wilma's young life, that is, the loss of her father through drowning, is revealed throughout her case study. One wonders how permanent the effects will be upon her developing personality. Opportunities to express her feelings freely would be helpful. A supportive home and school environment will alleviate much of the resulting emotional upset. But the shock of the tragedy will very likely remain with her in some form or other throughout her life. Perhaps she will always experience some emotional reaction to water and to sailboats. If she understands and accepts the reason for her fears, she may overcome any overt behavioral reaction. But a subconscious awareness is likely to remain with her, even after she has made adequate adjustments to her loss.

There is much evidence to establish the importance of past events on present behavior. Unconscious memory extends back considerably before age five. During psychoanalysis the effects of early experiences become evident, even when there is no conscious memory of the events.

A recent visitor to this writer's home asked, before coming, if there were any cats in the house. The woman is a mature and stable individual who commands the respect of all who know her. She is a fifty-year-old school principal with a strong personality and a keen sense of humor. She later related that she had been told that a cat had jumped into her carriage when she was an infant, and she retains this fear of feline animals to the present day!

The effects of infantile trauma are revealed in a case study done by an undergraduate student describing her neighbor's adopted boy, Eric. The child was adopted when he was one year old. The case study includes descriptions of behavior from that time through his third year. Here is the student observer's personal report of her first contact with the child.

It was Wednesday, two years ago, when Eric became a member of the Jones family. I remember the day well, because it had been a day that both the Jones family and my own family had waited for for some time.

Diane (Mrs. Jones) brought Eric out into the backyard minutes after they had arrived home from the adoption agency. I remember seeing Eric in a simple white tee shirt with diapers, sucking his thumb as he was carried out to the fence. Then, to my disappointment, Eric began crying at the top of his lungs when our eyes met! His arms and legs began kicking furiously and he screamed in anger. When Eric was taken into the house, his crying ceased. Not knowing what was wrong, we all attributed Eric's behavior to excitement and fatigue.

I made arrangements to visit the Jones's house later that evening. Upon my arrival Eric displayed the same reaction. This time, the child began beating his father's head and chest, and he had to be taken from the room. We discussed the fact that I wear glasses and this might be frightening to Eric. Diane put my glasses on and approached Eric. There was no crying reaction.

Eric soon began to go over to other strangers, but there seemed to be no hope that he would ever allow me to come near him. Of course, I was hurt, but I was determined to find out why Eric behaved like this with me.

The student observer was a frequent visitor at the Jones's home. She had been the baby-sitter for the two older girls in the family and had a close relationship with them. She tried in many ways to get Eric to accept her. She played ball with the sisters and gradually tried to include Eric in the game. She busied herself in the garden when Eric was playing nearby in the hopes that the child would get used to seeing her. After a year Eric still showed evidence of fear, but he tolerated her presence as long as she did not touch him. Once, when she offered to give him a balloon, he "grabbed it quickly and ran into the house, glancing back anxiously toward me without saying anything."

It was not until Eric was three that an incident occurred which changed his relationship to the student observer. One afternoon, while swinging in the swing, Eric fell off and hurt his head. He cried, and the student observer hesitatingly reached toward him. Eric seemed to forget about his past feelings and sought comfort for present hurts in her arms. After he stopped crying, he "realized he was in my arms, but did not struggle to get down. Instead he began to play with my lips and mouth as I talked to him. He laughed and I began to bounce him up and down. After several minutes I placed Eric back on the ground where he began to play. I bent down to kiss him good-bye (if he would let me), and, instead of rejecting me, Eric raised his arms and said, 'Carry me.' "

Eric's acceptance of the student observer was the result of her cautious and sensitive efforts to reach him. Had she rushed at him and tried to win him with displays of affection and attention, he would very likely have continued to resist her advances. But her success in establishing a relationship did not deter the student observer from further investigating. She decided to take the child and his mother back to the adoption agency to ask a few questions.

Upon our arrival Eric seemed to remember the place because he began to whimper. He had not been here for two years, but I sensed that he felt some insecurity and uneasiness that was associated with the place.

A new matron had taken over the agency. To my surprise she looked through the records and came up with some vital information that shed light upon Eric's behavior as it related to me.

When Eric was ten months old, he was boarded at a home, awaiting adoption. The woman who cared for him at this time was tall, fairly thin, wore glasses, and had long blond hair. (This description fits the appearance of the student observer also.) One day the woman went to take Eric from his crib to change him. He was crying wildly. As she pulled him from the crib, she swatted him across the backside. He cried harder and began to wiggle in her arms. He fell on the floor and received an injury that required eighteen stitches on his forehead, tongue, and mouth. All of this information was in the medical file at the agency. The family had not been informed of the incident at the time of adoption.

Eric had not seen the woman who had cared for him again. After the accident, according to the records, she had given up the child-care work. Eric never had the chance to overcome the fear that had built up in those few minutes when he fell from her arms.

There is little doubt that Eric's reaction to the student observer was caused by her resemblance to the woman associated in his mind with fear and pain. Eric had had a terrifying experience. Since he was only ten months old when it happened, it is not likely that he has any conscious memory of the event. But the fear associated with the woman who dropped him was carried over to his adoptive parents' neighbor, whom he met when he was one-year-old. The feelings persisted for two years in spite of the kindness of the student observer and the obvious warmth that was displayed toward her by the rest of the Jones family.

No doubt Eric has overcome his fear by now, and the accident is forgotten. But traumatic events in infancy have effects upon later behavior, and the impact of early experience is clearly demonstrated here. The student observer comments, at the conclusion of her report, "Eric will forget this all together, and it will become past history for the files and records kept for people like myself who do case studies." Hopefully, Eric's story will give the student observer, and other prospective teachers like her, a better understanding of some of the causes of children's behavior.

Projection

In the case study of Wilma Adams a great deal is revealed to the observer through the child's expressive artwork. Her first picture (first observation) was of a river into which a rainbow had fallen "terribly far," "crashing the water and spreading its colors all about." During the fourth observation Wilma constructed a boat for the teacher that "wouldn't ever sink." In the most dramatic of all of the observations Wilma worked with tension and remote concentration (seventh observation) to produce a sailboat with no one aboard, set among large blue and green waves.

In all of these examples, Wilma was using the medium of drawing or construction to externalize a deep-seated emotion related to the death of her father through drowning. The expressive acts and the comments she made about her works provided a means whereby she was able to project her thoughts to a neutral object. She was spared the pain of discussing the loss of her father directly, yet her deep feelings relating to this event were given some opportunity for release.

Projective techniques are frequently used in the diagnosis and treatment of emotional disturbance by psychologists and therapists. It is through the projection of thoughts and feelings onto relatively neutral objects that the individual reveals the structure of his personality and the nature of his problems. The Rorschach ink-blot test is, perhaps, the most well-known and effective projective technique used for this purpose. It is based upon the idea that perception is selective. The subject will see, in the nonstructured ink blots, those things that have meaning for him. He also perceives in a manner that is characteristic of his own style. Thus, some individuals are aware of the whole blot, while others notice detail first. For some the color and shading is important, while for others, it is not as significant in determining what they see. "Each person brings to the test his own personality, his own unique complex of feelings and his own unique history of experiences. And we find, therefore, that each person structures these ink blots in a way that distinguishes him from the next person."[3]

We are not suggesting that teachers use the Rorschach test to gain insight into their pupils. The test is difficult to administer and to score and takes much training and practice to use effectively. The discussion of Rorschach is included here simply as a means of demonstrating the manner in which personality and emotional disturbance are revealed through projection. Wilma did not need the stimulus of ink blots to start the process for her. Simply the

[3] Lucille Hollander Blum, Helen H. Davidson, and Nina D. Fieldsteel, *A Rorschach Workbook*, p. 5.

opportunity to "draw what you like," or the construction materials provided for building, gave her the opportunity to externalize some of the ideas and feelings that were disturbing her.

The student observer was not a trained psychologist. Yet he was able to sense the meanings of Wilma's expressions and was aware of the manner in which the drawings and construction revealed her inner being. The repetition of the theme of the sailboat indicated the obsessive hold that this image had upon the child.

Incidents reported by child analysts of patients in play-therapy sessions have often indicated the source of emotional disturbance in a similar way. In play therapy the child is given the opportunity to "play out" his feelings and problems, just as, in certain types of adult therapy, an individual "talks out" his difficulties. Kenneth, an eight-year-old patient described by the child analyst Dorothy Baruch had problems relating to a fear of acknowledging his maleness. His clay figures were phallic symbols that instantly were transformed to something else.

He made clay worms. Snakes. Guns. But always something happened to them. He blocked up the wall again and pushed back the wish to own up to having what every male must possess. Worms could not remain worms; nor snakes, snakes; nor guns, guns. The shape apparently was too telling. He had to turn them into eggs or cookies or cakes; boats, canoes, what not. . . . Inevitably he would put cracks or holes or hollows in these from which water would drip or splash.

One day he made a long cylindrical form, pointed at one end, a round knob of clay at the other end.

"It's a bomb with a ball kind of thing at the end," he stated. Then, daring more, he ventured in his mind to transform it with a revision quicker than the blinking of an eye.

"No. It's a wee-wee-er—a penis—with a ball kind of thing," pointing down at himself.

But this was obviously too much. "No, it's not. It's . . . it's . . . it's a long nose with somebody's head at the end."[4]

The clay used by Kenneth became material to be transformed into objects representing his thoughts. His fantasy was projected onto the neutral substance, the clay, in a manner similar to the way in which individuals project images onto the Rorschach ink blots.

Play-therapy rooms are well provided with clay, drawing paper, paints, construction materials, and puppets. The child is free to use what he likes in any way that he wishes to, as long as there is no injury to himself or to others. Paints may be splashed on the walls; dolls may be mutilated. The therapist accepts the child and places no value judgments upon his actions. A climate is established in which the child feels free to externalize his feelings, and in this way, he is helped to understand them.

Axline reports upon a case study of Tom, a twelve-year-old of above

---

[4] Dorothy Baruch, *One Little Boy*, pp. 65–66.

average intelligence who was seriously maladjusted both at home and in school.[5]

Tom used puppets in the play-therapy sessions to enact his relationships to his family and his feelings about himself. One puppet became "Ronnie, the bad boy," who was always getting into trouble. Another puppet was used to represent the authority figures of both the father and the school principal. Tom's resentment toward a younger half sister was displayed by his use of a girl puppet who constantly cried for "Mama." Tom's voice changed completely each time a different puppet spoke, and his dialogue was clever and amusing. He asked to put on some puppet shows for younger children. The appreciation which the six-year-olds had for his performance built up Tom's self-esteem to the point where he could look at his problems more objectively. Secure in the knowledge that he could not be blamed for what the puppets said, and well-hidden from his audience himself, his feelings could flow freely. Tom could delve deeply into the problems of his family relationships while still maintaining his dignity and self-respect.

Children do not always need external objects such as puppets on which to project their feelings. Nursery and kindergarten children often identify with characters in stories that are told to them. Perhaps every little girl imagines herself, at one time or another, to be *Cinderella*, and boys enjoy projecting themselves into characters like "Jack" who climbed the beanstalk and outsmarted the giant. The popularity of these tales persists throughout the ages. When a child identifies with a character in a story, he is likely to ask to hear it again and again.

Bettelheim describes the behavior of nine-year-old Mary, who came to the school for emotionally disturbed because of extremely antisocial actions. In the playroom Mary painted the face of an unhappy little girl who was just "any girl" and who had no name. Then she asked the counselor to read a story that she knew very well.

It was the story of a caterpillar (in Mary's words, an ugly worm) who, after many adventures, turned into a butterfly. Midway through the story her tension rose and she said, "Do you know what happens in the end?" "Yes," the counselor said, "but why don't you tell me?" So Mary told her excitedly how the ugly, unhappy worm turns into a beautiful, happy butterfly. It was the first time she had shown any positive emotion, and it was as if she had hope now that some day she, herself, might change from a nameless, just-any-girl, into a happy, distinct individual.[6]

Children do not need to be emotionally disturbed to make these identifications. The classroom is as good as the play-therapy room for some kinds of role play. Robbin, the shy first grader who is discussed in Chapter 5, amazed her class and her teacher when she dramatized her favorite story. She played the part of *The Little Match Girl*, who saw such beautiful images in the flame

[5] Virginia Axline, *Play Therapy*, pp. 30–52.
[6] Bettelheim, pp. 58–59.

of a match. "Robbin's face lit up, and her body unfolded. The movement was not big, but there was a change from the huddled position to the open one that started within the child."[7] No doubt Robbin was projecting herself into the person of *The Little Match Girl*. Story dramatization in the classroom gives many a child an opportunity to identify with favorite characters and thus provides the teacher with the chance to observe feelings being acted out.

Using play-therapy techniques in the classroom

During story dramatization the classroom teacher can gain understanding of her children. By observing kindergarteners as they act out family roles in the housekeeping corner, the teacher can have another opportunity for getting to know children's feelings. When the climate of the classroom is relaxed and open, children reveal themselves in many ways.

The teacher can learn a good deal from the play therapist about how to establish such a climate. Of course, the classroom is not the place for total freedom. Children may neither be destructive in handling equipment, nor may they use offensive language in expressing themselves. The classroom is not the place to probe deeply into emotional problems or difficult family relationships. But teachers should be as concerned about the feelings of children as they are about children's mastery of academic skills. Frequently, feelings are a determining factor in learning. A child who expresses resentment over little incidents, a child who inwardly withdraws, or one who fights constantly, might be a child handicapped in his social relations and in his academic learning. Many of the children discussed in this chapter had to overcome their emotional problems before they were ready to tackle academic tasks.

The rapport established between the teacher and her class has a great deal to do with the success of her teaching program. Children need to feel free to be themselves; they need understanding, recognition, and acceptance of their feelings in order to maintain their self-respect. Recently investigators have established the fact that growth and learning are directly related to the self-concept.[8] There are, therefore, significant implications for educational practices in the therapeutic approach.

We have discussed, in this chapter and in Chapter 5, the use of children's creative expressions as a tool for developing teachers' insight. But if the teacher is to help the child with his emotional adjustments, free expression by the child is not enough in itself. The teacher who tries to apply an approach similar to that used in nondirective play therapy must recognize the feelings the child has expressed. She must reflect those feelings back to the child in such a manner that the child gains insight into his behavior. This can be done to a great extent in any classroom situation if the teacher has an understanding of children and a sincere desire to help them. Many problems can be aborted

---

[7] Betty Rowen, *Learning through Movement*, p. 57.
[8] William W. Purkey, *Self Concept and School Achievement*.

before they develop into serious maladjustment if therapy techniques are applied.

Axline lists basic principles which guide play therapists in all of their interaction with children. The methods are very simple and can be used by classroom teachers to some extent and in some situations. It is to be remembered, however, that the classroom is not a play-therapy room, and the teacher is not a trained clinical worker. The principles are listed below, and teachers are advised to use them with discretion.

1. The therapist must develop a warm, friendly relationship with the child, in which good rapport is established as soon as possible.
2. The therapist accepts the child exactly as he is.
3. The therapist establishes a feeling of permissiveness in the relationship so that the child feels free to express his feelings completely.
4. The therapist is alert to recognize the feelings the child is expressing and reflects those feelings back to him in such a manner that he gains insight into his behavior. [An example of the use of this technique by a principal interviewing children is given in Chapter 4.]
5. The therapist maintains a deep respect for the child's ability to solve his own problems if given opportunity to do so. The responsibility to make choices and to institute change is the child's.
6. The therapist does not attempt to direct the child's actions or conversation in any manner. The child leads the way; the therapist follows.
7. The therapist does not attempt to hurry the therapy along. It is a gradual process and is recognized as such by the therapist.
8. The therapist establishes only those limitations that are necessary to anchor the therapy to the world of reality and to make the child aware of his responsibility in the relationship.[9]

Although these principles are not all practical for classroom use, there are some that can be readily applied in some types of situations, and others that, if used consistently, can decidedly improve classroom climate. A warm, friendly relationship with a child, for example, can make instruction appear to be individualized, even though there are forty other pupils in the class. A teacher can allow children to express their feelings freely and can encourage them to be themselves. Opportunities for such communication can be provided through group discussion or through creative writing. All teachers would benefit from the recommendation that children be allowed to participate in decision making, and that, at least at some times, children be allowed to "lead the way."

The teacher must have a degree of insight and understanding to recognize emotional problems. It may not be difficult to identify some types of disturbed behavior. The aggressive child who is disruptive in class is frequently referred to the school psychologist for examination. But the quiet child, who does his work with little enthusiasm and appears to be tired and apathetic most of the

[9] Axline, pp. 75–76.

time, is sometimes overlooked. When he is brought to the attention of school officials, his behavior pattern is often misinterpreted. Dorothy Baruch describes the principal's attitude toward her eight-year-old patient, Kenneth, in the following way.

Ken was doing poor work. That was all. He could not be promoted. It wasn't that the child had been absent too much because of his asthma. It wasn't because he was lazy. Though he wasn't ambitious either. He seemed to try to do his work, but in a half-hearted way.

"But the main thing, I believe, is that he just isn't as bright as the average child in this particular part of the city. So he falls below the average and can't keep up. Most of our children, you see, come from better class homes and are brighter. As you no doubt know, his family lives right on the borderline between our school district and the neighboring school district where the homes are smaller and the families aren't of such high caliber or income group. His I.Q. is a hundred and eight, whereas most of our I.Q.'s are above a hundred and twenty. So you see it's no wonder he can't keep up."[10]

Kenneth was suffering from problems of identity, and was helped considerably by his play-therapy sessions. (One of these, concerned with Kenneth's use of clay, is recorded above.) He turned out to be, not a child lacking in ability, but a very bright boy who was soon at the top of his class in academic achievement. At eight he almost failed second grade, but he was reading at an eighth-grade level by the time he reached fourth grade. The apathy he had shown in school was not the result of disinterest or inability but was a symptom of his emotional problems.

It would be difficult for a classroom teacher to spot Kenneth's disturbance. He was quiet and well-behaved. His features and bearing would not cause anyone to pay any particular attention to him. To the observant psychologist, however, the "droop of his shoulders" and the "hidden look in his eyes" gave the impression of a withdrawn and unhappy child. The classroom teacher might have discovered these same kinds of clues had she been trained in observational techniques and alerted to the implications of such characteristics.

Other children in need of therapy have been judged to be mentally retarded, autistic, or brain damaged. Axline's famous study of "Dibs" tells of a child who had been considered incurable by teachers, parents, and physicians.[11] At five he used no language. He attacked children who came near him. He spent his time in nursery school hiding under tables or crawling around the room, staying close to the wall. Yet this child, who could not communicate verbally, was already reading on an advanced level. Severe emotional disturbance caused him to remain locked up inside himself, unwilling and unable to relate to adults or to other children. How fortunate that one perceptive teacher sensed the desperate unhappiness of this child! She persuaded the parents to let Dr. Axline work with him instead of having him sent to a boarding school for the mentally retarded.

[10] Baruch, pp. 6–7.
[11] Virginia Axline, *Dibs.*

Some problems of emotional disturbance are easily identified. Sally, a child who was easily frustrated and frequently had temper tantrums in class, was very likely revealing an unfulfilled emotional need. Her family was very involved with a younger mentally retarded child, and Sally sometimes reverted to behavior patterns similar to her sister's, to get attention.

A seven-year-old boy, whose father used physical force on him and on his mother was disruptive in class and attacked both his teacher and other classmates. He did not respond to verbal reprimand and seemed to have little respect for women. Yet, when alone with his female teacher after school, he was affectionate and very anxious to please her. In cases such as these and in other examples of classroom behavior the teacher does not have to probe very deeply to sense emotional difficulties. Her awareness can help to guide her treatment of these children in class, and, when persistent problems occur, she can seek the advice of a consultant.

Children from inner-city ghettos frequently exhibit impulsive behavior that makes classroom management difficult. These children have not had the experiences that make impulse control rewarding for them. They are oriented toward the present, and they cannot postpone satisfactions for some future time. They are thus likely to strike out at offenders, and classroom brawls are not uncommon particularly in early adolescent years.

A good example of this behavior and a description of how to deal with it effectively can be found in E. R. Braithwaite's book, *To Sir, With Love*.[12] The incident of the attack by a child upon a teacher in this story was clearly provoked. However, the loss of control and the contagion of rage described in this scene reveal a syndrome sometimes found in socially and economically deprived children. Provocation for "acting out behavior" may come from inner fantasies, from distorted images of people in the child's world, which evoke tortured memories. A tone of voice, a seemingly harmless phrase, can set off a feeling of frustration that makes the child helpless. Rage is an overwhelming experience, and inability to cope with it can lead to tragedy. Braithwaite, the teacher who understood and related well to these children, used a therapeutic approach to their problems. He encouraged free expression of ideas and feelings in a discussion that took place long enough after the incident to allow the feelings of rage to subside. He revealed much of his own personal feelings, with which the boys could identify. Every teacher who works with deprived or disadvantaged children could benefit from the insights provided in this selection from literature.

Anger in young children can be of short duration and can frequently be released in a play activity. The kindergarten or nursery schoolroom has many materials that can be used for emotional release, and the teacher need not be a therapist in order to provide opportunities at a time when children seem to need them. Pounding clay and finger painting can be therapeutic. Water play is relaxing to most children under tension. The housekeeping corner offers a

---

[12] Incident from E. R. Braithwaite, *To Sir, With Love*. Selected and discussed in *Conflict in the Classroom*, eds. Nicholas J. Long, William C. Morse, and Ruth G. Newman (Belmont, Calif.: Wadsworth Publishing Company, 1965), pp. 5–12.

child a chance to act out his aggressive feelings toward family members without really doing any damage to anyone. Here is a scene in a nursery school as described by a student observer.

Upon my arrival Tuesday morning I was confused as to which child I wanted to observe. Within minutes I found a perfect subject. Four-year-old Billy is a very verbal and bright child. This morning he said nothing, but I could see that he was very angry. His walk was stiff—his face very tight. He struck out at objects as he walked by them. He made his way to the housekeeping corner. He took a doll and started to spank it—harder and harder—I thought he would never stop. Then he threw the doll down and sat in the "thinking chair." He looked angry, confused, and deeply involved in thought. He looked up and saw me watching him. He smiled and ran over to me. If I had not seen him ten minutes before, I never would have known that he was angry. He seemed to have worked off his frustration and aggression through his play.

If all teachers were sensitive to the emotional needs of children in their classroom, it is very possible that, in some cases, child therapy would not be necessary. If all teachers were capable of establishing a climate in their classrooms that is conducive to the growth of the individual, then it is likely that there would be less incidence of emotional disturbance. If all teachers were prepared through observational techniques to detect emotional problems when evidence of them first appears, perhaps children would become happier, healthier human beings.

REFERENCES

AXLINE, VIRGINIA. *Dibs: In Search of Self*. New York: Ballentine Books, Inc., 1964.

AXLINE, VIRGINIA. *Play Therapy*. Cambridge, Mass.: Houghton Mifflin Company, The Riverside Press, 1947.

BARUCH, DOROTHY. *One Little Boy*. New York: A Delta Book, Dell Publishing Co., 1964.

BETTELHEIM, BRUNO. *Love Is Not Enough: The Treatment of Emotionally Disturbed Children*. The Free Press, 1950.

BLUM, LUCILLE HOLLANDER, HELEN H. DAVIDSON, AND NINA D. FIELDSTEEL. *A Rorschach Workbook*. New York: International Universities Press, Inc., 1954.

HEATON, MARGARET. *Feelings are Facts*. New York: The National Conference of Christians and Jews, 1952.

JONES, RICHARD M. *Fantasy and Feeling in Education*. New York: New York University Press, 1968.

KESSLER, JANE W. *Psychopathology of Childhood*. Englewood Cliffs, N.J.: Prentice-Hall, Inc., 1966.

LONG, NICHOLAS J., WILLIAM C. MORSE, AND RUTH G. NEWMAN. *Conflict in the Classroom*. Belmont, Calif.: Wadsworth Publishing Co., 1965.

McNEIL, ELTON B. "Patterns of Aggression." *The Psychology of the Elementary*

School Child. Edited by Alfred R. Binter and Sherman H. Frey. Chicago: Rand McNally and Company, 1972.

MOUSTAKAS, CARL. *The Authentic Teacher: Sensitivity and Awareness in the Classroom.* Cambridge, Mass.: Howard A. Doyle Publishing Company, 1966.

MOUSTAKAS, CARL. *Children in Play Therapy.* New York: McGraw-Hill, Inc., 1953.

MOUSTAKAS, CARL. *Psychotherapy with Children.* New York: Harper & Row, Publishers, 1959.

PRESCOTT, DANIEL A. *Emotion and the Educative Process.* Washington, D.C.: American Council on Education, 1938.

PURKEY, WILLIAM W. *Self Concept and School Achievement.* Englewood Cliffs, N.J.: Prentice-Hall, Inc., 1970.

ROWEN, BETTY. *Learning through Movement.* New York: Teachers College, Columbia University, 1963.

14

Giftedness and creativity

The children we have discussed in the last three chapters are all confronted with some kind of problem which limits their ability to perform well in school or prevents them from becoming well-integrated individuals. Various causes have been cited that throw light upon their inability to fulfill their potential. For some, environmental deprivation lies at the source of the problem. For others genetic malfunction causes learning disability, while still others suffer from emotional problems relating to family relationships.

The children we will be viewing in this chapter all are functioning at a very high level. They do well in schoolwork and are considered to be gifted by their teachers. Does this superior ability present problems for some of these children?

Torrance claims that we have seriously neglected the education of the gifted.[1] Like the mentally ill, gifted children have been regarded as "mysterious, beyond human understanding." Their problems receive little attention because, it is believed that, since they have superior potential, gifted children will take care of themselves. Yet many of these children suffer from loneliness, from lack of understanding, and from frustration. They are frequently resented by certain teachers, who, because of their own insecurities, take out this resentment in a punitive way. In general, we tend to view deviation, at either end of the scale, with suspicion. We prefer the "average," the "regular guy" to the "egghead." This attitude, prevalent in our society, tends to create problems for some children with superior ability.

Defining "giftedness"

The means for identifying gifted children at the beginning of the century was teacher nomination. Under these circumstances, gifted children were those

[1] E. Paul Torrance, "Toward the More Humane Education of Gifted Children," *Creativity: Its Educational Implications*, comps. John C. Gowan, George D. Demos, and E. Paul Torrance (New York: John Wiley & Sons, Inc., 1967), pp. 53–54.

who were doing considerably better than their peers in schoolwork. Such a definition would rule out many whose high aptitude for conceptualization and reasoning does not manifest itself in high performance in school. Albert Einstein, Thomas Edison, and Winston Churchill would be among those who would not qualify as gifted.

Another, and perhaps the most prevalent, definition of the gifted child is stated in terms of rank on an intelligence test, frequently the Binet scale. The child whose level of cognitive development is advanced beyond that of children of comparable age is considered gifted. This standard was established by Lewis M. Terman, whose research served as a model for many subsequent studies.

The classic study by Lewis M. Terman, published in 1925, identified characteristics of children with high IQ scores. Terman, working in the public schools in California, selected children in the top 1, 2, or 3 percent as identified by the Binet scale. He called these children "gifted," and proceeded to investigate other qualities that are associated with exceptional intellectual ability. He found that the gifted sample were superior to the average in almost every dimension. Prior to this time the intellectually superior child was portrayed as unattractive, poorly coordinated but studious, a stereotype that still persists in caricature. But Terman's gifted students were found to be healthier than the average, more attractive personally, and better coordinated, as well as high achieving in school tasks.

Terman's findings have been supported by many investigators. But there is a range of differences that exists among those children with high IQ scores. Some are extremely conforming individuals, while others are remarkably independent. Some achieve in one area of special interest; others perform well in all areas. Some are leaders among their peers, while others are isolates. Getzels and Jackson claim that understanding of the gifted child has been hampered by the heavy reliance upon IQ as the distinguishing factor in identification. They state three limitations of this approach.

1. It suggests that intelligence tests represent all known cognitive abilities. [The ability to invent and to innovate is not measured, while recall and recognition play a significant role in IQ scores.]
2. It does not account for the discrepancies that exist between IQ and academic performance. [There are many instances of children with high IQ scores who do poorly in school work, and children with low or average scores who do well.]
3. The IQ concept has been immune to advances in our understanding of thinking and behavior. [Environmental influence is now considered to be a significant factor in intelligence.][2]

These investigators and others working in this area are raising some new questions. Are there qualities, not sampled in the conventional intelligence test, that are also representative of giftedness? A child who does not have a high

[2] Jacob W. Getzels and Philip W. Jackson, *Creativity and Intelligence*, chapter 1.

IQ may be accomplished in other respects. For example, what qualities are possessed by the artistically superior child who may not score well on verbally oriented IQ tests? Are there gifted children among the disadvantaged? Is academic achievement a necessary concomitant of giftedness?

We might broaden our definition of the gifted child to mean any young person whose development and behavior consistently demonstrates unusual traits, capacities, and achievements for his age. There are wide varieties of giftedness in children. Recognition of these differences can alleviate some of the problems that confront gifted children and can help them to develop to their fullest potential.

Creativity

In recent years new measures of intellectual ability have been designed which place a premium upon such characteristics as intellectual fluency, originality, flexibility, and foresight.[3] (See Appendix E for examples from such tests.) These tests attempt to assess creativity as opposed to mastery of cognitive skills acquired through memory or quick association. Both measures of IQ and measures of creativity appear to be essential in identifying giftedness. Children who obtain high scores on creativity but not such high ones on IQ measurements do as well in school as those whose ratings are high on IQ but not so high on creativity. But these two groups of children seem to exhibit differing personality traits and learning styles.

Getzels and Jackson selected subjects from the sixth grade through high school who exhibited these different types of cognitive excellence.[4] They then proceeded to identify varying characteristics of the highly intelligent (as measured by IQ) group and the highly creative (as determined by creativity tests) group. All of these children would be considered to be gifted, as they were selected from the enrollment at a private school whose admission policy was based upon academic performance. E. Paul Torrance replicated this study using various age groups—students from four elementary schools, students from a public high school, and two samples of students in graduate school. The results of all of these studies were similar. "Despite sizable differences in IQ, the two groups were equally superior in achievement to the population from which they were drawn."[5]

There were, however, striking differences in the values, attitudes, and aspirations of the two groups. The high IQ students valued and disvalued the same objects and ideals that they believed their teachers did. By comparing a "self-ideal" ranking with a "teacher-perception" ranking, it was seen that high IQ students desired for themselves the same qualities that they thought their

---

[3] See *The Torrance Tests of Creative Thinking* (Lexington, Mass.: Personnel Press, Inc., 1966).

[4] Getzels and Jackson.

[5] E. P. Torrance, as reported in Getzels and Jackson, pp. 25–26.

teachers valued. These students appeared to be highly success oriented. For the high creativity students, however, this correlation was low. The relationship between the qualities that they valued and those they believed would lead to success as adults was virtually nil.

It is not surprising, in the light of this evidence, to find that teachers tended to prefer members of the high IQ group to members of the creative group. Even though their scholastic performance was the same, the high IQ student was preferred over the average students by their teachers, while the creative students were not.

Creative students exhibited other distinguishing features as a group. There was more humor and more fantasy present in their writing. When presented with open-ended stories, high IQ students seemed to be stimulus bound and thus finished the story very much within the context of the ideas previously presented. The highly creative students, on the other hand, tended to structure the task in their own terms rather than merely complying with it in the terms given. They were thus more stimulus free, using the initial situation as a starting point for their own ideas.

All of these findings correlate highly with those of other investigators in the area of creativity.[6] Guilford describes "convergent thinking" as thinking which tends to be channeled or controlled in the direction of the answer. "Divergent thinking," on the other hand, is described as being less goal bound, with freedom to go in different directions. Maslow speaks of "safety" and "growth" and describes the "self-actualizing person" as the one who is willing to take risks. Carl Rogers discusses "openness to experience" as one of the essential elements of creativity.

According to some research, therefore, there appear to be two types of outstanding performers, the highly intelligent and the highly creative. Both convergent and divergent thinking are socially valuable, and children who excel in either style may be considered to be gifted. There need be no preference for the creative over the highly intelligent or vice versa. The distinctions are analytical and should be helpful to the classroom teacher in assessing varying qualities in achievement in order for her to bring out the best contributions from children who exhibit both kinds of thinking.

Ultimately, however, there are no types of children in the classroom. There are only individuals. Some may be more creative; some may be more conforming; and some may combine these traits in some unique way of their own. The individual differences among gifted students is as great as it is for any other group of students. Classification into groups may reveal some common characteristics, but qualitative differences are obscured. We, therefore, will present two case studies of children who can both be considered as gifted. Each child exhibits some characteristics of one of the types described in the research mentioned above.

6 J. P. Guilford, A. H. Maslow, C. R. Rogers, as cited in Getzels and Jackson, pp. 51–53.

A CASE STUDY OF BRIAN, NINE YEARS
AND ELEVEN MONTHS OLD

INTRODUCTION

To look at Brian you would see a healthy, alert boy. Comparing normally to those of his grade level in size, Brian gives not a husky but a robust appearance. He is slender and well-built and stands tall with sturdy confidence. Long, but carefully trimmed dark hair frames his boyish face. His eyes are clear and dark, often brightly darting to some new source of action, anxiously aware of all around him. From a warm and almost laughing smile comes a surprisingly deep and harsh voice, painfully grating to hear. At the age of nine years and eleven months he has completed more than half of his fifth year in elementary school.

Brian's family background looks just as healthy as he does. The third of three children, he is some years younger than his brother in prep school and his sister in boarding school. It is said he was an unplanned child. Brian's parents are prominent citizens in their community. His mother, having more than a casual interest in education, has earned a graduate degree from a leading university. His father, a very liberal-minded young executive, heads a large banking institution and has held a position on his district's school board, which accounts for his sincere concern for his youngest son's public education.

Brian speaks very little of his sister and in her absence seems to have forgotten her. He does, however, speak affectionately of his older somewhat "hippie" brother. He is extremely proud of his father and admires him with unfailing devotion. He speaks of him often and openly regrets not being able to spend more time with him. When they are together, they seem to get along fabulously, as if some magic bond were holding them. A good father-son relationship has developed, but due to heavy schedules, gets little exercise.

Brian speaks seldom of his mother, but when he does, it is with kindness. She has confessed she feels she has neglected him and not given him the time he deserves. When she seems to find time for her son, his teacher notes, she seems much more concerned with his educational growth than with his personal emotional and social development.

Although this occurs very rarely, one can sometimes detect a loneliness in Brian's feelings about his home life.

PHYSICAL

Brian is not big for his age, but rather he is quite tall and slender, his lanky legs stretching out from the Bermuda shorts uniform he wears nearly every day. His long arms swing in a rhythmic stride as he walks. His head is held in constant readiness to turn toward action.

Brian shows good coordination and ability in even difficult skills, and his long legs are a great asset in running games. At play he can hold his own with his classmates. Although not as interested in sports as his Little League neighbors, he does enjoy his physical-education class.

Brian is usually a willing participant, but as his physical-education instructor points out, he only seems to lack in one area—strength. He can perform well but with a lack of power that seems to frustrate him. True he is stronger than some in his class, but he falls far short of others. Upon seeing Brian in a fight one day with one of his peers, I had to sympathize with him. His determination to win far outweighing his ability to do so. He was almost too stubborn to accept the inevitable defeat, although he was "totally saturated" (a description he coined to describe his sweaty appearance). He just couldn't quit. So strong was his commitment to win.

His teacher feels Brian is somewhat annoyed by this weakness, which perhaps explains his frequent preference for nonphysical activities such as reading.

INTELLECTUAL

Brian's 139 IQ places him intellectually ahead of his peers. He is an excellent student in all areas and is greatly respected by his classmates and teachers.

Brian takes a serious interest in his studies and he is especially good in arithmetic, in which he works in an advanced class. In reading his capabilities place him well up in the junior high school level. He does not, however, take such a serious interest in cultural subjects such as art and music. His teachers regard Brian as a very intelligent person. His ability to think things through and to come up with good logical answers is just amazing.

Brian is a very good independent worker. Although he can work well in a group, he seems to function best when he is on his own. It is evident that he feels it is better to depend on himself to get the work done than to trust anyone else to do it. Not that his ideas are always that much better than others: it's just that he is more comfortable with his own efficient manner of organization.

There is one notable quality about Brian's work which can best be seen through his handwriting. Although this is a great joke to him, perhaps it may tell us something about this complex individual. This quality is the great speed at which he carries out his work. He is always in a hurry to get whatever he is doing done so he will be free to move onto his next task. He is always the first one finished. He just seems to lack the patience it takes for extended concentration. The quality of his work is sometimes affected by a few careless and frustrating errors. This quality of speed is most easily seen in his handwriting, or rather the scrawling, barely legible, almost physician-like code that he makes of it. It seems to tell us that his mind just works too fast to be bothered waiting for his hand to catch up.

As I mentioned, this is a source of great amusement as far as he's concerned, and, until recently, he had refused to try to improve. His mother's plea is the one he has chosen to answer. It seems that now he is out to please her as a way of recognizing his mother's sudden interest in him. In fact, upon recently being complimented on some minor improvement in his writing, he was elated at thinking how happy his mother would be to hear it.

Brian is, for the most part, a very verbal child. He is always talking —always wanting to be heard. I guess this explains why his class discussion grades far outweigh his written work assignments. His oral answers can even be somewhat surprising at times, as he is never afraid to speak up, voicing his opinion. Some of his teachers are greatly alarmed by this and feel that at times he offers too much information, thereby becoming a threat or a pest. One older and more traditional teacher, for example, is getting tired of what she believes to be his suggestions for improving her teaching methods.

No. Brian is not a fresh boy. He is just trying to be helpful in his own peculiar way. He has a lot "on the ball" and is just overly anxious to share his vast knowledge with everyone.

SOCIAL

Brian gets along well with others. Everyone seems to think so—his parents, his teachers, his principal, his friends, and even he, himself. After all, he's a very likable guy.

Brian is a good friend to most, but he maintains a carefully selected circle of close friends which undergoes very little change. He seems to feel more comfortable at play with this group and actually works well with them too, because they are also his intellectual equals. This does not mean that he excludes all others. On the contrary, he is sociable to all of his classmates, but when he has his choice of companions, whether for work or play, he is forever loyal to his group.

Brian is as greatly respected by his elders as they are by him. He is aware of their superior authority and does not challenge this. Although he somewhat reluctantly admits he is not all that sure about their intellectual ability, he does make the best of the situation. His cheerful personality makes everyone an immediate friend.

At school his principal and teachers are always calling on him to do tasks of responsibility. They know he can be trusted, and that they can depend on him. He has been asked to represent his school on occasion and is always eager to be chosen for special projects. You might say that Brian is the type who loves to be in the limelight—he doesn't want to miss a thing!

EMOTIONAL

Surely Brian is a very emotionally complex person, but his exuberant personality makes it difficult to see beyond the laughter. He is an enthusiastic boy—enthusiastic about life and about the role he plays in it. His attitude is a healthy one. His ideas are bright and alert. He always wears a smile. Brian seems to be in excellent control of his feelings. The only area in which he lacks control is happiness—he just seems to be happy all the time.

A struggle he seems to conceal beneath his smile is one involved with competition with a classmate of his similar standing. Ross has always been a threat to him and although Brian is much more mature than he is, it really bothers him to see Ross get ahead. He is aware of this position, and the rivalry is well known at home and at school.

Ross, on the other hand, is a little more hostile toward Brian— openly vying with him for attention and recognition. Brian seems to be secure in his own abilities because he never really confronts his competitor, although he is constantly aware of his every move.

Brian wants to be treated like a man in a way which strongly emulates his father. He is always ready to do what is expected of him and ready to keep up a strong front—never allowing himself to break down in front of anyone. I've never heard of any occasion when Brian has broken down. I doubt if he would ever admit to having cried.

Another sort of burden which he seems to carry is an underlying sense of loneliness. It's not that he has no friends. He does. It's just that this feeling seems to be related to his home life. He seems to have a sense of emptiness about his family life that he shelters like some carefully guarded secret. He rarely speaks of home and family activities, but when he does, there is evidence of a barely detectable void, a loneliness. He seems to be just dropping all unpleasantness from his jubilant attitude to keep up the image of Brian.

SUMMARY

Brian seems very well adjusted to life. He knows the score and he knows where he stands. He is a well-equipped individual. He is alert. He is ready for action.

I feel sure that he will do well in whatever world awaits him. He has the self-confidence and the ability to make whatever plans he holds for his future into reality.

He is strong in his convictions and I am sure he will not deter from the goals he sets for himself. He is determined to get things done to his satisfaction.

As Brian grows older and stronger, he will be able to handle problems close at hand. He will deal with things logically and intelligently. Brian will take very good care of himself.

It is so hard to tell what goes on beyond that smiling face that is Brian.

A CASE STUDY OF DAVID, TEN YEARS OLD

INTRODUCTION

David is a fifth grader in a suburban elementary school. He is a slender boy, somewhat taller than most boys of his age, with dark hair, and a medium complexion. His most distinctive feature is his eyes, which are unusually large and blue, and because of their size, they seem to protrude slightly. He would be considered to be a good-looking boy.

David has an older sister, Joan, age 13, who is an outstanding student with artistic abilities, particularly in the area of dance and dramatics. David, himself, is a gifted musician who can play several instruments by ear. He dislikes practicing but enjoys collecting classical records and singing in school choral groups. His schoolwork tends to be erratic. He does well in some subjects and poorly in others.

The family lives in a small house in a residential community. The father is a chemist who enjoys his work, and earns a moderate income. The mother had edited a local newspaper until the birth of her first child. At the present time she does some part-time work at home, reading manuscripts for a publishing firm.

The family seems to be a close-knit group. They enjoy camping trips together, and all share a love of nature and outdoor activities. Their house is littered with books and magazines and gives the general appearance of being lived in and not very neat.

INTERVIEWS

Mrs. B., David's mother, is a large handsome woman who seemed to be quite at ease in the interview. She was wearing jeans and a pullover sweater that was somewhat frayed. She invited me to have coffee with her. We sat in the kitchen, and I noticed that the breakfast dishes were still piled in the sink.

She was warm and gracious and talked freely about her family. She described it as "father centered," and said that her husband had many strong opinions and that he expected the children to respect them. I got the impression that Mrs. B. allowed the father to dominate the household, while at the same itme she made many decisions quietly behind the scenes. She has a good sense of humor and does not take herself or her role as a parent too seriously. She believes it is important to give children the best food and nourishment and to let them alone as much as possible. When asked if she talked to David about his school life, she replied, "He doesn't talk much, and I don't like to pry."

She enjoys her children- and feels that they are more "secure and independent" than she was at their ages. David has occasional disagreements with his father, but generally she feels that they have a mutual respect and love for each other. Their main area of disagreement concerns athletics. David is a good athlete but would rather "play baseball when he feels like it" than go out for team practice, which he thinks would take too much of his time. Mr. B. had been interested in working with the Little League until David dropped out, much to his father's disappointment. There are occasional "impassioned clashes" between father and son, but they continue to share an interest in many sports activities.

Another hobby shared by father and son is airplane model construction. David is quite skilled with his hands and can work for hours putting small pieces together with patience and concentration. His mother thinks this is particularly remarkable, since David is not patient and careful about many other things. His room is usually sloppy, and he does chores around the house in a careless manner. The rake used to sweep up the leaves on the front lawn might frequently be found in the driveway when he is finished, much to his dad's annoyance.

Mrs. B. is not overly concerned about David's erratic pattern of school performance. She knows he is capable and can do well at anything he tries. She recognizes his inherent good judgment and sense of values. She appreciates his humor and his love of music, both qualities which she admits he "gets from" her.

David's teacher told me a surprising thing when I saw her. She said that David had almost failed fourth grade and had been placed on probation in her fifth-grade class at the beginning of the term. His fourth-grade teacher had considered him "lazy" and "insolent." She felt that "the only way to make him buckle down" was to "teach him a lesson and fail him." His mother had not mentioned this, but she had said that David did not get along well with his teacher last year and likes his fifth-grade teacher much better.

David's teacher this term is a warm and friendly person, and her classroom is conducted with a relaxed and free atmosphere. The children frequently are allowed to work on projects of their own choosing. David, she said, is capable of intensive work and effort when involved in something he is interested in. He did a detailed drawing of the inner ear for a science project. He has been chairman of several committees and has proved himself to be a capable leader. His marks on tests vary considerably. He may get 100 on a math test one week and 50 or 60 the next week. In essay-type work his ideas are good, but he loses credit because of poor spelling and punctuation. She admits that David "could do better if he tried." He writes amusing and interesting stories and has had several of his compositions included in the school newspaper.

One of his stories concerned a boy who wanted "to get ahead in the world" but whose "only talent was a nice smile." He ended up posing for toothpaste ads on TV and made a lot of money.

Another story concerned a boy who wanted to know "who he was before he was born." He went to a doctor who decided to consult a number of animals about the problem. Each animal denied having any relation to the boy, because he was missing some distinguishing feature of that animal family.

The teacher feels that both of these stories show that David is thinking about his role in life, but he covers up his serious philosophical bent with humor. She thinks he is not as carefree as he, himself, would like to believe.

Before I attempted to get David's ideas about himself, I realized that he would not talk freely about his feelings and therefore I asked his teacher if I could administer a sentence-completion test to the entire class that was designed as a kind of self-rating scale. The class was also asked to write an autobiography as a writing lesson.

David's answers on the sentence completion reveal that he values independence highly. He wrote that "I feel happiest when—I am not having my personality pried into." When asked to state how he spent Sunday afternoons, he answered, "Playing piano is my hobby, and it's none of your business how I spend Sunday afternoons.

His opinion of himself seems to be adequate. He thinks that others regard him as "being O.K." or "being a card." "No matter what others may think, I, myself, know that—I can be funny." "I feel that my chief aim in life is to—not be obnoxious." Again, his humor is highly important to him, and he uses it to cover up when situations (such as personality tests) seem threatening.

His autobiography is more freely expressive of his feelings. He wrote that, "Our family goes places together and we have fun. We are together so much of the time that none of us can move a muscle without the rest of us having to twitch a little." His rivalry toward his sister is revealed by his description of her. "My sister is a little retarded —all she does is play the phonograph and talk on the telephone."

SUMMARY

David thinks of himself as an essentially worthwhile human being. He enjoys life and his family but resents any slight effort to push him in any direction. It is understandable that a highly directive teacher would antagonize him, and he would not do well in her class. He wants to be liked by his peers and values his wit highly. But he is not achievement oriented in the conventional sense. He would not want to be the boy in the toothpaste ad that he wrote about. He is secure enough not to be too upset when he does not do well in a school situation. I think he feels that his family is supportive of his and has confidence that he will lead a good life.

I was not able to find out what David's IQ score was, but I imagine it is well above average. His wit and originality show him to be a bright and creative person. He is well-liked by his classmates, and I feel he will be a popular boy with girls in a few years. In spite of some problems in school I think he will be successful in life if he finds the right outlets for his talents.[7]

ANALYSIS OF THE TWO CASE STUDIES

Both Brian and David are boys with superior abilities. The striking difference between them is in their attitudes toward achievement. Brian is determined to get ahead and to be a leader. David is more relaxed, less goal directed, and more concerned with maintaining his independence.

Brian might be considered to be the typical "All-American" boy. He exudes self-confidence as he "swings his arms in a rhythmic stride." He is a leader in school both in class and on the playground. Yet there is something

[7] This case study is a composite picture based upon Getzels and Jackson's studies, Torrance's studies, and this author's own observations.

about this boy that makes us take a second look. Is he happy in his role? Does he have to work too hard to maintain his prestigious position? Like a young lion he is constantly alert to spring. "His eyes are clear and dark, often brightly darting to some new sources of action, anxiously aware of all around him." He must win in a physical contest even against superior strength. He "conceals beneath his smile" his feeling of rivalry toward a student of equal ability. He always presents a "strong front—never allowing himself to break down in front of anyone."

David is less concerned about maintaining a leadership position. He is a good athlete but does not want to participate in team sports in spite of his father's urging. He seems to be relatively unconcerned about school achievement, and he wants to pursue his own interests for the values he finds inherent in them. He makes fun of "the boy in the toothpaste ad" and uses humor to debunk much that he considers to be pretentious and phony. Getzels and Jackson found a certain mocking attitude on the part of the creative children toward what they call the "All-American Boy"—a theme almost totally lacking in the stories of the highly intelligent group. In general, humor was much more prevalent with the creative group.

From the descriptions in the two case studies cited here, Brian appears to be a more stimulus-bound, intellectually gifted achiever, while David exhibits many of the characteristics attributed to creative individuals.

Relationships in the two boys' families seem to differ significantly. Brian's family is an outstanding one in the community. Brian maintains a healthy respect for his parents, but the student observer noted some "sense of emptiness about his family life that he shelters like some carefully guarded secret." Brian would never admit to any inadequacies in his family or in his life. Does Brian, therefore, strain to keep up an image that has been created?

David's family, on the other hand, seem to be less concerned with putting up a front. His mother was casual and relaxed during the interview and seemed unconcerned about the appearance of her house or of her person. She did not seem to worry about whether David got good grades, but she had confidence in his values and respected his independence.

These differences in family attitudes correspond with Getzels' and Jackson's study. The parents of the high IQ group seemed to be more concerned about financial security and success. Parents of highly creative children emphasized less conventional qualities, such as a child's "openness to experience," his "values," and his "interests and enthusiasm for life."

The contrasts between these two boys are particularly significant in the light of the reactions of today's youth to the society in which they find themselves. Brian might very well grow up to be the perfect "organization man," attaining material success and prestige in his work and his community. He might also, as have many other capable young men, ask himself if it is worth all of the effort, and if the values cherished by his family and the society in which they operate are worthy ones.

David, on the other hand, might never be willing to "join the establishment" in pursuit of goals he does not value. At the same time he may be able to survive while pursuing his own idea of the good life without open rebellion and hostility.

We cannot change society overnight, but we can remove some of the pressure to achieve, so that the "Brians" in our schools are not so intense and so driven. We can also admire the independence of creative students like David, and we can give them the respect that they deserve. The highly creative student often seeks personal goals quite different from those valued by adults. In some ways these goals may be different from those that teachers favor. We must, therefore, recognize these differences in value systems and in learning styles that exist among gifted children. The creative student must be allowed to be independent without being labeled "obnoxious." On the other hand, the intellectually achieving youngster must learn to accept himself as he is, to relax, to sense, to feel, and even to cry occasionally.

Pressure to achieve

The case study of Brian gives us a picture of a child who is determined to excel. But, in spite of his strong drives, Brian is essentially a well-functioning and healthy individual, who is admired by both his peers and his teachers.

Some precocious children, however, suffer from severe problems of emotional adjustment. Parents may have high expectation levels, using the child's accomplishments to fulfill their own needs for recognition. We have all seen some of the unpleasant effects upon behavior when parents insist that their children "show-off" their talents for all of the world to see. The child actor, used to adult acclaim, may become a person who is never content unless he is in the limelight. Academically precocious children may be unpleasant to have in class because of their superior attitudes toward their peers.

A student observer did a case study of a six-year-old boy whom she taught in a Sunday-school class. Charles is an only child, who was born to upper-middle-class parents at a late stage in their lives. The child began reading when he was three, and was able, even at that time, to discuss much of what he had read intelligently. Now, at six, he frequents the library often and reads books on any subject that he can find. His mother told the observer, "I knew he was smart, but never did I guess how smart!" Charles reads about complex theories in science and explains these ideas to his mother.

In Sunday school Charles varies the roles he plays throughout the morning. He may be happy or sad, fighting or passive, quiet or talking excitedly. He is not well coordinated and becomes easily frustrated when involved in physical activity. He enriches class discussion with his large fund of knowledge, which he freely contributes. Here is the student observer's description of his behavior.

His voice is high pitched and he gets very emotional. He displays his anger and his pleasure freely. He is easily frustrated, not only by his own short-comings, but also by the shortcomings of others. When upset, he resorts to physical displays of anger, often rather loud and violent. He can remain in his seat for no longer than two and a half to three minutes at a time.

Discipline must be handled with the utmost of care as Charles is prone to fits of anger and temper tantrums when he feels that he has failed to be perfect. This obsession with perfection is the key, I believe, to many of his problems. He has said, on more than one occasion, "I want to be like God —perfect."

The student observer, who was also Charles's Sunday-school teacher, said that she had to be very careful in order to keep Charles from hurting himself and other children. His physical assaults were in the form of kicking and punching and usually began without warning. He has been observed hitting himself on the head with his bag of books, because another child had said something that Charles knew to be incorrect. He was upset when the other child did not listen to him. Usually the other children accepted Charles but stayed out of his way when he was angry.

Charles has been referred to a psychologist and is being helped through therapy and tranquilizers. Hopefully, he will overcome his emotional problems, so that his superior ability will not be a handicap to healthy maturation.

The creative, independent student is frequently pressured to achieve. David, in the case study earlier in the chapter, was fortunate in that his mother had confidence in him and respected his sense of values. She was not overly concerned when he did not perform well in school and had not mentioned to the interviewer that he had almost failed his fourth-grade class. Many children like David are considered to be "underachievers" and are hounded at home and in school to work harder and to try to get higher grades.

E. Paul Torrance has received numerous letters from parents of gifted children, asking him for help in dealing with their problems.[8] One mother tells of a ten-year-old who seemed to be impervious to punishment. He "shows great capacity for school work when he wants to. He refused to finish addition and subtraction drills at school. It was thought that he didn't know the answers. Then multiplication was introduced, he surprised everyone by knowing the answers. His teacher reports that he is always raising his hand, walking up to her desk, even trying to instruct the class . . ."

Another mother wrote that her thirteen-year-old has had a steadily declining academic record. He daydreams in class constantly, and seems very withdrawn. Yet, at home, he displays a burning interest in electronics, and stays up all night performing experiments. He cannot join the science club at school because he does not have a *B* average!

Gifted children frequently reveal their feelings of loneliness and frustration through their writings. They express ideas about the absence of love and understanding in their lives. Adults expect them to conform to established patterns, and the children feel rejected when their own interests and drives are not recognized. But the creatively gifted are too independent and often too single-minded to change their ways to please adults! The drive to find out how

[8] E. Paul Torrance, "Toward the More Humane Education of Gifted Children," pp. 53–56.

things work in electronics or the need to express one's own feelings in poetry or in art are too strong. These children will not sacrifice the pursuit of their own objectives in order to meet externally imposed criteria for performance.

Relating to authority

As indicated in several of the examples given above, the gifted child frequently has difficulty relating to authority. It seems foolish to some to waste time on needless arithmetic drill when the answers are already known and understood! To others a preoccupation with a vital interest, such as electronics, is so all consuming that it makes other areas of learning boring. Teachers are frequently annoyed by the attitudes of children like this. The children seem impervious to punishment and show little concern about their teachers' opinions of them.

But these gifted children need recognition, as do all children. Teachers might give them opportunities to share their special projects with the class. Some kinds of assignments can be related directly to the child's interests. The artist can illustrate the social studies lesson for a display on the bulletin board. The gifted scientist can do arithmetic problems related to his science projects, rather than repeat useless drill in areas already well learned.

It is understandable why teachers often do not favor some of the gifted children that they meet in their classes. As we have seen, some are indifferent to criticism. Some refuse to do assignments. Some are outspoken in their opinions and even "try to instruct the class!" Teachers find these children difficult to control, and frequently the teachers themselves feel threatened by the presence of such children in their classrooms. It takes a secure adult to accept and to like a child who may be more knowledgeable or more capable, in some areas, than the teacher herself!

David, the ten-year-old in our second case study, was obviously not liked by his fourth-grade teacher, who considered him to be "lazy" and "insolent." This teacher may have used her authority to try to "make David work," and this approach would, very likely, create resistance in a boy like him. His fifth-grade teacher seemed to understand him better. She was amused by his stories and was favorably impressed with his abilities in several areas. David was doing above-average work in her class.

David also had some problems in his relationship with his father. His mother reported that there were "occasional impassioned clashes" between father and son mainly concerned with the boy's unwillingness to participate in sports activities. We have the feeling that there were, and will continue to be, other areas of disagreement. The father is reported to have "strong opinions." David's answers to the sentence-completion test reveal that he very much has a mind of his own and that he resents any efforts on the part of others to impose ideas upon him. Perhaps the permissive and accepting attitude of his mother serves as a buffer and allows David and his father to remain on good terms with only occasional flare-ups between them.

Skippy, the eight-year-old boy who wrote the story, "The Owl Who Went to Medical School," discussed in Chapter 5, was also a child who antagonized many of his teachers. His third-grade teacher loved his quick wit and his spontaneity. But discussion in the teachers' room revealed the fact that few teachers were anxious to have this child in their classes. His lack of respect for authority and his attitudes about teachers are clearly revealed in his story.

Finding sufficient challenge

Problems often result when gifted children are not given sufficient challenge in the classroom. Often the capable child is bored by constant repetition and drill of familiar material. He may resort to daydreaming or to disruptive behavior as the result of this boredom.

A five-year-old child was observed in a Head Start program. He had spent the previous two years in similar kinds of school settings, where he reportedly had done very well. But this term he was a problem to his teacher. Here is a student observer's report.

The children were busy repeating the names of letters of the alphabet that were being displayed on cards. Patrick named the letters several times then got up and began to play with a puzzle. The aide went to him and told him to go back to his seat. He went back and sat down, but he did not recite as the others were doing. He looked around at the other children and laughed aloud. This was annoying to the teacher. She said to him, "You are not saying your letters." He said, "I know it."

Patrick finished his coloring of the letters before anyone else. He got out of his seat and began looking at other children's papers, telling them what they did that was wrong. The teacher told him to stop annoying the other children, and Patrick answered, "Stop annoying me."

We can see that this little boy is already becoming a discipline problem and no doubt could be accused of being "fresh" and "insolent." But it is obvious that the activity presented to the class bored him. He could not sit still and was observed "playing with his shoe buckles, pulling off his shoes, and so on." Finally he resorted to disruptive behavior. This might have been avoided if the teacher recognized what was happening and gave Patrick something else to do while the others were finishing their work.

Parents of children who have attended nursery school frequently complain to teachers that their children are bored with their work in kindergarten. The parents want an accelerated program of reading and writing for these children. But there are many challenging activities within the kindergarten curriculum, if the teacher is resourceful enough to provide them. No child, whether precocious or slow, should find school boring. If we meet each child at his own level, regardless of age or grade, we can avoid problems that result when there is insufficient challenge in the classroom.

Artistic children sometimes are bored with schoolwork because there are insufficient opportunities for the development of their special talents. Often these children go unnoticed, and no one recognizes that they are, indeed, gifted. Their academic work may be average, and their participation in class discussion may be minimal. Many children with artistic abilities are not strongly verbal and appear to be quiet and shy.

In the action study with seven- and eight-year-olds done by this author and reported in Chapter 5, several such children were discovered.[9] Annette rarely volunteered an answer in class and was an average student. Yet in her movement responses and in her artwork, she revealed herself to be an unusually sensitive and perceptive child. She could catch a mood from a story, from a painting, or from music. She responded to changes in rhythm, tempo, and volume, and her graceful and lyrical movement was a delight to watch. Her feeling responses were of marked intensity.

Is a child like Annette to be considered "gifted"? Are there opportunities provided in the school setting which allow for the development of the aesthetic potential of such a child? Fortunately, Annette was exposed to an experimental program which was aimed at the development of aesthetic responses through movement. She excelled in this program and was recognized by her teacher and her peers. In later years she began writing poetry and was a frequent contributor to the school newspaper.

Guidelines for teachers of gifted and creative children

As we have seen in this chapter, gifted and creative children often have problems in school. But the problems frequently stem from the attitudes of teachers, and the children themselves cannot always be held responsible for them. Creative, independent children often challenge their teachers and are considered to be "insolent." Artistic children do not receive recognition in the schools and rarely have the opportunity to fulfill their potentials. Precocious children are bored and may become discipline problems. Even the conforming high achiever feels driven by parents and teachers to maintain his image, for he must always be "outstanding."

Many of these problems can be eliminated in classrooms where teachers provide a responsive environment and respect the unique potentials of each child. David did well in his fifth-grade class, whereas he almost failed fourth grade. Annette found an outlet for her giftedness through dance and poetry. Patrick's misbehavior could have been controlled if his teacher gave him activities which were of interest to him. Brian and Charles could become happier children if parents and teachers demanded less of them and allowed them to relax some of their intense efforts.

Torrance provides a checklist for teachers which can help them to provide an atmosphere in which the creative and gifted student can function well.

---

[9] Betty Rowen, "An Exploration of the Uses of Rhythmic Movement to Develop Aesthetic Concepts."

A Checklist for the Teacher

Don't be too "threatened" by the exceptional child or the unexpected response.

Pay attention to the "atmosphere" of the room.

Don't be too concerned about a higher noise level—if it's a "busy hum."

Remember the creative need to communicate—maybe the whisper is all right.

Don't be blinded by "intelligence" test scores—they don't tell the *whole* story.

Don't be afraid to wander off your teaching schedule—stay flexible.

Encourage divergent ideas—too many of the "right" ideas are stifling.

Be accepting and forgiving of the "mistakes."

Remember, the "obnoxious" child may simply be escaping from the tedium of your class.

Don't let your pride get in the way of your teaching.

Different kinds of children learn in different ways.

Let them "test their limits."

Don't let the pressure for "evaluation" get the upper hand.

Give them a chance to "warm-up" to producing ideas.

Respect the privacy of their responses (especially the less successful ones).

Criticism is killing—use it carefully and in small doses.

How about those "Provocative Questions"?

Don't forget to define the problem.

Don't be afraid to try something different.[10]

Gifted children would present fewer problems in the classroom if these factors were taken into consideration. We need to provide opportunities for children with unusual abilities to grow into healthy and productive adults. Too frequently it is the gifted youngster who becomes a school dropout. Communes and hippy villages are filled with gifted individuals who have a great deal to offer to society, but who have not found an atmosphere conducive to productivity in schools and in industry. We cannot afford to lose this talent. The gifted child must feel that he is accepted for what he is. He must be encouraged to make his own unique contributions in school and throughout life.

REFERENCES

CROW, LESTER D., AND ALICE CROW, eds. *Educating the Academically Able: A Book of Readings.* New York: David McKay Company, Inc., 1963.

GALLAGHER, JAMES H. *Teaching the Gifted Child.* Boston: Allyn and Bacon, 1964.

GALLAGHER, JAMES J., ed. *Teaching Gifted Students: A Book of Readings.* Boston: Allyn and Bacon, 1965.

GETZELS, JACOB W., AND PHILIP W. JACKSON. *Creativity and Intelligence: Explorations with Gifted Students.* New York: John Wiley & Sons, Inc., 1962.

[10] E. Paul Torrance, "Creative Teaching Makes a Difference," *Creativity: Its Educational Implications*, eds. John C. Gowan, George D. Demos, and E. Paul Torrance (New York: John Wiley & Sons, Inc., 1967).

GOWAN, JOHN C., GEORGE D. DEMOS, AND E. PAUL TORRANCE, ed. *Creativity: Its Educational Implications*. New York: John Wiley & Sons, 1967.

HALL, THEODORE. *Gifted Children: The Cleveland Story*. Cleveland: The World Publishing Company, 1956.

HILDRETH, GERTRUDE H. *Introduction to the Gifted*. New York: McGraw-Hill, Inc., 1966.

MIEL, ALICE, ed. *Creativity in Teaching*. Belmont, Calif.: Wadsworth Publishing Company, 1961.

ROWEN, BETTY. "Developing Aesthetic Concepts through Movement." Film made in conjunction with Cooperative Research Report. Available through ERIC National Audio-Visual Center, Washington, D.C.

ROWEN, BETTY. *An Exploration of the Uses of Rhythmic Movement to Develop Aesthetic Concepts in the Primary Grades*. Cooperative Research Report, No. ED 020770, USOE. Washington, D.C.: Government Printing Office, 1966.

TERMAN, LEWIS M. *Genetic Studies of Genius, Vol. I, Mental and Physical Traits of a Thousand Gifted Children*. Stanford, Calif.: Stanford University Press, 1925.

TORRANCE, E. PAUL. *Education and the Creative Potential*. Minneapolis: University of Minnesota Press, 1963.

TORRANCE, E. PAUL. *Guiding Creative Talent*. Englewood Cliffs, N.J.: Prentice-Hall, Inc., 1962.

TORRANCE, E. PAUL, ed. *Talent and Education*. Minneapolis: University of Minnesota Press, 1960.

WALLACH, MICHAEL A., AND NATHAN KOGAN. "Creativity and Intelligence in Children's Thinking." *The Psychology of the Elementary School Child*. Edited by Alfred R. Binter and Sherman H. Frey. Chicago: Rand McNally & Company, 1972.

WITTY, PAUL, ed. *The Gifted Child*. Boston: D. C. Heath and Company, 1951.

WITTY, PAUL, JAMES B. CONANT, AND RUTH STRANG. "Creativity of Gifted and Talented Children." Addresses given at the American Association of School Administrators, February 1959. New York: Teachers College Press, Columbia University, 1959.

15

Implications of the case-study approach

There is a story that has been told frequently at educational conferences that satirizes the traditional approach to the individual differences that we find in our schools. The story is concerned with animals, not children, but the implications are obvious.

The animals in the forest got together one day and decided to start a school. There was a rabbit, a bird, a squirrel, a fish, and an eel, and they formed a Board of Education. The rabbit insisted that running be in the curriculum. The bird believed that learning to fly was essential. The fish wanted swimming to be the main focus, while the squirrel considered tree climbing to be central to all education. They wrote a curriculum guide, which prescribed *all* of these subjects for *all* of the animals.

Although the rabbit got *A* in running, he had difficulty with tree climbing; he kept falling over backward. Soon he got to a point where he couldn't run well any more. Instead of receiving an *A* in running, he was now getting a *C*, and he continued to fail in tree climbing. The bird did well in flying, of course, but he kept breaking his beak and wings when he tried to learn to burrow in the ground. The fish had difficulty whenever he was out of water, so he dropped out of school. Only certain squirrels were able to master the art of flying. The eel did nothing very well, but he applied himself with diligence, and was able, after a while, to perform adequately in each of the subject areas. Consequently he was rewarded for his efforts, and at graduation, he was chosen to be the class valedictorian.

Have we been guilty of running an "Animal School" like the one described here? In spite of our concern for individual differences have we been requiring standard performances for all children regardless of their special talents and particular learning styles? Like the rabbit in our story there are some children who have become so frustrated trying to perform tasks that they are unable to do that eventually they lose the ability to do well even in the areas of their strengths. Like the bird there are children who are damaged by the educational process. There are others who, like the fish, are forced to drop out of a school that does not meet their needs. And, like the flying squirrels, there are some children in every minority group who do make the grade, and that makes it harder for those who cannot. Perhaps the members who function best in the school community are those who conform, to some extent, to all requirements. Are the mediocre pupils, like the eel, the most likely to succeed in our schools? Are we still trying to make everyone perform like everyone else?

It is time we begin to look at children first instead of giving priority to curriculum designs and to test scores. We claim to respect individual differences, but the ways in which we assess behavior negate our beliefs. It is not the score on a standardized test that tells us what a child is like. An analysis of the test in the light of the child's background, personality, and attitudes can tell much more. It is not what a child does that should be the sole criterion for evaluation. It is the reasons for his actions that must be taken into consideration. It is not his over-all performance that matters so much as his areas of special strengths that need to be identified.

Although we use the word frequently, there really are no *normal* children. "Norms" are standardized ways of behaving, and they represent no "flesh and blood" individual. It is true that through examination of numerous case studies and observations we can inductively arrive at some generalizations concerning behavior at various developmental levels. In Part II of this book this approach was used. The students who did the observations were not trained psychologists, and the children who were observed were selected at random. Yet, there were common characteristics that revealed themselves for various age levels of children. The findings of the student observers correlated highly with those of researchers in the field of child development. An observational approach, therefore, can be useful in arriving at generalizations regarding growth and development of children. But what makes one child unique can only be seen in perspective by contrasting his behavior with the generalized principles that have been established. No child's growth pattern follows these developmental principles in every aspect.

The case studies that were presented at the beginning of each chapter in Part III of this book represent unique individuals. Although their behavior may have some characteristics in common with other children who have similar problems, the profiles presented in these chapters are not representative of groups of children. Each case study is a report on an individual human being with attitudes and qualities that are distinctly his own. It may be helpful for a teacher to compare the behavior of a child she knows with that of a child described in a case study. She should not expect to find identical patterns in any instance.

Categories are hard to establish when we deal with human beings. It is the very individual nature of the combination of potentials that exist in each person that makes it difficult to predict his behavior. We all know of children who come from broken homes and poverty backgrounds who do well in school.

There are numerous cases of children with severe handicaps who are happy and productive individuals. And then there are instances of children who "have everything," but who are most difficult to deal with and manifest indications of deep unhappiness. Because a particular set of factors exists in combination does not mean that behavior patterns can be predicted. The complexity of the human mind and personality cannot be oversimplified.

The case studies in Part III of this book describe individuals. They must not be interpreted as new stereotypes—the environmentally deprived child, the learning disabled child, the emotionally disturbed child, the gifted child. Nor are the previous chapters to be considered as representing all areas in which developmental problems may exist. We have simply presented samples of problems which became evident to students who used a case-study approach to learn more about children.

We have not been concerned with tests of the reliability or validity of our findings. These are standard procedures when one is involved in research studies. Data can be analyzed in this way when a large number of subjects are being considered. Consistency of performance with individual children cannot be expected. Research of this nature usually presupposes that a number of factors have been controlled and the researchers have defined their variables. This is also an impossibility when dealing with individual children.

The case-study approach, therefore, does not claim to be a means of establishing proof of any research findings relating to child development. Its purpose is rather to help students and teachers to get to know individual children. If the cases presented in this book give some insight into the behavior of a few individuals, that is all to the good. But the case-study approach will be most effective when it is applied by teachers to children in their own classes.

The case-study approach in the classroom

Is it feasible to study individual pupils in the classroom? If teachers and administrators are convinced of the importance of knowing the child, means can be provided to facilitate such study. The case-study approach is a way of viewing the teaching role. If one has this approach, many opportunities present themselves for getting to know children. Informal contacts on the playground and in the lunchroom supplement insights gained from classroom observations and from children's school performance.

New trends and new forms of classroom organization require broad knowledge about individual pupils. The establishment of learning centers, team teaching, and pod-type classrooms are aimed at individualizing instruction. "Today, the major classroom tactic must be guided by child growth and development, and child individuality. The establishment of the Learning Center is directed toward this end. The Learning Center method focuses the teacher's sights on each child—enhancing the opportunities for meeting the personal needs of the learner."[1]

[1] Ralph Claude Voight, *Invitation to Learning.*

For this new approach to be successful it will be necessary for teachers to employ many techniques in order to know their pupils and to be able to guide them in their individual learning pursuits. Without such knowledge the large numbers of children in open-classroom settings can easily lead to confusion and lack of direction for both teachers and students. It is easier for the teacher in a small self-contained classroom to know each child. For many such teachers no special tools or observational devices are necessary. But for teachers, in new types of classroom settings, confronted with many pupils in a day, and having multiple teaching approaches to choose from, special techniques must be employed to make knowledge of the individual child possible.

Tests and scales have been developed to help the teachers in these settings to assess their pupils' level of operation in various areas. Reading abilities, for example, are broken down into their component parts, and children are assigned for practice sessions according to their assessed skills and deficits. But the chart listing each child and scoring his abilities is not enough. The teacher must view this information in its relationship to her total picture of the pupil. If she keeps a record of these scores in a folder along with samples of the child's work, she will have a broader view than a rating on an inventory can give her, no matter how carefully it was designed to indicate differences in learning styles. If she adds to this folder records of her own observations, notes on interviews with parents, and so on, she then has a collection of information that can help her in her task of assessment. (Methods involved in this kind of record keeping are discussed in Chapter 4.)

Pod classroom arrangements and team teaching free a teacher to do some direct observation. While her teammate leads the instructional program, she might focus upon one child, noting his verbal responses, his body movement, his facial expressions. These observations can then be placed in the child's folder and can add considerably to the teacher's understanding of the youngster.

A review of the children's folders from time to time gives the teacher the opportunity to assess each child's behavior and performance in the light of all of the evidence she has collected. She can then decide how well she knows this child, and if she is satisfied that she is providing the best possible learning environment for him.

Of course, it is not feasible to do an in-depth case study on every child in the class. But if a teacher keeps individual folders containing the types of information described above, she will have a fairly good picture of her pupils as individuals. She can determine which ones are puzzling to her and which ones might require a "second look." Case-study material can then be gathered about these special few.

Some of the factors which might influence her decision to make further investigation are.

1. Poor attendance either due to poor health or for unknown causes
2. Loss of interest in schoolwork or general apathy

3. Discrepancies in achievement either because of high potential and poor performance or because of inconsistencies of performance
4. Rejection by classmates and peers
5. Emotional behavior as evidenced by temper tantrums, withdrawal, and so on
6. Disruptive behavior in class or frequent demands for attention

Teachers are readily aware of some children's problems when they are disorderly and are difficult to deal with in class. Often these children are quickly referred for psychological examination or are sent to the principal for disciplining. But a further look at the child through a case-study approach might be more helpful. The principal and the school psychologist do not have the opportunities to view the child's behavior daily or to know him in various situations, as the classroom teacher does. Even where a referral is deemed necessary, the additional information provided by a case study and classroom observations would be very useful in putting together a more complete picture.

The case-study approach is even more valuable in instances where the child does not demand attention. Many quiet children go unnoticed in the classroom, where they must compete with others who are more outgoing and aggressive. When a teacher comes across a folder which provides her with little information, a case study might be called for. Perhaps this is a child she has hardly gotten to know. Perhaps there is hidden potential in this child which has not been tapped. Perhaps, like some children we have discussed in previous chapters, there are severe emotional problems which keep this child from expressing himself freely or from living up to his full potential.

It is always helpful to share views of individual children with colleagues and professional consultants. The faculty lunchroom is not the place for this kind of discussion. It must be conducted in a professional manner, possibly led by a guidance person. Administrators who are convinced of the importance of knowing the individual child can provide opportunities for such conferences. Nothing is more stimulating and enlightening than the sharing of ideas with various people who have had contact with the pupil. Teachers who had taught the child in previous terms may see him differently. Some may know the family or may have had experiences with sisters or brothers that increase the fund of information about the child. Periodic meetings of small groups of faculty members where a discussion of individual pupils could take place might be beneficial.

Inservice workshops can be organized where interested teachers can get together periodically for such discussions. On occasion outside consultants may be called in. School psychologists can offer information concerning test results and can add their insights to those of the classroom teachers. School boards in some communities have subsidized workshops of this nature, and have called in consultants from colleges and universities to conduct them. The workshop method has proved to be successful both in solving individual problems of students and in raising morale among teachers.

A pioneer program of this nature was initiated by Daniel A. Prescott and has been conducted by the University of Maryland Institute for Child Study for many years.[2] Teachers in a given school system who wish to participate in such a workshop are enrolled in child-study groups of approximately a dozen persons. Each participant selects a child whom he is teaching as a subject about whom he will gather information to be interpreted by the group. There is, therefore, an intense study made of as many children as there are participants in the workshop. Each teacher writes, in descriptive anecdotal form, accounts of several behavioral situations each week. These records are then shared with the other teachers in weekly meetings. A trained discussion leader works with the teachers, helping them to do objective reporting and suggesting additional sources for information.

After the recording of data has gone on for three or four months, the teachers begin to observe recurring patterns of behavior in the children they are studying. They then develop some hypotheses about the causes of this behavior, and they test them out in the light of further evidence. By eliminating the unreasonable explanations, the participants develop insights and begin to understand much about the children they are studying.

Child-study groups have been effective in parent-education programs. Some school administrators and some PTAs have organized voluntary meetings of groups of parents who get together regularly to discuss mutual problems of child rearing. Outside speakers and discussion leaders may be used from time to time. Often the parents themselves conduct the meeting, selecting a topic in advance and gathering information for discussion through observations of their own children. In cooperative nursery schools, where parents are directly involved in the operation of the school, these child-study meetings have been very effective in promoting understanding of children's behavior.

In schools where parents are used as aides in the classroom, in the lunchroom, or in the cafeteria such child-study workshops would be very helpful. Problems that arise during the performance of duties could be discussed, as well as individual children who are causing difficulties. Case-study files could be compiled with the cooperation of teachers and school authorities. Parents might gain understandings which would help both in their function as school aides and in their roles as parents with their own children.

The stress on parent involvement within the school setting has been emphasized in recent years. The case-study approach can be an effective means of bringing parents and teachers together to study children.

The case-study approach in teacher education

It goes without saying that, if teachers in the classroom need to know individual children, then they should be prepared in teacher-education programs with means to acquire that knowledge. Preservice programs for teachers have been mainly concerned with methods and materials of teaching. Of equal value in the education of prospective teachers are techniques for developing

[2] Daniel A. Prescott, *The Child in the Educative Process.*

the ability to know and understand children. John H. Fischer, president of Columbia University's Teachers College, has said, "The standard cliché-filled debate on whether the prospective teacher should learn what to teach or how to teach is a pointless waste of time. He obviously needs both, and more: he must also understand whom he teaches and why."[3]

Education majors in colleges and universities are usually required to take a course in child psychology or child development. To a large extent such courses consist of an examination of learning theories and a study of developmental patterns of children. Topics such as learning and motivation, and the characteristics of physical, social, emotional, and intellectual growth are discussed, and readings from authoritative sources are prescribed. The student ends up with a fund of information which she may or may not remember or apply when she goes out to teach.

She has not learned how to look at children or how to assess their growth and development as she does so. She has not gotten to know a real child. She has learned about "norms" and expected behavior patterns. Teacher education must become focused upon process, rather than dealing purely with product. The information is important, but the prospective teacher must learn how to acquire it for herself. Each child she will meet in her classroom will be different, and no understanding of "norms" will give her insight into any one child's unique personality and learning style.

How can we teach prospective teachers how to observe? Can insight be developed? Any skill is acquired through practice. We learn to observe by observing. Students can be required to do numerous observations of children at various age levels, as the student observers quoted so frequently in this book were required to do. The experience is a rewarding one, and the insights gained through group discussion of observations are significant. In evaluating the course taught by this author, one student stated, "Studying teaching methods before you get to know children is like taking a course in calculus without any background in arithmetic!"

After the college students, in these undergraduate classes in child development, have done a series of observations of children at various age levels, they are taken on a field trip to visit a clinic for children who have learning problems. The children in the clinic have various types of difficulties. They vary also in age, background, and personality. The clinic keeps extensive case histories on each child.

Students from the child-development class are asked to focus upon one of the children at the clinic and to do several ten-minute time samples. The college students spend an hour observing the children, and then they are taken to the office of the diagnostician. Each student gives her impressions of the child she had been observing, and this is then compared with the diagnostician's estimate of the same child. It is always surprising that so much of each child's problems and style of behaving is discernible to the student observers in so short a period of time. Knowing nothing about the children they were watching, most of the students are able to infer a good deal about

[3] John H. Fischer, "What—And How—To Teach Teachers."

them based purely upon the children's overt behavior. The inferences of the students in the child-development class closely match the analysis given by the diagnostician, which is based both upon her knowledge of the children and on the information in the case-history files. It is doubtful if the students could have been so astute in their judgments if they had not had extensive practice in observational techniques.

Study of child development based upon direct observation is more feasible today than in previous generations. College campuses and laboratory schools are well equipped with one-way viewing screens, videotape machines, and movie and slide projectors. Materials can be developed for classroom use which employ the multimedia equipment that is available. Vignettes of classroom action and of children's behavior can be analyzed and discussed. Students can be encouraged to make their own observations and to come up with their own inferences based upon what they see.

Students and teachers in the field agree, when asked, that the most valuable part of their teacher-education program was their term of student teaching. It is unfortunate that in most instances the prospective teacher must wait until her senior year in college before she has the opportunity to deal directly with children. Field experiences should begin much sooner. Freshmen interested in education as a career should be encouraged to work with community recreation groups, with after-school clubs, with children at summer camps. Teacher educators might require some volunteer activity of prospective teachers, and they should be available to discuss and evaluate these experiences with their students.

Hours of observations are frequently a component of some preservice education courses, but this practice should be extended and emphasized. Not only should methods of teaching be observed by the students, but children's reactions and learning patterns should be noted. Case studies can be required for college education courses, providing the student with direct knowledge of a child. But of even greater value is experience in developing the observational skills that can make her a more perceptive classroom teacher.

Another approach that, in this author's experience, has proved to be valuable, is a course designed expressly to increase awareness and sensitivity. Exercises to heighten sense perception and powers of observation make up a large part of the classroom activity. (This course, and its effects upon one group of graduate students, is reported in Chapter 3.) Teachers have found that their attitudes have changed and their insights have deepened as a result of this program. They claim to have greater empathy with the problems of children.

Recognizing the "exceptional child"

All children face some problems in growing up, and all need teachers' understanding and empathy. But some children are confronted with handicaps that impede their progress unless they are detected and help is provided. It is the classroom teacher who must recognize the child who faces these problems. In many instances she can secure the help she needs from sources within the school, but it is she who must work with the child to help him to overcome the blocks to learning that may occur.

The child may have a physical defect such as partial hearing, poor vision, or a speech problem. Too often inattention and poor learning abilities are caused by factors such as these. Sometimes giving the child special consideration in seating arrangements in the classroom or having him visit a clinic periodically can remedy the learning situation. A case-study approach can help the teacher to discover these problems. Once they are detected, the performance of the child in school often improves considerably.

The term "exceptional child" usually refers to that child who deviates sufficiently to be placed in a special class. Educators who have the training to work with handicapped children do not get to see them unless they are identified by the classroom teacher. In these instances case-study methods prove to be valuable both for the classroom teacher and for the special educator.

The "exceptional child" might also be the slow learner, the child with emotional problems, or the gifted child. The term refers to any child who may be guided to more effective performance if his difficulties are better understood.

To some extent every child is an exceptional child. But, some, more than others, have problems that loom so large on their horizons that they cannot function up to capacities. Some have special talents that are being ignored or blocked. Some have hidden disabilities that make them appear to be "lazy" or "underachieving." Some have been deprived of the kinds of experiences that prepare them for learning situations. We have had the chance to look closely at a few children like these in the case studies presented in Part III of this book.

These children, more than the others, will benefit most from an approach to teaching that emphasizes detailed observation of the individual and attention to his background. The "average" child will very likely learn and will get along well. The nonconformist or deviant may become lost to himself and to society if the school does not attend to his needs. The case studies provide ample evidence of children who suffer from indifference, from unrecognized limitations, from emotional trauma, and from pressures to achieve. For some, recognition of the problem in itself is enough to bring a solution. For others, the awareness of the teacher is the first step in a process that might, in time, remedy the situation. For still others, an accepting atmosphere in the classroom will help these children to develop their unique abilities.

The implications of a case-study approach are most clearly evident in these instances. If teachers can be trained to observe children, to investigate their backgrounds, and to view them in the light of all the evidence that is available, many children who fail may begin to achieve in school. Many others can be guided toward greater fulfillment.

The teacher's role

If a teacher views her role as one of releasing potentials that are within children, rather than that of solely imparting information to them, she can find great satisfaction in her profession. If she thinks of each child as an individual with unique qualities of his own, she can find that the discovery of those qualities is a special challenge to her. A well-known humorist who was a teacher, and in his thinking will always remain one, states his philosophy this way:

I believe that each newborn child arrives on earth with a message to deliver to mankind. Clenched in his little fist is some particle of yet unrevealed truth, some missing clue, which may solve the enigma of man's destiny. He has a limited amount of time to fulfill his mission and he will never get a second chance—nor will we. He may be our last hope. He must be treated as top sacred.

In a cosmos in which all things appear to have meaning, what is *his* meaning? We who are older and presumably wiser must find the key to unlock the secret he carries within himself. The lock cannot be forced. Our mission is to exercise the kind of loving care which will prompt the child to open his fist and offer up his truth, his individuality, the irreducible atom of his self. We must provide the kind of environment in which the child will joyfully deliver his message through complete self-fulfillment.[4]

A case-study approach to teaching can provide a means whereby the teacher can discover the "irreducible atom" that lies within each child. Hopefully, she will have the tools to "unlock the secret he carries within himself." If she can provide the empathy and understanding that each child deserves, perhaps the "clenched fist" will open and the child's message will be "joyfully delivered."

REFERENCES

ALMY, MILLIE. *Ways of Studying Children*. New York: Teachers College Press, Columbia University, 1959.

COHEN, DOROTHY H., AND VIRGINIA STERN. *Observing and Recording the Behavior of Young Children*. New York: Teachers College Press, Columbia University, 1958.

FISCHER, JOHN H. "What—And How—To Teach Teachers." *The New York Times Magazine* (September 9, 1962).

GORDON, IRA J. *Studying the Child in School*. New York: John Wiley & Sons, Inc., 1966.

LEVENSON, SAMUEL. *Everything but Money*. New York: Simon and Schuster, Inc., 1966.

MILLARD, CECIL V., AND JOHN W. M. ROTHNEY. *The Elementary School Child: A Book of Cases*. New York: Holt, Rinehart and Winston, Inc., 1957.

[4] Sam Levenson, *Everything but Money*.

PRESCOTT, DANIEL A. *The Child in the Educative Process*. New York: McGraw-Hill, Inc., 1957.

VOIGHT, RALPH CLAUDE. *Invitation to Learning: The Learning Center Handbook*. Washington, D.C.: Acropolis Books Ltd., 1972.

WHITE, VERNA. *Studying the Individual Pupil*. New York: Harper & Row, Publishers, 1958.

The Stern-Masling Teacher Preference Scale*

The following paragraphs describe characteristic teacher attitudes and gratifications. Students might be requested to select their order of preference, and list the paragraph numbers on a slip of paper. The selections can then be compared to the chart of teacher motives, gratifications, and attitudes, which is given later in this appendix.

Par. 1   I feel that teaching is an ideal career for me because it offers me the opportunity for a rich and varied life. I not only have the many satisfactions that come from teaching itself, but I also have the time to do other things that are important to me. Although there is not as much time as I would like, teaching makes it possible for me to read, relax, travel, have hobbies, be with my family and friends, and in short to be a versatile person and live a full life. I feel that this makes me a more mature and effective individual, and therefore a better teacher, more capable of understanding children and guiding them in their growth.

Par. 2   I have always wanted to be a teacher, for as long as I can remember. I like the kinds of people my fellow teachers represent, share the same kinds of interests they do, and enjoy doing things with them socially as well as professionally. Although a teacher's income isn't all it might be, we make it a point to attend plays and concerts whenever possible. I also try to keep informed in literature and art, since I'm conscious of my responsibility as a member of the teaching profession to help maintain standards of culture, learning and good taste. The teacher is an important influence in the community and I am proud to be one.

Par. 3   The children themselves are my greatest source of pleasure in teaching. I really love to see their eager faces every day, anxious to please and

* Only a part of the Teacher Preference Scale is reproduced here for use in teacher education settings. Further information can be obtained from The Psychological Research Center, Syracuse University, Syracuse, N.Y.

grateful for affection. Of course, they're not all the same, and they can sometimes be very trying, but I can truthfully say that there are very few children I haven't felt warmly towards. It gives me a great deal of pleasure to look after them, helping them in the ways that only a person genuinely concerned with their welfare really can. I've sometimes given more time than I should to a child for this reason, including after-school hours, but I've never regretted this because there is nothing more satisfying to me than to be able to contribute to a child's happiness and well-being.

Par. 4   I feel most rewarded as a teacher when my pupils have become so involved in their own pursuit of learning that my presence is almost superfluous. It has always seemed to me that pupils learn very little by being told what the teacher knows. Real learning is a personal experience, and the best teacher is the one who can succeed in bringing pupils to the threshold of their own minds. You have to respect the child's personal integrity to do this, letting his interests and not the teacher's determine the learning experience. I encourage my youngsters to be independent and self-reliant right from the beginning, and am better satisfied with the child who stands up and disagrees with me when he thinks I'm wrong than the one who looks to me to tell him what to think.

Par. 5   Although there are many aspects of teaching which are of concern to me, I have come to feel that the most urgent task is to work for the improvement of the school system and the advancement of teaching as a profession. There is much to be done in educating not only the public but other members of the profession as well. Too many pay lip-service to the needs of the schools and of teachers, but are unwilling to commit themselves to concrete action. There are times when I've wondered if it has been worth the personal sacrifice: the rewards are few, and your intentions are often misunderstood. But when I think of the importance of the problems involved I know there is nothing else I can do.

Par. 6   The most enjoyable part of my day is the time I spend with my pupils. Childhood is such a wonderful period, and it's wonderful to be able to help youngsters appreciate it to the fullest and to share it with them. When I think of some of the adults I know, it seems to me that there are many virtues they could learn from children, instead of the other way around. I know I've learned a lot from my pupils, listening to their talk and watching them behave. There isn't much about their interests and feelings I haven't come to understand, and one of my greatest satisfactions in teaching is when a youngster begins to see me as a friend and confidant rather than as an outsider.

Par. 7   I like to have my classes run smoothly, with a minimum of confusion or distraction. Youngsters like to have things spelled out, and they are most comfortable when there are rules and procedures which everyone can follow in order to do things in the right way. I enjoy helping the children see the purpose behind many of the rules they regard as arbitrary, but the most important thing is that they learn to pay attention to the rules, and that they begin to develop habits of punctuality, neatness, cleanliness, and order early in life. In the arrangement of the materials in my classroom, and in my own personal behavior, I constantly try to set an example for them. I take pride in the thought that my pupils are being well-prepared for their future responsibilities in adult life.

Par. 8   My greatest satisfaction in teaching comes when someone who is competent to judge tells me I've done a good job. I feel a very solid sense of achievement when the principal or supervisor compliments me on the progress of my class. Of course, much of the credit belongs to them for the help and support they provide. It's good to be a member of the educational team, when everyone works together for the same end. I am constantly encouraged by the thought that my own efforts and the guidance available from competent supervision bring me ever closer to the ideal of being a good teacher.

Par. 9   My greatest satisfactions in teaching come from my successes in captivating the interest and attention of the children. The most important problem in education is to motivate the student and, it seems to me, the best way to do this is to make the material of real interest to him. When the teacher is vivid, exciting and colorful, the children can't help but become aroused themselves. I like to use demonstrations, dramatizations and other techniques which help to make the lesson entertaining, and I try to introduce as much freshness and originality as possible into my teaching. In the final analysis it's the impact of the teacher as a personality that makes for the difference between successful and unsuccessful teaching.

Par. 10   The most important part of a teacher's job is to prepare children for adult life. As youngsters, they think that everything is play, but they will soon enough learn differently. It is the responsibility of the teacher to make them ready for their later responsibilities by teaching them obedience and respect for authority, self-control and hard work. The teacher must be firm if the pupils are to be kept on the right path, but it is for their own good. The real rewards in teaching come from the knowledge that you have done your part in developing the citizens and soldiers of tomorrow, devoted to God and country.

A SUMMARY OF TEN TEACHING ROLES IN TERMS OF MOTIVE, GRATIFICATION, AND ATTITUDE COMPONENTS

Motives	Gratifications	Attitudes
1. Practical	Instrumental rewards	Detachment
2. Status-striving	Prestige	Professional dignity
3. Nurturant	Children's affection	Providing love
4. Nondirective	Children's autonomy	Encouraging self-actualization
5. Rebellious	Promoting teachers' rights	Reforming schools
6. Preadult-fixated	Vicarious participation	Identification with children
7. Orderliness	Obsessive compulsions	Developing good pupil habits
8. Dependency	Support from superiors	Cooperation with authority
9. Exhibitionistic	Children's admiration	Showmanship
10. Dominance	Children's obedience	Maintaining discipline

Flanders' Categories for Interaction Analysis

The observer is to memorize the categories listed below. Then, while listening to a tape-recording or observing in an actual classroom setting, she is to decide which category best represents the communication just completed. About every three seconds, she is to write down the category number, while simultaneously assessing communication during the next period. This is to be continued at the rate of twenty to twenty-five observations per minute, keeping the tempo as steady as possible. The notes, therefore, are merely a sequence of numbers written in a column, top to bottom, preserving the original sequence of events. Occasional margin notes might explain class formation, or communication pattern of subject under discussion.

Interaction analysis consists simply of observing, recording, and counting events as they occur. Purposes of observation must be clearly defined to fit the needs of the group or individual who is observing. Categories can be changed and designed to fit the purposes of the observation.

Comparisons between two or more categories might reveal the proportion of pupil-initiated responses that follow teacher's direct or indirect influences. Thus, the observer might be able to construct a general pattern of possible behavioral cause and effect.

CATEGORIES FOR INTERACTION ANALYSIS

INDIRECT INFLUENCE

1. ACCEPTS FEELING: accepts and clarifies the tone of feeling of the students in an unthreatening manner. Feelings may be positive or negative. Predicting or recalling feelings are included.

2. PRAISES OR ENCOURAGES: praises or encourages student action or behavior. Jokes that release tension, but not at the expense of another individual, nodding head or saying "um hum?" or "go on" are included.

3. ACCEPTS OR USES IDEAS OF STUDENT: clarifying, building or developing ideas suggested by a student. As teacher brings more of his own ideas into play, shift to category 5.

4. ASKS QUESTIONS: asking a question about content or procedure with the intent that a student answer.

DIRECT INFLUENCE

5. LECTURING: giving facts or opinions about content or procedure; expressing his own ideas, asking rhetorical questions.

6. GIVING DIRECTIONS: directions, commands, or orders which students are expected to comply with.

7. CRITICIZING OR JUSTIFYING AUTHORITY: statements intended to change student behavior from unacceptable to acceptable pattern; bawling someone out; stating why the teacher is doing what he is doing; extreme self-reference.

8. STUDENT TALK-RESPONSE: talk by students in response to teacher. Teacher initiates the contact or solicits student statement.

9. STUDENT TALK-INITIATION: talk initiated by students. If "calling on" student is only to indicate who may talk next, observer must decide whether student wanted to talk.

10. SILENCE OR CONFUSION: pauses, short periods of silence and periods of confusion in which communications cannot be understood by the observer.

(Left margin labels: TEACHER TALK, STUDENT TALK, SILENCE)

Source: N. A. Flanders, *Teacher Influence, Pupil Attitudes and Achievement*, Co-operative Research Monograph, No. 12 (Washington, D. C., U. S. Office of Education, 1965), p. 20.

Suggested Checklist To Identify Interferences in the Learning Pathways*

	Never	Seldom	Often
AUDITORY			

Function
  Following directions
    frequent request for repetition
  Spelling errors
    vowel substitutions (notably e/i)
    difficulty with blends
    omissions in multi-syllabic words
  Inattentive or daydreaming
    in large or noisy room
    with teacher out of direct sight
    when lesson is completely oral
    when near a noisy child, fan, etc.
  Speech errors (unrelated to tongue or age)
    substitutions
    omissions
Memory
  sequence errors (shakemilk for milkshake)
  immediate but not long-range recall
  inaccurate recall of new names, terms

VISUAL
Function
  covers an eye when reading or writing
  tires easily when reading or writing
  works too close to material
  misreads

* Permission for use granted by Educational Guidance Services, Inc., 7200 S. S., 39th Terrace, Miami, Florida, 33155.

AUDITORY	Never	Seldom	Often
small words (a or the)	___	___	___
similar words (three for there)	___	___	___
sequence errors (was for saw)	___	___	___
needs to point when reading	___	___	___
loses place when reading	___	___	___
makes errors copying from the board	___	___	___
reading improves with large type	___	___	___
misses word when scanning a page	___	___	___

Memory
recalls concrete data (verbal or pictures)	___	___	___
but not symbols	___	___	___

MOTOR
Function
does not cross midline of body			
in writing	___	___	___
in reading	___	___	___
bumps into desk, door frame, etc.	___	___	___
drops materials, pencils, etc.	___	___	___
poor catching, batting	___	___	___
illegible writing	___	___	___
tight pencil grip	___	___	___

Memory
must "see" to correct writing errors	___	___	___
many erasures on papers	___	___	___
directionality errors in writing	___	___	___
copy better than writing	___	___	___
slow in forming letters, words	___	___	___

LANGUAGE
following directions
recalls words but does wrong action	___	___	___
requests clarification	___	___	___
good grades in language arts,	___	___	___
but poor in content subjects	___	___	___
difficulty writing complete sentences	___	___	___
misuses words (lock for key)	___	___	___
knowledge is rote	___	___	___

Summary of Findings:

Check if further, in-depth testing is indicated.

Auditory	___function	___memory
Visual	___function	___memory
Motor	___function	___memory
Language	___use	___memory

The Denver Developmental Screening Test*

The Denver Developmental Screening Test is used in clinical settings as a device to determine whether a child's behavioral patterns warrants further investigation or testing. A vertical line is drawn on the chart at the point corresponding to the age (in years and months) of the child being observed. Activities commonly performed by children of that age are listed, with various shadings to indicate the percentage of children of that age level who have performed the task successfully. The performance of the child being observed can then be compared to others of his age level. A significant developmental lag is indicative of need for further testing.

This screening test cannot be administered accurately without obtaining a manual of instructions and testing materials.* Any deviations from the correct manner of presentation and interpretation jeopardizes the norms that are presented on the test form. However, students might familiarize themselves with these norms, and might simulate some of the activities described in the directions below, while doing observations of children. This screening device is included here as a guide to observations, and comparisons to the norms listed on the chart cannot be considered as valid unless further information concerning procedures is obtained.

* Can be obtained from Ladoca Project and Publishing Company, East 51st Ave. and Lincoln St., Denver, Colo. 80216.

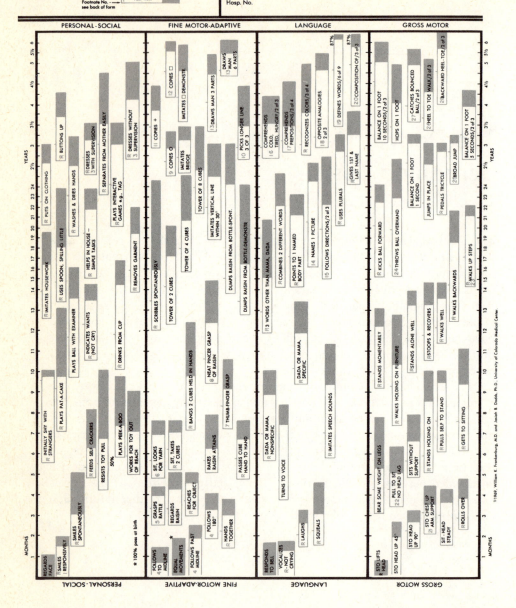

1. Try to get child to smile by smiling, talking or waving to him. Do not touch him.
2. When child is playing with toy, pull it away from him. Pass if he resists.
3. Child does not have to be able to tie shoes or button in the back.
4. Move yarn slowly in an arc from one side to the other, about 6" above child's face.
   Pass if eyes follow 90° to midline. (Past midline; 180°)
5. Pass if child grasps rattle when it is touched to the backs or tips of fingers.
6. Pass if child continues to look where yarn disappeared or tries to see where it went. Yarn
   should be dropped quickly from sight from tester's hand without arm movement.
7. Pass if child picks up raisin with any part of thumb and a finger.
8. Pass if child picks up raisin with the ends of thumb and index finger using an over hand
   approach.

9. Pass any enclosed form. Fail continuous round motions.
10. Which line is longer? (Not bigger.) Turn paper upside down and repeat. (3/3 or 5/6)
11. Pass any crossing lines.
12. Have child copy first. If failed, demonstrate

When giving items 9, 11 and 12, do not name the forms. Do not demonstrate 9 and 11.

13. When scoring, each pair (2 arms, 2 legs, etc.) counts as one part.
14. Point to picture and have child name it. (No credit is given for sounds only.)

15. Tell child to: Give block to Mommie; put block on table; put block on floor. Pass 2 of 3.
    (Do not help child by pointing, moving head or eyes.)
16. Ask child: What do you do when you are cold? ..hungry? ..tired? Pass 2 of 3.
17. Tell child to: Put block on table; under table; in front of chair, behind chair.
    Pass 3 of 4. (Do not help child by pointing, moving head or eyes.)
18. Ask child: If fire is hot, ice is ?; Mother is a woman, Dad is a ?; a horse is big, a
    mouse is ?. Pass 2 of 3.
19. Ask child: What is a ball? ..lake? ..desk? ..house? ..banana? ..curtain? ..ceiling?
    ..hedge? ..pavement? Pass if defined in terms of use, shape, what it is made of or general
    category (such as banana is fruit, not just yellow). Pass 6 of 9.
20. Ask child: What is a spoon made of? ..a shoe made of? ..a door made of? (No other objects
    may be substituted.) Pass 3 of 3.
21. When placed on stomach, child lifts chest off table with support of forearms and/or hands.
22. When child is on back, grasp his hands and pull him to sitting. Pass if head does not hang back.
23. Child may use wall or rail only, not person. May not crawl.
24. Child must throw ball overhand 3 feet to within arm's reach of tester.
25. Child must perform standing broad jump over width of test sheet. (8-1/2 inches)
26. Tell child to walk forward, ⊂∞∞∞∞➤ heel within 1 inch of toe.
    Tester may demonstrate. Child must walk 4 consecutive steps, 2 out of 3 trials.
27. Bounce ball to child who should stand 3 feet away from tester. Child must catch ball with
    hands, not arms, 2 out of 3 trials.
28. Tell child to walk backward, ◄⊂∞∞∞⊃ toe within 1 inch of heel.
    Tester may demonstrate. Child must walk 4 consecutive steps, 2 out of 3 trials.

DATE AND BEHAVIORAL OBSERVATIONS (how child feels at time of test, relation to tester, attention
span, verbal behavior, self-confidence, etc,):

Selections from the Torrance Tests of Creative Thinking*

Samples are given below of questions similar to those that appear on the Torrance Tests of Creative Thinking. Answers to these types of questions are scored for "fluency" (the number of relevant responses), "originality" (a rating given based upon the uniqueness of the response), and "flexibility" (determining the diversity of the responses). Scoring directions are given in a manual, and are quite complex. No attempt should be made by students to administer a formal test, or to try to evaluate results. The questions are given here simply to illustrate the kind of thinking that is related to creativity, according to Torrance. Students might use the questions, or adaptations of them, in interview sessions with children, and might approximate, on the basis of their own subjective judgment, the creative potential that the child has exhibited.

* Torrance Test Demonstrator is reproduced with permission of Personnel Press, Lexington, Mass., publisher of the Torrance Tests of Creative Thinking.

Part 2

List all the
questions you can
think of about
this picture.

1 _____

2 _____

3 _____

4 _____

5 _____

6 _____

Part 1

List all the ways you can think of to improve the toy.

1 _____

2 _____

3 _____

4 _____

5 _____

6 _____

Prepared by

Personnel Press, Inc., Princeton, N. J.
A Division of Ginn and Company

Part 3

List all the uses you can think of for junk autos

1 _____

2 _____

3 _____

4 _____

5 _____

6 _____

7 _____

8 _____

Part 4

Add lines to the incomplete figures to sketch some interesting objects.

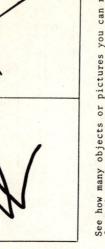

See how many objects or pictures you can make from the triangles below.

INDEX